Following the attack on Pearl Harbor, the Navy obtained approximately 700 vessels from private owners, armed them, designated them as patrol yachts (PY) or patrol craft (YP), and sent them to sea. The vessels spanned the spectrum from yacht to waterfront work horse—fishing vessel, whaler, tug, and freighter. San Diego tuna fishermen—including those that would be aboard their boats at the Battle of Midway, and at Guadalcanal supporting the 1st Marines—donned Navy uniforms without the benefit of "boot camp" training and went off to war. They were joined by fishermen and yachtsmen from ports and harbors all across America, as well as men straight from cities and rural towns. Officers and crewmen who took vessels into harm's way received the Navy Cross, and other awards for valor for acts of heroism performed under fire. Officers aboard the yachts *Fisheries II* and *Maryanne* were awarded Navy Crosses for their actions during the defense of the Philippines—three posthumously, as they died while prisoners of war. Three men aboard the *YP-346*—sunk by the Japanese light cruiser *Sendai*—also earned Navy Crosses, and the *YP-346* and two other former tuna boats at Guadalcanal received the Presidential Unit Citation for heroism. YPs and PYs at Saipan, Okinawa, Iwo Jima, Leyte, and Balikpapan earned battle stars for combat; the ex-halibut boat *YP-251* was credited with sinking a Japanese submarine in Alaskan waters, and the patrol yacht *Siren* earned a battle star during one of the most successful series of attacks on a convoy by a single German submarine. Others did not fare so well; the *YP-389* and patrol yacht *Cythera* were lost to German U-boats in infamous "Torpedo Junction" off North Carolina. All of the unheralded vessels served when called, and like militiamen of old, they were mustered out when no longer needed.

Battle Stars for the "Cactus Navy"

Also by David D. Bruhn

Ready to Answer All Bells

Wooden Ships and Iron Men: The U.S. Navy's Ocean Minesweepers, 1953–1994

Wooden Ships and Iron Men: The U.S. Navy's Coastal and Motor Minesweepers, 1941–1953

Wooden Ships and Iron Men: The U.S. Navy's Coastal and Inshore Minesweepers, and the Minecraft That Served in Vietnam, 1953–1976

MacArthur and Halsey's "Pacific Island Hoppers"

Battle Stars for the "Cactus Navy"

America's Fishing Vessels and Yachts in World War II

David D. Bruhn

HERITAGE BOOKS
2014

HERITAGE BOOKS
AN IMPRINT OF HERITAGE BOOKS, INC.

Books, CDs, and more—Worldwide

For our listing of thousands of titles see our website at
www.HeritageBooks.com

Published 2014 by
HERITAGE BOOKS, INC.
Publishing Division
5810 Ruatan Street
Berwyn Heights, Md. 20740

Copyright © 2014 Cdr. David D. Bruhn, USN (Retired)

Heritage Books by the author:

Battle Stars for the "Cactus Navy": America's Fishing Vessels and Yachts in World War II

MacArthur and Halsey's "Pacific Island Hoppers:" The Forgotten Fleet of World War II

Wooden Ships and Iron Men: The U.S. Navy's Ocean Minesweepers, 1953–1994

Wooden Ships and Iron Men: The U.S. Navy's Coastal and Motor Minesweepers, 1941–1953

Wooden Ships and Iron Men: The U.S. Navy's Coastal and Inshore Minesweepers, and the Minecraft that Served in Vietnam, 1953–1976

All rights reserved. No part of this book may be reproduced or transmitted in any form or by any means, electronic or mechanical, including photocopying, recording or by any information storage and retrieval system without written permission from the author, except for the inclusion of brief quotations in a review.

International Standard Book Numbers
Paperbound: 978-0-7884-5573-5
Clothbound: 978-0-7884-6001-2

To the late Carolyn L. Barkley, genealogist and author

Contents

Foreword by Melville Owen.. xiii
Foreword by August Felando... xv
Acknowledgments.. xix
Preface.. xxi
  1. The "Cactus Navy" at Guadalcanal................................ 1
  2. War Plan-Rainbow No. 5... 29
  3. Overview of the Patrol Yacht and "Yippie" Fleets............... 39
  4. Japan's Submarine Offensive off America's West Coast........... 47
  5. West Coast Defense Measures and the Navy's "Q-Ships"........... 59
  6. War in the Aleutians... 79
  7. The Battle of Midway... 99
  8. Loss of Guam and the Philippines.............................. 109
  9. Cutter *McLane* and YP-251 Sink Submarine in Alaskan Waters... 123
 10. U-boat Attacks in Torpedo Junction............................ 131
 11. Gulf, Panama, and Caribbean Sea Frontiers..................... 163
 12. Additional Tuna Clippers Sent to the South Pacific............ 197
 13. Consolidation of the Southern Solomon Islands................. 207
 14. Occupation and Defense of Cape Torokina....................... 219
 15. Breaking the Bismarck Islands Barrier......................... 233
 16. Tarawa.. 241
 17. The Marianas—Saipan, Guam, and Tinian......................... 245
 18. The Leyte Landings and Aftermath.............................. 255
 19. The Assault and Occupation of Iwo Jima and Okinawa............ 261
 20. Mine Clearance at Balikpapan, Borneo.......................... 269
Postscript... 273
Appendices
  a. Yard Patrol Craft (YP).. 277
  b. Patrol Yachts (PY).. 293
  c. Coastal Patrol Yachts (PYc)................................... 295
  d. Vaughn, Murphy, and Nevle Navy Cross Medal Citations.......... 297
  e. Raymond, Petritz, and Strand Navy Cross Medal Citations....... 301
  f. YP-389 Crew List.. 303
  g. Patrol Yacht, Converted Yacht, and YP Unit Awards............. 305
  h. Letter from the Secretary of the Navy to A. Donham Owen....... 307

{x} Contents

Bibliography 309
Notes 311
Index 343
About the Author 377

Photos

Preface-1: *YP-438* under way. xxii
Preface-2: *Donald Amirault* before conversion to *YP-438*. xxiii
 1-1: *Night Action off Tulagi* (painting by Richard DeRosset) xxvi
 1-2: Skippers of San Diego tuna clippers 7
 1-3: *YP-346* with destroyer *Tucker* under tow. 12
 1-4: Tuna clipper *Challenger* following service as *YP-239*. 24
 3-1: Ernest Borgnine in his Navy uniform. 40
 3-2: *YP-625* under way. 44
 5-1: Motor yacht *Norwester*, following her service as *YP-165*. 62
 5-2: Motor yacht *Pat Pending* under way in San Francisco Bay 66
 5-3: Q-ship *Normandie II* under way off southern California 72
 6-1: *YP-72*, the flagship of the Alaska Patrol 83
 6-2: *Sub and Yippy Tie Up* (painting by William F. Draper) 86
 6-3: *YP-92* in the Aleutians covered in snow. 97
 7-1: Midway Atoll 100
 8-1: Patrol yacht *Isabel* at Hankow, China 112
 9-1: Halibut schooner *Foremost* before her conversion to *YP-251* 124
10-1: Fishing schooner *Cohasset* before her conversion to *YP-389* 146
10-2: Patrol yacht *Cythera* in port 157
11-1: Patrol yacht *Siren* under way 194
12-1: Bora Bora, Society Islands 200
13-1: *YP-516* under way. 214
14-1: *YP-415* under way. 225
16-1: Patrol yacht *Southern Seas* under way 242
17-1: *YP-56* at Coco Solo, Panama Canal Zone 247
18-1: *YP-421* under way. 258
19-1: *YP-42* at Builder's Yard 266
Postscript: *YP-520* aground at Buckner Bay, Okinawa. 275

Maps

1-1: Solomon Islands ...3
1-2: Guadalcanal area, Solomon Islands ...15
6-1: Aleutian Islands ...87
7-1: Outlying Hawaiian Islands ...102
8-1: Mariana Islands ...110
8-2: Manila Bay area of the Philippines ...114
9-1: Southeast Alaska ...126
11-1: Caribbean Sea ...189
11-2: Southeast Caribbean Basin ...192
12-1: Western Pacific Islands ...203
13-1: Espiritu Santo and Guadalcanal ...213
14-1: Bougainville, Solomon Islands ...221
15-1: New Britain in the Bismarck Archipelago ...234
15-2: Cape Cretin area of New Guinea ...237
16-1: Funafuti Atoll, Ellice Islands ...242
16-2: Tarawa Atoll, Gilbert Islands ...243
17-1: Kwajalein Atoll, Marshall Islands ...251
18-1: Leyte, Philippine Islands ...257
19-1: Okinawa, Ryukyu Islands, and Iwo Jima, Nanpo Islands ...262
20-1: Borneo ...271

Foreword

The history recounted in this book is little known outside the families of the boat owners whose vessels were requisitioned by the government in the very early days of World War II. Our family's experience started well before Pearl Harbor and continued well past the delivery of our 50-foot cabin cruiser *Pat Pending* to the United States Navy at Treasure Island on San Francisco Bay on 9 December 1941.

In early 1941, the Navy realized that its shortage of patrol boats would require the acquisition and conversion of civilian boats to military use. Boats of all sizes, from 40-foot pleasure craft to 80-foot fishing vessels to 150-foot yachts, would be needed to fill the void. In fact, the Navy "requested" some of these boats as early as the summer of 1941. I recall that we were asked to sell *Pat Pending* that summer. As we were using the boat every weekend, and there was no emergency, we declined.

However, everything changed on 7 December when we learned of the attack. By 10 a.m. the next morning, the Navy was calling and ordering the delivery of *Pat Pending* by noon on Tuesday, 9 December, for military duty. Clearly, the Navy had been preparing lists of qualified boats, their owners and contact information, knowing that these boats would be needed in a hurry.

A number of other boat owners at the Oakland Yacht Club received the same call and by Monday night, all the owners were at the yacht club removing their personal equipment and supplies. I recall some of the owners, in an effort to avoid the need to carry their liquor home, drank as much as possible.

Once the Navy had the boats, it was grey paint on all outside surfaces and an ugly green on the interior. The government then sent a team of appraisers to set the price to be paid for the requisitioned boats. In our case, we received a check for $7,000 on 7 April 1942. That was close to what we had paid for *Pat Pending* when we acquired it in October 1940. I recall that there was an appeal process for those that felt they did not receive a fair price.

Pat Pending was assigned to the Tiburon Net Boom Depot, outfitted with a depth charge cage on the middle deck, and a deck gun on the bow. Her duty was to patrol the newly installed submarine cable net across the entrance to San Francisco Bay. The boat was on station twenty-four hours a day, with the refueling and changing of crew handled from a 146-foot navy tug called the *Eider*. She and a sister ship, the *Dreadnought*, were stationed at each end of a 1,000-yard log boom that was pulled open and shut to allow our ships to enter and exit port. By late 1943 the Navy had built enough patrol vessels to retire *Pat Pending* and similar boats. They were put "on the dry" (beached) in Alameda to await disposal. At that time the law required auctioning of all military surplus. My father was concerned that this regulation might mean that we would not have *Pat Pending* back in the family. He also felt that it was unfair to the former owners not to have the first chance to buy back their boats. To cure the problem, Dad asked his congressman to introduce a bill requiring that these requisitioned boats be offered to the former owners before any auction was held. *Pat Pending* was the first boat returned under Public Law 305 of 1944. We offered $10, but the War Administration in charge of sales countered at $100, which we paid.

By summer of 1945, nine months and $24,000 later, *Pat Pending* was better than new. In the sixty-six years since that time, we have made improvements and completed a major rebuild in 2000, thus ensuring that *Pat Pending* will continue to enjoy civilian life on San Francisco Bay for many years to come.

Melville Owen
Belvedere, California

Foreword

While managing the affairs of the American Tunaboat Association (ATA) in San Diego between October 1960 and September 1991, I had numerous conversations with men who had served aboard the tuna clippers that were converted to U.S. Navy YPs during World War II. Most of these talks concerned the movement of the Tuna YPs from San Diego to the Canal Zone for picket duty off the Panama Canal Zone during the months of February and March 1942; the activities of Tuna YPs in waters off Hawaii, Samoa, and Midway Island between April and July 1942; the trips of Tuna YPs in the Solomon Islands (Tulagi, Guadalcanal, and Bougainville) during the critical months of mid-1942 and 1943; and the loss of Tuna YPs during a typhoon off Okinawa in October 1945.

On business trips for the ATA, I visited Guadalcanal, Papua New Guinea, New Caledonia, Western Samoa, American Samoa, New Zealand, Australia, Guam, and Saipan. In Honiara, Guadalcanal, I examined papers and obtained maps relative to the war on Guadalcanal, and then took a brief fly-over of Tulagi Island. Armed with the maps of Tulagi and Guadalcanal that I had secured in Honiara, I talked with Edward and Joe Madruga about their memories of operating *YP-289* (ex-*PARAMOUNT*). During trips to Noumea, New Caledonia, I became familiar with the unique anchorage aspects in the port of Noumea, as well as the aged facilities once used by those in command of our military during WW II. These visits increased my understanding of the Pacific-wide distribution of Tuna YPs, but also made me curious as to why so few people, even within the U.S. Tuna Industry, were familiar with the role of Tuna Clipper YPs during WW II. Necessarily, I started to ask my friends at the ATA more about the Tuna Clipper YPs.

My search included visits to the Navy Department Library, part of the Naval History and Heritage Command at the Washington Navy Yard, during my many business trips to Washington, D.C. I was surprised by this facility's limited collection of data and photos relating to the commercial fishing vessels converted to YPs during WW II. Much work remains to be done to complete the story. David Bruhn's work is an excellent example of what can be accomplished.

The first high seas tuna clipper was built by Japanese immigrants in San Pedro, California, during 1924. It was equipped with a diesel marine engine, a machine that was relatively new to the U.S. commercial fishing industry. *PATRICIA I* made history when it became the first vessel to fish successfully for tuna off Baja California and then return its refrigerated catch directly to tuna canners located in Southern California. This round trip capability was unique. Prior to this historic event, the small tuna boats transferred their catch to tuna tenders or tuna mother-ships in near shore waters. The larger vessels then would deliver the catch to the tuna canners located in the ports of San Pedro or San Diego. Stimulated by the success of the *PATRICIA I* and other similar tuna baitboats, a new-style tuna vessel was developed in Southern California. This new construction was rapid, fundamental, and driven by fishermen, shipyards, canners, and diesel engine manufacturers. By 1929, U.S. flag tuna clippers were fishing in waters off Cocos Islands, Costa Rica, and off Galapagos Islands, Ecuador. By the end of 1930, fishing at Galapagos Islands had become routine. Significantly, the construction of tuna clippers with new capabilities to make fishing voyages, lasting months, to distant places in the eastern Tropical Pacific started again in the mid-1930s. In San Diego, navy officials carefully observed this development, particularly noting the size of the diesel engines, the methods and equipment used to refrigerate the tuna, and the navigational and seagoing skills of the men aboard the tuna clippers. They were aware that the areas where U.S. tuna clippers operated were seasonally affected by tropical storms and hurricanes. They learned that the fishermen exercised difficult seamanship skills when taking live bait in shallow areas along the coasts and islands, or when searching for new tuna fishing grounds.

After the Japanese naval attack at Pearl Harbor, the U.S. Navy searched for American commercial fishing vessels capable of operating on the high seas, and ordered tuna clippers to leave their fishing grounds and make port at the Panama Canal Zone or at ports in Southern California. Later, the U.S. Navy made the wise decision to ask the tuna fishermen to serve on the tuna clippers that were being converted to military service. Hundreds of fishermen agreed. Fifty-two tuna clippers were acquired by the military; almost all converted for service as YPs. Twenty-one of these vessels did not return home to the U.S. tuna industry after the war because of ordered destruction, sinking, foundering, or the effects of battle engagements.

The number of tuna fishermen who died in the service of this YP fleet is currently unknown. We know that *YP-345* (ex-*YANKEE*) was lost with all hands in waters southeast of Midway Island. The U.S. tuna industry is proud that the United States Marine Corps awarded the Presidential Unit Citation to the following three former tuna clippers: *YP-239* (ex-*CHALLENGER*), *YP-284* (ex-*ENDEAVOR*), and *YP-346* (ex-*PROSPECT*), and that Battle Stars were awarded to the following five tuna clippers: *YP-236* (ex-*EUROPA*), *YP-284* (ex-*ENDEAVOR*), *YP-514* (ex-*AMERICAN BEAUTY*), *YP-516* (ex-*QUEEN AMELIA*), and *YP-517* (ex-*ST. ANN*).

August Felando
President, American Tunaboat Association, 1960-1991

Acknowledgments

The catalyst for this book was correspondence I received in June 2006 from retired Master Chief George Johnson, USN, inquiring if I had researched and written about "the other Iron men and their wooden ships like the Gloucester fishing schooners and beam trawlers that were all they had to fight with on [America's] east coast in 1942." At the time, I was unaware that the YP designation had been associated with anything other than the training craft used to instruct prospective officers in seamanship and navigation. Discussions with renowned maritime artist Richard DeRosset—whose magnificent painting, *Night Action off Tulagi*, is the cover art for this book—revealed that San Diego tuna boats had served in the Southwest Pacific during World War II. Richard had some knowledge of the service of these vessels in the Solomon Islands, and provided me a copy of a diary kept by Kenneth Adams, the commanding officer of one of them. Research led me to Ronald Gilson—the author of *An Island No More*, a memoir about growing up in Gloucester, Massachusetts, during the war and his association with its famous fishing fleet—who generously provided much information. Next, I became acquainted with August Felando of San Diego, whose decades' long involvement with the American tuna industry includes personal experience as a commercial fisherman, boat owner, and, since the late 1950s, as a maritime lawyer. His article, "The Errand Boys of the Pacific: Tuna Clippers and World War II," published in *Mains'l Haul* in 2008, paid long-overdue tribute to the war service of approximately 600 members of the San Diego fishing community. I am greatly indebted to him for his considerable assistance with the book and for allowing me to use data that he had compiled on the characteristics of West Coast fishing vessels taken into military service during the war.

I am also very appreciative to King Graver and Melville Owen for allowing me to use photographs of their beautiful classic wooden motor yachts, the *Norwester* and *Pat Pending*—which served as the YPs *165* and *119* respectively during the war—in this book. John Wayne was an earlier owner of the *Norwester* and Hollywood director Lloyd Bacon of the latter yacht. Mr. Owen was kind enough to pen a foreword for the book, and to provide much information about the Navy's acquisition of the *Pat Pending* and his father's repurchase of it after the war.

In the appendices, the tables devoted to patrol yachts and patrol vessels are derived largely from shipbuilders' records compiled by Tim Colton, a naval architect, as well as from official U.S. Merchant Marine and Navy information. Captain Jerry Mason, USN (Ret.), the host of www.u-boat.net, also lent assistance based on his considerable knowledge of German U-boat operations. Similarly, Bob Hackett and Sander Kingsepp, the hosts of www.combinedfleet.com/sensuikan.htm, have compiled information on the war patrols of Japanese submarines.

Many other individuals also contributed to or influenced the book. For the sake of brevity, I have omitted the use, where appropriate, of military rank: Vincent Battaglia, Brendon Coyle, Robert Cressman, King Graver, Frank J. Guidone, Jon T. Hoffman, Joe Hoyt, Augustus P. Johnson, Mark A. Kelso, Nicholas John Lavnikevich, John R. Lewis, Mike McCarthy, James Clair Nolan, George K. Petritz, Justin M. Ruhge, Robert P. Sables, Leonard Skinner, Peter Tare, Joaquin S. Theodore, Kemp Tolley, N. G. Wade, David Walkinshaw, J. W. Wickham, and Donald J. Young.

I am particularly grateful to the late Carolyn L. Barkley, genealogist and author, for her work as the editor of this text. Her discerning eye and pen contributed eloquence and substance to the work. Finally, Jo-Ann Parks has created another handsome book owing to artistic talent and prowess in design and typesetting.

Preface

This was the roughest duty I ever had in the Navy in three wars; it was hell up off the Grand Banks in winter with the ice and cold. Our cook had an old cast iron range and burned wood to cook our chow. They finally converted his stove to kerosene and he was one happy guy the stove also heated the crew's quarters. We had three 20mm guns and some depth charges and small arms to go out and fight the German U-Boats. My ship [YP-438], the Donald Amirault, was a Gloucester fishing schooner taken by Navy, which removed her masts and mounted guns. They should have left them. The old diesel engine we had could not be relied upon [and was] always breaking down. If we had her masts we still could have sailed. We sank down off Florida due to a [engine] break down and [grounding on a] coral reef.

Right after Pearl Harbor the Navy was in bad shape and was desperate for any type of ship or craft they could get their hands on. They took over all large yachts, fishing vessels, and just about anything they could get. My neighbor had a forty-foot yacht and I know it went to the Coast Guard. The steel beam trawlers were converted to carry a three-inch gun in a false deck house on the main deck and also depth charges.

My ship operated out of [the] East Boston section base. That is until we were ordered south to Florida as the U-boats were having a field day sinking our tankers [bound] from the Gulf of Mexico headed north.[1]

George Johnson, BMCM, USN (Retired)

The fishermen who volunteered for U.S. Navy service, and went to war aboard the boats in which they had fished during peacetime, were used to hard, spare conditions in relatively small vessels that offered few amenities and, particularly in the days before the advent of modern GPS navigation, radar, and up-to-date localized weather forecasts, the possibility of being taken by the sea. Navy men were also accustomed to a mariner's life, albeit aboard larger ships. Ronald Gilson recalls well the *Donald Amirault* and the modifications made to prepare her for naval service. She entered a shipyard where

YP-438, a demasted former Gloucester fishing schooner, was lost after her engine broke down and she grounded on a submerged breakwater off the entrance to Port Everglades, Florida.
Courtesy of BMCM George Johnson, USN Retired

workers removed her raised bow (which Gloucester fishermen called a "whaleback") and her wooden foremast and mainmast, as being schooner-rigged for commercial fishing, vice; these lofty spars were not needed for her upcoming military role. Her fishing gear, four deck gallows frames, winch and deck bollards were returned to Gloucester and kept in storage in Gorton's warehouse on the waterfront in expectation of her return after the war. However, the *YP-438* proved to be one of the "ships that sailed for sunny isles, but never came to shore."[2]

Gilson described the characteristics of such vessels and what it was like to fish aboard them during that era:

> [T]he cast iron, wood fired "Shipmate" fo'c'sle stove in the crew's quarters forward on the *Donald Amirault* . . . was the standard, the only one used in our offshore fishing vessels of the '40s. It was all we had available. Only later did they devise a little oil burner fixed to a plate, bolted to the ash pit door, usually to the left of the stove as you faced its front. I know it was tough aboard that vessel, roaming the Grand Banks in the winter, Gulf of Maine, and Bay of Fundy. Locals today have no conception of a fishermen's life in the '40s, when living on these vessels was almost primitive.
>
> The old diesel engine [fitted in the *Donald Amirault*] was probably a 250-300hp Atlas six-cylinder heavy duty machine. . . .They were the most popular engine in the fleet at the time, closely followed by the Cooper Bessemer diesel.[3]

He also recalled the nightly "black outs" required all along the eastern seaboard to reduce German U-boat slaughter of merchant ships and smaller craft, including fishing boats, should they become silhouetted against the coastline by the lights of towns and cities:

> I well remember during this time that those of us living close to the water in Gloucester were forced to blacken our windows with tar paper, afraid of subs immediately off our eastern shore. My dad patrolled the shoreline as a volunteer in the USCG Reserve, looking for submarine activity within sight of land. It was a very dangerous time; our fishermen were real targets in the early years of WW II.[4]

The *Donald Amirault* was but one of the approximately 700 privately owned or commercial vessels taken for service during the war, including yachts, fishing vessels, whalers, tugs, Coast Guard patrol boats and lightships—basically anything large enough to be fitted with machine guns and depth charges. In the ensuing chapters, readers will go to sea (vicariously) aboard vessels similar to the *YP-438* in the American and Pacific Theaters of war. The first chapter is devoted to the heroics of former San Diego tuna clippers in the Solomon

Photo Preface-2

Gloucester fishing schooner *Donald Amirault* before Navy acquisition and conversion to *YP-438*.
Courtesy of BMCM George Johnson, USN Retired

Islands during the summer and autumn of 1942. Chapters 2 and 3 provide a description of Rainbow-War Plan No. 5, the catalyst for the acquisition of these vessels, as well as an overview of the service of navy patrol yachts (PY/PYc) and patrol craft (YP).

The U.S. Navy had some large steel-hulled patrol yachts (PY) left over from World War I and acquired a few more. Smaller, mostly wooden-hulled, yachts were classified as coastal patrol yachts (PYc), even smaller ones as patrol vessels (YP). These craft joined the myriad of other types of ships and craft that made up the "Yippie" fleet. Readers not requiring the level of detail provided in Chapters 2 and 3, may wish to go directly to Chapter 4, returning to the earlier sections if they require more background information.

After its opening in the Solomon Islands, the book returns to the waters off America's West Coast, where in December 1941, Japanese submarines launched an offensive against merchant shipping. Japanese and United States Navy confrontations continue as the action moves to Alaskan waters for the Aleutians Campaign portion of the Battle of Midway, and then to Midway Island itself. Referred to locally as "YP boats" or fishboats," YPs serving in the Aleutians provided support for Catalina seaplanes. The mettle displayed by the pilots of these patrol aircraft as they attacked Japanese fleet units resulted in Admiral Chester Nimitz ordering them to "bomb the Japanese out of Kiska." Four former San Diego tuna clippers, a long way from home, served as tenders/oilers for the Catalina seaplanes during the Battle of Midway.

The loss of Guam and the Philippines in the western Pacific is discussed, including information about a classified operation that President Roosevelt personally directed commander-in-chief Asiatic Fleet to undertake. During hearings held in 1945, members of Congress stated their belief that this operation, in which an ill-equipped patrol yacht was sent to reconnoiter Cam Ranh Bay with its heavy concentration of Japanese warships, had been intended to provoke a war with Japan in early December 1941. The small-ship action then returns to Alaskan waters and the cat-and-mouse battle between a submarine and the small Coast Guard cutter *McLane* and *YP-251*. The two ships were credited with sinking the Japanese *RO-32*, although it now appears that the submarine was, in fact, Russian.

The second half of the book traces the death and destruction wrought by German submarines off the Eastern Seaboard, in the Gulf of Mexico, on the Atlantic side of the Panama Canal, and in the Caribbean, which caused hundreds of merchant—and some navy ships—to be sent to the bottom. Two of the latter were the *YP-389*, a 110-foot former fishing trawler drawn into a one-sided battle with the German submarine *U-701* off Hatteras, and the patrol yacht *Cythera*, sunk off North Carolina by the *U-402*. The narrative follows the U-boats of Admiral Donitz to the Gulf of Mexico and Caribbean, where the Allies had to battle the submarine threat while also worrying about the "Vichy French" in the region, perhaps leading to the purposeful sinking of the Free French submarine *Surcouf*. She was lost amidst much speculation and rumor among British and American naval forces that she might go rogue and torpedo American convoys en route Europe, or attempt to defect to "Vichy" French territory in the West Indies or Central America. After leaving Bermuda on 12 February 1942, the *Surcouf* was never seen again; rumors about her demise persist.

From the Caribbean, readers travel back to the Central and Southwest Pacific for the final drive toward the Japanese home islands. YPs and/or patrol yachts earned battle stars at Tarawa, Saipan, Leyte, Iwo Jima, Okinawa, and—in the final amphibious landing of the Pacific War—at Balikpapan. The activities of the *YP-421*, a former Massachusetts fishing trawler, are particularly noteworthy. The Battle of Leyte Gulf was the first time that the Japanese used organized kamikaze attacks, and efforts to defeat the Allies through the use of the suicide planes, essentially pilot-guided explosive missiles, as well as conventional aircraft, would continue. During air strikes on shipping off Leyte, the *YP-421* shot down two Japanese bombers, and a few months later worked with Lt. Comdr. Leonard Goldsworthy, RAN, the Australian Navy's premiere mine disposal expert and its most highly decorated officer, at Balikpapan, Borneo. There were other encounters with enemy aircraft, particularly by the YPs *41*, *42*, and *56*, 98-foot ex-Prohibition-era Coast Guard cutters that had been converted to survey ships. Termed "harbor stretchers," they were among the first naval vessels to arrive, following the capture of a beachhead by the Marines, to facilitate harbor developments. The *YP-41* shot down a Japanese plane at Okinawa. The portion of that battle, both above and on the sea, was characterized by repeated massed kamikaze attacks, resulting in scores of Navy ships sunk, damaged beyond repair, or knocked out of action for thirty days or more.

Readers interested in learning more about a particular YP or patrol yacht will find information in the first three appendices. Summaries of ship characteristics and names of commanding officers, if known, appear throughout the book. This information, gleaned from thousands of pages of individual war diaries, is not readily available—nor is the history of the ships.

A comparison can be made between the 700 vessels drafted for service as patrol yachts and YPs, and the "state navies" during the American Revolutionary War, the latter consisting of shallow-draft barges, galleys, gunboats, and a few small deep-water vessels that could prey upon British merchant ships. The World War II equivalents of these vessels were the former tuna clippers, beam trawlers, and Coast Guard cutters that served with the Pacific Fleet. Following the war's end, the YPs and a majority of the patrol yachts were returned to their owners or otherwise disposed of, and the men that had taken them into harm's way were, like militiamen of old, quietly mustered out and sent home.[5]

Photo 1-1

Night Action off Tulagi by Richard DeRosset depicts the destruction of USS *YP-346* (the former San Diego tuna clipper *Prospect*) by the Japanese light cruiser IJN *Sendai* off Guadalcanal on 8 September 1942.

1

The "Cactus Navy" at Guadalcanal

> *It was only a small action that met little resistance, but it can be argued that the raid on Tasimboko saved the First Marine Division on Guadalcanal and set up the turning point in World War II.*
> —Capt. Frank J. Guidone, USMC (Ret.), commander of Company Able, 1st Raider Battalion, on Guadalcanal[1]

In the early evening of 7 September 1942, the rifle companies of the U.S. Marine Corps' 1st Raider Battalion embarked in the destroyer-transports *Manley* (APD-1) and *McKean* (APD-5) and the patrol craft *YP-239* and *YP-346* at Kukum on the north coast of Guadalcanal, en route to a site twenty miles to the east to launch a raid on Japanese forces occupying Tasimboko village. The YPs were former San Diego tuna boats sent to the Solomons by the U.S. Navy for duty as supply ships. Normally engaged in hauling food, fuel, supplies, and occasionally personnel from Tulagi to Guadalcanal across the span of water separating the two islands, they had been drafted as a last resort, after APDs *Little* (APD-4) and *Gregory* (APD-3) had been sunk by the Imperial Japanese Navy (IJN) destroyers *Yudachi*, *Hatsuyuki*, and *Murakumo* two days earlier in the waters between Guadalcanal and Savo Island.[2]

The *Manley* and *McKean* were the only two remaining units of Transportation Division 12, initially comprised of the five destroyer-transports *Manley* (APD-1), *Colhoun* (APD-2), *Gregory* (APD-3), *Little* (APD-4) and *McKean* (APD-5), which had been sent to the Solomons, following the Battle of Savo Island, to deliver badly-needed supplies and support to the Marines on Guadalcanal. The APDs were converted World War I era flush-deck destroyers whose current mission was to deliver a company-sized combat unit to a location off a hostile landing beach. They would then stand off and provide gunfire support as needed while Higgins boats delivered the Marines to shore. As the *Little* discharged stores on the Guadalcanal beach on 30 August, she witnessed the destruction of *Colhoun* during a Japanese air raid as the APD patrolled offshore. Successive plane attacks sent the destroyer-transport to the bottom with fifty-one crewmen killed and eighteen wounded. The *Little* herself, as well as the *Gregory*, would be lost to enemy destroyer gunfire on 4 September while returning to their anchorage at Tulagi Island after transporting a Marine Raider Battalion to Savo Island. The Japanese, after direct hits from gun salvos left the APDs ablaze and sinking, steamed between the stricken ships firing shells and strafing survivors in the water. The *Gregory* sank about 0140, and *Little* some two hours later. Admiral Chester Nimitz, commander-in-chief Pacific Fleet, paid tribute to the destroyer-transports: "With little means, the ships performed duties vital to the success of the campaign."[3]

THE TOKYO EXPRESS

The three destroyers which attacked and sunk the two American APDs on 4 September were part of the so-called "Tokyo Express," fast ships that by night transported food, reinforcement personnel, supplies and equipment to Japanese forces operating in and around New Guinea and the Solomons. The enemy had initiated use of the Express to counter the air superiority established by the Allies in the South Pacific in late August 1942 after Henderson Field became operational on Guadalcanal. Recognizing that its slow transports were vulnerable to attack by day, the IJN devised an alternative plan whereby warships of the Tokyo Express would make all deliveries in darkness and return to their originating bases prior to dawn in order to prevent daylight interception by Allied aircraft. A majority of the participating ships were part of the Eighth Fleet operating from Rabaul, New Britain, and Bougainville, Solomon Islands. (Rabaul, 565 nautical miles westnorthwest of Guadalcanal, was the largest center of Japanese military activity in the South Pacific.) Some units from the Combined Fleet, home-based further north at Truk Atoll in the Caroline Islands, were often attached temporarily. Express operations, which began soon after the Battle of Savo Island on 9 August 1942, continued until 25

November 1943. On that date, five American destroyers, under the command of Capt. Arleigh Burke, USN, interdicted and almost completely destroyed three IJN destroyer-transports escorted by two destroyers in the Battle of Cape St. George. The sea battle, fought in waters between Cape St. George, New Ireland, and Buka Island (now part of the North Solomons Province in Papua, New Guinea), marked the end of Japanese resistance in the Solomon Islands.[4]

Map 1-1

Groups of Japanese warships termed the "Tokyo Express" made nightly runs from their bases at Rabaul, New Britain, and Bougainville in New Guinea, down the slot between the northern and southern Solomon Islands to deliver food, reinforcement personnel, supplies and equipment to Japanese ground forces operating in and around New Guinea and the Solomons.
Source: http://www.lib.utexas.edu/maps/historical/pacific_islands_1943_1945/solomon_islands.jpg

IMPENDING TASIMBOKO RAID

Following the destruction of three units of Transportation Division 12 within only five days, and with only two destroyer-transports left to provide troop lift, Marine Col. Merritt A. "Red Mike" Edson drafted YPs *239* and *346* to participate in the raid on Tasimboko after he observed them working the Tulagi Harbor. When the ships formed at Kukum on 7 September 1942, the stark differences between the APDs and YPs were very apparent. While the destroyer-transports sported a coat of jungle-green paint and camouflage nets to help them blend in against tropical backdrops, the former fishing vessels were a dull navy gray.⁵ Another contrast was the ride the ships offered; Marines aboard the 815-foot destroyer-transports were much happier during the ensuing wet, cold transit in rough seas than those in the two diminutive vessels. A member of Able Company later remarked that the most miserable night of his life was the one he spent between 7 and 8 September while embarked in the *YP-346*. He described the conditions thus:

> The stack of that YP poured sparks [emitted by the laboring diesel engine] into the air all night. We were extremely crowded . . . so we huddled in a sitting position and attempted to brace ourselves to catnap. . . . It was cold! The rolling vessel made some seasick and as they heaved we were all awash in cold sea water and vomit.⁶

The Guadalcanal Campaign, of which the impending raid would be only a small part, was spurred by the Japanese occupation of Tulagi, a small island nestled in a bay at Florida Island opposite Guadalcanal, on 3 May 1942. In response to the enemy having established a toehold in the strategically-located island chain, U.S. naval forces began to build a base on nearby Espiritu Santo Island three weeks later. Japan wanted an air field in the Solomons from which its land-based bombers could provide air cover for the advance of Imperial land forces to Port Moresby, the capital city of Papua and the site of an Allied base (the territories of Papua and New Guinea were combined after World War II into a single territory that today is known as Papua New Guinea). The thousands of troops based there were the Allies' last line of defense before Australia. Having found Tulagi fit only for a seaplane base, on 5 July Japanese forces landed on Guadalcanal, twenty miles across the New Georgia Sound (which Allied servicemen referred to as "The Slot") from Tulagi, and began the rapid construction of Lunga Point Airfield from which the empire's planes could menace the shipping lanes to Australia.⁷

In an effort to prevent that eventuality and gain control of the Solomons, 11,000 members of the 1st Marine Division landed at Guadalcanal on 7 August, and captured the airstrip at Lunga Point, as well as the Japanese encampment at Kukum on the west side of Lunga Point the following day. That same afternoon, after fierce fighting, Marines discharged at Tulagi took the Japanese-held Island, as well as the smaller islands of Gavutu and Tanambogo. The captured airstrip on Guadalcanal was renamed Henderson Field, and its occupation and use by Allied forces temporarily halted Japanese expansion in the

South Pacific. The significance of American control of the island—from which the Allies could expand their presence in the South Pacific while thwarting the Japanese thrust—was not lost on the enemy. Guadalcanal became a pivotal piece of island real estate, one that both sides wanted to control and to which they were willing to commit large numbers of forces. By day, aircraft from Henderson Field controlled the skies, allowing U.S. Navy transports and small vessels to operate in the area with some degree of safety. At night, however, control of these waters shifted as IJN warships, then safe from air attack, raced down the slot between the northern and southern Solomons with supplies and troops to resupply Japanese land forces—and to assault Allied ships caught outside the protected harbor of the fortified island of Tulagai.[8]

FISHING VESSELS TO THE FORE

How did the tuna boats from San Diego come to be plying the dangerous Solomon Islands waters during the summer of 1942? A few weeks after the attack on Pearl Harbor on 7 December 1941, Comdr. W. J. Morcott, USN (Ret.), the U.S. Navy's port director, met with San Diego tuna fishermen to inform them that the Navy needed them and their boats to support the war effort. About 600 fishermen signed up that day—men with good Portuguese names like Madruga, Gonsalves, Rosa, Theodore, Mascarenhas, Soares, Perry, and Freitas, mixed with Italian names like Ascuito, Scandinavian ones like Rasmussen, and others like Green. Many of the fifty-two clippers that went to war were acquired by the military under a "Bare Boat Charter." Such charters required a vessel to be returned to its owner in a condition as least as good as when acquired, less ordinary wear and tear based on use of the vessel for naval purposes. Other vessels were purchased from their owners, private individuals as well as subsidiaries of tuna canners and shipyards. A majority of the clippers were ordered to the South Pacific for employment as small supply vessels, or to the Panama Canal Zone for assignment to anti-submarine patrol duties. The term "tuna clipper" originally applied to tuna baitboats greater than 100 gross tons and, since all large YPs were tuna baitboats, the term was appropriate to describe the YPs acquired from the San Diego tuna fishing community. A majority of the tuna clippers were operated by captains of Portuguese descent, followed by those of Japanese, Italian, and Dalmatian origins. A number of smaller vessels from the major

California fishing ports, including San Diego tuna baitboats/sardine seiners, San Pedro seiners/tuna baitboats, and sardine seiners from Monterey and San Francisco, were also taken into service to serve as naval district patrol craft.[9]

The tuna clippers were especially prized for their refrigeration capabilities and economical diesel engines. Sporting new coats of dull slate-gray paint over their former brilliant white hulls, and fitted (typically) with a 20mm cannon forward, as well as .50-caliber (sometimes .30-cal.) machine guns and depth charges, the boats were quickly pressed into service as the "errand boys of the Pacific."[10]

The fishermen who volunteered for duty quickly donned navy uniforms; there was no requirement for the experienced mariners to attend boot camp. The skippers and chief engineers of the boats received commissions as chief warrant officers, and crewmen were given petty officer ratings, compensatory with their age and knowledge. The experience of Vincent Battaglia is fairly representative. After joining the Navy on 1 May 1942 as a machinist's mate second, he reported aboard the *YP-346* (the ex-tuna clipper *Prospect*) on 6 May, and left San Diego aboard her that same day. The skipper, Joaquin Theodore, had remarked to a lieutenant commander, while arranging his own entry into the Navy, that he did not even know how to salute, to which the officer replied: "Mr. Theodore, we don't care how you salute; we want you because of your seamanship." His ship was armed with two .50-caliber machine guns, one atop the pilothouse and the other in the stern near where depth charges were stored on a rack. The men aboard believed that the barrel-shaped explosives would provide little protection against submarines, and the depth charges made them uneasy, as a collision with another ship while in convoy—always a possibility at night—could blow their boat to pieces.[11]

After standing out of San Diego harbor, the *YP-346* joined a group of thirteen other YPs departing San Diego for the Hawaiian Sea Frontier in company with the patrol yacht *Almandite* (PY-24). All of the vessels were raised-deck tuna clippers destined for use as refrigerated supply ships in the Hawaiian Islands or in the South or Southwest Pacific. Kenneth G. Adams, the commanding officer of the *YP-347* (formerly the *Star of the Sea*), described the transit to Hawaii, during which the ships ran at night with navigation lights extinguished to help avoid the possibility of detection by enemy forces:

Photo 1-2

Former skippers and chief engineers of San Diego tuna clippers newly commissioned as naval officers, most as boatswain or machinist warrant officers. Pictured, upper row, left to right, are Boatswains Victor Rosa and Frank Gonsalves, Ens. Antonio Mascarenhas, Boatswain John Tosso, Machinists Robert Hargreaves, James Burk, Mike Ascuitto, V. I. Simian, W. A. Robbins, and L. E. Wiley, all USNR. Lower row, left to right, with officers of the 11th Naval District port director's office, Machinist John Turner, Boatswain Edward Madruga, Machinist Manuel Enrique, USNR, Comdr. W. J. Morcott, USN Ret., Lt. J. F. Piotrowski, USN Ret., Lt. Comdr, J. E. Kemmer, USN Ret., Boatswains Ed Varley and E. Quallin, USNR.
Courtesy of the San Diego Portuguese Historical Center

When clear of Point Loma [San Diego], all fifteen boats fell into their previously assigned station, and the Yippie [YP] fleet was Pearl Harbor bound. Keeping station was a nightmare. My tub was either too fast or too slow. So it was a case of crawling up on the ship ahead or falling back too far. Fortunately ours was the last ship in the column; else we surely would have been rammed....

Then there was the nighttime, during the dark of the moon, and complete blackout, without even a feeble stern light to help the following ship. Daytime was bad enough, but darkness was simply hell. Only by the grace of God did we avoid collision with the ship ahead.

Pearl Harbor was an astonishing, appalling sight that the folks back home were never told about. There were wrecked ships all over the bay and at the docks. The water was thick with oil. The [battleship] *Arizona* lay on her side. One ship at the dock had a hole clear through her. We were issued gas masks and ordered to carry them at all times. The civilian population did likewise, right down to every child.¹²

Upon arrival, the 185-foot patrol yacht reported for duty to the Hawaiian Sea Frontier, and thereafter operated in and out of Pearl Harbor for the duration of the war. Her duties included patrolling the harbor entrance and escorting other ships on runs from Oahu to other Hawaiian islands, as well as to Johnston and Palmyra Atolls located quite a distance southwest of Pearl Harbor. She also served as a weather station in the Hawaiian area. The fourteen YPs entered U.S. Navy Yard, Pearl Harbor in the early afternoon of 17 May. Six of the former tuna clippers (identified by asterisks in the following summary of ship characteristics) would not return home from the war. The abbreviation Bos'n denotes the rank of Warrant Officer Boatswain.

Ship Designation/ Former Name	Year Built	Length Feet	Commanding Officer(s)
YP-237/*Anna M.*	1941	101.2	BM1 John R. Bruce/Lt. (jg) M. S. Morgan
YP-239/*Challenger**	1940	113.7	Howard H. Branyon/Ens. G. E. Shannon
YP-240/*Conte Bianco*	1934	111.7	At war's end, Lt. (jg) M. S. Carroll
YP-277/*Triunfo**	1937	116.0	Pete Dias
YP-284/*Endeavor**	1940	131.3	Christian Rasmussen
YP-289/*Paramount**	1937	110.1	Bos'n Edward X. Madruga
YP-290/*Picaroto*	1937	127.9	Bos'n Victor Rosa/Lt. A. B. Goldman
YP-292/*Azoreana*	1937	130.4	Bos'n Ed Varley/Ens. W. H. Tidman
YP-345/*Yankee**	1939	105.9	G. J. Brocato
YP-346/*Prospect**	1938	108.7	Bos'n Joaquin S. Theodore
YP-347/*Star of the Sea*	1930	107.0	Bos'n Kenneth G. Adams
YP-348/*Cabrillo*	1935	126.0	Virgil Pash/Bos'n V. DiPaixio
YP-349/*Queen Mary*	1938	134.0	George Reeves
YP-350/*Victoria*	1937	129.0	Manuel Freitas¹³

The former San Diego tuna clippers did not remain idle for long. A few other YPs were present in the Hawaiian Islands, but being relatively small, they had been assigned to the local defense force. These craft included five former Japanese-owned fishing boats—*YP-173* (ex-*Kasuga Maru*), *YP-174* (ex-*Nachi Maru*), *YP-186* (ex-*Tenjin Maru*), *YP-225* (ex-*Kiyo Maru*), and *YP-226* (ex-*Tenjin Maru II*)—as well as the ex-*Seamonger* (*YP-123*) and the ex-*Islander* (*YP-327*), built in 1924 in Malmo, Sweden, and in 1931 by the Sampson Fishing Boat Co. of Honolulu, Hawaii, respectively. The larger, more seaworthy ex-tuna boats were dispatched with provisions and supplies to areas farther out in the island chain. Four YPs—*284, 290, 345,* and *350*—cleared the harbor at 0700 on 20 May 1942 en route to Lisianski and Midway, west-northwest of Honolulu. A second group—the *237, 239, 277,* and *348*—set off for French Frigate Shoals, 260 miles to the southeast of Midway, to deliver provisions, spare parts, and fuel to a Motor Torpedo (PT) Boat squadron detained there en route to Midway. The YPs and PT boats were part of a larger Pacific Fleet effort to prepare Midway for an anticipated Japanese attack. Cryptanalysts had broken Japan's top secret naval code on 15 May 1942 and were able to piece together that Adm. Isoroku Yamamoto, the architect of the attack on Pearl Harbor, planned to occupy Midway Island and the Aleutians. Nimitz immediately ordered the reinforcement of Midway.[14]

YPS ORDERED TO THE SOUTH AND SOUTHWEST PACIFIC

Amid such efforts, on 17 June Nimitz assigned five of the former tuna clippers to Vice Adm. Robert. L. Ghormley, the newly appointed commander, South Pacific Area and South Pacific Force. Three of the YPs—*240, 289,* and *292*—were then at, or en route to, Samoa, and *YP-239* and *YP-346* were en route to Efate, two links in a recently-developed vital supply line to Australia. Shipping bound from Bora Bora in French Polynesia to Australia had to pass through or close to the Cook Islands, then the Samoa, Tonga and Fiji groups, and finally, approximately a thousand miles from the Australian coast, the New Hebrides group and New Caledonia. These island bases were generally poor, offering little more than a small airfield and a protected anchorage for ships while they took on fuel or supplies from service vessels. Efate, a part of the joint British-French colony of New Hebrides, however, hosted a large military base. Initially established as an outpost to support New Caledonia, 300 miles to the southwest, and the Fiji Islands, 600 miles to the east, it subsequently served as a minor air and naval base for offensive operations. With the U.S. Army already in New Caledonia and the Japanese moving into Guadalcanal, 700 miles to the north, top military brass had deemed it critical to open airfields in the New Hebrides to facilitate bombing enemy forces on Guadalcanal and to prevent completion of a Japanese airfield on Lunga Point. In July YPs *284* and *290* were hurriedly deployed to the Southwest Pacific.[15]

The earlier group (YPs *239*, *240*, *289*, *292*, and *346*) had left Hawaii with orders to the Efate/Samoan Defensive Area; with YPs *284* and *290* ordered to Auckland, New Zealand. The latter two vessels arrived at Tongatabu, Tonga Islands, following stops en route at Palmyra, and Suva, Fiji. From there, necessities of war sent the *YP-290* to Auckland, New Zealand, and the *YP-284*, following her arrival at Espiritu Santo, to Guadalcanal along with YPs *239* and *346*.

Ship(s)	Assigned Location
YP-290	Auckland, New Zealand
YP-239, *YP-284*, and *YP-346*	Guadalcanal, Solomon Islands
YP-240, *YP-289*, and *YP-292*	Samoan Islands[16]

The voyage of YPs *239* and *346* to Efate was representative of those of the other ships. After returning from French Frigate Shoals, the two YPs had stood out of Pearl Harbor in the late afternoon of 9 June and set a course south for Palmyra, an atoll halfway between Hawaii and Samoa and the site of a naval air station. The crews of the former tuna clippers typically numbered about seventeen men, usually nine ex-fishermen and eight "regular Navymen," who included an experienced gunner's mate to maintain the ship's armament. Leaving Palmyra on 15 June, the vessels continued sailing south, bound for Tutuila, Samoa. Upon arrival there eight days later, the ships' captains, Chief Warrant Officers Branyon and Theodore, reported for duty under Vice Admiral Ghormley. It is unclear whether the two vessels then continued to operate together or separately. The *YP-346*'s next stop was Fiji, where its crew found, much to their delight, that liquor was only six cents a shot. Following this respite, the *346* set a course west-northwest for Espiritu Santo, New Hebrides, the site of a supply and support base as well as a naval harbor and an airfield.[17]

LOSS OF THE DESTROYER *TUCKER*

As the *YP-346* neared Espiritu Santo in the early evening of 3 August, a Navy destroyer challenged her via flashing light message. Following receipt of the correct response, the DD, also bound for Espiritu Santo, signaled "Good luck to you guys." The YP entered Segond Channel an hour past midnight and thereafter sighted a wrecked ship ahead that was breaking in two and folding up like a jackknife—the same one with which she had exchanged signals the previous night. After having bid them farewell, the *Tucker* (DD-374) unknowingly entered a defensive minefield laid the previous day by the minelayers *Gamble* (DM-15), *Breese* (DM-18) and *Tracy* (DM-19), and struck a mine at 2145. The destroyer was unaware of the danger, as she had received no radio warning regarding the existence of the new field. The explosion broke the *Tucker*'s back, killing three crewmen, with an additional three missing and presumed lost. In an effort to keep the DD from breaking in two, her captain ordered topside weight jettisoned, and sailors heaved depth charges, torpedoes, 20mm shells, and other portable gear overboard. Upon arrival at the scene, Theodore took the 346 into the field in an attempt to save the beleaguered warship:

> And so when I got there, the captain asked me if I could give him a tow, causethey're in deep water, to go into shallow water. . . . So I went alongside him, [and] he give me a line.[18]

The YP was able to get the foundering *Tucker* clear of the minefield, fortunately without detonating any more mines, but despite her best efforts she was unable to beach the destroyer. The DD later grounded in the surf off the northwest coast of Malo Island, set there by strong wind and seas. In the interim, those aboard were either taken off or abandoned ship. On her arrival on scene around noon, the minelayer *Breese* found that most of the survivors had already been put ashore. The *YP-346* had taken about half the crew off and the tanker *Nira Luckenbach* another dozen, while others had abandoned ship in the destroyer's whaleboat and life rafts. The minelayer took aboard the remaining thirty-eight men and three officers and, in the late afternoon, offered the services of three of its own officers to guide the *YP-346* and *Nira Luckenbach* through the field. The YP stood into port, while the merchantman chose to turn around, proceed out the channel, and make passage south of Malo Island. The beached destroyer later broke apart and sank after shifting offshore.[19]

After reaching Espiritu Santo, the *YP-346* offloaded frozen food for the base and, over the next few days, did whatever else was asked of her including retrieving a downed flyer from the sea and towing a barge. On 28 August Rear Adm. John S. McCain, commander Aircraft South Pacific Forces, directed that the YPs *346, 239*, and *284* take aboard aviation gasoline, and Rear Adm. Richmond K. Turner,

Photo 1-3

YP-346 with the *Tucker* (DD-374) under tow at Espiritu Santo, New Hebrides, on 3 August 1942. The destroyer had struck a mine while turning from Bruat Channel into Segond Channel, breaking her keel.
US Navy photo # NH 77030 from the collections of the Naval History and Heritage Command, http://www.navsource.org/archives/14/31346.htm.

commander Task Force 62 (Amphibious Force, South Pacific Force), ordered the destroyer *Helm* (DD-388) and three YPs to form Task Unit 62.2.3 and proceed to Guadalcanal. Upon arrival the former tuna clippers were to report for duty to Major Gen. Alexander Vandegrift, commanding general 1st Marine Division. The *Helm* got under way in the early evening of 29 August, but due to darkness, could not locate the three ships she was to escort. The DD stood westward through Bougainville Strait, then northwestward to pass south of San Cristobal Island before proceeding for Lengo Channel leading to Guadalcanal. She eventually made contact and the group arrived at its destination in the mid-afternoon of 31 August.[20]

YP DUTY AT GUADALCANAL/TULAGI

The offloading of cargo from the YPs began the next morning. Around noon, as a Japanese air raid arrived overhead and bombs began falling on the beach and in the anchorage, the little ships hauled in their anchors and put out to sea as fast as possible. Baptized by enemy attack, the YPs would subsequently serve as tugs, dispatch boats, rescue craft, troop and supply ferries, and transports for minor amphibious operations in dangerous waters. Because "Cactus" was the military code word for Guadalcanal, the YPs, and other ships that shuttled food, supplies, and ammunition between Tulagi and Lunga Point, Guadalcanal, were referred to as the "Cactus Navy."[21] Vincent Battaglia, a former *YP-346* crew member, summarized that duty and the fighting between American and Japanese forces on Guadalcanal and Tulagi:

> Our anchorage was Tulagi. It was maybe a two-hour run [20 nautical miles] from Guadalcanal to Tulagi....There were three YPs, the *Endeavor,* the *Challenger,* and the *Prospect.* Our duty was between Tulagi and Guadalcanal, back and forth, carrying troops from here to here, load with food, or whatever it was.
>
> [There was] a lot of fighting at Tulagi. In two or three days it was all over with. It shifted and about a month later it was down in Guadalcanal. The Japanese started reinforcing. . . . At night a Jap ship would come down the channel. The next day an American ship would come up. The big battles were fought two months after we got there.[22]

MARINE RAID ON TASIMBOKO VILLAGE

In early September, native scouts and aerial reconnaissance discovered that Japanese troops had come ashore on Guadalcanal at Tasimboko, eighteen miles east of Lunga Point. The scouts correctly estimated that the enemy force (which would prove to be a reinforced brigade) was several thousand in number. The Marines believed enemy strength to be about 500 men, and that the 1st Raider and 1st Parachute Battalions under Colonel Edson would be sufficient to deal with them. In any event, there was little time to respond to the threat. After occupying a village near the shore and setting up a supply base, the brigade, led by Major General Kawaguchi, had begun advancing inland towards the Marine defense perimeter around Henderson Field.[23]

At 1800 on 7 September, the rifle companies of the 1st Marine Raiders embarked from Kukum, Guadalcanal, in *McKean, Manley, YP-239,* and *YP-346* for a night transit east to Taivu Point. Approaching the landing point just prior to dawn, a group of ships they hoped were not units of the Japanese fleet appeared on the horizon. Happily, the group proved to be the transport *Fuller* (AP-14) and cargo ship *Bellatrix* (AK-20), escorted by warships and engaged in unrelated business. A Japanese rear guard of 300 men, left behind to guard the brigade's supplies, also sighted the ships and mistakenly thought they were part of a larger landing force. Alarmed, the soldiers withdrew into the jungle, abandoning individual weapons, supplies and 37mm antitank guns at water's edge, and leaving the landing site only lightly defended.[24]

Prior to the landing of Marines by Higgins boats, the destroyer-transports and planes of Marine Aircraft Group 23 shelled and strafed enemy strong points inland. However, as the Marines came ashore and moved into the underbrush, they took fire from .25-caliber rifles and machineguns, followed by 75mm artillery. Baker Company silenced the enemy fire and attacked Tasimboko from the west along the beach, as Able Company moved into the jungle and came in from the south. Enemy resistance was light; the raiders suffered only two killed and six wounded while advancing toward the village. (Meanwhile, *McKean* and *Manley* had shuttled back to Kukum and returned with the balance of the raiders, the weapons company of the 1st Raider Battalion and the 1st Parachute Battalion.) On their arrival at Tasimboko Village, the Marines found it stockpiled with cases of food and sacks of rice, medical supplies, and more than 50,000 rounds of ammunition. Having gone without eating for over twelve hours and hungry after the cold, wet transit, the raiders ate some of the food, including delectable canned crabmeat, drank whatever was available, including Saki, and then destroyed the large quantities of supplies, ammunition and equipment. Before re-embarking in the destroyer-transports and YPs in the early evening, Marines stripped the breach blocks off large artillery pieces and threw them into the sea, and used Higgins boats to drag the smaller guns offshore into deep water.[25]

By that time, word of the raid had reached the Japanese Navy's high command, and an angry Tokyo Express, led by the light cruiser IJN *Sendai*, was proceeding down the slot between the northern and southern Solomon Islands to exact vengeance. Meanwhile, the APDs and YPs had returned to Lunga Point to disembark the Marines where, in the rain and amidst rough seas, leathernecks began boarding boats for the short trip to shore. As the *Manley* unloaded, she received orders to clear out at highest speed as a raid by enemy surface units was expected momentarily. With 200 Marines still embarked, she hoisted aboard all boats and, accompanied by the *McKean*, headed out Lengo Channel at 2110 hours. The YPs were told to make haste for Tulagi, about twenty miles away, which offered an enclosed harbor defended by shore guns. However, sanctuary for the ex-tuna boats, which were only able to make 10 knots, was a long two hours away and the *YP-346* did not make it.[26]

Map 1-2

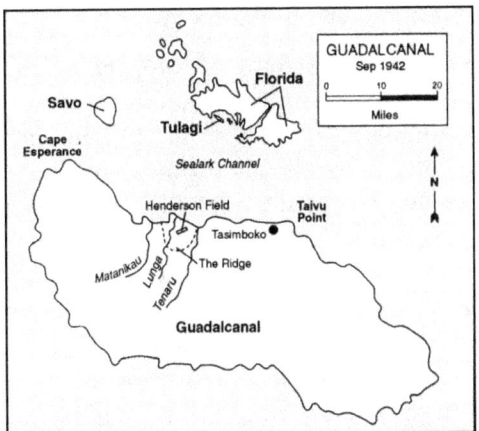

Told while disembarking Marines at Lunga Point to clear out at highest speed, since a raid by Japanese enemy surface units was expected momentarily, the former tuna clippers *YP-239* and *YP-346* made haste for Tulagi about twenty miles away. The latter was just short of the sanctuary of the harbor when she came under fire from an enemy light cruiser.
Source: http://www.nps.gov/history/history/online_books/npswapa/extContent/usmc/pcn-190-003130-00/sec6.htm

Vincent Battaglia described being warned of the impending raid, and the ensuing attack by the *Sendai*, which caught the *YP-346* alone in the channel ten minutes from safety, as her sister ship—*YP-239*, only 300 yards ahead—was beating into the harbor:

> Hey, you guys, you better get out of here. There is a cruiser and two destroyers in the channel.... Now we are going to Tulagi, "Hail Marys" [praying] all the way. When we get there it is about midnight. The Japanese cruiser shoots up a star [shell, an illumination round], shoots its flares up and lights up the whole bay. In the spotlight they find us and start shooting at us.... That ship was so close you could hear the blowers [that push air into the propulsion boilers] on the ship.
>
> They hit us twice. They hit the pilothouse. One guy was blown off the pilothouse; he is dead. [The commanding officer] Theodore

looks like he got wounded; one Marine got wounded here; one guy got his arm shot off. To make a long story short, I went over the side because of the ammonia. Theodore said, "Get off of this thing." Ammonia gas [used for freezing fish] is very deadly. Theo manages to get the boat in the right direction to go towards the beach. We are in the water while the boat beaches itself. That is how they got Theodore off and they got these other guys off, but we were in the water.[27]

The Japanese cruiser, having overhauled the *YP-346*, opened fire on the wooden vessel with its 5-inch main battery and anti-aircraft guns shooting fragmentation rounds. The first salvo hit the magazine and fire swept the deck of the little ship. The blast from a gun round destroyed the pilot house, fatally wounded Electrician's Mate First Lehman and blew him over the side. (His body was found two days later.) A hit aft punctured a section of piping associated with the fish freezing system, releasing deadly ammonia gas into the boat. Shrapnel from an anti-aircraft round struck Joaquin Theodore between the shoulder blades, causing the commanding officer to collapse on deck. (He was fortunate that the entry wounds were to the left of his spinal cord and that most of the metal shards exited his body on the right side of his chest). When able to look up, Theodore noted the helmsman, Roy C. Parnell, a gunner's mate second, was staggering near the wheel with a dazed look on his face as a result of one of his hands having been shot away, and sent him below for treatment. Years later, the former ship's captain described the brutal attack and his order to beach the *YP-346*:

> I took one and beside that I told everybody to take shelter, who don't belong on deck, so they did. All of them. The only guys on top of the deck was me. I was on the bridge and the other guy at the wheel. . . . He got a piece of shrapnel in his arm, he cut his arm, broke his arm. I hollered over there to somebody for help. I had two Marines that were on my ship, they were gunners and they came out and I told them, "Beach the ship."[28]

With no chance against the cruiser, having only .50-caliber machine guns for self-defense, and his ship aflame such that a distant Marine could see the channel illuminated by it, Theodore chose his best and only option to save the crew from almost certain death:

> But what are you going to do? You have a little ship there, you can't defend yourself. What are you going to do? The first thing I thought

of was beach the ship. Get it away from the line of fire and I think it saved a lot of the guys. We lost one guy there. He was my electrician on the ship. . . . He got hit with a piece of shrapnel, I guess.[29]

"Beach the ship" may have been the last order the incapacitated captain uttered. Following a direct hit in the engine room, Chief Machinist's Mate Charles Vaughn went on deck to make a damage report and on arriving topside, found the bridge shot away, a Marine at the helm, and was told that Theodore was dead. Marine Private 1st Class John Murphy, who had been asleep in his bunk until awakened by the cook for general quarters, had run topside with Private 1st Class Gerard Nevle to man their gun. Unable to get near it due to shells exploding in the magazine below the gun, the Marines quickly took up new, more pressing duties. Nevle entered the demolished bridge, set the *YP-346* on a heading toward land, and ministered first aid to the helmsman. After the ship veered off course, he re-manned the helm and, despite there being only three broken spokes still fixed to the hub of the wheel, grounded the vessel off the beach in shallow water. Nevle then got the wounded gunner's mate over the side, helped him to swim ashore, and leaving his charge safely on the beach, returned aboard to assist other crewmen.[30]

While these efforts were underway, Chief Vaughn returned to the engine room and aided by Murphy, secured the ammonia system in an effort to protect ship's company from being incapacitated or killed by the deadly, colorless gas. Vaughn then told Murphy to "take off." Emerging on deck the Marine was knocked flat by an exploding fragmentation round and shrapnel gouged away a chunk of his arm. Despite his wound, he picked up a lifejacket and slipped over the side, entering the water about fifty yards from shore. After making the beach, Murphy assisted in transporting Parnell to a field hospital for medical attention. For their courageous actions under fire, which almost certainly saved the lives of the gravely injured captain and other members of ship's company, Vaughn, Murphy, and Nevle received the Navy Cross. The medal, the second highest American decoration for valor, is awarded for extraordinary heroism not justifying the Medal of Honor. (Copies of their award citations are provided in Appendix D.)[31]

The sailors and two Marines, some wounded, found no shelter from the elements ashore except for a small cave, unable to accommodate more than a single person, near the beach. After placing the grievously wounded commanding officer inside the cave, the men huddled on the beach in the rain until rescued, after first witnessing the final destruction of their little ship, the former tuna boat *Prospect*, the following night.³²

Following the first engagement, the Japanese erroneously believed that the *YP-346* had been destroyed. An officer aboard the *Sendai*, Lieutenant Kaboshima, reported at midnight on 8 September:

> No enemy at Lunga, we advanced to Tulagi. Sighted two destroyers in harbor [probably the two YPs], shot them. One sunk.

The cruiser then left the area, believing that she had dispatched her prey, and the tiny ship thus escaped obliteration. Her luck would not continue. The *Sendai* returned the following night around midnight, sighted the *YP-346* aground at a point on Tulagi Island, and began shelling it. One of the rounds struck a bait box used to store ammunition in the after part of the ship and the resulting explosion and fire finished off the vessel.³³

Battaglia described the event:

> The Japanese cruiser comes in again that night at midnight, and the same thing [happened]. They run a light across the beach and they see the ship on the beach. . . . It was already beached and I didn't think we could salvage it. Ernie and I were about 100 yards away from the ship and they started blowing it out of the water. The Japanese sank the same ship twice. Do you want to know where the Japanese navy was September 9, 1942? They were at Tulagi sinking a fishing boat.³⁴

Theodore's description of having "taken one" during the action was understated. Initially evacuated to Pearl Harbor for medical treatment, he was later sent stateside to Oak Knoll Naval Hospital in Oakland, California, where surgeons removed his dead right lung, which contained shrapnel. Following recovery, the Navy assigned him to tending anti-submarine nets at the entrance to San Diego harbor for the duration of the war. Afterwards Theodore worked the fuel dock in San Diego—unable, due to the injuries he had sustained, to return to fishing.³⁵

LOSS OF THE TUG *SEMINOLE* AND PATROL CRAFT *YP-284*

> *They only had small guns on them, you know. The Japanese destroyers picked them off like wooden ducks.*
>
> —Larry Canepa, skipper of a San Diego tuna clipper during World War II, describing, in an interview in 1988, the disparity between YPs and enemy warships operating in the South Pacific.

Six-and-a-half weeks after the loss of the *YP-346*, three Japanese destroyers sent the *YP-284*, along with the fleet tug *Seminole* (AT-65), to the bottom on the morning of 25 October 1942 during the second battle for Henderson Field. *Akatsuki*, *Ikazuchi*, and *Shiratsuyo* opened the action against the destroyer-minesweeper *Trever* (DMS-16) from a range of five miles. The *Trever* and her sister ship *Zane* (DMS-14) were both former World War I destroyers with only modest armament. Two hours earlier, they had received a warning that three Japanese destroyers were headed their way. However, there was work to be done providing support for Motor Torpedo Boat Squadron 3. One of the squadron's divisions was already present at Tulagi and a second—comprised of *PT-37*, *PT-39*, *PT-45*, and *PT-61*—had arrived earlier that day.[36]

The *Trever* was ferrying torpedoes, ammunition, and gasoline across the channel to Guadalcanal with two motor torpedo boats in tow astern, and the *Zane*, in company behind her, was similarly burdened when the Japanese destroyers appeared and took them both under fire. The three DDs were eastbound, passing a stretch of water at the southern end of the slot between Guadalcanal, Savo Island, and Florida Island termed "Ironbottom Sound" by Allied sailors due to the large numbers of ships and planes already sent to the ocean floor there during the relatively young Guadalcanal Campaign.[37]

Bracketed by gun salvos, the minesweepers cut their tows adrift in an effort to evade the Japanese ships. Lt. Comdr. Dwight A. Agnew, commanding officer of the *Trever* and the senior officer of the two ships, ordered his three-inch guns to commence firing and turned the two ships hard left into the shoal-ridden Nggela Channel in a futile attempt to escape the enemy's five-inch guns. The *Zane* was hit by a salvo at 1035, killing three crewmen, wounding nine, and disabling one gun mount. As four fighter aircraft from Henderson Field appeared overhead, the 1st Assault Unit destroyers, under Comdr. Yusuke Yamada, changed course to fight off the attack. The minesweepers—making more than 29 knots in an endeavor to flee almost certain destruction—proceeded into Indispensable Strait.[38]

The salvation of the *Trevor* and *Zane* brought about the ruin of the *YP-284* and *Seminole*, which had arrived at Lunga Point, Guadalcanal, from Tulagi with cargoes of howitzers, ammunition, aviation gasoline and 146 embarked Marines. The fleet tug had discharged about 200 drums of gasoline and four howitzers, while the *YP-284* stood by awaiting lighters to put out from the base, when, at about 1015, the two vessels received orders from Naval Operating Base, Guadalcanal to abandon unloading and run for Tulagi. The *Seminole* and *YP-284* immediately ceased transferring men and materials ashore and set off, making maximum turns, hoping the enemy would remain occupied with the minesweepers. Such was not to be. The tug was a little short of mid-channel and the slower YP only some five miles off Guadalcanal when the Japanese destroyer line broke contact with *Trever* and *Zane*. Both ships immediately recognized their increased peril and took evasive action. The *Seminole* changed course and headed for Lengo Channel, while *YP-284* did an about face and started to run for Guadalcanal.[39]

With the ultimate result of the coming fight obvious to all aboard the *YP-284*, Lt. Christian Rasmussen engaged the enemy with his meager three-inch bow gun. The one-sided battle was short. The Japanese DDs opened fire on the YP at about 1050. The second salvo set fire to her cargo and a direct hit to the engine room damaged the refrigeration system ammonia receivers, filling the ship with fumes. Rasmussen then ordered engines stopped and all hands including the Marines aboard to abandon ship. The enemy continued firing and the YP sank within minutes, about five miles east of Lunga Lagoon off Koli Point, carrying three Marines to the bottom. One section of Battery "I" of the 10th Marines, numbering about forty-five officers and men, was aboard, having been unable to disembark at Guadalcanal. No crewmen were killed, although many suffered wooden splinter wounds.[40]

Having dispatched the YP, the Japanese destroyers turned their attention to the *Seminole*. During the preceding battle, she had changed course, trying to close the shore and get under the protection of the Guadalcanal shore batteries. Naval gunfire found the *Seminole* at about

1115, followed by two additional salvos that set fire to the drums of aviation gas on deck. Five minutes later she was ablaze with burning gasoline pouring into the ship's interior through the shell holes. Lt. Comdr. William G. Fewel gave the order to abandon ship, and shortly afterwards the tug slipped beneath the surface in twenty fathoms of water, a half mile offshore between Lunga and Koli Points. As a majority of the gun rounds had passed through the *Seminole*'s sides without exploding, casualties were much lighter than they would have been otherwise; only one sailor killed and two wounded. For their actions, the officers and men of the *YP-284* and *Seminole* received a battle star to affix to their Asiatic-Pacific Campaign Medals.[41]

The vanquishers of the two little ships did not emerge from the action unscathed. Off Lunga Point, Marine shore batteries and F4F aircraft from Marine Fighting Squadron 121 damaged the *Akatsuki*, F4Fs the *Ikazuchi*, and U.S. Army Air Force P39s the *Akatsuki* and *Shiratsuyo*.[42]

YP-239 STEPS UP HER EFFORTS

Following the enemy action on 25 October, only the *YP-239* remained of the three ex-tuna clippers which had formed the core of the Cactus Navy, and she now worked even harder to provide crucial support to troops on Guadalcanal. A former Marine described his role in assisting the YP in ferrying gasoline to Guadalcanal and being caught aboard her out in open waters at the commencement of the naval battle of Guadalcanal on 12 November 1942:

> We were assigned working parties on most days, the more common being retrieving 55-gallon drums of gasoline from Tulagi harbor. Supplies were coming more frequently now and Guadalcanal had no harbor. Additionally, the Canal [Marine slang for Guadalcanal] would be subject to three or four bombings a day and was more dangerous. Supply ships would enter Tulagi harbor under cover of darkness and dump their load of gasoline which was destined for the airplanes at Henderson Field as well as for the PT (motor torpedo) boats. The base for the PT boats was hidden under large trees at the far end of Tulagi harbor nearest Florida Island. The supply ships could unload rapidly that way and try to get as far away as possible before sunrise since any ship caught in daylight was sure to be sunk. We would swim out into the harbor, grab a gasoline drum, and holding the drum with both hands we would kick our feet to propel ourselves to the small dock. This was rather tiring work....

It would take quite a while to retrieve the drums and then we would load them onto the old YP boat, also kept hidden at the far end of the harbor, and take them over to the Canal after dark. [Due to her shallow draft] the YP boat could come closer ashore than the supply ship. We would then roll the drums overboard while other Marines stationed on Guadalcanal would move them ashore onto the beach. While this procedure took about the whole Company on the Tulagi end, only a few of us were needed aboard the YP boat for the night crossing.

I made the night crossing three or four times. Usually the crossings were without incidence, but on one occasion it got pretty exciting. It was the night of November 12th and we were about halfway across en route to Guadalcanal when I could feel the boat increase to top speed, turning back to Tulagi as it did so. A sailor came running by and I asked him what was up. He said they had just received a radio message that said the Japanese fleet was heading south and the U.S. fleet was traveling north. They were due to meet right about here, right about now. He had not more than said those words when both fleets opened fire with us right between them, and shells were roaring overhead going in both directions.

Of all the ships out there, our little boat was absolutely at the bottom of the list of targets, which I kept telling myself. On the other hand, we were a wooden-hulled boat armed with only a machine gun. Even though traveling at top speed, we were only going about ten miles an hour. Every inch of our deck was covered with drums of high octane aviation fuel, except for where I was sitting on the fantail. My seat was a rack of highly explosive depth charges used to fight submarines. Although we didn't amount to anything, I was afraid someone would pop off a small round at us just for the fun of it. Top speed also meant sparks were flying out of our stack, which illuminated us quite nicely, though it was not necessary as both fleets were firing starshells overhead which lit up the night sky. It was an hour before we entered Tulagi harbor and I knew we had made it.[43]

The Japanese made several attempts to retake Henderson Field between August and November 1942. The naval and land battles, and the smaller skirmishes and raids of the Guadalcanal Campaign culminated in the naval battle of Guadalcanal fought between 12 and 15 November. The battle was the last Japanese attempt to land enough troops to retake Henderson Field, but it was unsuccessful. The inability of the Japanese to capture Henderson Field doomed their effort on Guadalcanal, and they evacuated their remaining forces by 7 February 1943, conceding the island to the Allies. The importance of the Guadalcanal Campaign was summarized by Adm. William F. Halsey, Jr., USN, commander, South Pacific Force and South Pacific Area:

> Before Guadalcanal the enemy advanced at his pleasure—after Guadalcanal he retreated at ours.[44]

LAURELS FOR THE CACTUS NAVY

For his heroic actions in command of the *YP-239*, Chief Warrant Officer Howard H. Branyon, USN, received the Navy Cross. The associated citation reads:

> The President of the United States takes pleasure in presenting the Navy Cross to Howard H. Branyon, Chief Boatswain, U.S. Navy, for extraordinary heroism and devotion to duty in action against the enemy while serving [as the] Commander of Patrol Ship *YP-239*, in the waters between Tulagi and Guadalcanal, Solomon Islands, during the period from 1 September 1942 to 2 November 1942. Chief Boatswain Branyon was in command of a small auxiliary naval craft used in transporting essential men and supplies. His craft averaged at least one trip a day, many of the trips having been made under heavy enemy fire, and at night, under the most trying circumstances. In spite of the obstacles and great danger present, Chief Boatswain Branyon carried out his missions with extreme courage and skill, setting an example to his command. His unflinching leadership resulted in an uninterrupted flow of reinforcements and supplies without which the ground troops would have been greatly hampered. The conduct of Chief Boatswain Branyon throughout this action reflects great credit upon himself, and was in keeping with the highest traditions of the United States Naval Service.[45]

In late August when YPs *346*, *284*, and *239* arrived at Guadalcanal to take up their duties, their officers and crew members numbered approximately fifty, as each had a ship's company of some seventeen men. Two members of this small group, Branyon and Vaughn, received Navy Crosses, as did Marine PFCs Nevle and Murphy, who served as gunners aboard the *346* during the Tasimboko Raid. One third of the group, the officers and crewmen of the *YP-284*, earned a battle star for combat with enemy destroyers. The Secretary of the

Photo 1-4

Tuna clipper *Challenger* featured in an advertisement in the *Pacific Fishermen* (January 1945). The Atlas Imperial Diesel Engine Co. highlighted that the tuna clipper's achievements as *YP-239* included: towing to safety eleven damaged warships, shelling enemy positions, shooting down Japanese bombers, putting raiding parties ashore, landing vital supplies on Guadalcanal under fire, and rescuing survivors of sunken ships.

Navy, Frank Knox, awarded the 1st Marines on Guadalcanal the Presidential Unit Citation, the highest award a military unit may receive, and the equivalent, in degree of heroism, to the Navy Cross for an individual.

Citation:

The officers and enlisted men of the First Marine Division, Reinforced, on August 7 to 9, 1942, demonstrated outstanding gallantry and determination in successfully executing forced landing assaults against a number of strongly defended Japanese positions on Tulagi, Gavutu, Tanambogo, Florida and Guadalcanal, British Solomon Islands, completely routing all enemy forces and seizing a most valuable base and airfield within the enemy zone of operations in the South Pacific Ocean. From the above period until 9 December 1942, this Reinforced Division not only held their important strategic positions despite determined and repeated Japanese naval, air and land attacks, but in a series of offensive operations against strong enemy resistance drove the Japanese from the proximity of the airfield and inflicted great losses on them by land and air attacks. The courage and determination displayed in these operations were of an inspiring order.

The Marine Corps later added the *YP-239, 284,* and *346* in gratitude for the support provided it by the intrepid little ships.[46]

SHIP LOSSES

Almost all the tuna clippers that served as YPs during World War II were from San Diego, and a majority of the boats were from the Portuguese community, with many sons of Portugal aboard. As 1942 drew to a close, the community had already suffered the destruction of four of its boats: YPs *346* and *284* at Guadalcanal, *YP-277* (ex-*Triunfo*) to a mine at French Frigate Shoals, and *YP-345* (ex-*Yankee*) to unknown causes, but most likely an enemy submarine, near Midway Island. The commanding officer of the latter ship, Chief Warrant Officer G. J. Brocato, and his crew of seventeen all perished at sea. Six more tuna clippers would be lost in subsequent years. An explosion of unknown origin sank *YP-235* (ex-*California*); *YP-279* (ex-*Navigator*) and *YP-281* (ex-*San Salvador*) foundered in storms or heavy weather; and *YP-239* (ex-*Challenger*), *YP-289* (ex-*Paramount*), and *YP-520* (ex-*Conte Grande*) sank or were destroyed during a typhoon off Okinawa in 1945.

Over the course of the war, 41 of the approximately 700 YP and patrol yachts would be lost, or damaged beyond repair, due to enemy action, storms or groundings:

- *YP-284* and *YP-346* were sunk by Japanese surface ships;

- Patrol yacht *Cythera* (PY-26) and *YP-389* were sunk by German submarines;
- *YP-345* sank due to an unknown cause, but most likely a Japanese submarine;
- *YP-277* was lost to a sea mine;
- YPs *26*, *235*, *405*, and *577* were destroyed by undetermined explosions;
- Converted yachts *Fisheries II* and *Maryanne* were destroyed to prevent capture at Corregidor, Luzon, Philippine Islands;
- *YP-97* was lost due to the Japanese occupation of the Philippine Islands;
- *YP-16* and *YP-17* were lost due to the Japanese occupation of Guam;
- YPs *279*, *281*, and *331* foundered in heavy weather;
- Coastal patrol yacht *Moonstone* (PYc-9), and YPs *47*, *74*, *77*, *383*, *387*, and *492* were sunk by collision;
- YPs *72*, *73*, *88*, *94*, *95*, *128*, *183*, *205*, *270*, *336*, *422*, *426*, *438*, *453*, and *481* were destroyed by grounding.[47]

ADDITIONAL ACCOLADES

Three patrol yachts—*Isabel* (PY-10), *Siren* (PY-13), and *Southern Seas* (PY-32)—and the converted yachts *Fisheries II* and *Maryanne* would each earn a battle star, and thirteen YPs—*41, 42, 56, 236, 251, 284, 415, 417, 421, 456, 514, 516,* and *517*—would garner another nineteen. The *Siren* received its battle star for convoy escort duty in the American Theater; all the others were awarded for combat in the Pacific.[48]

The diversity of the vessels awarded battle stars illustrates how thoroughly Navy representatives scoured America's numerous ports and harbors as well as the Service's own backwaters for remnants from World War I laid up in "mothballs" for vessels. The *Isabel*, the oldest, was commissioned on 28 December 1917, and was a veteran of World War I. The *Southern Seas* was laid down on 4 August 1920 as motor-yacht *Lyndonia* for Mrs. Cyrus Curtiss (the wife of the owner of the *Saturday Evening Post*). The yacht was later sold to Pan American Aviation Company, renamed *Southern Seas*, and subsequently sold to the Army on 30 December 1941 for use as a troop transport. After reefing at Tauria Pass, Cook Islands, on 22 July 1942, the Navy salvaged her for duty as a patrol yacht. The *Siren* was laid down in 1929 as the *Lotosland*, and was outfitted with a seaplane (a five-passenger Sikorsky).

The Navy bought the yacht from Col. Edward A. Deeds on 16 October 1940, and converted her to a coastal minelayer (CMc-1) before reclassifying its new acquisition as a patrol yacht on 15 November 1940.[49]

Of the YPs, *41*, *42*, and *56* were 98-foot long former Coast Guard cutters acquired by the Navy in the 1930s following the end of Prohibition and the associated need to use them to chase rum runners. Five of the ships were wooden-hulled former San Diego tuna clippers— *YP-236* (ex-*Europa*), *YP-284* (ex-*Endeavor*), *YP-514* (ex-*American Beauty*), *YP-516* (ex-*Queen Amelia*), and *YP-517* (ex-*St. Ann*)—and three others were steel-hulled Massachusetts fishing trawlers—*YP-415* (ex-*Swell*), *YP-417* (ex-*Calm*), and *YP-421* (ex-*Surf*). The record of the smallest YP was particularly impressive. The *YP-251*—a 79-foot former halibut schooner—and the 125-foot Coast Guard cutter *McLane* (WSC-146) were credited with sinking the Japanese submarine *RO-32*. The YP was commanded by a Dane who at age fifteen had run away from his Fresno, California, home, rode a freight train headed up the northwest coast, and joined a sailing ship to begin his career at sea.[50]

2

War Plan-Rainbow No. 5

Those who plan do better than those who do not plan even though they rarely stick to their plan.

—Winston Churchill, British Prime Minister

War Plan-Rainbow No. 5, issued by the Chief of Naval Operations on 26 May 1941 in anticipation of America's probable entry into war in the European and Pacific theaters, was the catalyst for the Navy's acquisition of civilian and commercial vessels. Under this plan (destined to be the basis for American strategy in World War II), there would be early deployment of United States forces to the eastern Atlantic, and to either or both the African and European continents, followed by offensive operations to defeat Germany and Italy. A strategic defensive was to be maintained in the Pacific until success against the European Axis Powers permitted a major transfer of fleet units to the Pacific for an offensive against Japan.[1]

The war plan detailed the initial naval organization, the composition of operating forces, and the tasks of the supporting naval establishment. One section of the document established Naval Coastal Frontiers, defined their boundaries, and specified the numbers and types of vessels and aircraft that would comprise the operating forces assigned to the commanders of the frontiers. The Naval Coastal Frontier Forces were to be formed on M-day (a military code word for the day on which mobilization would begin, or was due to begin) or sooner if directed by the Chief of Naval Operations. M-Day might precede a formal declaration of war by the United States or the occurrence of hostile acts. As a precautionary measure, the War and Navy Departments might initiate certain features of the plan prior to M-Day.[2]

Each Naval Coastal Frontier Force included a subordinate Coastal Force and a Local Defense Force. The vessels of the former were to operate well offshore near the outer boundaries of the frontier, while those of the latter were to cover the nearshore and inshore areas. Since the Navy had insufficient forces to provide the commanders of local defense forces with the ships and craft necessary to carry out their responsibilities, it assigned them mostly "X" vessels instead. Virtually non-existent at the outbreak of the war, these vessels (designated by the letter X preceding their normal ship classification) were to be acquired from sources other than the Navy or Coast Guard. When directed, commanders were to lease or purchase privately-owned and commercial vessels and prepare them for military service. In preparation for this possibility, naval district representatives began scouring their local waterfronts to identify candidate craft for conversion.[3]

During the First World War, the Navy had augmented inadequate naval forces with civilian ships, but the practice dated back to the Revolutionary War. The colonies, having declared their independence, needed far more than the thirty-one vessels of the Continental Navy to contest the Royal Navy's control of the seas successfully. To increase the paltry fleet, they issued commissions as privateers and letters of marque to privately-owned, armed merchant ships which were outfitted as warships to prey on enemy merchant ships. Over the course of the war, the sixty-four ships of the Continental Navy captured 196 enemy ships. These impressive numbers, however, pale in comparison to the collective efforts of the 1,697 privateers, who accounted for an additional 2,283 vessels. Nearly a century and a half later in 1916 during the First World War, the Navy began a registry of the privately-owned pleasure craft and yachts available for patrol service in the event the United States was drawn into the prolonged fighting in Europe. After Congress declared war on 6 April 1917, the service obtained many of the vessels and designated them as Section Patrol (SP) Craft. A majority of the SPs were returned to their owners, or disposed of, after the war. The Navy did retain a few; some served during World War II as YPs or other type naval vessels.[4]

"X-VESSELS"

In anticipation that, in the event of war with Germany and/or Japan, the fleets would need every capital ship available, the war plan directed commanders of the naval frontiers and naval districts to meet their needs for vessels through the "militarization" of ships and craft obtained from private owners:

Designation	Type Vessel	Designation	Type Vessel
XAG	Station ship	XPC	Submarine chaser
XAM	Minesweeper	XPG	Gunboat
XAMb	Base minesweeper	XPY	Patrol yacht
XAMc	Coastal minesweeper	XPYc	Coastal patrol yacht
XAOb	Base oiler	XYP	Yard patrol craft
XCMc	Coastal minelayer	XYF	Covered lighter[5]

PROJECTED VERSUS ACTUAL WARTIME QUANTITIES

Following the attack on Pearl Harbor, Japan and Germany immediately began submarine offensives off America's West and East Coasts. The Navy, recognizing that its frontier commanders possessed inadequate forces to stop, or even impede, the massacre of shipping, took steps to remedy the situation. Few viable options were available. The fleet commanders could spare no ships, and the delivery of "new construction" patrol craft and submarine chasers was still months away. Accordingly, top brass ordered more World War I remnants returned to service, and re-canvassed ports, harbors, and boat and shipyards to acquire additional existing vessels as well as ones under construction or on the ways. Ultimately, three times as many patrol yachts and patrol craft served during the war than had been projected; YPs comprised most of the increase. (A few YPs were redesignated as PYcs, or vice versus, resulting in some double-counting in the following table.)

Type Vessel	Projected Quantities	Actual Wartime Service
Patrol yacht (PY)	24	21 (*PY-10*, PY *12-29*, PY *31-32*)
Converted yacht	0	2 (*Maryanne* and *Fisheries II*)
Coastal patrol yacht (PYc)	43	52 (*PYc-1* through *PYc-52*)
Patrol craft (YP)	166	639 (YPs *3-99*, YPs *102-189*, YPs *191-192*, YPs *194-615*, YPs *617-646*)
Totals	233	714[6]

The Navy assigned all the patrol yachts and patrol craft specified in the plan to either the Western Atlantic or Pacific Area. There were no ships or craft allocated to the Philippine Coastal Frontier due to a belief that the small Asiatic Fleet in the Philippines could not hold out against a Japanese invasion. The plan instead directed the frontier to acquire "Such suitable vessels as are locally available and additional vessels and aircraft as assigned by Commander in Chief, U.S. Asiatic Fleet." Admiral Thomas C. Hart, the fleet commander, was to support the defense of the Philippines as long as possible, and to "shift base to British or Dutch ports at discretion." This bleak prognosis of future events proved correct. On the same day that Japan forces attacked Pearl Harbor, bombers from Formosa and Saipan struck the Philippines and Guam, respectively, and American navy units unable to escape southward, or not already scuttled to deny them to the enemy, were destroyed or captured when the islands fell.[7]

NAVAL COASTAL FRONTIER BOUNDARIES

The boundaries of naval coastal frontiers were clearly defined, and each frontier, with the exception of the Hawaiian and Philippine ones, was subdivided into defense sectors. Each sector was the responsibility of a commandant of a naval district or commanding officer of an operating base.

Western Atlantic Area

North Atlantic Coastal Frontier (commandant, Third Naval District)
Northern boundary: Northern boundary of the United States, as well as American bases in Newfoundland
Southern boundary: Diamond Shoals Lightship, Hatteras Inlet inclusive, southern and western boundary of Dare County, North Carolina, Albemarle Sound, Chowan River, Virginia-North Carolina boundary to the west, all inclusive.
Defense Sectors:
- Newfoundland (commander, Naval Operating Base, Newfoundland)
- New England (commandant, First Naval District at Boston, Massachusetts)
- New York (commandant, Third Naval District at New York, New York)
- Delaware-Chesapeake (no dedicated sector naval commander; responsibility for operating forces was shared by the commandants of the Fourth and Fifth Naval Districts, headquartered at Philadelphia, Pennsylvania, and Naval Operating Base, Norfolk, Virginia, respectively)

Southern Coastal Frontier (commandant, Sixth Naval District)
Northern boundary: Diamond Shoal Lightship, Hatteras Inlet, exclusive; southern and western boundary of Dare County, North Carolina, Albemarle Sound, Chowan River; Virginia-North Carolina boundary to the west, all exclusive.
Southern boundary: The Rio Grande. The coastal zone extends southeastward and southward to the northwestern boundary of the Caribbean naval coastal frontier, so as to include the Gulf of Mexico and such parts of Bahaman waters and the Caribbean Sea as to lie to the northward of that boundary.
Defense Sectors:
- Carolina Florida (commandant, Sixth Naval District at Charleston, South Carolina)
- Gulf (commandants of Seventh and Eighth Naval Districts at Miami, Florida, and New Orleans, Louisiana, respectively)

Caribbean Coastal Frontier (commandant, Tenth Naval District)
Boundaries: All United States territories and possessions, and United States military and naval reservations and activities on shore located within an area bounded as follows:
Beginning at latitude 18° 05' North, longitude 87° 32' West thence by a line bearing 63° true to the 25th parallel of latitude thence by the 25th parallel of latitude to the 65th meridian of longitude, thence by a line direct to latitude 2° North, longitude 49° West, thence by a line direct to the place of beginning. The coastal zone includes all of the waters within these boundaries, as well as the sea lanes and focal points beyond, but near, the eastern boundary.
Defense Sectors:
- Guantanamo (commander, Naval Operating Base, Guantanamo, Cuba)
- Puerto Rico (commandant, Tenth Naval District at San Juan, Puerto Rico)
- Trinidad (commander, Naval Operating Base, Trinidad): Caribbean possessions, territories, reservations, and United States naval activities in Venezuela, British Guiana, Surinam, and French Guiana

Panama Coastal Frontier (commandant, Fifteenth Naval District)
Boundaries: All United States territories and possessions, and United States military and naval reservations and activities on shore located within the following area: British Honduras, Guatemala, Honduras, El Salvador, Nicaragua, Costa Rica, Panama, Colombia, and Ecuador,

all land areas between the southwestern boundary of the Caribbean coastal frontier and the coasts of Central and South America; and all land areas between the coasts of Central and South America and a broken line drawn from the Mexico-Guatemala border to a point in latitude 5° South, longitude 95° West, and thence to Peru-Ecuador border. The coastal zone includes all the waters within these boundaries, as well as the sea lanes beyond, but near, the western and southern boundaries.

Defense Sectors:
- Atlantic (commandant, Fifteenth Naval District at Balboa, Canal Zone)
- Pacific (commandant, Fifteenth Naval District)

Pacific Area

Pacific Southern Coastal Frontier (commandant, Twelfth Naval District)
Northern boundary: Northern boundary of California.
Southern boundary: Southern boundary of the United States. The coastal zone extends southeastward to abreast the southern boundary of Mexico.
Defense Sectors:
- Southern California (commandant, Eleventh Naval District at San Diego, California)
- Northern California (commandant, Twelfth Naval District at San Francisco, California)

Pacific Northern Coastal Frontier (commandant, Thirteenth Naval District)
Northern boundary: Northern boundary of Washington except that Alaska is part of the Pacific coastal frontier.
Southern boundary: Northern boundary of California.
Defense Sectors:
- Northwestern (commandant, Thirteenth Naval District at Seattle, Washington)
- Alaskan (commandant, Thirteenth Naval District; later, commandant, Seventeenth Naval District at Kodiak, Alaska)

Hawaiian Coastal Frontier (commandant, Fourteenth Naval District)
Boundaries: Oahu and all of the land and sea areas required for the defense of Oahu. The coastal zone extends to a distance of 500 miles

from all the Hawaiian Islands, including Johnston and Palmyra Islands and Kingman Reef.

Far East Area

Philippine Coastal Frontier (commandant, Sixteenth Naval District)
Boundaries: Luzon and all of the land and sea areas required for the defense of Luzon. The coastal zone includes all of the sea approaches to the coastal frontier.[8]

NAVAL COASTAL FRONTIER AND DISTRICT FORCES

The war plan allocated the more capable ships assigned any particular naval coastal frontier to its coastal force and the remaining craft to the local defense forces of the subordinate naval district(s). Coastal forces included Navy patrol vessels (PE), patrol yachts (PY), and gunboats (PG), as well as a few Coast Guard vessels. The Panama, Pacific Southern, Pacific Northern, and Hawaiian Coastal Frontiers were allocated a division of World War I-era destroyers; several frontiers had a patrol bomber squadron (VPB) supported by a seaplane tender. The war plan also assigned the North Atlantic Coastal Frontier, a blimp (ZNP); the Caribbean Coastal Frontier, submarine chasers (PC); and the Pacific Northern Frontier, two antiquated "S-boats"—World War I vintage submarines—and a submarine rescue ship in case its services were needed. Local defense force commanders were provided with YPs, PYcs, various types of minecraft—minesweepers (AM), coastal minesweepers (AMc), base minesweepers (AMb), and coastal minelayers (CMc)—and station ships to support them.[9]

NAVAL COASTAL FRONTIER FORCE TASKS

The tasks assigned to the coastal frontier forces in the Western Atlantic and Pacific Areas were nearly identical:

Western Atlantic Area

- Defend the North Atlantic, Southern, Caribbean, and Panama Naval Coastal Frontiers;
- Protect and route shipping;
- Support the U.S. Atlantic Fleet;
- Support the Army and associated forces within the coastal frontiers;

- The Naval Coastal Frontier Forces of the Panama Naval Coastal Frontier to provide support to the U.S. Southeast Pacific Force.

Pacific Area

- Defend the Pacific Southern Frontier, Pacific Northern Coastal Frontier (which included the Alaskan Sector and Unalaska Island in the Aleutians, site of Dutch Harbor), and the Hawaiian Naval Coastal Frontier;
- Protect and route shipping;
- Support the U.S. Pacific Fleet;
- Support the Army and associated forces within the coastal frontiers.[10]

A primary duty of coastal frontier commanders was to protect and route non-combatant shipping, whether transiting singly or in convoy, along the sea routes within their frontiers. Commandants of naval districts were responsible for routing the vessels sailing from one port to another within their own districts. A variety of means might be used to protect shipping within coastal frontiers and districts, including sea or air escort, covering operations, patrol, dispersal of vessels, shifting of routes, or a combination thereof.[11]

NAVAL SEA FRONTIERS REPLACE COASTAL FRONTIERS

Existing coastal frontiers overlapped the boundaries of the naval districts, and naval operations took place in coastal zones in which both the Army and Navy exercised control. Thus, new commands called "sea frontiers" were established on 6 February 1942. The designated areas, which included the existing coastal zones as well as the land areas of the coastal frontiers, were created by a joint Army-Navy agreement, the Army charged with the defense of the land areas while the Navy maintained inshore and offshore patrols. Associated changes included the realignment of some districts between frontiers, the addition of two new sea frontiers, and the deletion of the Philippines frontier, reflecting its loss to Japan. The numerals in the following summary associate naval districts with their parent frontiers: "7", for example, signifies the Seventh Naval District, originally a part of the Southern Atlantic Coastal Frontier, and later a subordinate command of the Gulf Sea Frontier.

Former Coastal Frontiers and Subordinate Naval Districts	New Sea Frontiers and Subordinate Naval Districts
North Atlantic Coastal Frontier (1, 3, 4, 5)	Eastern Sea Frontier (1, 3, 4, 5, 6)
Southern Atlantic Coastal Frontier (6, 7, 8)	Gulf Sea Frontier (7, 8)
Caribbean Coastal Frontier (10)	Caribbean Sea Frontier (10)
Pacific Southern Coastal Frontier (11, 12)	Western Sea Frontier (11, 12, 13)
Pacific Northern Coastal Frontier (13)	combined into above sea frontier
Hawaiian Coastal Frontier (14)	Hawaiian Sea Frontier (14)
Panama Coastal Frontier (15)	Panama Sea Frontier (15)
Philippine Coastal Frontier (16)	eliminated
	Alaskan Sea Frontier (17)
	Moroccan Sea Frontier

The most significant change was the creation of separate Western and Alaskan Sea Frontiers, in lieu of a single Pacific Northern Coastal Frontier, and the establishment of an entirely new Moroccan Sea Frontier (sometimes called the North Africa Sea Frontier) on the east coast of French Morocco under the command of Rear Adm. John L. Hall, Jr., USN. With the exception of the Moroccan Sea Frontier, the sea frontiers generally began at the shore of the United States and extended into the sea for a nominal distance of two hundred miles. The frontier commanders had control and responsibility for the convoys within their areas, had their own forces for convoy and other uses, and worked closely with the U.S. Army Air Force in defense of the frontiers. They were also charged with sea-air rescue, harbor defense, shipping lane patrol, minesweeping, and air operations.[12]

NAVAL DISTRICTS

To help ensure the defense of shorelines and inland waterways, the United States and its territories and island possessions were divided into sixteen naval districts (plus two river commands that existed only during the war). Later, following recognition of a need for a dedicated naval district for Alaskan and Aleutian waters, another district, the Seventeenth, was created.

Number	District	Headquarters
First	New England, less Connecticut	Boston, Massachusetts
Third	New York, Connecticut, and upper New Jersey	New York, New York
Fourth	Pennsylvania, lower New Jersey, and Delaware	Philadelphia, Pennsylvania

Number	District	Headquarters
Fifth	Maryland, Virginia, West Virginia, and north coastal region of North Carolina	Naval Operating Base, Norfolk, Virginia
Potomac River Naval Command	The Potomac River Area, including the District of Columbia, and certain bordering counties in Maryland and Virginia	Navy Yard, Washington, D.C.
Severn River Naval Command	Anne Arundel County, Maryland	United States Naval Academy, Annapolis, Maryland
Sixth	North Carolina (except north coast), South Carolina, Georgia	Charleston, South Carolina
Seventh	Florida, except portion of northern Florida lying west of the Apalachicola River	Miami, Florida
Eighth	South Central States	New Orleans, Louisiana.
Ninth	North Central States	Great Lakes, Illinois
Tenth	Caribbean possessions, territories, reservations, and United States naval activities in Venezuela, British Guiana, Surinam, and French Guiana	San Juan, Puerto Rico
Eleventh	Southern third of California, Arizona, and New Mexico	San Diego, California
Twelfth	Northern two-thirds of California, Nevada, Utah, and Colorado	San Francisco, California
Thirteenth	Washington, Oregon, Idaho, Montana, Wyoming	Seattle, Washington
Fourteenth	Hawaiian Islands-Midway Area	Pearl Harbor, Territory of Hawaii
Fifteenth	Panama Canal Zone	Balboa, Canal Zone
Sixteenth	Philippine Islands	Cavite, Philippine Islands
Seventeenth	Alaska and the Aleutians	Kodiak, Alaska[13]

3

Overview of the Patrol Yacht and "Yippie" Fleets

> *The YP, [Naval] District [Yard] Patrol Craft, with a district stretching over the entire world, gets everywhere—the South Pacific, the South West Pacific, Central Pacific, Northern Pacific, Atlantic, North Atlantic, Mediterranean, and the Caribbean. They steam between islands, continents, atolls, and in many an instance cover spans of ocean far beyond the limits for which they were originally designed. They work as small reefers, cargo ships, coastal transports, and submarine [hydrographic] survey ships—not to mention their intended job, district patrol craft. They have carried everything that would go down the hatch or on the deck—frozen meat, provisions, mail, ammunition, and personnel. The [U.S. Navy] Bureau may still class them as Yard Patrols, but it is a yard that has expanded out of all proportion to the size of the ship.*
>
> —J. W. Wickham, *The Story of the Yippee Fleet*, Wartime Press[1]

The characteristics of the private yachts that the Navy acquired for war service were very similar; clean lines, steam or sail propulsion, and refinements reflecting their designers' efforts to combine eloquence and comfort with handling and performance. The main differences between the patrol yachts (PY) and coastal patrol yachts (PYc) were size and age. The patrol yachts—spanning 154 to 245 feet, and displacing 500 to 1,220 tons—were larger than the coastal patrol yachts and generally older, built between 1906 and 1931. Almost all were of steel, which, along with their size, allowed for the installation of heavier armament than was possible in svelte coastal patrol yachts built of wood. The *Chalcedony* (PYc-16), at a robust 195 feet, was an exception. The smallest coastal yacht was the 96-foot *Patriot* (PYc-47). A product of famed yacht builder Herreshoff Manufacturing of

Bristol, Rhode Island, she displaced a mere eighty-three tons. Most of the PYcs were of 1920s through 1940s vintage. The oldest was the *Truant* (PYc-14) which, built by Herreshoff in 1892 had been both well-fabricated and well-maintained. (Appendices B and C provide a summary of the characteristics of the patrol yachts and coastal patrol yachts.)[2]

Shortly after America's entry into the war, it became evident that additional anti-submarine patrol vessels were desperately needed to combat U-boats off its coasts. On 17 June 1942, the Chief of Naval Operations ordered the commanders of the Eastern and Gulf Sea Frontiers to acquire all civilian craft capable of remaining at sea at cruising speed for forty-eight hours and, preferably, able to carry four 300-pound depth charges and a .50-caliber machine gun. Some of the vessels obtained were yachts, sold for a nominal fee, loaned, or donated to the Service. While their previous owners probably winced as they watched hand-rubbed mahogany, scoured teak and gleaming bright-work disappear under thick coats of gray paint, many of these same individuals also donned a Navy uniform and traded their luxurious offices for a pitching deck.[3]

Photo 3-1

Ernest Borgnine served aboard the patrol yacht *Sylph* (PY-12) during World War II, rising from seaman to gunner's mate first class during his naval service, and later became an acclaimed film and television actor.
Courtesy of the Naval History and Heritage Command, www.history.navy.mil/bios/borgnine_e.htm

Most of the men who served in the patrol yacht force came from more modest backgrounds; some achieved much acclaim and notoriety after the war. Ernest Borgnine, a crew member aboard the *Sylph* (PY-12), became a famous actor, with roles in dozens of acclaimed films as well as television shows to this credit, most notably the popular series *McHale's Navy* (1962–66). During his service in the Navy, he rose from seaman to gunner's mate first.[4]

COMPOSITE OF THE "YIPPIE FLEET"

While the YP fleet included both lavish yachts and less well-appointed pleasure craft, such as cabin-cruisers, most of its members were waterfront workhorses: tuna clippers, purse seiners, draggers, and trawlers, as well as a few freighters and whalers. Rounding out this group were some former Coast Guard and reclassified Navy vessels, U.S. Fish and Wildlife Service craft, U.S. Naval Academy training craft, and sampans and other types of fishing boats confiscated from their Japanese owners. Thirty 128-foot Navy YPs, built specifically for offshore patrol, joined the fleet between 1944 and 1945.[5]

FORMER COAST GUARD, NAVY, AND OTHER GOVERNMENT VESSELS

The first substantial Navy acquisition of YPs occurred in 1933. Following the end of Prohibition and its associated requirement to maintain a "whiskey barrier" to decrease waterborne smuggling of alcohol, the U.S. Coast Guard transferred fifty-three 75-foot patrol craft (known as "six-bitters," a variation of "six bits," Depression-era slang for seventy-five cents) to its sister service. Two years later, eight larger 98-foot cutters joined them. Expanding its search to other government agencies, the Navy obtained seven boats from the Fish and Wildlife Service.[6]

The Navy, as it was prone to do when in need of more of one thing and less of something else, converted twenty-one base minesweepers, nine coastal minesweepers, and nine other craft (a mixture of motor torpedo boats, coastal patrol yachts, and sub-chasers) to patrol craft. Navy brass also ordered the use of fifteen 75-foot YPs, assigned to the U.S. Naval Academy to train midshipmen in seamanship and navigation, to patrol inshore waters near Annapolis, Maryland. While thus employed, they came under the Severn River Naval Command. The 151 YPs listed below would, however, ultimately account for a little less than one-fourth of the Yippie Fleet.

Vessel Type	Hull Numbers	Length Feet	Displ Tons	Year Built	Qty
ex-USCG patrol craft	5–40, 44–55, 57–60, 67, 72	75	37	1924–25	53
ex-USCG cutters	41–42, 56, 61–64, 69	98	210	1925–26	8
ex-U.S. Fish & Wildlife craft	194–200	various	various	1913–38	7
ex-USN base minesweepers	360–380	various	various	1929–41	21

Vessel Type	Hull Numbers	Length Feet	Displ Tons	Year Built	Qty
ex-USN coastal minesweepers	381–389	various	various	1936–41	9
ex-USN PT boat	110	81	52	1940	1
ex-USN PT boats	106, 107	72	40	1941	2
ex-USN coastal yachts	261, 425, 454	various	various	1922–30	3
ex-USN sub-chasers	77, 105	various	various	1927, 31	2
Midshipmen training craft	78–82, 99	75	51	1941	6
Midshipmen training craft	583–591	75	50	1943	9
YP-617 class	617–646	128	403	1944–45	30
Total number:					151[7]

ACQUISITION OF HAWAIIAN SAMPANS

Amidst growing tensions between the United States and Japan during the 1930s, the U.S. military viewed the fishing fleet in Hawaii, long dominated by Japanese immigrants, as a serious threat to national security. In 1935, the Japanese operated more than 140 fishing sampans off Oahu, Maui and the Big Island. The largest and most impressive type was the aku boat, which on a good day might haul in 40,000 pounds of fish, capable of spending up to a week at sea. These "Hawaiian sampans" were painted blue and had evolved from the traditional Japanese design due to the addition of a sponson for better stability in heavy seas, as well as a deckhouse to provide protection from rough weather, and a raised bow. The launching of a newly-built boat was accompanied by the chanting of sutras and offerings of sake. In 1941 twenty-six of these large vessels plied the seas for yellowfin and skipjack tuna. They delivered their catches directly to a waterfront cannery in Kewalo Basin, a boat harbor that hosted a shipyard and served as home for the Honolulu fishing fleet.[8]

The Navy suspected that Japanese-operated boats might be spying, performing reconnaissance for a much-feared invasion of Hawaii by sea. Thus, when the Japanese government arranged for many of the fishermen to attend fishing schools in Japan, there was concern that these men were being interrogated by Japanese Navy officials regarding hydrographic conditions in Hawaii. Accordingly, even before the attack on Pearl Harbor in December 1941, the Navy had begun confiscating sampans and repurposing the larger aku boats. Repainted white and with rebuilt engines, they were sent out on patrol.[9]

Following the outbreak of war, American authorities confiscated the remaining sampans and commandeered their supporting infrastructure for military use. The Navy requisitioned additional large fishing vessels for use as YPs, converted the tuna cannery in Kewalo Basin into a plant for the assembly of airplane fuel tanks, and used the nearby shipyard for the maintenance of military craft. (A listing of the former Japanese vessels—whose names generally end in maru; a common suffix for ship names—and the other members of the Yippie Fleet are provided in Appendix A.)[10]

COAST GUARD-MANNED PATROL CRAFT

Under an agreement made between the Commandant of the Coast Guard and the Chief of Naval Operations, the Coast Guard agreed to provide officers and enlisted men to operate a number of Yard Patrol Craft, beginning on 14 December 1941. Ultimately Coast Guard crews manned forty of the smaller YPs employed for inshore and harbor patrol activities. These craft remained commissioned Navy vessels under Navy operational control as the Coast Guard had become a part of the Navy on 1 November 1941, in preparation for anticipated war. Guardsmen manned 351 Navy ships—which they termed "cutters," in the tradition of their service—during the war.[11]

DUTY ABOARD A YIPPIE

Unlike other specific types of Navy ships, there was great variance among the YPs, spanning the spectrum from modest cabin-cruiser to yacht, fishing boat to whaler, in addition to a few freighters and other types. Most were of wood construction, some of steel, and a few were a combination of both materials. Some were single or double-masted, although the Navy fitted engines in sailing vessels (and removed the masts on some boats) during their conversion. The designation "YP" denoted "Yard Patrol Craft" because the Navy believed that, due to their small size and limited storage for fuel and food, the small vessels would only be able to operate for a few days from a yard or base before having to return for support. However, the necessities of war resulted in many operating far from home and, within a relatively short time, commanders referred to YPs as patrol vessels, and in some areas as patrol ships. Fleet sailors used the moniker "Yippies," "Yippees," or

"Yippy-boats." Vessel paint schemes reflected varied duties, geographic locations, and whims of individual captains. Some boats sported standard Navy gray paint, while others were dark blue, two-toned blue and gray, or an assortment of shades from green to black.[12]

Most YPs, propelled by a single screw coupled to a single diesel propulsion engine of modest horsepower, could make only 8 to 10 knots. Crew size varied from around a dozen officers and men on the small boats to upwards of thirty aboard larger vessels. Two or three officers commonly comprised the wardroom of the *YP-617* class ships, with the captain usually doubling as navigator and communications officer, and the executive officer as first lieutenant and gunnery officer. Boatswains' mates, aided by six or seven seamen, performed topside maintenance; machinist's mates and motor machinist's mates, assisted by four or five firemen, kept the ship running. The duties of other ratings—gunners' mates, signalmen, quartermasters, and radiomen—focused on ship's operations and self-defense. A cook, and a pharmacist's mate if assigned, rounded out the crew.[13]

Photo 3-2

The *YP-625* under way. She was one of thirty newly constructed, 128-foot YPs based on the proven tuna clipper design. Courtesy of the Tacoma, Washington Public Library: http://search.tacomapubliclibrary.org/images/dt6n.asp?un=3&pg=1&krequest=YP&stemming=On&phonic=&fuzzy=&maxfiles=5000.

Aboard most of these type YPs, each man was assured of a bunk (in lieu of a hammock, often stacked several high aboard large Navy ships) and plenty of locker space. Additionally, berthing spaces in some vessels were located above the main deck, allowing for sunshine and natural ventilation. Morale is often highest aboard ships known to be "good feeders," and with only a few crewmen to serve, the cook usually could provide a variety of meals that were impossible to find on larger ships, particularly as former fishing boats and *YP-617* class vessels, with large cargo refrigeration holds and capacious ice boxes, often had plentiful fresh foods, meats, and vegetables on hand.[14]

However, the wonderful duty that existed aboard YPs in port, or when the vessels were operating in calm inshore waters, usually disappeared after standing out to sea. The sailors aboard a diminutive ship being tossed about by wind and wave—like a cork adrift, twisting and turning, as green water broke over the deck—were forced to eat sandwiches standing up, with an arm around the nearest stanchion to avoid a nasty fall. Seasickness was common, and nothing to be ashamed of, as men newly reported from boot camp and old salt alike often stood their watches with a bucket close at hand. Returning to harbor, sailors were apt to forget the bruises they had acquired, and the spam sandwiches on which they had subsisted, and once again take comfort in the knowledge that their duty was enviable. There were, however, few recreational opportunities aboard a Yippy. The messdecks was the only place where the men could read, write a letter, play poker, or listen to the radio, and the "small stores" and ships store items taken for granted aboard most Navy ships were nonexistent. Occasionally, however, crew members had the opportunity to go aboard a larger naval vessel for a movie or to enjoy some "gedunk" (snacks items offered at the canteen or snack bar). When anchored out, a rowboat served as the YP's liberty launch, although a few aristocrats in the Yippie fleet boasted motorboats.[15]

4

Japan's Submarine Offensive off America's West Coast

> *The sub didn't chase us into port exactly. We zigzagged around, maneuvering always to present the smallest target possible. The sub circled and dodged, trying to get broadside of us, but never succeeded. As we neared land and the sub fired the last of its eight shots—four of which splashed water onto the deck—it quickly submerged.*
>
> —Frederick Goncalves, captain of the tanker S.S. *Agwiworld*, following an attack by the Japanese submarine *I-23*, some twenty miles off Monterey Bay, California, on the afternoon of 20 December 1941

AMERICAN FREIGHER *CYNTHIA OLSON* SUNK

Commander Minoru Yokota, the commanding officer of the Imperial Japanese Navy submarine *I-26*, surfaced at dawn on 7 December 1941 to confirm the nationality of a merchant ship he had been tracking, the 2,140-ton *Cynthia Olson* with a cargo of army supplies en route to Honolulu from Tacoma, Washington. Having verified that she flew an American flag, he fired a warning shot meant to convey "stop your engines and do not transmit a warning." The master of the lumber freighter ordered an SOS sent and lifeboats lowered, but courageously ignored the warning and continued to make way. Yokota fired eighteen 5.5-inch rounds from his deck gun at a range of 1,000 meters and, having set the ship aflame without sinking it, submerged and, from a distance of 450 yards, fired a torpedo which passed astern of the *Cynthia Olson*. Frustrated, he surfaced and fired another twenty-nine rounds after which the then critically damaged freighter began to settle. The submarine remained on the scene for another two hours before Yokota, convinced that the ship could not be saved and concerned about a possible attack from Hawaiian Island airfields, decided to depart the area. The freighter went to the bottom at 33° 42'N, 145° 29'W, the first American merchantman lost to a Japanese submarine in World War II.[1]

Yokota had encountered the ship the previous day 300 miles off the California coast, but had been under orders not to commence hostilities until the time of the planned attack on Pearl Harbor (0330 on 8 December, Tokyo time). Thus, he stalked the freighter until 0800 on 7 December (Hawaiian time). *Cynthia Olson*'s radioed SOS indicating that it was under attack by an enemy submarine was received by the steamship *Lurline*, but no rescue effort ensued as by then attention was focused on the bombing of Pearl Harbor 1,000 miles to the southwest. Accordingly, the freighter's thirty-three-man crew plus the two Army soldiers who had been aboard, perished after abandoning ship in lifeboats.[2]

Newly commissioned and assigned to the Sixth Fleet's Submarine Squadron 1, the *I-26* had departed Yokosuka, Japan, on 19 November on her first war patrol. She was one of the new 356-foot Type B1 submarines, which were fast (23.5 knots surfaced and 8 knots submerged), had a very long range (14,000 miles at 16 knots), and carried a Yokosuka E14Y seaplane in a small hangar fitted in front of the conning tower. Along with the *I-10*, she was assigned to collect intelligence in the Aleutians area, with orders to reconnoiter American bases and report the presence of any U.S. naval forces to the fleet commander. Yokota was then to proceed to an area midway between Hawaii and San Francisco and report any U.S. Navy units heading towards Hawaii with reinforcements, and finally, following commencement of the attack on Pearl Harbor, to attack American shipping.[3]

ADDITIONAL ENEMY SUBS ORDERED TO AMERICA'S WEST COAST

Two days after the attack on Pearl Harbor, the *I-6* sighted a carrier (the *Enterprise*, Halsey's flagship) and two heavy cruisers near Kauai Channel southeast of Pearl Harbor, heading northeast at 20 knots. On receipt of this intelligence, Vice Adm. Mitsumi Shimizu, commander-in-chief of the Japanese Sixth Fleet, ordered Squadron 1 units to pursue and sink the carrier, thought to be bound for the West Coast of the United States. The nine subs were then to take up positions at designated sites off the Pacific coast and to begin attacking American merchant shipping. The Imperial General Headquarters staff subsequently directed the IJN to shell West Coast shore installations. Shimizu identified coastal cities and lighthouses to be targeted, and, as a climax to the operation, directed the submarines to take their designated target under fire and then retire to Kwajalein in the Marshall Islands, the headquarters of the Sixth Fleet, where Shimizu waited aboard the light cruiser IJN *Katori*.[4]

Following the carrier's escape, the I-boats set courses for the West Coast. Based on pre-war intelligence, four subs were ordered to locations thought to offer the best opportunity to attack shipping lanes commonly used by merchant vessels. The *I-19* took up a position off Los Angeles Harbor, *I-15* off San Francisco Bay, *I-25* off the mouth of the Columbia River, and *I-26* off the Strait of Juan de Fuca. Ironically, the remaining five submarines—which were assigned to areas considered less important—would see the most action. The *I-9* took station off Cape Blanco on Oregon's southwest coast, and progressing south along the California coast, the *I-17* positioned itself off Cape Mendocino, *I-23* off Monterey Bay, *I-21* off Estero Bay, and *I-10* off San Diego.[5]

While hunting in the Astoria region off the Columbia River estuary after dark on 18 December 1941, the *I-25* encountered the *L. P. St. Clair* and fired ten rounds at the southbound Union Oil tanker; all missed. Reacting quickly, the startled master made a hard turn to port and escaped up the Columbia River. That same day, the freighter *Samoa*, en route to San Diego with a load of lumber, was attacked by the *I-17* and by good fortune also emerged unscathed. The submarine had been patrolling on the surface about fifteen miles off Cape Mendocino when a lookout spotted the approaching ship. Commander Kozo Nishino opened the action with gunfire, but after five rounds missed due to the *I-17*'s pitching deck—which caused the shots either to fall short of or to sail over the target—he fired a torpedo at the freighter from a seventy-yard distance. The master of the *Samoa* described witnessing the seemingly impending destruction of this ship:

> We saw the telltale wake of a torpedo coming directly at us amidships. It was too late to do more than just wait for our destiny. [Then] the miracle happened. The torpedo went directly beneath us, didn't even touch the hull and continued beyond. A short distance away it exploded.[6]

In the gloom, Nishino was unable to see whether the torpedo had hit the ship. He brought the sub in to within about forty yards of the *Samoa* and then moved away again, believing the vessel was sinking due to her heavy port list and missing lifeboat. He later reported that he had sunk an American ship. However, unbeknownst to Nishino, the *Samoa*'s engineers had been shifting water in ballast tanks at the time of the attack, inadvertently creating the list. The lifeboat had been lost in a storm a few days earlier, not taken by crewmen abandoning the ship as Nishino believed. The freighter hove to until daybreak and then made best speed for San Diego, arriving safely there on 20 December 1941.[7]

TANKER *EMIDIO* LOST

Two days later, in early afternoon, the *I-17* got another chance to attack an American merchant vessel, the 6,912-ton Socony-Vacuum oil company tanker S.S. *Emidio*, which, twenty-five miles off Cape Mendocino, was returning empty to San Francisco from Seattle. Her master, Clarke A. Farrow, on receiving a report of a submarine a quarter mile astern and closing, ordered full speed, but to no avail as the *I-17* was making 20 knots. He ordered the radio operator to send an SOS, upon which the sub opened fire, the first shot carrying away the radio antenna. Two more rounds struck the *Emidio*, one destroying a lifeboat hanging in its davits. Farrow stopped the engines and hoisted a white flag, then ordered the crew to take to the lifeboats. One boat was hit, spilling three crewmen, R.W. Pennington, Fred Potts and Stuart McGillivray, who were attempting to launch it into the water. By the time other lifeboats were able to slip their falls to search for the men, they had perished.[8]

With the exception of four crewmembers still aboard—the radioman Foote, who purposely remained, and three engineers on watch, who likely had not heard the order to abandon—the ship's company rowed away. The submarine fired a parting shot at the boats, but did not pursue them, and submerged just as a PBY Catalina seaplane approached. A unit of Patrol Squadron VP-44 from Naval Air Station, Alameda, the plane, piloted by Lt. (jg) "Pappy" Samuel O. Cole, had been flying near the California-Oregon border searching for enemy sightings when it came upon the *I-17*. A member of the plane crew recalled the incident:

As we approached we saw a Japanese submarine on the surface. We started an attack, the submarine dove and we dropped depth charges. We never knew if we were successful with our attack. We circled the ship, the tanker *EMIDIO*, [and then] we continued on our patrol and never heard any more about the incident.[9]

The first depth charge failed to damage the *I-17*, and Nishino decided to risk disclosing his position to the aircraft in order to take a torpedo shot at the abandoned tanker. While watching the area where the sub had disappeared, men in lifeboats saw a periscope slowly emerge above the ocean surface, and then the trail from a torpedo as it sped towards the *Emidio*. Aboard the tanker, Foote, having rigged a makeshift antenna, was preparing to send a second SOS when the torpedo struck. Undaunted, he added the words "torpedoed in the stern" and sent the message before proceeding to the main deck and jumping over the side. The engine room team, Oiler B. F. Moler, Fireman Kenneth Kimes, and 3rd Engineer R. A. Winters, were performing their duties when the torpedo penetrated the engine room bulkhead, churned past Moler and exploded on the other side of the space, killing the other two men. Moler, despite three broken ribs and a punctured lung, made his way up and out of the flooded space and leapt overboard. He and Foote were picked up by lifeboats.[10]

The thirty-one survivors rowed their boats for sixteen hours through a driving rainstorm until recovered the following day by the Coast Guard cutter *Shawnee* (WAT-54) a few miles off Humboldt Bay. The *Emidio*, abandoned but still afloat, drifted north and broke up on the rocks off Crescent City, a small town on the California north coast twenty miles south of the Oregon border, named for a nearby crescent-shaped stretch of sandy beach. Wave action later deposited the remains of the first American ship to be sunk by the Imperial Japanese Navy's submarine force along California's coast in World War II in the city's harbor. One site, marked by a plaque, is now a California Historical Landmark.[11]

Nishino was not finished attacking American shipping. On 23 December, the *I-17* surfaced southwest of Cape Mendocino and took the 7,038-ton tanker S.S. *Larry Doheny* under fire from a range of a mile and a half. Four rounds hit the ship and set the bridge area aflame. The arrival of a land-based aircraft forced the submarine to crash dive, but Nishino fired a torpedo at 0729 and heard the warhead explode ninety seconds later. It must have detonated prematurely, however, because the vessel made port safely. (The tanker's luck later ran out on 6 October 1942 when the *I-25* sank her off Cape Sebastian, some twenty miles north of the California-Oregon border. She would be the last American ship lost as a result of the Japanese submarine offensive off the West Coast.)[12]

THREE MORE MERCHANTMEN ATTACKED

The Japanese submarines *I-19*, *I-21*, and *I-23* each attacked a merchant ship between 20 and 23 December 1941. Mid-afternoon, on the 20th, as the *Emidio* survivors had begun rowing to safety, the *I-23* was stalking the S.S. *Agwiworld* 330 miles to the south off Santa Cruz. The first warning of an existing peril that Frederick Goncalves, master of the Richfield Oil Company tanker, had was the crack of the submarine's deck gun from astern his ship; it prompted him to run to the bridge. To minimize the cross-section of the large 6,771-ton vessel, he ordered the helm hard to port to bring the bow around quickly and point it at the submarine. But after a second round from the closing sub, Goncalves shifted the rudder to present the ship's stern to the enemy and fled. Although the *I-23*'s top speed was greater than that of the tanker, Lt. Comdr. Genichi Shibata could not close on the *Agwiworld*—which was desperately zigzagging as it fled towards Santa Cruz—without rolling even more in the heavy surface swell, further degrading the accuracy of gunfire. He fired a half-dozen or more rounds from a distance of about 500 yards, but the fishtailing merchantman made good its escape.[13]

Two days later, on 22 December, the *H. M. Storey* emerged unscathed from an encounter with the *I-19* off Point Arguello, some fifty-five miles north of Santa Barbara. After an hour's chase, the submarine fired two torpedoes at the 10,763-ton Standard Oil Company tanker, and then a third, after a "fish started a hot run" in its tube and had to be jettisoned for crew safety. All three torpedoes missed and the tanker escaped, aided by the timely appearance of two Navy aircraft. A woman on the shore at Point Conception described witnessing the ensuing aerial attack:

> Navy bombers arrived overhead only a few minutes after the submarine, lying less than two miles off shore, fired its first torpedo. The planes dropped depth charges. The bombs were so heavy that when they exploded they shook the ground where I was standing. The explosions raised big columns of water.[14]

The *H. M. Story* would, like the *Larry Doheny*, later fall victim to the *I-25*. Shelled and torpedoed on 18 May 1943 while en route to San Pedro, California from Noumea, New Caledonia, she went to the bottom with the loss of two crewmen.[15]

On 23 December 1941, the day after *H. M. Story* escaped the *I-19* off Point Arguello, the *I-21* found and shelled the tanker S.S. *Idaho* near Piedras Blancas on California's central coast. The *Idaho*, although damaged, suffered no casualties.[16]

TANKER *MONTEBELLO* SUNK

The Union Oil Company tanker *Montebello* did not fare as well in an encounter with the *I-21* that same day. The submarine, having sighted her proceeding north from Port San Luis, California, to Vancouver, British Columbia, fired two torpedoes at her. One hit and exploded, breaching the tanker's number two hold and, as sea water entered, the thirty-eight-man crew abandoned her in lifeboats. To hasten the ship's demise, Comdr. Kanji Matsumura also fired several gun rounds into her, and the *Montebello* sank within an hour, four miles south of the Piedras Blancas light.[17]

The 440-foot tanker had loaded a cargo of 73,571 barrels of Santa Marina crude at the Union Oil Company's facility in Port San Luis the previous day. Merchant mariners were now well aware of the danger that existed outside the sanctuary of a port. Around midnight, amid several reports of submarine sightings off the coast, the ship's captain resigned, leaving command to First Mate Olof Ekstrom. The ship cleared the Port San Luis breakwater at 0130 and proceeded northward. Two hours later, on learning that the *Larry Doheny* had been attacked to the north of the *Montebello*'s position, Ekstrom ordered crewmembers to put on lifejackets and individuals not on watch to stand by lifeboat stations.[18]

At 0530, Ordinary Seamen Richard Quincy and William Srez spotted the silhouette of a submarine low in the water, running in the tanker's wake. The *I-21* repositioned to landward, off the tanker's starboard quarter, and then fired a torpedo into the vessel. Ekstrom described the events preceding his order to abandon ship twenty-five minutes later:

> The sub began shelling us. There was from eight to 10 [gun] flashes. One hit the foremast, snapping it. Another whistled by my head so close I could have reached out and touched it. But there was

> no panic, no hysteria. We got all four lifeboats into the water. Splinters from one of the shells struck some of the boats, but by some kind of miracle, none of us was wounded.

Eckstrom, hopeful that the *Montebello* could be saved, ordered the lifeboats to stand off a short distance and wait. Just as dawn broke, however, the tanker slipped beneath the surface and the men began rowing for shore.[19]

Although the term "lifeboat" would seem to denote a degree of safety, the men were not out of harm's way, as the *I-21* opened fire on the boats with machine guns until poor visibility forced her to retire. Some rounds struck the boat carrying Eckstrom, Srez, and four others, but luckily no one was wounded. Srez recalled the hard pull to make the beach:

> Machinegun bullets hit our boat, and she began leaking like a sieve. We began rowing shoreward, with some of us leaning on the oars for all we were worth and the others bailing.[20]

At 0930 the first boat arrived off Cambria, a seaside village on a rocky section of coast midway between San Francisco and Los Angeles, and residents assisted the men ashore. The damaged boat, the last to arrive, landed below the village at noon. Srez explained:

> We were caught in the surf and the lifeboat capsized.... Some of the boys were scratched up, and the captain nearly drowned.[21]

A team of marine researchers found the wreck of the *Montebello* off the southern Big Sur coast nearly fifty-five years later in November 1996. Film taken by a small two-man submarine revealed the derelict ship, upright and cobwebbed with snagged fishing lines and nets. Researchers believed that two of her ten oil storage tanks had been ruptured when she sank, and that remaining ones, which appeared undamaged, might still hold thousands of barrels of heavy crude. If so, the likely eventual escape of the oil posed an environmental risk to the adjacent Monterey Bay National Marine Sanctuary and the pristine coastline and offshore ecosystem.[22]

However, fears of a massive spill after deteriorating tank shells gave way were alleviated on 9 February 2012. Following a week of high-tech imaging and drilling into the side of the wreck, scientists reported the tanks held only harmless seawater. A Coast Guard spokesman aptly summarized the disappearance of enough oil to fill the gas tanks of approximately 70,000 cars:

> It could have been a slow gradual leak over many years since 1941. It could have all come up the day the ship was sunk in 1941. Basically, who knows? We'll probably never know."[23]

JAPANESE SUBMARINES CONTINUE ATTACKS

The *I-19*, *I-23*, and *I-25* attacked three freighters and a tanker between 23 and 27 December, bringing to thirteen the number of American merchant vessels ambushed by six Japanese submarines (*I-17*: 3, *I-19*: 3, *I-21*: 2, *I-23*: 2, *I-25*: 2, *I-26*: 1) in 1941.

On the morning of Christmas Eve, the *I-19* unsuccessfully attacked the lumber schooner *Barbara Olson*. Steaming quietly towards San Diego, she was rocked by a violent blast 100 feet off her starboard side, after a torpedo passed under her and exploded on the opposite side. Lookouts aboard the patrol yacht *Amethyst* (PYc-3), off the Los Angeles Harbor entrance about four miles distant, heard the blast and sighted smoke and spray being propelled high into the air. The vessel's commanding officer ordered general quarters set and began a search for the enemy submarine. An hour later, after a fruitless effort, he ordered material readiness relaxed to Condition Baker, released the crew from battle stations, and resumed patrol duties.[24]

By 1000, the *I-19* was ideally positioned a few miles north off Point Fermin, San Pedro, when the McCormick Steamship Company's 5,700-ton freighter *Absaroka*, bound for San Diego, passed through the area. Joseph Scott, a merchant seaman, was the first person aboard the lumber carrier to sight the *I-19*:

> It was midmorning and all hands were up, when I looked off to starboard and saw a whale. At least I was about to say "look over yonder, a whale," when I changed my mind and yelled, "There's a Jap submarine!"
>
> She was coming head-on. Then her periscope went up and she shot a torpedo. . . . It went wide, but right on its heels came another [which] I could see . . . was going to get us.
>
> In those other torpedoing's [reference to the four ships torpedoed out from under the 48-year-old veteran during World War I], as I recall 'em, there was always a bang or blast and a bump. But this

one was a sort of slow jar, with nothing but a rumble because she hit well below the waterline.[25]

The torpedo struck about fifty feet aft of the beam and the resulting explosion knocked three crewmen, Harry Greenwald, Marshall Mansfield, and Herbert Stevens, who were working on the starboard side of the *Absaroka*, into the sea. The remaining man, Joseph Ryan, was able to ride out the blast. Within a matter of seconds, Greenwald was back on deck, the ship having rolled so far over that he had been able to grab the deck railing, and was carried up as the *Absaroka* shuddered and righted herself; Mansfield pulled himself back on board by a rope. Stevens, whose leg had been injured, yelled for help. Ryan threw him a line and had begun to draw him toward the freighter when a stack of lumber, its lashings severed by the explosion, toppled on Ryan, killing him instantly.[26]

Other crewmen had lowered the lifeboats, and as the *Absaroka* began to settle deeper in the water, her captain and crew abandoned ship. The radio operator had sent out a distress call. Within a short time aircraft arrived overhead and dropped bombs on the last reported position of the submarine. The *Amethyst* arrived next and began dropping depth charges. However, neither the bombs nor the pattern of thirty-two depth charges produced any evidence of harm to the sub, which had again escaped. The master, Louie Pringle, and seven crewmen later reboarded the still afloat lumber carrier, and a Navy tug came alongside and towed the ship to shore, beaching it on a strip of sand below Fort MacArthur.[27]

One month later, in the 26 January 1942 issue of *Life* magazine, movie actress Jane Russell was featured in the "Picture of the Week," standing in the huge hole created in the *Absaroka's* hull by the torpedo. In the picture she was holding a famous war poster that warned: "A slip of the lip may sink a ship," with the words "may sink a ship" crossed out and replaced by "may have sunk this ship."[28]

Nearly 300 miles up the California coast, the *I-23* attacked the S.S. *Dorothy Philips* off Monterey on Christmas Eve. Apparently not wanting to expend a torpedo on the small 2,119-ton American steamship, which lookouts aboard the surfaced submarine had initially misidentified as an old gunboat, Genichi Shibata opened with his deck gun, damaging the *Dorothy Philips*' rudder. Unable to maneuver sufficiently to avoid shoal water, she ran aground.[29]

By 27 December most of the Japanese I-boats off the Pacific coast had depleted their fuel reserves, and Vice Adm. Shimizu cancelled the planned shelling of cities and lighthouses. The *I-25*, however, had sufficient fuel and opportunity to conduct that day the final attack by a Japanese submarine in America's home waters in 1941. After sighting the running lights of the 8,684-ton tanker *Connecticut* off Cape Disappointment, Oregon, Comdr. Meiji Tagami initiated a twenty-minute chase to close on her. Once satisfied with his position, he fired a single torpedo which hit the merchant vessel and exploded, setting her aflame as she began to sink. The ship's master, however, cheated both the submarine and the "Graveyard of the Pacific"—which, studded with shipwrecks lay off the treacherous Columbia River bar—by making a run for it and grounding the *Connecticut* at the river's mouth.[30]

JAPANESE WEST COAST SUBMARINE OFFENSIVE CONCLUDES

Following the Japanese submarine attacks in December 1941, merchantmen suffered only four I-boat attacks off America's Pacific Coast in 1942, and none during the remainder of the war. On 3 February, the *I-17* was ordered to return to the West Coast, and before departure from Kwajalein, she received a list of potential targets to shell, including the San Francisco and Castroville, California, waterfronts. Arriving off the coast on 20 February, Comdr. Nishino Kozo rejected all of the targets except for an oil refinery in Ellwood City, near Santa Barbara, California. During the evening of 23 February, he fired armor-piercing rounds at the refinery for twenty minutes and then withdrew, with only minor damage to a pier and an oil well derrick to his credit. He also made an unsuccessful attack five days later on the 8,298-ton tanker *William H. Berg* off Cape Mendocino, the westernmost point on the California coast. Kozo heard an explosion and assumed that the torpedo he had fired had sunk her. However, the tanker escaped unscathed, apparently due either to a premature or late detonation of the warhead. The *I-17* ended its unproductive war patrol on arrival at Yokosuka on 30 March.[31]

Two other submarines, the *I-25* and *I-26*, operated off North America's Pacific Coast from late spring through early summer 1942. The *I-25* would return alone in the late summer. Collectively, the two submarines torpedoed four ships, shelled coastal installations, and conducted the first-ever bombing attack against the continental United States. Japanese military planners hoped that a massive forest fire in the Pacific Northwest, combined with fear of a possible invasion, might induce the Navy to redirect its fleet from Pearl Harbor to defend the homeland. However, incendiaries dropped by a seaplane from the *I-25* failed to set ablaze a southern Oregon forest sodden with recent rain.[32]

5

West Coast Defense Measures and the Navy's "Q-Ships"

> *Immediate consideration is requested as to the manning and fitting-out of Queen repeat Queen ships to be operated as an antisubmarine measure.*
>
> —Portion of a paraphrased coded dispatch sent by Adm. Ernest King, commander-in-chief United States Fleet, to commander Eastern Sea Frontier on 20 January 1942, suggesting commencement of a "Q-Ship Program" to help combat German U-boats off America's East Coast.[1]

The Japanese submarine attacks on merchant shipping and shore installations in late 1941 and early 1942, like the U-boat offensive off the Eastern Seaboard, spurred urgent effort by naval sea frontiers and naval districts to acquire additional forces and to implement measures to provide merchant ships with greater protection. Along the West Coast, while the scant Western and Northwestern Sea Frontier forces performed patrol and escort duties out to sea, local defense forces of the Eleventh, Twelfth, and Thirteenth Naval Districts helped ensure the safety of ports, harbors and approaches, and escorted merchantmen in inshore and nearshore waters.

The activities at San Pedro, California, a part of the Eleventh Naval District, were representative of measures implemented at other West Coast ports and harbors to provide greater safety for shipping. While patrol craft and lookouts ashore scanned ocean waters for any sign of the enemy, magnetic cable loops on the sea floor detected vessels passing nearby. Detections coordinated with the sightings of friendly ships were discounted; the rest were investigated as possible submarines. Ships entered port through channels swept by coastal and harbor minesweepers, and passed through nets and booms intended to deny entry to enemy vessels, as well as a harbor entrance control point that monitored all inbound and outbound traffic. These and other related activities are summarized below:

- Coastal Lookout System
- Detection Defenses (Point Fermin West Loop, and Sunset Beach East and South Loops)
- Harbor Entrance Control Point
- Pilotage Section
- Captain of the Port
- Nets and Booms (net tenders and gate vessels)
- Operations (minesweepers, patrol craft, and the Zeppelin airship *ZNR-L* based at Goodyear Field in Los Angeles)[2]

NAVAL DISTRICT RESPONSIBILITIES AND UNITS ASSIGNED

The following pages identify the patrol yachts, patrol craft, and coastal and harbor minesweepers of the Eleventh, Twelfth, and Thirteenth Naval Districts, which were responsible for operations shoreward of the Western Sea Frontier and for inland waters. Ship lists provide an overview of the ex-yachts/fishing vessels employed as PYcs, YPs, AMcs and AMbs in particular areas, as well as context for explanations of their duties.

Commander, Western Sea Frontier
Vice Adm. John W. Greenslade, USN

Commandant, Eleventh Naval District
Rear Adm. Ralston S. Holmes, USN

Eleventh Naval District Inshore Patrol: Capt. M. R. Pierce, USN

Ship Name or Designation (Former Type Vessel/ Name and Name of Commanding Officer if Known)	Length Feet	Displ Tons	Year Built
San Diego Section: Comdr. C. Craig, USN			
Jasper PYc-13 (ex-yacht *Stranger*)	134	395	1938
YP-37 (ex-Coast Guard patrol boat *CG-273*, Army *Q-173*)	75	37	1925
YP-38 (ex-Coast Guard patrol boat *CG-269*)	75	37	1924
Sanderling AMc-11 (ex-purse seiner *New Conte de Savoia*, Lt. Louis H. Gwinn, USNR)	72	94	1937

Ship Name or Designation (Former Type Vessel/ Name and Name of Commanding Officer if Known)	Length Feet	Displ Tons	Year Built
Firecrest AMc-33 (ex-purse seiner *S. G. Giuseppe*, Ens. Charles S. Judson, Jr., USNR)	69.8	92	1937
San Pedro Section: Capt. J. H. Everson, USN			
Amethyst PYc-3 (ex-yacht *Samona II*, Lt. Herman Reich, USNR)	147	525	1931
YP-33 (ex-Coast Guard patrol boat *CG-253*)	75	37	1925
YP-34 (ex-Coast Guard patrol boat *CG-258*)	75	37	1925
YP-39 (ex-Coast Guard patrol boat *CG-276*)	75	37	1925
YP-111 (ex-yacht *Blue Moon*)	56	27	1927
YP-147 (ex-*Celia*)			1937
YP-164 (ex-yacht *Saxon III*)	69	33	1929
YP-165 (ex-wooden motor yacht *Chiro*, *Norwester*)	75	67	1932
YP-275 (ex-*Segelen*)	100	154	1929
Courser AMc-32 (ex-*Nancy Rose*)	71.7	86	1938
Grouse AMc-12 (ex-fishing boat *New Bol*, Lt. (jg) Theodore L. Bergen, USNR)	73.2	127	1938
Plover AMc-3 (ex-wooden hulled trawler *Sea Rover*)	78.3	117	1936
Roadrunner AMc-35 (ex-purse seiner *Treasure Island*)	74.4	108	1939[3]

Section bases at San Pedro and San Diego provided logistics support, repair and maintenance for Eleventh Naval District inshore patrol craft, and were responsible for district utility craft. While Navy destroyers escorted convoys offshore and Coast Guard cutters performed anti-submarine patrols near Santa Catalina Island, in the Santa Barbara Channel, and in the vicinity of Point Conception, vessels of the Inshore Patrol conducted daily harbor defense patrols and sweeps of the harbor approaches.[4]

The coastal minesweepers were all former fishing vessels, while the YPs were a mixture of ex-Coast Guard patrol boats and yachts. One, *YP-165*, was a classic wooden motor yacht built in 1932 for Charles Gilbert by the Willis Reid Shipyard in Winthrop, Massachusetts. An avid deep sea fisherman, Gilbert had instructed naval architect Frank Munroe to design a vessel capable of running "in any seas in any weather." The resulting *Chiro* was not fanciful (a newspaper account of her launch noted "she is of plain design but well worked out"), reflecting Gilbert's desire for a purposeful boat. The yacht passed through the Panama Canal in 1937, was renamed *Norwester*, and thereafter remained under private ownership until Navy acquisition in 1941. She served as a YP in southern California waters for the duration of the war, and later as John Wayne's yacht.[5]

JOHN WAYNE'S YACHT *NORWESTER*

The late John Wayne's beloved yacht *Wild Goose* was a former World War II wooden-hulled 136-foot minesweeper (*YMS-328*). Less well known is that before he acquired her, he was a co-owner of the 75-foot *Norwester*, which his business manager Bo Roos purchased shortly after the war. The actor entered into a partnership with Roos in 1955, after which the yacht received a facelift. Changes included the addition of a large day room and wheel house forward of the original salon and increased headroom to accommodate Wayne's 6' 4" height and his habit of wearing a hat while inside. Other modifications included solid bulwarks, covered side decks, and new upper decks. After Wayne purchased the larger *Wild Goose* in 1963, Roos retained ownership of the yacht until his passing in 1974. His daughter thereafter maintained the yacht for nearly twenty years before selling the *Norwester*. After its sale, it passed through the hands of a number of private owners and organizations, but today still plies Pacific Northwest waters and is available for charter.[6]

Photo 5-1

Motor yacht *Norwester*, which served during World War II as YP-165 and later belonged to John Wayne, cruising off Anacortes, Washington, where she is normally moored.
Courtesy of owner, King Graver.

COASTAL MINESWEEPER *ROADRUNNER*

The coastal minesweeper *Roadrunner* (AMc-35) was more representative of the types of former private and commercially-owned vessels acquired by the Eleventh Naval District. The 74-foot wooden vessel was built in 1939 by Western Boat of Tacoma, Washington, for August Felando of San Pedro. Prior to Pearl Harbor he employed her as a purse seiner in the sardine and tuna fishery off Mexico and Southern California. Following the war's end and the return of the former *Treasure Island*, Felando restored the vessel as a tuna baitboat during the summer of 1945 to fish for albacore off the West Coast of the United States, Canada, and Mexico. He later converted it to engage in the trawling of the dogfish liver fishery off Oregon, Washington, and Alaska. Upon her return to San Pedro in late 1945, Felando converted the vessel to a purse seiner engaged in fishing for sardine, mackerel, bluefin, yellowfin, and skipjack off California and Mexico.[7]

SUBMARINE SIGHTINGS AND A DEPTH CHARGE ATTACK

The principal duty of the YPs assigned to Section Base, San Pedro was the protection of merchantmen in local waters. On 1 March 1942, the *YP-164* was assigned to anti-submarine patrol and escort duty at El Segundo, a coastal town on Santa Monica Bay. The town's name, which means "the second" in Spanish, had been chosen as it was the site of the second Standard Oil refinery on the West Coast (the first being at Richmond, California). Three days later, the *YP-34* left San Pedro around noon to help guard the tanker *Standard Service* by conducting an anti-submarine patrol while it loaded at El Segundo. This duty was particularly important that day as earlier the section base had received a report of a sub sighted one mile off San Clemente, a town to the south, midway between Los Angeles and San Diego, renowned for its ocean and mountain views, pleasant climate, and Spanish colonial-style architecture.[8]

During the late morning of 5 March, the Coast Guard cutter *Hermes* (WPC-109) and *YP-34* rendezvoused with the tankers *J. C. Donnell* and *K. R. Kingsbury* southwest of Point Vicente, escorted them to El Segundo, and took up an anti-submarine patrol while the ships were loading. On completion, *YP-34* accompanied the vessels south to San Pedro while the cutter escorted the *Standard Service* west to the 100-fathom curve. Two days later, an army corporal reported sighting a submarine at 0505 off Gaviote, a town about thirty miles west of Santa Barbara. Two naval aircraft investigated waters up the coast from the community, with negative results.[9]

Two weeks later, on 23 March, Section Base, San Pedro received yet another report of a submarine, this time a periscope sighting off White Point (the southern tip of Palos Verdes Peninsula, which forms the northern boundary of San Pedro Bay) about one-half mile due south of the Palos Verdes Coast Guard lighthouse. The cutter *Cahoone* (WSC-131), *YP-33*, and a naval aircraft were sent to investigate. A little before noon, the *YP-33*'s sound gear detected the strong signature of a submarine one-half mile off Point Vicente, bearing 160 degrees true, but then lost it. The *Cahoone* ordered her to conduct a depth-charge attack after regaining contact. *YP-33* found the sub again, but the noise originating from ten degrees off the YP's port bow was insufficient to fix the position of the enemy for an attack. At a little past noon, the cutter *Diligence* (WSC-135) stood out of San Pedro to join in the hunt. With both cutters circling their prey, *YP-33* obtained a stronger sound contact twenty degrees off her port bow, and dropped two depth charges at 1409. At 1443 the *Cahoone* deployed a single depth charge, which failed to detonate. Five minutes later, the YP detected a signature between the two cutters, moving to cross the bow of the *Cahoone*. The cutter launched two depth charges, but apparently caused no harm to the submarine; two minutes later the *33* detected a strong propeller signature dead ahead. She rolled two additional depth charges off her stern above the submarine's suspected location, following which all sound ceased. However, no evidence, such as an oil slick or debris, of the demise of the sub appeared. The *Diligence* was assigned to all-night listening duty off White Point, with negative results.[10]

TWELFTH NAVAL DISTRICT

Twelfth Naval District, which encompassed the northern two-thirds of California including the expansive San Francisco Bay, required large local defense forces. Although the small fishing ports of Monterey and Eureka required protection, the San Francisco Bay was most important because, in addition to the shipping entering and leaving it daily, the area hosted many military bases, creating a "target rich environment." The bay, the naval base on Treasure Island, and those along its shoreline, would have been wide open to Japanese submarines except for a net stretched across the Golden Gate from Point

Sausalito almost to the St. Francis Yacht Club on the San Francisco Marina. In anticipation of war, the three mile-long, 6,000-ton net had been constructed at the nearby Tiburon Net Depot and was in place on 7 December 1941.[11]

In 1904 the Navy had acquired the property on the eastern shore of the Tiburon Peninsula for use as a coaling station because the adjacent bay water was of sufficient depth to moor battleships, which then would be protected from an attack via the Pacific by the hills and other landforms of Marin County. In addition, the site was only seventeen miles by water from the Mare Island Navy Yard. Steaming coal for the Pacific Fleet was brought by colliers (ships) from the East Coast and stored in large bunkers on an L-shaped wharf-trestle. In 1908 Teddy Roosevelt's Great White Fleet—sixteen new battleships of the Atlantic Fleet, painted white except for gilded scrollwork on their bows—refueled there before continuing on its fourteen-month round-the-world cruise. The station closed during the Depression after oil replaced coal as ship fuel, and in 1931 the Navy loaned the property to the State of California to establish a school to train Merchant Marine officers. The Nautical School, renamed the California Maritime Academy, relocated to Vallejo in 1940, and the Navy reclaimed the base for use as a net depot for construction and storage of anti-submarine and anti-torpedo nets.[12]

Six YPs were based at Tiburon to provide support for the depot by patrolling the cable net strung across the bay. A member of this group, *YP-119*, was the former yacht *Lightnin*. The stately craft had been built in 1929 by Lake Union Dry Dock of Seattle, Washington, for Lloyd Bacon, a film director for Warner Brothers. He had entertained many celebrities aboard; his daughter recalled sitting in the cockpit captivated by Bing Crosby singing and telling jokes. Bacon also enjoyed long distance predicted log racing and he entered the boat in a race from Long Beach to San Francisco in 1931. He thought he had won the race, but was awarded second place on a technicality. Out of frustration he sold the boat in San Francisco. The boat passed through the hands of two owners before it was purchased by Don Owen on 12 October 1940 and renamed *Pat Pending*. The Navy acquired her two days after the attack on Pearl Harbor. Following modification, the vessel sported a coat of gray paint over her former pristine white hull and teak house with an ugly green interior. The *YP-119* was fitted with a deck gun—most likely a .30-caliber or .50-caliber machine gun—on her bow, and depth charges on the middle deck.[13]

Photo 5-2

Motor yacht *Pat Pending*, the former *YP-119*, under way for "opening day on the bay," marking the official start of San Francisco's Boating Season. Courtesy of Melville Owen

In May 1942, the local defense forces of the Twelfth Naval District included the following patrol craft, coastal minesweepers, and harbor minesweepers:

Commandant, Twelfth Naval District
Vice Adm. John W. Greenslade, USN

Twelfth Naval District Local Defense Forces

Ship Name or Designation (Former Type Vessel/ Name and Name of Commanding Officer if Known)	Length Feet	Displ Tons	Year Built
Naval Station, Treasure Island			
Bunting AMc-7 (ex-*Vagabond*)	79.3	115	1935
Chatterer AMc-16 (ex-*Sea Breeze*)	75.3	112	1936
Grosbeak AMc-19 (ex-purse seiner *Del Rio*, Ens. Thomas F. Martin, USN)	78.1	110	1935
Hornbill AMc-13 (ex-fishing vessel *J. A. Martinolich*)	85	160	1940
Killdeer AMc-21 (ex-fishing boat *Rainbow, Jenny Rose, Vindicator*)	97	191	1930
Waxbill AMc-15 (ex-purse seiner *Leslie J. Fulton*, Ens. Edward L. Holtz, USNR)	76.2	112	1936
Hull AMc-146 (ex-purse seiner *Lina V.*/reclassified YP-384)	79.3	108	1940
Hull AMc-147 (ex-*Pacific Star*/reclassified YP-385)	81.3	144	1940
Hull AMc-148 (ex-*Lina B.*/reclassified YP-386)	79.3	134	1936
AMb-2 (ex-purse seiner *Auroa*/reclassified YP-360)	79.3	122	1940
AMb-5 (ex-purse seiner *Santa Rosa*/reclassified YP-363)	75.9	106	1940
AMb-8 (ex-purse seiner *San Jose*/reclassified YP-366)	71.5	96	1940

Ship Name or Designation (Former Type Vessel/ Name and Name of Commanding Officer if Known)	Length Feet	Displ Tons	Year Built
AMb-9 (ex-purse seiner *Belle Haven*/reclassified YP-367)	70	98	1939
AMb-11 (ex-purse seiner *Stella Maris*/reclassified YP-369)	71.2	105	1939
AMb-12 (ex-purse seiner *Dante Alighiere*/reclassified YP-370)	75.3	105	1939
AMb-13 (ex-purse seiner *Redeemer*/reclassified YP-371)	78	114	1940
AMb-14 (ex-purse seiner *San Giovanni*/reclassified YP-372)	75.2	106	1939
AMb-16 (ex-purse seiner *Belvedere*/reclassified YP-374)	71.2	95	1939
YP-112 (ex-*Pez Espada II*)	41' 11"	42	1934
YP-113 (ex-motor yacht *Elogrier*)		20	1929
YP-117 (ex-motor yacht *Xanadu*)	59' 6"	37	1935
YP-118 (ex-motor yacht *Jasmine, Skeeter*)	30	23	1930
YP-121 (ex-cruiser *Bobanet*)	43		1929
YP-124 (ex-*Intrepid*)			1927
YP-131 (ex-wooden motor yacht *Sobre las Olas*)	105	122	1929
YP-136 (ex-yacht *Mary Anne, Memory*)	66		1919
YP-137 (ex-recreational boat *Motap*)	57		1941
YP-138 (ex-*Sadye Lynn*)			1924
Section Base, Eureka			
YP-129 (ex-*Felica*)	67		1922
YP-139 (ex-*Beautyrest*/reclassified small boat)			1919
San Luis Naval Patrol Detachment			
AMc-143 (ex-purse seiner *St. James*/reclassified YP-381)	87.9	149	1940
AMc-144 (ex-purse seiner *Twin Brothers*/reclassified YP-382)	75.5	106	1940
AMb-3 (ex-purse seiner *Exposition King*/reclassified YP-361)	75.4	105	1939
AMb-4 (ex-purse seiner *Western Star*/reclassified YP-362)	74.8	118	1939
AMb-6 (ex-purse seiner *New Hope*/reclassified YP-364)	75.5	107	1940
YP-132 (ex-wooden motor yacht *K'Thanga*)	92		1926
Monterey Patrol Detachment			
AMb-7 (ex-purse seiner *Cutino Brothers*/reclassified YP-365)	78.1	114	1940
YP-128 (ex-*Bonnie Dundee III*)	66		1935
Naval Ammunition Depot, Mare Island			
YP-147 (ex-*Celia*)			1937
Naval Net Depot, Tiburon			
YP-119 (ex-yacht *Lightnin, Pat Pending*/reclassified small boat)	50	17	1929
YP-123 (ex-*Seamonger*/reclassified small boat)			1924
YP-125 (ex-*Spinster*/reclassified small boat)			1926
YP-126 (ex-cruiser *Mabi II*/reclassified small boat)	43		1931
YP-141 (ex-cruiser *Folderol*/reclassified small boat)	48		1936
YP-145 (ex-yacht *Ballyhoo Fourth*/reclassified small boat)	40		1927
Captain of the Port, San Francisco			
YP-114 (ex-motor yacht *Adventuress*)	45	32	1940
YP-115 (ex-motor yacht *Bee, Kennylee*/reclassified small boat)	48		1930
YP-116 (ex-*Balboa*/reclassified small boat)			1928
YP-120 (ex-yacht *Grathea II, Borenna II*)	57		1928

Ship Name or Designation (Former Type Vessel/ Name and Name of Commanding Officer if Known)	Length Feet	Displ Tons	Year Built
YP-122 (ex-motor yacht *Mary Kay*/reclassified small boat)	45		1929
YP-127 (ex-gas yacht *Lila M., Alma R., Elizabeth, Bounty*/ reclassified small boat)	44		1929
YP-130 (ex-gas yacht *Junemma*/reclassified small boat)	44		1931
YP-134 (ex-recreational boat *Cherie II*/reclassified small boat)	43		1930
YP-135 (ex-*Armador II*)	40	28	1931
YP-140 (ex-wooden motor yacht *Thor, Cormorant*)	52	27	1925
YP-142 (ex-motor yacht *Hermit*)	68	44	1927
YP-143 (ex-motor yacht *Indolence*)	50	26	1926[14]

Each day at dawn, four coastal minesweepers (or occasionally three, augmented by an AMb) conducted a routine sweep of the main ship channel seaward of the Golden Gate Bridge, searching for magnetic and acoustic mines. Less frequently, they performed minesweeping out to the 100-fathom curve, and occasionally served as escorts for inbound tankers. Japanese submarines were capable of carrying and deploying mines as well as torpedoes, but their commanders—like their American counterparts—preferred to carry all torpedoes in lieu of a mixture of mines and torpedoes and to attack shipping with gun or torpedo versus laying mines in coastal waters. Believing that Japanese subs posed a bigger threat to merchant vessels well offshore, the Navy reclassified five AMcs as YPs and assigned them to patrol duties with the Western Sea Frontier Force.[15]

Naval administrative actions resulted in other changes. The service revoked the YP designation of seventeen vessels on 18 April 1942 and reclassified them as small boats. A week later, a similar action reclassified an equal number of district base minesweepers (AMbs) as patrol craft. Following these changes, there were thirty-eight YPs assigned to the local defense force in May 1942. These numbers were bolstered when the frontier commander later transferred six YPs—*360, 372, 382, 384, 385,* and *386*—to the local defense force. Four of these craft were equipped and had been used exclusively for minesweeping—leaving insufficient space for depth charges for antisubmarine warfare—and the other two as supporting guard and Dan buoy-laying boats.[16]

AFTERMATH

Following the war, the Navy removed the nets that had shielded the San Francisco Bay, returned them to Tiburon for storage in case of any future need, and inactivated the net depot. The depot was reactivated during the Korean War and eventually closed in 1958, after which the components of the barrier were discarded. The nets went to scrap dealers for salvage and the massive 12-ton concrete plugs used to anchor the nets were used for shoreline protection at the depot. Many of the huge floats served as beehives throughout California—a few others still support houseboats on the Sausalito waterfront—and the Gantry cranes were removed. Today, the former site of the net depot hosts the Tiburon Upland Nature Reserve and Paradise Beach County Park, the National Oceanographic and Atmospheric Administration Tiburon Laboratory, and Romberg Tiburon Center run by San Francisco State University.[17]

Following her service as *YP-119*, the Navy sold the former *Pat Pending* back to Don Owen for $100, and he invested over $24,000 in her restoration. In June 1997, the boat was found five feet down by the bow, and ready to settle to the bottom at her berth at the San Francisco Yacht Club in Belvedere. Today, following a lengthy three-and-one-half year restoration, she still plies San Francisco Bay waters as a classic wooden-hulled yacht under the stewardship of the Melville Owen family. By the time the boat was relaunched in October 2000, she had all new frames, planks, and decks, new electrical systems and plumbing, and a redesigned interior. A new Crusader "Captain's Choice" 8.1 liter 8-cylinder gas engine was installed in 2001, replacing the 6-cylinder twin-ignition Hall-Scott Invader that had propelled the *Pat Pending* for seventy-two years.[18]

Another famous yacht, the *Sobre las Olas*, served as the *YP-131*, at Treasure Island, San Francisco. She too is still afloat today as one of the largest antique classics on the West Coast; among her owners were J. Paul Getty and William Randolph Hearst. The wooden motor yacht *K'Thanga*—which as the *YP-132* had been assigned duty with the San Luis Naval Patrol Detachment—was for decades one of San Francisco's classic yachts, before burning up while serving as a "live aboard".[19]

WESTERN SEA FRONTIER

The Eleventh and Twelfth Naval District local defense forces were a part of the Western Sea Frontier Forces under Vice Adm. John W. Greenslade, USN:

- Task Force 51 (Surface Forces, Southern Sector): Rear Adm. Ralston S. Holmes, USN, Destroyer Division 70—*Amethyst* (PYc-3), *Hermes* (WPC-109), *Perseus* (WPC-114), and *Cahoone* (WPC-131).
- Task Force 52 (Surface Forces, Northern Sector): Rear Adm. Hugo W. Osterhaus, USN (Ret.), Destroyer Division 83—*Ariadne* (WPC-101), *Daphne* (WPC-106), *Alert* (WSC-127), *Pulaski* (WSC-149), and *Shawnee* (WAT-54), plus the destroyer *Talbot* (DD-114).
- Task Force 53 (Local Defense Forces, Eleventh Naval District)
- Task Force 54 (Local Defense Forces, Twelfth Naval District)
- Task Force 55 (Aircraft, Western Sea Frontier): Rear Adm. John S. McCain, USN, (temporary commander), Navy, Marine Corps, and Coast Guard aircraft.[20]

Although comprised of five "task forces," Greenslade's organization was anything but impressive. His two "destroyer divisions" were made up of seven Coast Guard cutters, one tug, one coastal patrol yacht, and one Navy destroyer. Beyond that, he had only small district craft and some land-based aircraft to patrol California's 840-mile coastline and to protect shipping from Japanese submarines. The challenge he faced was daunting—finding an elusive enemy in a huge area stretching two hundred miles off the coast and spanning thousands of square miles. After considering ways to deal with this problem, he decided to use the aircraft tender *Pelican* (AVP-6) as "bear bait" to attract Japanese submarines.

Q-SHIP PROGRAM

Several books have been written about the U.S. Navy's World War II employment of Q-ships, heavily armed merchant ships with concealed weaponry, designed to lure enemy submarines into making surface attacks against seemingly defenseless vessels, thus providing the ships with an opportunity to open fire and sink the subs. The basic ethos of every Q-ship was to be a wolf in sheep's clothing. The literature on the subject is devoted to the five units of the Eastern Sea Frontier—*Eagle* AM-132/*Captor* PYc-40 (former fishing trawler *Harvard*, *Wave*), *Atik* AP-100 (former cargo vessel S.S. *Carolyn*), *Asterion* AP-101 (former cargo vessel S.S. *Evelyn*), *Big Horn* AO-45 (former tanker S.S. *Gulf Dawn*), and *Irene Forsyte* IX-93 (ex-Canadian schooner *Irene Myrtle*). They were a part of a "Mystery" or "Q" ship project that Admiral King, in response to pressure from President Roosevelt, had reluctantly organized to combat the heavy losses of merchantmen off the East Coast.[21]

A Q-ship on the Western Sea Frontier was disguised to look like a tuna boat. This ship, the *Normandie II*, was the former minesweeper *Pelican* (AM-27); commissioned on 10 October 1918, the Navy had reclassified her as a small seaplane tender in 1936. The *Pelican* entered Navy Yard, Mare Island on 13 March 1942 to be reconfigured for her new role. Over the next six weeks she received raised bulwarks around the bow, a new foremast just forward of the bridge, and an extra cabin behind the bridge. Her disguise was completed by covering her two 3-inch guns forward, building a fake bait tank on the fantail that housed a Seagull floatplane, adding a crow's nest on the mainmast, and fitting prominent tuna boat ratlines on both masts. The *Normandie II* left the yard on 24 April.[22]

She operated in southern California waters that summer, a perfect area for a very large 187-foot "tuna clipper" to blend in with the San Diego fishing fleet. Her activities, however, remained highly classified. The commanding officer of U.S. Fleet Training Base, San Clemente Island—in his 13 June 1942 war diary entry following her arrival at the island off California's coast about fifty miles southwest of Los Angeles—noted only:

> At 1510 the U.S.S *Normandie II* anchored at Pyramid Cove in accordance with previous radio advices. Mission unknown.

The Q-Ship visited San Clemente Island again five weeks later, when, at 0610 on 20 July, she arrived at Wilson Cove with a Marine Corps plane (J2F5, No. 00733) and its crew of three enlisted men. The Grumman single-engine amphibious biplane (used primarily for utility and air-sea rescue duties) belonged to Squadron 242 of the Base Marine Air Wing stationed at Goletta, California, and had been salvaged near Santa Cruz Island. The *Normandie II* departed at 0705 after offloading the aircraft.[23]

The *Pelican* apparently retained her original name during her tenure as a Q-Ship, although she likely had *Normandie II* displayed on bridgewing name boards or transom in keeping with her role of tuna clipper. The commanding officer of U.S. Fleet Training Base, San Clemente Island, and the task force commander of the Eleventh Naval District Local Defense Forces, referred to her as *Normandie II*; other naval correspondence cited her as *Pelican*.[24]

Photo 5-3

Seaplane tender *Pelican* (AVP-6) under way off the southern California coast between May 1942 and April 1943 after conversion to the "tuna boat" Q-ship *Normandie II*.
Photo No. NH 96553, Courtesy of the Naval History and Heritage Command, http://www.shipscribe.com/usnaux/AVP/pelican2b-08.jpg

Sixty years after the clandestine service of the *Normandie II*, scant information exists about her activities during 1942 and 1943. The commander, Western Sea Frontier war diary entry for 31 March 1943 cited *Pelican* being under his operational control for "operations under emergency conditions and in training therefore." The *Normandie II* ceased to exist with the transfer of the *Pelican* to the Atlantic Fleet in May. She arrived at U.S. Naval and Drydock Repair Facility, San Juan on 2 May where, over the next eight days, yard workers removed the ship's float plane, hanger and false work around the guns and, for good measure, overhauled her engines and gave the entire ship a glistening new coat of paint. Assigned to commander, Caribbean Sea Frontier, the *Pelican* alternated tending seaplanes with serving as a convoy escort until reporting to the Navy Fleet Sound School in March 1945. Once there she assisted in experiments with new anti-submarine warfare gear. Ordered to Charleston Navy Yard for decommissioning after the war, the former Q-ship was struck on 19 December 1945 and sold for scrap eleven months later.[25]

The Eastern Sea Frontier Q-Ship program proved a dismal failure. During her shakedown cruise following modification, the *Atik* was torpedoed on 26 March 1942 by the German submarine *U-123* with the loss of all hands. With the exception of the *Big Horn*, the other Q-ships did not encounter any U-boats during their cruises, and the former tanker, which sailed in several convoys attacked by enemy submarines, was not credited with any kills. After heavy weather opened the seams of the *Irene Forsyte* during her maiden voyage south from New London, Connecticut, to Bermuda in late September 1943, the Navy appointed a Board of Investigation to determine responsibility for the material failure of the vessel. Admiral King's written review of the subsequent report (and of the program generally) concluded with the statement: "The practice of granting to Frontier Commanders and District Commandants uncontrolled authority to implement projects of this nature has been discontinued." In an associated action, on 14 October 1943 King directed commander, Eastern Sea Frontier to decommission the *Irene Forsyte* on her return from Bermuda, and to take other steps which would lead to the conclusion of all antisubmarine patrols by Eastern Sea Frontier vessels disguised as merchant vessels.[26]

NORTHWEST SEA FRONTIER AND THE THIRTEENTH NAVAL DISTRICT

Vice Adm. Charles S. Freeman, USN, headquartered at Seattle, Washington, commanded both the Northwest Sea Frontier—comprised of the Northwestern and Alaskan Sectors—and the Thirteenth Naval District. The vessels serving as local defense forces reflected their acquisition from the Pacific Northwest area. With commercial fishing and logging as the main industries, and plentiful straight-grained, old-growth timber available for boat building, a majority were wooden-hulled former fishing vessels. There were, however, several unique ships, including two former Coast Guard lightships and a small 37-foot patrol boat, three antiquated Fish and Wildlife vessels, one vintage steel-hulled trawler, and a yacht previously owned by movie actor John Barrymore. Amongst the district's coastal minesweepers were some new *Accentor* and *Acme*-class ships. Recognizing that requirements for AMcs would soon exceed the availability of fishing vessels that could be converted to perform minesweeping duties, the Navy had rapidly designed its own, based on the proven fishing boat model, and rushed them into production.

The YPs were commanded by junior officers or, in the case of some smaller craft, senior enlisted men (chief boatswain's mates). A majority of the commanding officers (titled "officers in charge" aboard some vessels) were Navy, some were Coast Guard, and one was an officer of the U.S. Coast and Geodetic Survey. Their names, if known, are included in the following disposition of coastal minesweepers, patrol yachts, and patrol craft in the Northwestern Sector on 15 May 1942. Three of the craft listed, the *AMc-149* and YPs *396* and *397*, were placed in service later in the month. (Vessels of the Alaskan Sector are identified in the following chapter, entitled "War in the Aleutians".)

Commander, Northwest Sea Frontier, and Commandant, Thirteenth Naval District
Vice Adm. Charles S. Freeman, USN

Thirteenth Naval District Inshore Patrol: Capt. E. Friedrick, USN

Ship Name or Designation (Former Type Vessel/ Name and Name of Commanding Officer if Known)	Length Feet	Displ Tons	Year Built
Northwestern Sector Section Base, Seattle			
Affray AMc-112 (*Acme*-class coastal minesweeper, Lt. Robert I. Thieme, USNR)	89	205	1941
Agile AMc-111 (acquired by Navy while under construction, Lt. (jg) John G. Turbitt, USNR)	96	215	1941
Frigate Bird AMc-27 (ex-fishing boat *Star of San Pedro*)	73.5	112	1935
Goshawk AMc-4 (ex-steel freighter *Echmuhl, Lexington, Penobscot*, Lt. (jg) Allan Dwight Curtis, USNR)	150	585	1919
Liberator AMc-87 (*Accentor*-class coastal minesweeper, Lt. (jg) James W. Dawnes, USNR)	97	195	1941
Nightingale AMc-149 (ex-purse seiner *St. Francis/YP-150*, Lt. (jg) Donald W. Deits, USNR)	85.3	168	1940
Phoebe AMc-57 (ex-fishing trawler *Western Robin*)	98	205	1941
Pintail AMc-17 (ex-fishing vessel *Three Star*)	77.7	126	1937
YP-7 (ex-Coast Guard *CG-272*, James Joseph Hall, Chief Boatswain's Mate, USN)	37	75	1925
YP-96 (ex-USC&GS *Pratt*, Lt. E. F. Hicks, Jr., USC&GS)	78.1	107	1922
YP-154 (ex-purse seiner/bait boat *Aletta B.*)	85.1	154	1936
YP-166 (ex-purse seiner *Majestic, Nightingale* AMc-18, Lt. (jg) Charles Fredrick Wilson, USNR)	74.1	93	1934
YP-198 (ex-FWS *Eider*, John F. Rasmussen, Chief Boatswain's Mate, USCG)	78.3	152	1913
YP-333 (ex-M.V. *Amelie*, Ens. W. E. Stevenson, USNR)	85	78	1925
YP-337 (ex-purse seiner *San Juan*, William M. Lowry, USNR)	71.9	72	1930
YP-338 (ex-*Discover*, Lt. J. K. Carpenter, USNR)	91		1933
YP-396 (ex-lightship *Umatilla* LV-88 Ens. C. R. Brink, USCG)	135' 5"	683	1907
YP-397 (ex-lightship *Swiftsure* LV-113, Ens. Richard E. Walker, USCG)	133' 3"	630	1929

Ship Name or Designation (Former Type Vessel/ Name and Name of Commanding Officer if Known)	Length Feet	Displ Tons	Year Built
Section Base, Neah Bay			
Amber PYc-6 (ex-yacht *Infanta, Polaris*, Lt. William B. Combs, USNR)	120	260	1930
YP-84 (ex-purse seiner *Ketchikan*)	69.6	94	1937
YP-89 (ex-purse seiner *Challenger*)	69.1	91	1937
YP-149 (ex-purse seiner *Farallon*)	79.9	137	1931
YP-153 (ex-purse seiner *Waldero*)	78.1	130	1936
Section Base, Port Angeles			
YP-83 (ex-purse seiner *Rio del Mar*)	71.2	94	1937
YP-90 (ex-purse seiner *Montara*)	71.3	99	1937
Section Base, Astoria			
Radiant AMc-99 (*Acme*-class coastal minesweeper)	97	228	1941
Section Base, Port Townsend			
Crow AMc-20 (ex-purse seiner *Jadran*)	71.9	104	1935
YP-87 (ex-purse seiner *Valiant*)	70.4	102	1937
YP-199 (ex-FWS *Kittiwake*, Lt. (jg) R. K. Keller)	73	30	1908
YP-200 (ex-gas yacht/FWS *Widgeon*, Lt. (jg) Vernon Grant Impett, Jr.)	75	38	1913[27]

The district's inshore patrol units were distributed among its six section bases, two in Oregon and four in Washington. Section Base, Coos Bay was 110 miles north of the California-Oregon border; the one at Astoria was on the Columbia River forming the Oregon-Washington border. The four bases in the State of Washington—Neah Bay, Port Townsend, Port Angeles, and Seattle—lay on the Strait of Juan de Fuca, or Puget Sound. After entering the strait from sea, ships bound for Seattle passed Neah Bay on the south side, then Port Angeles and Port Townsend, before proceeding in a southeasterly direction through the Sound to reach the Port of Seattle.

EX-LIGHTSHIPS *UMATILLA* AND *SWIFTSURE*

As the war progressed, the Navy continued to acquire almost any type vessel for use as YPs. Eventually, after having exhausted available sources, the service recognized that the Coast Guard had a number of lightships, very fine vessels designed to endure long periods at sea in the worst weather imaginable. The lightship *LV-88*, built in 1907, was withdrawn from its duty at Umatilla Reef off the Washington coast and stationed at Seattle as an "examination vessel." At that time most lighthouses were blacked out to prevent their beacons from silhouetting merchant vessels against the shoreline during night passage; lightships were withdrawn from their stations to avoid becoming "sitting ducks" for enemy submarines. Lightships were then commonly assigned the task of Examination Ships, positioning themselves at a harbor entrance and surveying all vessels within visual range. In particular, inbound craft required early sighting, positive identification, and timely reporting. Although usually at anchor, at some locations lightships patrolled their area while underway. To provide the *LV-88* a means of self-defense, she was fitted with one 3-inch gun forward (the standard anti-aircraft gun for United States destroyers through World War I and the 1920s) and one "Y" gun depth charge-projector on her stern.[28]

Lightship *LV-113*, launched in 1929 at Albina Marine Works in Portland Oregon, was a modern diesel-electric propelled, steel-hulled vessel with steel deckhouses, two masts with lantern galleries, and a smokestack amidships. Following delivery in 1930, the Coast Guard had assigned her to the Swiftsure Banks station, roughly fourteen miles northwest of Cape Flattery along the Washington Coast, where she remained until 1942 when the station was closed. Following acquisition by the Navy, she entered a Seattle yard for conversion, receiving heavy armament as well as anti-submarine capabilities before her assignment in mid-June to Juneau, Alaska. At completion, she boasted a monster 4-inch gun mount forward (the standard low-angle, quick-firing gun for destroyers throughout World War I and the 1920s), .50-caliber machine guns on her bridge wings, and a .30-caliber machine gun atop the aft deckhouse. The now slate-gray YP was also fitted with JK-9 sonar and a "Y" gun back aft with seventeen depth charges stored on deck.[29]

Leaving the yard, the *YP-397* departed Seattle and proceeded to Port Townsend (the location of the new Coast Guard "boot camp" Training Station) to fill out her crew complement. With six officers and forty-two enlisted, she then sailed north through the Inside Passage, stopping briefly at Ketchikan before continuing on to Juneau. Richard E. Walker, formerly of the U.S. Lighthouse Service, which had become a part of the Coast Guard in 1939, was the ship's commanding officer. Although former masters and mates, such as he, were to have been integrated into the new service with commensurate rank, this reassignment had seldom occurred. The commanders of lighthouse service vessels were almost invariably seasoned master mariners of long experience and great skill, yet most were given the rank of chief petty officer, chief warrant officer or, at the very best, ensign or lieutenant (junior grade) on merging with the Coast Guard.[30]

Following her arrival in Juneau, the *YP-397* was dispatched without fanfare or delay to an area of Icy Strait in Southeast Alaska (connecting Glacier Bay to the Pacific) between Cape Spencer and Indian Head Light. Her orders were to maintain station, identify all ships, and assist in the formation of convoys in the strait. Mindful that vessels making the crossing independently to Kodiak or Dutch Harbor were easy pickings for Japanese submarines, Northwest Sea Frontier Force units convoyed merchantmen to help ensure their safety in the Gulf of Alaska as well as other Alaskan and Aleutian waters.[31]

6

War in the Aleutians

[They] would sink if rammed by a barnacle.
—Comdr. Charles E. Anderson, USNR, Dutch Harbor captain-of-the-port, remarking on the state of a group of World War I-era destroyers and former fishing boats (YPs) that comprised the so-called "Alaskan Navy" in early 1942[1]

Within days of the attack on Pearl Harbor, Japan swallowed up Guam, Indochina and Thailand, and by Christmas had taken Wake Island and Hong Kong. Within two months, her forces had occupied Manila, Singapore, and British Malaya (now called Malaysia). In March 1942 the Allies lost Java and Burma, and Japanese armies were in the Owen Stanley Mountains of New Guinea, with the coast of Australia almost in sight. In May, Corregidor surrendered, the Philippines fell, and Japan invaded the Solomon Islands. The Allies were in desperate straits, and not just in the Pacific. German U-boats had sunk almost five hundred ships off America's East Coast, and Japanese submarines had sunk a few vessels and shelled refineries and installations on the West Coast. United States naval forces in the Pacific were driven back to Hawaii and the West Coast, and Japan knew that U.S. strategy was limited to holding a line of defense that began in New Guinea, extended northward through Samoa and Midway, and was anchored at Dutch Harbor in the Aleutians.[2]

One bright moment for America occurred on 18 April 1942 when a group of U.S. Army Air Force B25s, led by Lt. Col. James H. ("Jimmie") Doolittle, launched from the carrier *Hornet* (CV-8) in the Central Pacific and bombed Tokyo. While the damage inflicted by the sixteen bombers was small, the psychological effect of an air raid on

Japan was huge. The Japanese high command disagreed about the site from which the raid had originated. Some argued that the bombers had been launched from carriers, while others believed their origin to be an airfield in Alaska. Flying such a distance through the pervasive inclement weather of the Aleutians, which included harsh winds and blizzards, however, would have been impossible. Attu, the westernmost island in the Aleutians, lay 1,746 nautical miles from Tokyo. However, the nearest U.S. base was located on Umnak Island, 260 miles further east, 2,006 long miles from Japan's capital city. In preparation for the Doolittle raid, engineers had taken desperate measures to increase the fuel storage aboard the bombers. Modifications included removing tail guns to create space for a rubber fuel tank in the tail section (and installing broomsticks painted like machine gun barrels to provide the impression of a defensive capability), and loading ten five-gallon gas cans aboard for manual addition to gas tanks while in flight. These actions increased the range of the planes to 2,000 miles under optimum flying conditions—no headwinds, storms, or navigation errors.[3]

Following the raid, Yamamoto, who was already obsessed with destroying American sea power, expanded his plans to include offensive operations against U.S. military installations in the Aleutians. His first attempt to destroy the American fleet had taken place in early May in the Battle of the Coral Sea, during which Japanese torpedo and dive bombers sank the carrier *Lexington* (CV-2) and damaged the *Yorktown* (CV-5). His new strategy focused on both Midway Island and the Aleutians. Japanese carrier aircraft would strike Dutch Harbor, Unalaska Island, while further west, occupational forces landed on Adak, Kiska, and Atu. Yamamoto envisioned that this first strike would draw the American fleet away from Pearl Harbor and north towards Alaskan waters, enabling his combined fleet to engage it near Midway after having captured the island for use by his own planes.[4]

SUBMARINES *I-25* AND *I-26* RETURN TO AMERICA'S WEST COAST

In preparation for the planned invasion of Midway, Japanese submarines *I-25* and *1-26* left Yokosuka on 11 May 1942 to conduct reconnaissance in the Aleutians before taking up patrol off the northwest coast of the United States. During a flight over Kodiak on 27 May, the *I-25*'s float plane sighted an American cruiser and two destroyers.

Intelligence obtained about U.S. Navy ships in the area was considered so vital to planning an attack on Dutch Harbor that the *I-26* was positioned, with her hanger empty, to recover the aircraft should something happen to the *I-25*. Three days later, at dawn on 30 May, as the *I-25* prepared to launch the floatplane, her lookouts sighted an approaching American cruiser. The sub could not dive with the small plane on deck, but the warship passed without detecting her low silhouette in the mist. While the *I-25* conducted surveillance flights, the *I-26* reconnoitered Kodiak, Chirikof, and Sitkanak Islands.[5]

At the completion of this assignment, the submarines set course to arrive off Seattle, Washington, and the coast of Oregon, respectively. Shortly after her arrival on 7 June, the *I-26* shelled and sank the 3,286-ton American ship *Coast Trader* about thirty-five miles southwest of Cape Flattery near the entrance to the Strait of Juan de Fuca. The cargo ship's fifty-six survivors were rescued by the Canadian corvette HMCS *Edmunston* (K106) and the *Virginia I*, a fishing vessel. The *I-25* arrived off Oregon a week later and employed a number of false bamboo periscopes to confuse the anti-submarine vessels in the vicinity.[6]

CODEBREAKERS LEARN OF YAMAMOTO'S PLANS

The Japanese offensive planned for early June would not be a surprise. A team of Pacific Fleet cryptanalysts broke Japan's top secret naval code on 15 May and were able to piece together Yamamoto's plan to occupy Midway and the Aleutians. Informed of this intelligence, Nimitz established Task Force 8 under Rear Adm. Robert A. Theobald (who had been serving as his commander of Pacific Fleet destroyers) on 21 May. Nimitz had only two operational carriers available, the *Enterprise* and *Hornet* (repairs to *Yorktown* were not expected to be finished before August) and required the majority of his fleet to oppose the Japanese at Midway. He was thus only able to provide Theobald with a force of five cruisers—*Indianapolis* (CA-35), *Louisville* (CA-18), *Honolulu* (CL-48), *St. Louis* (CL-49), and *Nashville* (CL-43)—and units of Destroyer Division 11—*Gridley* (DD-380), *McCall* (DD-400), *Reid* (DD-369), and *Humphreys* (DD-236). Theobald would also have command of the sparse U.S. Navy, Army, and Canadian forces already based in Alaska. These forces consisted of the so-called "Alaskan Navy" commanded by Capt. Ralph C. Parker,

USN; nearly two hundred planes (mostly Army bombers and fighters) under Maj. Gen. Simon B. Buckner, Jr., USA; and the twenty Navy Catalina PBY seaplanes of Patrol Wing 4. Having received his orders to prepare Alaska against a Japanese attack, Theobald left Pearl Harbor aboard the destroyer *Reid* bound for Kodiak, headquarters of the Alaskan Naval Sector.[7]

THE ALASKAN NAVY

Five years before the war, Alaska was virtually undefended. Its only naval facility was a seaplane base at Sitka, a seaport on Baranof Island in the Alaska Panhandle that faced the Gulf of Alaska. As a result of recommendations made by the Hepburn Board, which reviewed America's national defense structure, new construction followed, and by September 1941 bases at Sitka, Kodiak, and Dutch Harbor had been commissioned as naval air stations, with the latter two ready to receive submarines. In mid-1940 the Army sent Colonel Buckner to Alaska to prepare the territory for the possibility of war with Japan. The Navy quickly followed suit by creating an Alaskan Sector under the Thirteenth Naval District and appointing Parker to command it.[8]

The associated allocation of forces to Parker was, to be very generous, "modest"—a single ship, the *Charleston* (PG-51). Between 6 November 1940 and 27 November 1941, the 328-foot gunboat made five cruises, patrolling the long section of coastline from Seattle to Aleutian and Alaskan waters. During a cruise from 23 January to 15 March 1941, an embarked survey party put ashore in a series of small ports found a scarcity of existing infrastructure and little hint of the build-up in Army personnel. A crewman observed in his diary that there was nothing at Hunter Bay or Latouche, nothing at Sawmill Bay except for sawmills, and absolutely nothing at Cold Bay. He humorously described Petersburg as "just a little burg too," Juneau as "still just Juneau," Sitka as "still [a] mud-hole," and Yakutat as also "just a little burg." The flagship encountered few units of the Alaskan Navy during the expedition, except for YPs based at Dutch Harbor.[9]

Captain Parker had only the *Charleston* until he was able to procure three Seattle fishery boats—the *YP-72* (ex-cannery tender *Cavalcade*), the *YP-73* (ex-cannery tender *Corsair*), and the *YP-74* (ex-purse seiner *Endeavor*)—and outfit them for use as patrol craft. The "YP boats" operated from Dutch Harbor under local command of Comdr.

Charles E. ("Squeaky") Anderson, USNR, a Swede and Alaskan, said to be the only sailor alive who really knew Aleutian waters, whose nickname was a pun on his loud, piercing voice. By May 1942, Parker's navy had grown to include two old World War I four-stack destroyers, three Coast Guard cutters, and a few more YPs, none, except for the *Charleston*, fitted with sonar or guns larger than three-inch. The YPs were among a group of halibut and purse seiners converted in 1941 by Olson & Winge Marine Works of Seattle, Washington—the first yard in the Pacific Northwest to undertake a full program of Army-Navy repair and adaption work—for Navy use as supply ships. These fifteen vessels, whose hulls were sheathed with ironbark, a tropical wood, would range up and down the Pacific Coast from the Canal Zone to the Aleutians and into the Bering Sea. Standard modifications included accommodations for additional crewmen, transformed stowage space for military uses, and mounted armament.[10]

Photo 6-1

Prior to World War II, the *YP-72*, former purse seiner *Cavalcade*, served as the flagship of the Alaska Patrol. During the Aleutians Campaign portion of the Battle of Midway, the 87-foot wooden vessel carried out picket ship, patrol and other duties that included towing a propeller-less PBY-5A Catalina into Port Moller.
Official Navy photograph #239470, courtesy of NavSource, http://www.navsource.org/archives/14/31072.htm

ADDITIONAL YPS SENT NORTH

By May 1942 the number of YPs operating in the Alaskan Sector as units of the local defense force had increased significantly. A summary of the duties or status of these vessels as of the fifteenth of the month follows:

Ship Name or Designation
(Former Type Vessel/Name and Name of Commanding Officer if Known) — Length Feet — Year Built — Assigned Duty/Status

Section Base, Cordova

Ship	Length Feet	Year Built	Assigned Duty/Status
YP (*Northern Light*)			in repair at Cordova

Section Base, Dutch Harbor

Ship	Length Feet	Year Built	Assigned Duty/Status
YP (*Washington*)			patrol section waters
YP (ex-motor vessel *Point Reyes*)			patrol section waters
YP-86 (ex-purse seiner *Pacific Fisher*)	73.6	1937	patrol section waters
YP-88 (ex-purse seiner *Adventure*)	74.6	1937	patrol section waters
YP-93 (ex-purse seiner *Margaret F.*)	69	1937	patrol section waters
YP-94 (ex-purse seiner *Western Chief*)	76.4	1936	patrol section waters

Section Base, Ketchikan

Ship	Length Feet	Year Built	Assigned Duty/Status
YP (ex-fishing vessel *Hiram*)			patrol section waters
YP-197 (ex-FWS *Brown Bear*)	114' 10"	1934	in repair at Seattle
YP-250 (ex-gas fishing boat *Spencer*)	64	1913	in repair at Seattle
YP-251 (ex-halibut schooner *Foremost*, Jack L. Hull, Chief Boatswain's Mate, USCG)	79' 8"	1924	in repair at Seattle
YP-401 (ex-*Monterey*)	110	1917	en route to Seattle

Section Base, Kodiak

Ship	Length Feet	Year Built	Assigned Duty/Status
YP-72 (ex-cannery tender *Cavalcade*)	87	1940	patrol section waters
YP-74 (ex-purse seiner *Endeavor*)	72.1	1937	in repair at Cordova
YP-95 (ex-purse seiner *Nordic Pride*)	74.8	1940	in repair at Seward
YP-148 (ex-purse seiner *Western Queen*)	85	1940	patrol section waters
YP-151 (ex-purse seiner *Sunrise*)	80.2	1931	patrol section waters
YP-152 (ex-purse seiner *Western Traveler*)	78.8	1937	patrol section waters
YP-155 (ex-purse seiner *Storm*)	74.7	1939	patrol section waters

Section Base, Sitka

Ship	Length Feet	Year Built	Assigned Duty/Status
YP (ex-*Bendora*)			patrol section waters
YP-73 (ex-purse seiner *Corsair*)	84.5	1937	patrol section waters
YP-85 (ex-purse seiner *Nick C. II*)	72.1	1939	patrol section waters
YP-92 (ex-purse seiner *Helen B.*, Lt. Harold Wright)	72.3	1938	patrol section waters [11]

Together, the Alaskan Sector and Northwestern Sector comprised the Northwest Sea Frontier, commanded by Vice Adm. Charles S. Freeman, USN, who was also the commandant of the Thirteenth Naval District and thus controlled both sea frontier and local defense forces. Captain Parker still had too few YP boats available for patrol of Alaskan and Aleutian waters. This shortfall was partially alleviated on 25 May when twenty-two YPs—*72-73, 83-84, 86, 88, 94-96, 148-149, 151-155, 197, 333, 338, 396-397,* and *401*—were reassigned to the Northwest Sea Frontier from local defense forces of the Thirteenth Naval District. That action was prompted by a Navy directive limiting local defense force vessels to those craft that could not be used in the open sea under favorable conditions. A rigorous selection of craft was to be made for transfer from local defense forces to sea frontier forces on a temporary basis. The justification for the action was the Navy's desire to "keep on top of enemy subs." Commanders were to make every effort to keep the vessels at sea two-thirds of the time. On 28 May 1942, the YPs began operations as a part of Task Force 8.[12]

PRELUDE TO BATTLE

Rear Adm. Theobald arrived at Kodiak on 28 May and immediately called a conference of his commanders to explain his general plan of organization and operation and to allow them to review his draft operation plan. In attendance were Maj. Gen. Simon B. Buckner, Jr., USA (commanding general Alaskan Defense); Brig. Gen. William O. Butler, Air Corps, USA (commanding general Eleventh Air Force); Capt. Ralph C. Parker, USN (commander Alaskan Sector); and Capt. Leslie E. Gehres, USN (commander Patrol Wing 4). The overarching guidance of the OpPlan was brief and to the point:

> This force will, in coordination with the Army, oppose the advance of the enemy in the Aleutian-Alaska Area, taking advantage of every favorable opportunity to inflict strong attrition.[13]

Based on information gleaned by his codebreakers, Nimitz provided Theobald with the projected composition of the Japanese Northern Force expected to attempt to seize bases in the Aleutian Islands area. Theobald subsequently received intelligence that this force would arrive off Kiska on 31 May or 1 June 1942, that Unalaska Island was the objective, and that he should expect an air attack on Dutch Harbor between 31 May and 3 June, followed by a landing attack between 1 and 4 June.[14]

DEPLOYMENT OF SCOUTING FORCES

All shipping was ordered out of the Umnak area in anticipation of the Japanese attack, and on 30 May, Task Force 8 units—the submarines *S-34* and *S-35*, gunboat *Charleston*, minesweeper *Oriole*, seaplane tenders *Casco*, *Williamson*, and *Gillis*, and Coast Guard cutters and YPs—were en route to their stations in Aleutian Peninsula waters. The two "S-boats" were units of Submarine Division 41, comprising the Submarine Group, and the tenders were support ships for the seaplanes and three scouting planes of Patrol Wing 4. These aircraft, along with one flight of Army Bombardment Squadron 36, comprised the Air Search Group. The Surface Search group was made up of the *Charleston*; *Oriole*; cutters *Haida* (WPG-45), *Onondaga* (WPG-79), *Cyane* (WPC-105), *Aurora* (WPC-103), and *Bonham* (WPC-129); and fourteen YPs.[15]

Photo 6-2

Oil painting by William F. Draper, titled *Sub and Yippy Tie Up*, depicts a quiet inlet of the Bering Sea in 1942, with a YP receiving a coat of paint and an old S-type submarine receiving fuel and provisions.
Courtesy of the Naval History and Heritage Command, www.navsource.org/archives/08/08123.htm.

Theobald had initiated seaplane patrol flights a day earlier before deployment of the patrol craft to picket stations on the Pacific and Bering Sea approaches to Dutch Harbor. Information about the YP boats assigned to the Surface Search Group is sketchy, as is information about conditions and any enemy forces they encountered. However, the experiences of the flagship *Charleston* were likely typical. A meeting of ships' commanding officers with representatives of commander, Alaskan Sector, on 29 May finalized arrangements for establishing the surface patrol lines. The *Charleston* left Dutch Harbor the following morning for Akutan Pass, which separates Unalaska from Umnak Island. Arriving on her station in the early morning on 31 May, she found the weather misty, with visibility decreasing at times to 200 yards, rough seas, and strong winds. The weather in the Aleutian Islands, especially toward the western part, is among the worst in the world. When sudden blasts of cold dense wind, called "williwaws," sweep down from snow and ice fields of coastal mountains, winds may increase to gale proportions and speeds of 100 knots are not uncommon. When these conditions occur, heavy seas and strong currents running through passes and channels near jagged island shorelines and shoals make navigation extremely hazardous. Rain is common even on good days and when it is not raining, there is normally fog. Moreover, it is a peculiarity of the area that fog and wind may persist together for many days at a time.[16]

Map 6-1

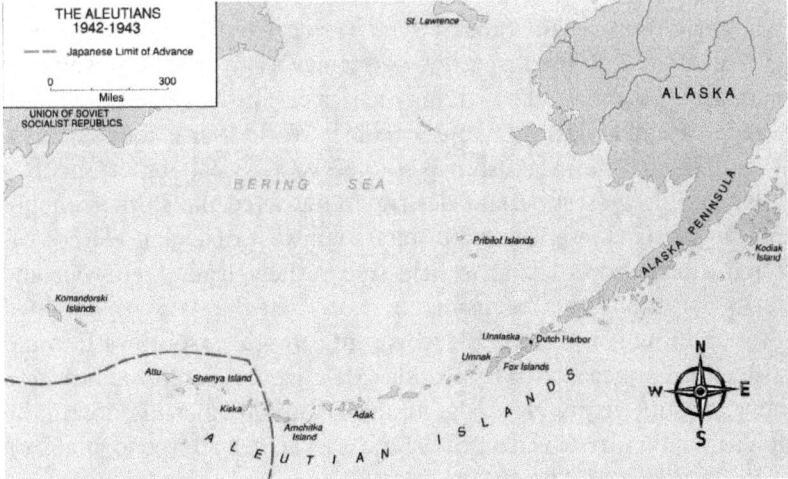

PBY Catalina seaplanes and YPs patrolled fog-shrouded Aleutian waters in search of the Japanese fleet during the Battle of Midway.
Source: http://www.lib.utexas.edu/maps/historical/aleutians_1942-43.jpg

The first day of June found the *Charleston* patrolling in misty fog, which allowed occasional stretches of visibility up to ten miles, and a cloud ceiling that varied in height from zero to 1,500 feet. In early evening, winds increased to gale force and the seas became rough. The following day, there were gale force winds with a 2,000 foot ceiling and 10 mile-maximum visibility; both decreased over the course of the day during which the patrol ship saw and heard nothing. On 3 June the seas were fairly smooth, with an overcast sky blocking any sunlight; visibility was between one-half and three miles. That night the sky was dark, and there was no indication of enemy forces in the vicinity. The following morning, crewmen felt a heavy thud against the ship's hull, believed due to a submarine-fired torpedo that failed to explode. There was, however, no sighting of an enemy submarine, aircraft, or ship. The weather worsened during the forenoon, with winds reaching gale force, creating long swells.[17]

DISPOSITION OF TASK FORCE 8

Theobald, embarked in the cruiser *Nashville* (CL-43), departed Kodiak in company with the oiler *Sabine* (AO-25) on the afternoon of 1 June to rendezvous at sea with other units of the main body. Having dispatched his submarines, patrol planes, and surface picket vessels to scout for the Japanese force, and having positioned the Destroyer Striking Group—*Case, Brooks, Sands, Kane, Dent,* and *Humphreys*—at Makushin Bay, Theobald intended to use Army land-based aircraft and, as opportunity allowed, his own cruisers to engage the enemy. The *Case*, a new destroyer, and five older World War I "four stackers" were to remain in Makushin Bay to serve as "weapons of opportunity." While almost certain destruction awaited the ships if caught out by the Japanese, the large inlet southwest of Dutch Harbor offered a backdrop of land to help screen them from enemy air and radar detection. The defensive air patrol that the Army maintained over its airfield on Umnak Island, seventy-five miles southwest, would also afford a measure of protection. Meanwhile, should the Japanese advance sufficiently close, the destroyers might have an opportunity to dash out under the cloak of darkness to launch a torpedo attack on enemy cruisers and transports.[18]

Theobald, who believed that the Japanese would try to seize Dutch Harbor by landing troops ashore somewhere between Umnak in the eastern Aleutians and Cold Bay on the tip of the Alaska Peninsula, positioned his small force south of Kodiak in order to defend the eastern Aleutians and Alaska. He did not yet have all his allocated ships as some were still en route from other parts of the Pacific. By 2 June the destroyer *Humphreys* had joined the *Nashville* and *Sabine* to screen them from enemy submarines; the light cruiser *St. Louis* and destroyer *Gilmer* arrived later that day. The only contact sighted that day was the submarine *S-27*, which crossed in front of the formation. The next morning, a group of four ships—the cruisers *Indianapolis* (CA-35) and *Honolulu* (CL-48), and destroyers *Gridley* (DD-380) and *McCall* (DD-400)—appeared on the horizon and proceeded to take their positions in the main body.[19]

ENEMY OFFENSIVE

In darkness a few hours earlier, Rear Adm. Kakaji Kakuta's Second Mobile Force—the light carriers *Ryujo* and *Junyo* and two heavy cruisers, screened by destroyers—had made a run in toward Dutch Harbor in preparation to launch an attack. His primary object was to strike Dutch Harbor, and thereby deflect Nimitz's forces from Midway. However, he also had orders to destroy installations that might facilitate an air invasion of Japan, and to cover and support the Kiska and Adak-Attu occupation forces. The carriers reached their launch position, 165 miles south of Dutch Harbor, undetected around 0250, having eluded both the search planes and the picket line of Coast Guard cutters and YPs. The same fog that shielded the enemy hindered aircraft in navigating over water. The *Junyo* attack group turned back half-way to the target, while the *Ryujo*'s planes found clear skies over parts of Dutch Harbor, allowing them to strike targets ashore. Many of the planes, though, were unable to find their way back to their ships and, once their fuel was expended, fell into the sea.[20]

FIRST ATTACK ON DUTCH HARBOR

At 0645 Theobald received a dispatch from Naval Air Station, Dutch Harbor stating that it had been attacked by a group of torpedo-bombers and fighter aircraft. The planes appeared without warning, but the air base had been at dawn battle stations daily and heavy anti-aircraft fire opened immediately. Enemy fighters strafed a Catalina seaplane taking off for Kodiak, resulting in two crewmen killed and another injured, and damaged another four PBYs nearby. Bombers hit fuel tanks, a radio station, warehouses, and barracks at Fort Mears, setting fire to some structures and increasing casualties to eighteen soldiers, three sailors, one Marine, and one civilian killed.[21]

During and immediately after the strike on Dutch Harbor, there were numerous contacts between Catalinas and enemy aircraft, mostly as PBYs were returning to base to refuel before resuming their patrols. Slow and ungainly by comparison, the flying boats wisely tried to avoid exposure to enemy fighters. The pilot of one Catalina did encounter two adversaries more to his liking—a pair of unarmed single-engine observation planes. He shot one down, and later apologized for letting the other escape.[22]

Following the first attack, Theobald's orders to the main body—the destroyers at Makushin Bay and six submarines under his command—remained, "Exploit favorable opportunity to deliver attrition attacks upon enemy forces..." A greater number of enemy bombers with their fighter escort were sent against Dutch Harbor the following day. Although Catalinas made occasional contact with Japanese ships, U.S. Army bombers, flying from Cold Bay and Umnak to the west of Dutch Harbor, had been unable, due to the conditions, to make effective attacks on the enemy carrier force.[23]

ARRIVAL OF ADDITIONAL PATROL CRAFT

Prior to the first attack, five additional patrol vessels—the cutter *Onondaga* and YPs *72*, *74*, *151*, and *155*—had arrived at Dutch Harbor on the morning of 3 June and then had stood out to sea: the *YP-74* in company with the destroyer *Talbot* (DD-114) to proceed to her station, seaplane tender *Gillis* with the YPs *72*, *151*, and *155* for a special mission, and *Onandaga* to clear the harbor until it was safe to return. Dispatched to rescue two aircraft forced down east of Akutan Island, the *Gillis* searched that area and in the vicinity of Tigalda Island with negative results. She then proceeded through Unimak Pass to examine the north side of Akun Island, again without success. The *Gillis* next received orders to locate and recover a plane shot down fifteen miles southeast of Scotch Cap lighthouse on Unimak. She searched those waters and the coastlines of all the islands in the area to no avail. The cutter *Nemaha* had retrieved the plane, but had not reported its recovery in order to maintain radio silence. The *Gillis* returned to Dutch Harbor during the afternoon of 4 June and moored at the oil dock to receive much needed fuel. There were few ships in port; available destroyers had been absorbed by Task Force 8, and YPs and other small craft were engaged in patrol and mercy activities.[24]

SECOND ATTACK ON DUTCH HARBOR

At 1635 the air station alert sounded. *Gillis* set general quarters and, after clearing the fuel dock, was directed to provide protection for the *President Fillmore* and the *Morlen*, which were just getting underway. At 1751, as she was leaving port with the two ships in trail, the seaplane tender sighted a formation of approximately twenty-six Japanese aircraft approaching through Akutan Pass to attack Fort Mears and Dutch Harbor.[25]

The *Gillis* opened fire with her forward 3-inch mount, diverting the aircraft from the *Fillmore* and *Morlen*. The formation then split into smaller groups of high altitude bombers, dive bombers, and fighters. Dive bombers made a run at the fuel tanks at the dock where the seaplane tender had been only a few minutes earlier, setting them aflame, but did not emerge unscathed, as one plane was hit streaming smoke as it pulled out of its dive. Two aircraft mounted a strafing attack on the *Fillmore*, which proved to be anything but an easy target. In addition to her normal ship armament, the Army troop transport had a deck-loaded battery of 37mm guns consigned for delivery to Cold Bay, giving her twenty-two antiaircraft guns. Once in action their combined muzzle flashes made it appear to an observer off the ship that she was on fire. Having found the transport a "tough slog," the planes broke off and attacked the *Gillis*. Her 20mm and .50-caliber gunfire forced them to retire with one trailing smoke as it rounded Priest Rock on its way out of Akutan Pass. The tender's 3-inch guns had kept horizontal bombers at a high altitude, and sent into the sea one of three planes attempting to approach undetected by flying low along the shoreline. Thereafter, all Japanese aircraft withdrew.[26]

While the damage inflicted by the enemy was not sufficient to knock out Dutch Harbor as an operating base, aircraft destroyed four fuel tanks, demolished a wing of the hospital, damaged an uncompleted hanger, and partially destroyed the old steamship S.S. *Northwestern*. The dilapidated vessel (constructed in 1889 in Chester, Pennsylvania, as the *Orizaba*) was beached for use as a barracks ship. Fort Mears suffered the destruction of four bombers, three fighters, and two seaplanes; casualties increased the death list to forty-three. A group of enemy fighters made a strafing run on Fort Glenn, sixty-five miles west on Umnak Island. Army pursuit planes from Otter Point airfield shot down two of the aircraft and the remaining seven withdrew without inflicting any damage.[27]

As soon as the raid developed, Army and Navy planes had initiated a search for the enemy carriers and made contact with Japanese ships several times. However, on almost every occasion, the enemy was able to vanish into fog banks before large air forces could be concentrated against them. Theobald had envisioned that Catalina scout planes would locate and maintain contact with the enemy until heavy bombers, if available, could mass an attack. The practice of the PBYs was to send contact updates until forced to withdraw to refuel, and to launch an attack before their departure, with enemy carriers being the most important target.²⁸

TASK FORCE COMMANDER VISITS KODIAK

On learning of the second attack on Dutch Harbor, Theobald ordered the commanding officer of the *Indianapolis* to take command of the main body, and the admiral set out in the *Nashville* for Kodiak, accompanied by the *Gridley*. En route he received a succinct update just prior to midnight:

> 11 bombers and 7 fighters attacked Dutch Harbor at 1808 W [local time]. SS *Northwestern* and warehouses lost. Details will follow.²⁹

Following his arrival at Kodiak on the morning of 5 June, Theobald went ashore to confer with the commanders of the Air Search Group, Air Striking Group, and Alaskan Sector. During the meeting he emphasized the absolute necessity to concentrate planes of the Air Striking Group for immediate attack following location of the enemy, and to keep the task force commander informed of operations. Theobald had ordered the units of the main body to maintain radio silence in order to prevent the enemy from pinpointing their location through use of high-frequency direction-finding equipment. However, this policy prevented him from transmitting timely instructions, which instead had to be delivered to the recipient by a ship detached from the main body. Following the conference, Theobald returned aboard the *Nashville* and left Women's Bay at 1605.³⁰

SEAPLANE AND FLIGHT CREW CASUALTIES MOUNTING

After leaving the meeting, commander, Air Search Group sent a dispatch to Theobald informing him of the steady degradation of the Catalinas, their nearly expended stamina of pilots and crews, and an existing, desperate need for additional planes:

> Originator declares not more than 14 doubtfully effective Catalinas remaining now. Operational and combat losses in maintaining contact are mounting and Army air has not yet struck effective blow. Pilots and crews at limit of endurance after 48 hours continuous flying and fighting despite usual Aleutian weather. This night will just about end them. Must have replacements or these Japs will give us the slip.³¹

The *Nashville* and *Gridley* rejoined Task Group 8.6 south of Kodiak on 6 June, and Theobald resumed command of the main body. In the late afternoon of the following day, he received a dispatch from Naval Air Station, Kodiak summarizing air attacks on enemy forces, and offering the good news that all but one crew of downed aircraft had been recovered. The message conveyed in part:

> Latest count of attacks 4 June one torpedo by Catalina ineffective due engine failure. Bombing of CV [aircraft carrier] by Catalina repulsed by AA [anti-aircraft] hits. Dive bombing on CV with torpedo by B26 ineffective [.] Torpedoes on CA [heavy cruiser] by 2 B26 2 hits claimed. Torpedo on CV by B26 repulsed by AA. Bombs on CV by B17 results undetermined.
>
> 14 Catalinas now effective including 2 replacements received 5 June. . . . All lost Catalina crews except 1 definitely recovered by [seaplane] tenders or fish boats [YPs]. Exception last seen 4 June with fish boat nearby.[32]

No enemy contacts were made the following day due to heavy fog, and all plane crews were experiencing extreme fatigue due to constant alerts, lack of proper facilities at dispersal points, and endless flying.[33]

ENEMY OCCUPATION OF ATTU AND KISKA

Meanwhile, on 6 June, under cover of fog, Japanese forces had begun the occupation of Attu and Kiska whose only military installations were meteorological outposts. Reports from these stations ceased the next day, and while it was not unusual for either station to miss broadcasting one or more weather updates, it was curious for both stations to miss all of them. On 10 June, after the fog had abated somewhat, a PBY reported substantial Japanese forces on both islands: four ships in Kiska harbor, one probably a cruiser and one a destroyer; and at Attu, a tent camp and numerous small boats and landing barges.[34]

That evening, having learned that Japanese forces had occupied Kiska and Attu, Captain Gehres sent a dispatch to the *Gillis* directing that all seaplanes out on night patrol return to base by way of Kiska and, fuel state permitting, drop their bombs on the enemy. The seaplane tender was then at Atka, 350 miles west of Dutch Harbor, having relocated there earlier that day to tend PBY Catalinas scheduled to operate from the small island.[35]

NIMITZ ORDERS CATALINAS TO BOMB JAPANESE OUT OF KISKA

On the evening of 11 June, Nimitz ordered commander, Patrol Wing 4 to bomb the Japanese out of Kiska, superseding Theobald's employment of the PBYs as primarily a search group, with Army bombers as the strike force. On receipt of these orders, Captain Gehres directed every unit operating with the wing to attack the enemy in Kiska continuously with bombs and torpedoes. The "Atka-Kiska-Gillis bombing shuttle" had actually begun earlier that day when, at 0345, Gehres (embarked in *Gillis*) started sending planes with 500-pound bombs to Kiska as quickly as they could be loaded. Aircraft from Patrol Squadrons VP-41, 42, and 43 arrived at Atka from Cold Bay, Dutch Harbor, and Otter Point (on Amnak Island) in execution of the operation, described thus by Gehres:

> For the next forty-eight hours there occurred what I believe to be one of the most remarkable exhibitions of pure tenacity of purpose that has ever occurred in any military or naval force. Every plane available to Patwing Four shuttled almost continuously from Dutch Harbor to Kiska, back to Atka for refueling and rearming thence back to Kiska. This was kept up day and night until *Gillis* has issued all her supply of bombs and every pumpable gallon of aviation gasoline. She was then relieved by *Hulbert*.[36]

By 12 June, enemy forces and anti-aircraft installations at Kiska had increased sufficiently that it was extremely hazardous for seaplanes to attempt to enter the harbor either under the overcast or from above through breaks in the cloud cover. Gehres summarized the damage that the planes had sustained and described the tactic adopted by pilots to minimize losses. Their strategy entailed plummeting downward through solid cloud cover, finding a target visually upon breaking through, and immediately dropping their bombs and pulling up to minimize the possibility of taking fire or crashing:

> [Three] planes . . . returned from bombing raids so riddled with machine gun fire and anti-aircraft shell fragments that they would not float. Two sank on landing. One was beached, but it was necessary to burn and abandon it. Despite this heavy anti-aircraft damage only one crew member was killed and two wounded.
>
> The attacks were invariably made diving through the overcast at the speed, unheard of for PBY's, of 250 knots and dropping the bombs by "seaman's eye" method, then making a four-hand pullout

back into the overcast. During this two day period of continuous bombing, there were contacts, bomb hits, and combats too numerous to list in detail.[37]

Having been recalled from picket ship duties, the units of the Surface Search Group were conducting normal patrol and escort duty from section bases under the direction of commander, Alaskan Sector. Some YPs were also searching for crews of downed Catalinas and performing general salvage work amid challenging conditions. One "fishboat," in urgent need of fuel, water, and provisions, approached the *Charleston* which was patrolling nearby. However, rough seas and force-six winds prevented her from coming alongside for replenishment. The gunboat ordered the YP to proceed to Dutch Harbor via Unalga or Akutan Pass for supplies and then return to station.[38]

On the afternoon of 23 June, the *Gillis* reported that her gasoline would be expended that night, and she was ordered to evacuate the Aleuts living on Atka and "scorch" the earth before her departure from the island. However, with 24 seaplanes moored in Nazan Bay at one time, and 68 officers and over 170 men on board resting while their aircraft were refueled and rearmed, a Japanese scout plane suddenly appeared over the harbor and then departed hastily westward to avoid pursuit. With both her location and that of her charges now disclosed to the enemy, the tender received orders to evacuate immediately. Gehres described the subsequent actions:

> Planes still unfueled and armed were apportioned the *Gillis*'s remaining gas and bombs as rapidly as possible. Those refueled with sufficient gas to make the trip immediately took off for Dutch Harbor via Kiska. Others had barely enough gas to reach Umnak and had to go direct. Five planes were left at the buoys with no gas for them until the *Hulbert* could arrive at 2000. Leaving these planes at the moorings, the *Gillis* proceeded to another anchorage, sent ashore [a] party of men who obtained gasoline from a cache which was useless for planes, spread it on the village of Atka and burned the village.[39]

The *Gillis* removed the school teacher and his wife, Mr. and Mrs. McKee, but could not evacuate the village natives as they had scattered to the hills when the Japanese aircraft appeared. Meanwhile, the *Hulbert* had arrived and refueled the remaining planes as the *Gillis* loaded them with bombs, and the PBYs set off for Dutch Harbor via

Kiska. Late that night, at 2340, the *Gillis* departed bound for Kodiak, arriving at the air station in the early evening of 15 June.[40]

The first army bombers had arrived over Kiska on 12 June and were quickly initiated by the Japanese. During the initial attack, the flight leader of a group of five B24s made the mistake of attempting a long, straight-away bombing run at 1,700 feet in the face of heavily concentrated anti-aircraft fire. Struck by gunfire in the bomb bay, the lead plane exploded and disintegrated in the air. Eight drops were made by the other planes near a cruiser with no apparent damage. The four B24s then dropped six bombs from a safer 18,000 feet, and observed resultant fires on a cruiser. Three heavy cruisers, two light cruisers, and twelve seaplanes were present in the harbor with two light cruisers or destroyers entering port, and a carrier ten miles to the north.[41]

The Aleutian portion of the Battle of Midway ended in mid-June 1942 with enemy forces occupying two islands of little value. Theobald's expectation of a fleet action had not materialized and the Aleutians battle became a contest of air power, as had Midway. Reconnaissance flights during the latter part of the month revealed that while a majority of the Japanese ships had apparently withdrawn, the remaining strong landing forces on Kiska and Attu were digging in and establishing advance bases on the barren islands. Amid the stalemate in the Territory of Alaska, the Navy dispatched two additional flag officers to the theater. On 22 June Rear Adm. W. W. Smith, who had been Nimitz's chief of staff, reported to commander, Task Force 8, embarked aboard the *Indianapolis*, and assumed command of the main body. Theobald and his staff then relocated to Naval Air Station, Kodiak. Four days later, Rear Adm. John W. Reeves, Jr., formerly commander, Northwest Sea Frontier, relieved Capt. Ralph C. Parker as commander, Alaskan Sector.[42]

AFTERMATH

In spite of some American concerns that the enemy occupation of Attu and Kiska signaled a Japanese intention to push eastward, there was no plan to invade the Alaskan mainland, Canada, or the United States. Although the Aleutian offensive was conceived by Yamamoto as a diversion to draw American naval forces away from Pearl Harbor, it was also defensive. Control of the western Aleutians by Japan would deny the United States the capability to launch air strikes against the empire from the islands as a prelude to an invasion. However, the brutal weather conditions and challenging terrain of the region that made sea, air, and land operations so formidable, also made an Aleutians-Alaska invasion route unattractive to both American and Japanese strategists. Major General Buckner succinctly characterized the implausibility of such means to reach the United States:

> They might make it, but it would be their grandchildren who finally got there; and by then they would all be American citizens anyway![43]

There was, of course, great public sentiment against relinquishing a part of the Alaska Territory to the enemy, no matter how worthless. However, no immediate major countermove was possible due to the commitment of a large part of the Pacific Fleet to the impending campaign in the Solomon Islands.[44]

Photo 6-3

Crewmen of the 72-foot *YP-92*, former purse seiner *Helen B.*, on deck after a snowstorm at sea.
Courtesy of Earl W. Mundy, Jr., NavSource: www.navsource.org/archives/14/31092.htm

During the Aleutians campaign, additional YPs had arrived in Alaskan waters to augment existing patrol forces. On 15 June 1942, twenty-five YPs were operating from six section bases, while two from Ketchikan were undergoing repairs at Seattle. Called "YP boats" or "fish boats," these YPs would continue to carry out unheralded and sometimes heroic tasks for the duration of the war. The patrol craft, largely former seiners 75 to 104 feet in length, were commanded by young reserve officers, often on their first tour of sea duty. Operations around Kodiak and Dutch Harbor, and the uncharted reefs and rocky beaches of the bleak Aleutians, tested the mettle of these little ships, particularly when they were iced down and wallowing in masthead-high seas.[45]

7

The Battle of Midway

> *Our citizens can now rejoice that a momentous victory is in the making. Perhaps we will be forgiven if we claim we are about midway to our objective.*
>
> —Adm. Chester Nimitz, June 1942

The mental picture that many Americans likely have of the Battle of Midway is an air battle in which U.S. Navy carrier aircraft sank several Japanese carriers, resulting in a pivotal change in the course of the war. Some people may recall that seaplanes located the enemy force, and that there were also submarines, PT boats, and other small craft present, as well as Army and Marine-Corps land-based aircraft. Few are likely aware that Catalina PBYs, supported by YPs, made unsung contributions to the Aleutians Campaign and the Battle of Midway.

Midway, located 1,141 nautical miles west-northwest of Honolulu, is actually a coral atoll, six miles in diameter, comprised of three islands: Sand, Eastern and Spit. The atoll's name is said to come from its location midway between San Francisco and Tokyo. It was first discovered in 1859, and the United States, recognizing its strategic importance, claimed it eight years later, in 1867, when Capt. William Reynolds, commanding the screw sloop-of-war *Lackawanna*, raised the American flag over the atoll. Under Navy direction, the construction of facilities for Catalina seaplanes began in March 1940, and Naval Air Station, Midway was commissioned on 18 August 1941. Despite its small size, the station hosted an airstrip on Eastern Island, as well as a hanger for seaplanes and other facilities on larger Sand Island.[1]

Midway Atoll, 24 November 1941. Eastern Island, then the site of Midway's airfield, is in the foreground. Sand Island, location of most other base facilities, is across the entrance channel.
Official U.S. Navy photograph from the National Archives, U.S. Navy photo 80-G-451086, www.history.navy.mil/photos/events/wwii-pac/midway/mid-1a.htm

STRATEGIC IMPORTANCE OF THE ROCKY ATOLL

Two Japanese destroyers shelled the island on the night of 7 December 1941, withdrawing at 2200 after killing four men and wounding ten, damaging some buildings, and destroying one patrol plane. The token attack signaled that Midway held little interest to the enemy. However, two weeks later, the fall of Wake Island—a U.S. territory hosting a naval base two thousand nautical miles west of Honolulu— dramatically increased the strategic importance of Midway to the United States, and thereby to Japan as well. Located 1,027 nautical miles northeast of Wake and nearer Pearl Harbor, the atoll then became the westernmost American outpost in the Central Pacific. From Midway shore-based seaplanes could fly patrols toward the Japanese-held Marshall Islands and Wake, checking on enemy activities and guarding against further attacks on Hawaii. The Japanese coveted Midway for use as a base from which empire forces could launch attacks on Pearl Harbor. However, because Midway lay beyond the range of Wake Island-based search planes, the enemy could not monitor U.S. naval activity on or near the atoll.[2]

BUILD-UP OF STATION DEFENSES

Nimitz visited Midway in early May 1942 to inspect its defenses and confer with the local commanders. As the Japanese threat became more eminent, he dispatched more ground and air forces to the atoll, crowding Eastern Island with Marine Corps, Navy, and Army-Air Force planes. On 29 May, the seaplane tender *Ballard* (AVD-10) and PT boats of Motor Torpedo Boat Squadron 1 arrived at Midway to bolster seaward defenses, and four ex-San Diego tuna clippers arrived to augment local defense forces. In anticipation of an impending air battle, the YPs were positioned near some small islands southeast of the station to refuel aircraft and rescue downed aviators. The *YP-284* (ex-*Endeavor*) was allocated to Lisianski, *YP-290* (ex-*Picaroto*) to Laysan, *YP-345* (ex-*Yankee*) to Gardner Pinnacles, and *YP-350* (ex-*Victoria*) to Necker. Other local defense force units were stationed near Midway or at other nearby lesser islands, reefs or shoals:

Midway Island	*PT-20*, *PT-21*, *PT-22*, *PT-24*, *PT-25*, *PT-26*, *PT-27*, and *PT-28*
Kure Island	*PT-29*, *PT-30*, and four small patrol craft
French Frigate Shoals	*Thornton* (AVD-11), *Ballard* (AVD-10), *Clark* (DD-361), and *Kaloli* (AOG-13)
Pearl and Hermes Reef	*Crystal* (PY-25) and *Vireo* (ATO-144)

By 4 June, the military forces stationed on or around Midway were as ready as possible to face the oncoming Japanese.[3]

LOSS OF THE PATROL CRAFT *YP-277*

During preparations to organize Midway for battle, other YPs (from the group of ex-tuna clippers that had arrived at Pearl Harbor from San Diego on 17 May) ferried aviation fuel and did whatever else was asked of them to assist in this effort. One of these vessels, the *YP-277* (ex-*Triunfo*)—part of a group of four YPs transporting provisions, parts, and fuel to Motor Torpedo Boat Squadron 1—became the first U.S. Navy ship lost to an American minefield in the Pacific. The PT boats had broken down at French Frigate Shoals, 487 nautical miles northwest of Honolulu, while en route to Midway. Arriving at the atoll in the early morning of 23 May, the YPs stood in towards the anchorage near La Perouse Pinnacle which jutted up between the tips

Map 7-1

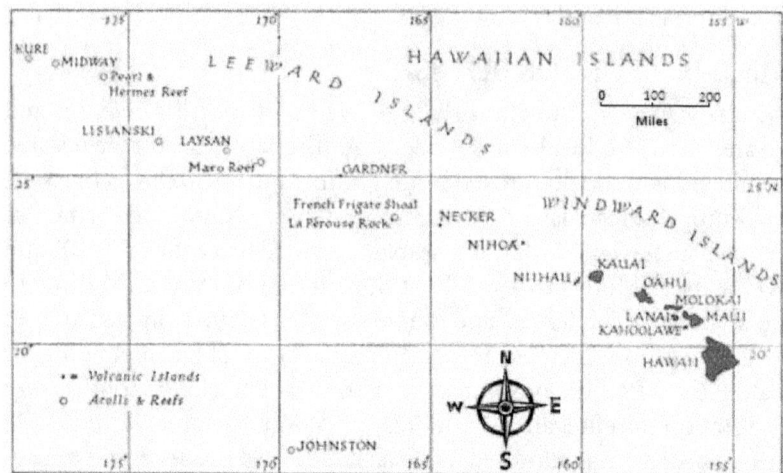

Some of the former San Diego tuna clippers acquired by the Navy provisioned outlying Hawaiian Islands after arriving at Pearl Harbor. Four of them—YPs *284* (ex-*Endeavor*), *290* (ex-*Picaroto*), *345* (ex-*Yankee*), and *350* (ex-*Victoria*)—would serve as support ships for PBY Catalina seaplanes during the Battle of Midway.
Source: http://www.lib.utexas.edu/maps/historical/pacific_islands_1943_1945/hawaiian_islands.jpg

of a crescent-shaped reef. The *YP-239* (ex-*Challenger*) led the other vessels—*348*, *277*, and *237*—along a nautical track that it believed would skirt a defensive minefield. The purpose of the field, laid seven weeks earlier by the minelayers *Pruitt* (DM-22), *Preble* (DM-20), *Sicard* (DM-21), and *Tracy* (DM-19), was to prevent enemy submarines from using the area as a refueling point for flying boat raids on Oahu.[4]

While proceeding toward the anchorage, the third ship in the column, *YP-277*, exploded a mine that blew her stern off and set her deck cargo of high octane fuel ablaze. John R. Bruce, the commanding officer of the vessel astern, brought the *YP-237* (ex-*Anna M.*) to within seventy-five feet of her, and quickly lowered a boat. Then, in spite of the danger presented by the field and exploding gasoline drums and ammunition aboard the stricken vessel, he entered the area to search for survivors. Bruce rescued Seamen Second Class John Elijah Callin and George Alonzo Hazzard, and recovered the body of another crew member. For his courageous action, he was awarded the Navy and Marine Corps Medal.[5]

BATTLE JOINED

> *In the first six to twelve months of a war with the United States and Great Britain I will run wild and win victory upon victory. But then, if the war continues after that, I have no expectation of success.*
>
> —Adm. Isoroku Yamamoto, commander-in-chief of the Japanese Navy (1940)

Like the PBY Catalinas that participated in the Aleutians Campaign, the seaplanes at Midway were charged with scouting for the enemy and, as required, functioning as a reserve striking force. James Clair Nolan, a Catalina pilot, described action between seaplanes and two-engine Japanese land-based planes operating from Wake:

> Just about ready to turn in when we got the word that the four of us PBYs (the "reserve striking force") were going out immediately on a night torpedo attack. The B-17s reported the Japs bearing 261, distance 572 miles at about three o'clock that afternoon. We were to go out and get as many as possible—with PBYs!
>
> Climbed in our planes and took off at 8:30 p.m. . . . About 400 miles out we thought we saw anti-aircraft fire on our right, but due to the rotten weather we couldn't see anything on the water. Soon the moon started to show through the clouds once in a while. When we reached the 520-mile mark about 1:30 Thursday morning and started to turn around, the waist hatch gunners spotted a plane tailing us. It blinked a red identification light at us a few times, so we knew it was a Jap, as our planes don't carry red identification lights. Just as we were about to fire on him he disappeared.
>
> Can't understand why he didn't fire at us. A few seconds later anti-aircraft fire started going off around us. We circled looking for some ships, but could see nothing—pitch black. Thought we'd go back to where we saw the first anti-aircraft fire as the Japs should have been closer to Midway in 10 hours than 520 miles. . . . Started back, hoping to run into the Japs at about the 400-mile mark—but there was nothing we could see. The Eastern sky started to get light. . . . About 5:30 it turned light and about 6 the sun came up. About 6:30 our radio started to hum—the morning patrols out of Midway were spotting Japs North, West and South.[6]

Nolan failed to locate any enemy warships and low on fuel, headed back to Midway, worried that his seaplane would be shot down by a carrier-launched Japanese bomber or fighter or, alternatively, that it would run out of fuel and end up in the sea:

> A report came through of a large body of Jap planes headed for Midway—we figured out they were only about 50 miles behind us. Would we beat them to Midway, or would they catch us and shoot us down? And, incidentally, where was the goddammed atoll called Kure Island, which we were supposed to pass over before approaching Midway? Our gas was getting low, the air and sea were swarming with Japs, and we weren't positive of our position, due to the impossibility of taking drift sights at night. [We] were beginning to feel desperate when I spotted Kure Island off to our right on the horizon. No one else could see it, even after flying toward it for 10 minutes.
>
> As we got to Kure (with sighs of relief from all hands) and turned toward Midway (about 30 miles away over the horizon) I got a jolt—there, rising from the island which was just below the horizon, were the initial columns of dirt and smoke indicating exploding bombs. Our base was being bombed! And now the smoke was rising in dense billows while new plumes of dust and sand continued to shoot skyward. We couldn't see the Jap planes however. How we had missed contacting each other I shall never know—my luck was with me.[7]

Having avoided contact with one or more heavily armed, and maneuverable Japanese aircraft, which would have likely resulted in certain death, Nolan's priority was to liaison with the *YP-284* at Lisianski to refuel. She and the other three YPs each had about 3,000 gallons deck-loaded in drums for just that purpose:

> Headed for Lisianski Island, where a YP boat was supposed to be available for fueling...but could see nothing due to the heavy rain squalls. [We] circled around helplessly with an awful feeling in our hearts. Suddenly, below us, through the rain, I spotted the light blue water that indicates a submerged coral head. I knew then that we were right on top of the island. A few more circles and through a break we spotted the island—about 100-by-50 yards of coral covered by sand, with millions of birds flying about and a few seals sleeping on the sand. Circled looking for the YP boat and after 15 minutes of futile searching, decided to take our last chance and try for Laysan Island—120 miles away and we had only about 110 gallons of gas left—it would be close.

An hour's flying brought us to Laysan and, thank God, there was a YP boat [the *YP-290*] with a pair of planes already fueling from her. We had six gallons left.

Landed in the fairly rough water with a few nasty jolts, but luckily popped no rivets from the hull. Settled down to wait for our turn to fuel. I climbed up onto the top wing in the sun and, peeling off my shirt, went blissfully to sleep. After many hours of waiting we finally started fueling late in the afternoon. It continued 'til after dark. Decided to stay tied to [the] YP tender overnight.

Climbed up onto top wing about 9 p.m. and turned in.[8]

The following morning, Nolan took on additional fuel and then radioed Midway for instructions, which were to return to Pearl Harbor. He arrived there to a celebration of the Navy's decisive victory in the second of five naval battles in the Pacific in which aircraft would play the predominant role:

Awoke in the morning. Took on another 100 gallons, giving us nine hundred in all. Radioed Midway for instructions. They ordered us to return to Pearl Harbor. . . . Got a greasy egg sandwich from the tender [*YP-290*]. . . . Took off with a few mighty crashes on wave tops. Headed home and arrived at dusk.

The newspapers are all howling over "our great victory at Midway." Seems as though the Japs got a good pasting. That's the first fight I've been in with them that my side won.[9]

BATTLE SUMMARY

The air battle of 4 to 7 June, conducted by Task Forces 16 and 17 formed around the carriers *Yorktown* (CV-5), *Enterprise* (CV-6), and *Hornet* (CV-8), brought about the resounding defeat of the Combined Fleet. Admiral Yamamoto suffered the loss of four carriers, *Akagi*, *Kaga*, *Soryu*, and *Hiryu*, with all their aircraft and many crew members (estimated at 275 planes, 2,400 men). Two, and probably three, battleships were also damaged, two heavy cruisers sunk, three or more heavy cruisers and one light cruiser damaged, three destroyers sunk, and four transport and cargo vessels hit, with an estimated total loss of 4,800 personnel. The U.S. Navy lost only the *Yorktown* and the destroyer *Hammann*, with 92 officers and 215 men killed, and about 150 planes lost or damaged beyond repair.[10]

The thirty-one Catalina seaplanes assigned to Naval Air Station, Midway played a key role in the battle. A flight of the scout planes made contact with the Japanese support force 700 miles west of Midway on 3 June and in darkness early the following morning, made a high-level bombing attack against it. Three hours later, at 0430, both sides launched scout planes to search for one another's carriers. American PBYs spotted the Japanese carriers at 0520. However, pursued by Zero fighters and immersed in a deadly game of "cat and mouse" in the clouds above the Japanese fleet, the scouts were unable to make a contact report until 0545. Twenty minutes later, a second and more detailed report followed. In the interim, Midway radar detected an incoming air raid and scrambled all planes still on the island. Battle was soon joined, the most significant part of which culminated at 1020 when dive-bombers from the *Yorktown* and *Enterprise* arrived over the Japanese carriers, whose fighter protection had been spent destroying previous waves of attackers. This circumstance left the flattops, crammed with fully armed and fueled strike aircraft that had yet to launch, defenseless against the American raiders. In a span of five minutes, the strike fleet, and Japan's dreams of victory and empire, were engulfed in flame and destruction. Although correct in his assertion that the tide would eventually turn in the favor of the U.S. Navy, Yamamoto's timeline had been incorrect. It occurred less than six months after the Japanese attack on Pearl Harbor.[11]

LOSS OF THE PATROL CRAFT *YP-345*

The patrol yacht *Crystal* (PY-25) departed Pearl and Hermes Reef on 9 June to return to Pearl Harbor via Lisianski, Layson, Gardner Pinnacles, and Necker—joined by YPs en route. After the group arrived at Pearl Harbor, the *YP-284* was ordered to Guadalcanal, where Japanese destroyers would sink it on 25 October. In late autumn, the *YP-345* left Pearl Harbor on 29 October for French Frigate Shoals en route to Midway, but failed to arrive at her destination as expected. The *Allen* (DD-66) was dispatched to search an area eighty miles northeast of Laysan Island. The destroyer arrived on scene late at night on 1 November, but darkness precluded any real action until daybreak. After failing to find any sight of the YP or survivors by mid-afternoon, Naval Air Station, Midway Island directed her to cease the search. The existing winds and seas varied from fresh breeze to strong gale and the ocean's surface from heavy swells to rough seas. As the former tuna clipper was built for and had operated in much worse conditions, the belief was that her loss due to foundering was unlikely, and that instead she had probably fallen victim to a Japanese submarine.[12]

8

Loss of Guam and the Philippines

> *We proclaim herewith that our Japanese Army has occupied this island of Guam by the order of the Great Emperor of Japan. It is for the purpose of restoring liberty and rescuing the Whole Asiatic people and creating the permanent peace in Asia. Thus our intention is to establish the New Order in the World.*
>
> —Opening statement of a proclamation dated 10 December 1941, issued by the Japanese commander-in-chief, following the capture of the island of Guam that same day[1]

Deprivation—starvation, beatings, and sometimes death—was endured by thousands of soldiers, sailors, and Marines taken prisoner by the Japanese when the Philippines and Guam fell. Among them were the officers and men of the *YP-16*, *YP-17*, *YP-97*, and the converted yachts *Maryanne* and *Fisheries II*.

PRELUDE TO PEARL HARBOR

The purchase of the Philippine Islands from Spain in 1898 drew the United States into Far Eastern power politics, ultimately making war with Japan very difficult to avoid, if not inevitable, due to the latter country's military expansionism and quest for national self-sufficiency. Making the situation worse was the U.S. failure at the time to acquire from Spain islands in the approaches to the archipelago from which a hostile country could launch an invasion. Although the U.S. did obtain the island of Guam, its value to the defense of the Philippines was negligible without ownership of nearby Saipan and Tinian. These islands were acquired by Japan in 1921, along with the remainder of the Marianas (except for Guam) and all the Marshall and Caroline Islands, when

Map 8-1

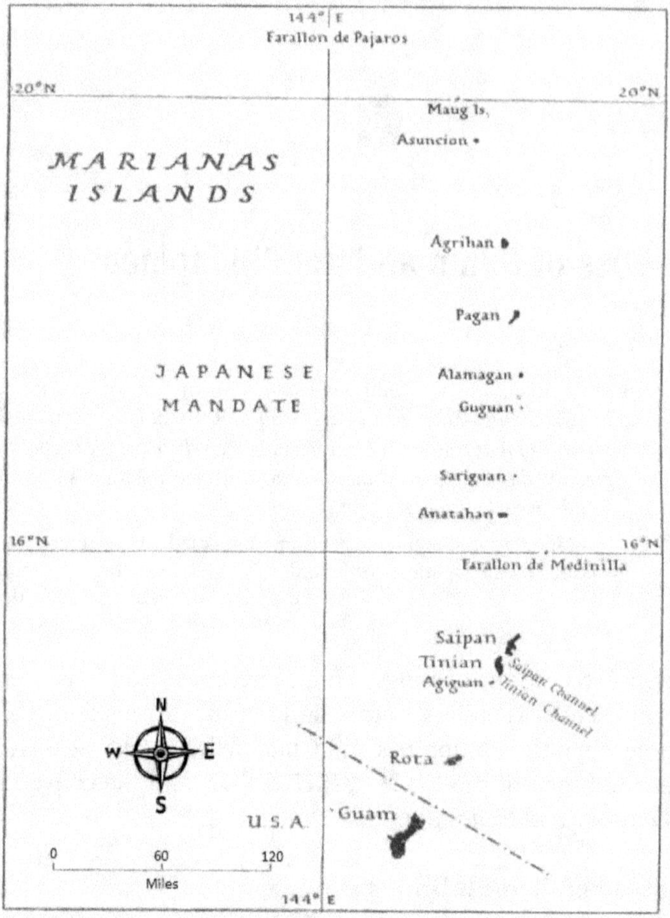

```
                    144° E
              Farallon de Pajaros
20°N                                              20°N
                          Maug Is.
                          Asuncion •

    MARIANAS
    ISLANDS
                          Agrihan ▶


                          Pagan ♪

    JAPANESE              Alamagan •
    MANDATE               Guguan ·


                          Sariguan ·

                          Anatahan ▪
16°N                                              16°N
                          Farallon de Medinilla


                          Saipan
                          Tinian  Saipan Channel
                          Agiguan · Tinian Channel


                          Rota

          U.S.A.     ·Guam

    0    60    120
        Miles
                    144° E
```

The value of Guam to America's defense of the Philippines was negligible without ownership of nearby Saipan and Tinian which Japan had acquired in 1921 along with the remainder of the Marianas, except for Guam.
Source: http://www.lib.utexas.edu/maps/historical/pacific_islands_1943_1945/marianas_islands.jpg

the League of Nations turned over the former German territories to Japan in recognition of its allying itself with Britain during World War I. The availability of these strategically located islands would later facilitate Japan's rapid conquest of the Philippines, Guam, and Wake, and aid in the seizure of Hong Kong, Thailand, North Borneo, Singapore, and the entire Netherlands East Indies.[2]

As part of America's response to Japanese expansionism and in an attempt to deter further aggression, the Navy realigned its forces in the Pacific. This strategy was in response to Congressional reluctance to fund armaments for the defense of U.S. possessions and territories that might never be used as well as a general aversion of the American people for war. The "Battle Fleet," the Pacific component of the existing United States Fleet, moved from the west coast of the U.S. to Pearl Harbor during the summer of 1940. That fall the Asiatic Fleet relocated from China to Manila Bay to strengthen the defense of the Philippines. These actions were followed on 1 February 1941 by a reorganization of the United States Fleet into three separate components: the U.S. Pacific Fleet, based at Pearl Harbor; the U.S. Atlantic Fleet (the former "Scouting Force" that comprised the Atlantic presence of the U.S. Navy), headquartered at Newport, Rhode Island; and the very small U.S. Asiatic Fleet, with no ship larger than a cruiser, at Manila Bay. The Asiatic Fleet retained its status as a force independent of the U.S. fleet, charged by the existing war plan to support the U.S. Army presence in the Philippines as long as the defense of the islands continued. However, due to its small size, all that could be reasonably expected should Japanese forces invade the archipelago would be for it to retire or fight a delaying action. Ultimately both actions occurred. Following receipt of Navy Department orders on 20 November 1941 to fall back, Adm. Thomas C. Hart began to move his fleet southward leaving, on 8 December (the 7th in Pearl Harbor), only four destroyers, one submarine, six river gunboats, five *Lapwing*-class minesweepers, two fleet oilers, the floating dry dock *Dewey*, and a few tugs at Manila Bay. Japanese planes raided Clark Field that day and Manila on 10 December.[3]

ROOSEVELT ORDERS PATROL YACHT *ISABEL* ON SECRET MISSION

On 1 December 1941 (a week before the attack on Pearl Harbor) as the threat of war grew ever larger, President Roosevelt sent a message with a highest-secrecy classification and precedence to Admiral Hart, ordering the establishment of a "defensive information patrol" of three small ships off the coast of French Indochina. The message directed this action executed "as soon as possible and in two days if possible" and designated the patrol yacht *Isabel* as one of the trio of vessels. Then the reserve flagship of the Asiatic Fleet, the Navy had acquired *Isabel* in 1917 while she was under construction as a 930-ton steam yacht for service during World War I. Decommissioned after the war, she was placed back in commission in July 1921 and sent to Asia. She arrived at Hong Kong in November to begin two decades of Far Eastern service. As flagship of the Yangtze River Patrol, she operated on that river and along the China coast during most of the 1920s. Late in that decade the *Isabel* became the part-time flagship for the U.S. Asiatic Fleet, and spent the 1930s and the first two years of the 1940s cruising in Philippine waters and off China. Roosevelt, who had served as Assistant Secretary of the Navy from 1913 to 1920—and thus knew ships—presumably selected her for a clandestine mission due to her antiquated appearance, typical of the small merchantman that sailed the China coast.[4]

Photo 8-1

Patrol yacht *Isabel* (PY-10) at Hankow, China, on 14 May 1937. She is "dressed overall" in honor of the coronation of King George VI of England and flies the four-star flag of Commander in Chief, U.S. Asiatic Fleet.
Courtesy of the Naval Historical Foundation. Collection of Admiral Harry E. Yarnell, USN, U.S. Navy photo NH 83530, http://www.navsource.org/archives/12/1310.htm

The planned use of the other two vessels never came to fruition. The schooner *Lanikai* was acquired and commissioned, but the start of the war resulted in the cancellation of her participation; the schooner *Molly Moore* was never taken over by the Navy. Thus, on 3 December, the *Isabel*, under the command of Lt. John Walker Payne, Jr., sailed alone for Camranh Bay (then part of French Indochina) to gather intelligence on the concentration of Japanese warships located there. If queried, his cover story was that he was searching for a PBY Catalina flying boat missing off the Indochinese coast. Admiral Hart directed the *Isabel* to remain painted white and her running lights dimmed at night to give the appearance of a fishing vessel. Vessel preparation included removal of excess topside weight, replacement of her motorboat by a pulling whaleboat, fueling and provisioning, and offloading all her codebooks except for one prearranged cipher.[5]

Payne was under orders to approach the coast under the cover of darkness and report on Japanese ship movements. If detected and engaged by the enemy, he was to fight back as best he could and try to escape, but if necessary, destroy the *Isabel* rather than allow the Japanese to capture her. At 0700 on 5 December, while the spy ship was still forty miles from Camranh Bay, a floatplane from the seaplane carrier *Kamikawa Maru* sighted her. Aircraft shadowed the *Isabel* for the remainder of the day, and that evening, on Hart's urgent orders, the patrol yacht reversed course and headed back to Manila Bay.[6]

Questions later arose about Roosevelt's motivation for ordering three ill-equipped and marginally armed vessels to operate near the Japanese bastion at Camranh Bay; some believed his secret operation was intended to provoke a war with Japan. Representative Frank B. Keefe of Wisconsin told the Joint Committee on the Investigation of the Pearl Harbor Attack in 1945: " . . . Admiral Hart was already conducting reconnaissance off that coast by planes from Manila." (He therefore, presumably, had information on Japanese ship movements.) Grilled by Michigan's Senator Homer Ferguson before the same body, Adm. Royal E. Ingersoll (former assistant to the Chief of Naval Operations) repeatedly testified that the message was wholly the President's idea, that Admiral Stark (the Chief of Naval Operations at the time) would not have initiated such a movement and was satisfied with the information that Hart already was furnishing. Ferguson's final question was "Could you tell us whether or not these were really men-of-war, so that if they had been fired on it would have been an overt act against the United States?" "It would have been," replied Ingersoll."[7]

DISASTER IN THE PHILIPPINES

Some eight or nine hours after Gen. Douglas MacArthur was informed of the attack on Pearl Harbor, his planes were caught grounded on their Philippine fields when two flights of Japanese bombers from Formosa struck Baguio and the Tugugarao airfield in northern Luzon at 0930 in the morning of 8 December. This attack was followed

Map 8-2

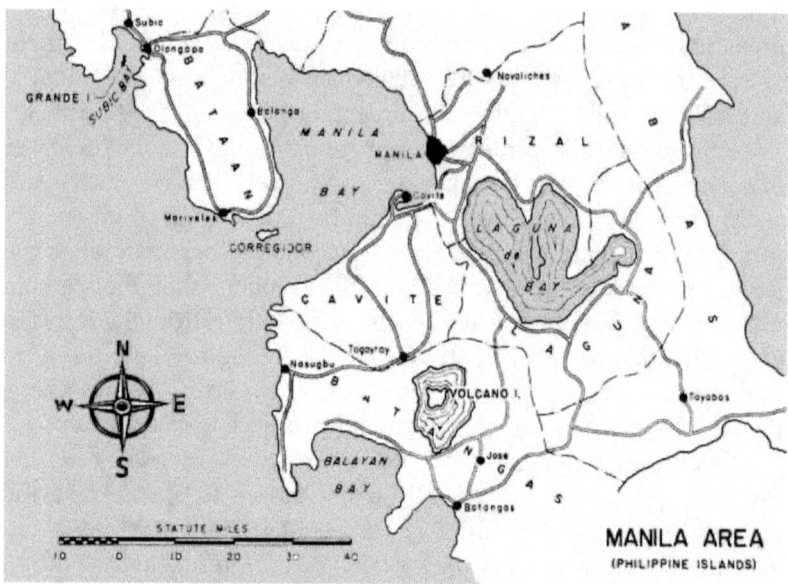

Manila Bay area of the Philippines.
Source: http://www.ibiblio.org/hyperwar/USN/Building_Bases/maps/bases2-p391.jpg

just after noon by the first of a group of 108 bombers, escorted by 99 fighters. The destruction of the Far Eastern Air Force (formerly the Philippine Army Air Corps) was complete. On 10 December, having eliminated the possibility of a defense or counterattack against its air forces, Japan sent an 80-bomber and 52-fighter group against Cavite to neutralize the airfield and destroy the navy yard together with the remaining ships of the Asiatic Fleet. Flying back and forth at 20,000 feet while dropping ordnance at will, high-level bombers sank the submarine *Sealion* (SS-195), damaged the destroyers *Peary* (DD-226) and *Pillsbury* (DD-227), and destroyed the minesweeper *Bittern* (AM-36). Too badly damaged for repair, the burned hulk of the sweep was stripped of usable items by sailors from other minecraft and later scuttled in Manila Bay. Eight bombs, all duds, ringed the *Isabel*'s fantail, and she brought down one of the attackers.[8]

With Philippine waters no longer safe, those Asiatic Fleet ships that could do so sailed for points south within the next few days, and with the remnants of the fleet falling back on Java, there was no point in Admiral Hart remaining. He turned over local naval command to Rear Adm. Francis W. Rockwell, commandant Sixteenth Naval

District, and on 26 December departed southward aboard the submarine *Shark* (SS-174). Having made her way to Java, the *Isabel* was assigned, as a member of the short-lived ABDA (American-British-Dutch-Australian) command, to convoy escort duties in the Dutch East Indies. On 7 February 1942, she rescued all 187 survivors of the 4,519-ton Dutch passenger ship *Van Cloon*, which after being shelled by the Japanese submarine *I-55*, was sinking off Bawean Island, Java. As the yacht fished survivors out of the water, the sub fired a torpedo at her and then surfaced nearby. The torpedo missed, and the *Isabel* drove the *I-55* under water with gunfire and then, assisted by a Dutch PBY Catalina on patrol nearby, dropped depth charges to drive it from the area.[9]

In March 1942, following a decisive victory by the Japanese in the Battle of Java Sea on 27 February, the *Isabel* joined other surviving Allied warships that were retreating to Australia. She operated out of Fremantle for the duration of the war, supporting the U.S. submarines based there.[10]

SHIPS AND DISTRICT CRAFT UNABLE TO ESCAPE THE PHILIPPINES

> *For the President of the United States:*
>
> *It is with broken heart and head bowed in sadness, but not in shame, that I report to Your Excellency that I must go today to arrange terms for the surrender of the fortified islands of Manila Bay: Corregidor (Fort Mills), Caballo (Fort Hughes), El Fraile (Fort Drum), and Carabao (Fort Frank).*
>
> *With anti-aircraft fire control equipment and many guns destroyed, we are no longer able to prevent accurate aerial bombardment. With numerous batteries of the heaviest caliber employed on the shores of Bataan and Cavite out ranging our remaining guns, the enemy now brings devastating cross fire to bear on us.*
>
> *Most of my batteries, seacoast, anti-aircraft and field, have been put out of action by the enemy. I have ordered the others destroyed to prevent them from falling into enemy hands. In addition we are now overwhelmingly assaulted by Japanese troops on Corregidor. There is a limit of human endurance and that limit has long since been past. Without prospect of relief I feel it is my duty to my country and to my gallant troops to end this useless effusion of blood and human sacrifice . . .*
>
> *With profound regret and with continued pride in my gallant troops I go to meet the Japanese commander.*
>
> *Good-by Mr. President.*
>
> —Lt. Gen. Jonathan Wainwright's last official communication (radio message) with President Roosevelt on 6 May 1942

Chapter 8

Back in the Philippines, on 21 December 1941, Rear Adm. Francis W. Rockwell established new headquarters in a tunnel on Corregidor, nicknamed "The Rock," supported by equipment and staff members transported there by the minesweeper *Tanager* (AM-5). On Christmas Eve, MacArthur decided to evacuate Manila and deploy his army in the Bataan Peninsula for the defense of the Philippines. On 11 March 1942, on orders from Washington, Lt. John D. Bulkeley's Motor Torpedo Boat Squadron 3 transported MacArthur, his family, members of his staff, and Rockwell to Mindanao, from which B17s flew them to Australia.[11]

The end was near for the remaining units of the Asiatic Fleet and large numbers of district craft. On 6 May, Lt. Gen. Jonathon M. Wainwright, USA, surrendered Corregidor and Manila Bay forts and all of the armed forces in the Philippines to the Japanese. A bitter pill to swallow, intended to prevent further effusion of blood, this action followed an epic struggle by Filipino and American soldiers to withstand, for more than three months, the constant and grueling fire of a superior enemy. Besieged on land and blockaded by sea, cut off from all sources of help in the Philippines and in the U.S., the intrepid fighters had endured all that they could. The river gunboats *Oahu* (PR-6) and *Luzon* (PR-7), built for service on the Yangtze River in China, and the minesweeper *Quail* (AM-15) were scuttled by U.S forces off Corregidor to prevent their capture, and the converted yachts *Fisheries II* and *Maryanne*, and converted small patrol craft *Perry* were destroyed. Also lost to Japanese occupation of the Philippines were the *YP-97* and sixty-two district craft.[12]

The reserve flagship of the Asiatic Fleet, *Isabel*, with captain and crew aboard, had made good her escape from the Philippines. Men assigned to the converted yachts *Maryanne* (the flagship for the section base commander, Lt. Fred L. Raymond, USNR) and *Fisheries II*—which were too small to put out to sea—were not so fortunate. Lt. (jg) Fred Rising Newell, Jr., the commanding officer of the *Maryanne*, was awarded the Navy Cross posthumously for his heroic actions during the defense of the Philippines. The citation reads:

> The President of the United States of America takes pleasure in presenting the Navy Cross to Lieutenant, Junior Grade Fred Rising Newell, Jr., United States Naval Reserve, for heroism during combat with the enemy during the period 7 December 1941 to

7 March 1942, and 19 - 28 April 1942, while on board the U.S.S. *MARYANNE*, in the Philippine Islands. While exposed to frequent horizontal and dive bombing attacks by enemy Japanese air forces, Lieutenant, Junior Grade, Newell directed the fire of his anti-aircraft battery and participated in operations of strategic importance in the Manila Bay area involving hazardous missions such as to reflect great credit upon the United States Naval Service.

Most of the vessels remaining in the Philippines were engaged, from 12 April 1942 until the islands fell, in hazardous duty involving the night sweeping of safe passages through mine fields south of Corregidor and night patrols to intercept enemy landing parties.[13]

Ens. George K. Petritz, a naval reserve officer, commanded the *YP-97*. After the attack on 8 December, when presumably the patrol craft was knocked out of action, he served as the commanding officer or executive officer of the *Fisheries II*. Ens. Lowell H. Strand, USNR, was the other officer aboard. Newell, Raymond, Petritz, and Strand were captured after the fall of Corregidor on 6 May 1942. (When General Wainwright finally surrendered, following continuous bombardment of Corregidor by artillery from Bataan as well as naval and aerial bombing, 173 naval officers and 2,317 enlisted men were left to face the horror of forced labor and Japanese prison camps for the duration of the war.) Only Petritz survived captivity. Raymond and Strand, like Newell, were awarded Navy Crosses posthumously. (Their medal citations are provided in Appendix E.)[14]

Petritz was a POW for over two years until he was able to escape from a prison ship that, bound for Japan, was damaged during an Allied air attack while still in Subic Bay. At Cabanatuan Prison Camp No.1, where he was originally taken in May 1942, he witnessed brutal beatings of starving prisoners who were barely subsisting on portions of rice mixed with corncobs, eggshells, bones, and banana peels. Petritz believed the Japanese guards treated prisoners like vermin based on their cultural belief that surrender was the ultimate disgrace. He was moved to the Bilibid Prison Camp on 13 October 1944, where conditions deteriorated dramatically as the United States began to dominate the war.[15]

At Manila on 13 December 1944, Petritz and 1,619 other prisoners, many suffering from tropical diseases including dysentery, were herded onto the *Oryoku Maru*, a gray-green former passenger ship gutted to transport troops. The Japanese intended the POWs to serve as slave laborers in its worker-starved factories. The men, steamy and sweaty, were squeezed into three different deep holds. With no space to lie down, many were forced to stand. Japanese civilians and Taiwanese and Japanese soldiers occupied cabins. With no ventilation, temperatures soared, and many men died from dehydration or suffocation as their tongues swelled in their throats. The following morning, dive-bombers from the carrier *Hornet* (CV-12) attacked the unmarked *Oryoku Maru* as it crept along the jagged edge of Luzon Island. A bomb hit the water and the explosion ripped a hole in the ship's hull, allowing sunlight and air to reach grateful prisoners. Damaged by the air strikes, the *Oryoku Maru* put into Olongapo Bay and the Japanese civilians and soldiers disembarked for movement ashore. The Taiwanese soldiers were left aboard to guard the prisoners in the hold.[16]

Dive-bombers attacked the ship again on the morning of 15 December. A direct hit in the aft hold killed about 100 men and wounded 150 more. The panicked survivors rushed up the long ladders leading out of the holds and jumped overboard. Japanese guards manned tripod-mounted machine guns along the beach and shot anyone attempting escape. After leaving the ship, Petritz swam directly away from the beach for about two miles. A banca (outrigger canoe) picked him up about 200 yards off Banicain, and the local boy and his grandmother aboard it took him to their barrio, where villagers hid him in the woods and gave him a good dinner. There he met another escapee, Darnell Kadolph. That night, the two men were transferred by banca to Tibawa. Kadolph remained there by choice and on the night of 5 January Petritz moved to Filipino guerrilla Camp D. On 29 January, the guerrillas led him to a beach where two Navy patrol boats whisked him away.[17]

Petritz was very lucky to have escaped the fate of many of the other 1,619 men that boarded the "hell ship" on 13 December. Approximately 100 of them died from suffocation or dehydration during the two nights aboard, while nearly 200 others were killed during the bombing or were shot in the water as they tried to escape. Surviving prisoners were assembled at nearby tennis courts and then moved to San Fernando, Pampanga. While in San Fernando, fifteen weak or wounded prisoners were taken to a nearby cemetery, beheaded, and dumped into a mass grave. About a thousand of the remaining prisoners were loaded on the *Enoura Maru*, while the rest boarded the smaller *Brazil Maru*. Both ships reached Takao (now Kaohsiung) harbor in Formosa on New Year's Day, and the smaller group of prisoners was transferred from the *Brazil Maru* to *Enoura Maru*. On 9 January, the *Enoura Maru* was bombed and disabled in the harbor, killing about 350 men. The remaining survivors were returned to the *Brazil Maru* which arrived in Moji, Japan, on 29 January 1945. Only 550 of the over 900 prisoners who had sailed from Taiwan were still alive, and more would die in the coming months in Japan, Taiwan, and Korea, leaving only 403 survivors of the original 1,620 to be liberated from camps in Kyushu, Korea, Manchuria, and Taiwan in August and September of 1945.[18]

Petritz was awarded the Navy Cross, as well as the Purple Heart, and was promoted to full lieutenant shortly after his return to the United States:

> The President of the United States of America takes pleasure in presenting the Navy Cross to Ensign George Karl Petritz, United States Naval Reserve, for extraordinary heroism in combat with the enemy during the periods 7 December 1941 to 7 March 1942, while on board the U.S.S. *FISHERIES TWO*, in the Philippine Islands. While exposed to frequent horizontal and dive bombing attacks by enemy Japanese air forces, Ensign Petritz directed the fire of his anti-aircraft battery and participated in operations of strategic importance in the Manila Bay area involving hazardous missions such as to reflect great credit upon himself and the United States Naval Service.[19]

DESTRUCTION OF THE "GUAM NAVY"

On the same day that Japan attacked the U.S. military installations at Pearl Harbor and in the Philippines, it also launched an air raid against the facilities and small group of Navy vessels located at Guam, the most formidable of which was the minesweeper *Penguin*. Two miscellaneous auxiliary vessels, two patrol craft, thirteen lighters, one dredge, and three self-propelled water barges formed the remainder of the "Guam Navy." Warned by a motor launch (as the ship's radio did not work) on the morning of 8 December that the war had begun, her commanding officer ordered the Ensign flown upside down (an international symbol of distress) and set an outbound course for the mouth of Apra Harbor. At 0815, nine Japanese bombers launched from Saipan, 125 miles north-northeast of Guam, arrived over Agana and commenced its destruction twelve minutes later. After bombing and strafing shore targets and the Piti Navy Yard, a group of planes attacked the *Penguin* outside the harbor. Although the ship did not receive any direct hits, exploding bombs and ammunition killed one of her officers and wounded over sixty crewmen, including the captain. Remaining crewmembers transported their injured shipmates to shore in life rafts and, to prevent the still seaworthy vessel from unavoidable capture, scuttled the minesweeper in deep water off Orote Point and swam ashore. A former crewman recalls watching his ship disappear into the ocean's depth:

> The last thing that went down was the American flag. It was like a fantasy world. This isn't happening, this couldn't happen. No one would ever attack the USS *Penguin* or any other (American) ship. It was just all unreal. We went through the motions and started to swim to get back to shore and from then on, it was just unreal.[20]

Two days later a Japanese attack force commanded by Rear Adm. Goto Aritomo came ashore on Guam. The force was comprised of the South Seas Detachment, a unit of about 5,500 army troops, and a special Navy landing force of about 400 men drawn from the Fifth Defense Force stationed in Saipan. Following fierce fighting and the surrender of the island territory by its governor, Capt. George J. McMillin, USN, the sailors spent the remainder of the war as POWs, first in a camp on Guam and then in Japan.[21]

At the time of the attack, Guam's only military defense consisted of 153 Marines, 271 naval personnel, 134 civilian construction workers, and 247 members of the local militia and the Insular Forces. The U.S. Navy had resurrected the Insular Force Guard unit in April 1941, to defend Guam. Guardsmen were, however, neither well-trained nor properly armed.[22] Four ships—as well as seventeen additional smaller District craft—were scuttled, destroyed, or captured:

Commandant, Navy Yard Piti: Capt. George J. McMillin, USN

Ship Name/Designation	Commanding Officer
Robert L. Barnes (AG-27)	Lt. J. L. Nestor
Penguin (AM-33)	Lt. J. W. Haviland
YP-16	Chief Boatswain's Mate Philip Earl Saunders, USN
YP-17	Chief Boatswain's Mate Homer Lamar Townsend, USN[23]

YARD PATROL CRAFT *YP-16* AND *YP-17*

The *YP-16* and *17* were 75-foot former Coast Guard cutters (*CG-267* and *CG-275*, respectively), built in 1925 by Lake Union Dry Dock and Machine Works of Seattle, Washington. They had arrived at Apra Harbor on 20 October 1940 aboard the oiler *Ramapo* (AO-12) to augment the local defenses of Guam and to provide surveillance and reconnaissance in the waters around the island. During the invasion of Guam, efforts to prevent useful material from falling into Japanese hands were only marginally successful; the *YP-16* was burned, but *YP-17* was only damaged and captured. The Japanese later made use of the *Robert L. Barnes* and *YP-17*.[24]

The captured Americans, including the crews of the YPs, were held on the island until shipped to Japan on 10 January 1942.

YP-16

Name	Rating	POW Camp
Henry Jay Ashton	Boatswain's Mate Second, USN	Hirohata, Japan
Donald Adair Binns	Coxswain, USN	Zentsuji, Japan
Arthur Benedict Dahlsted	Machinist's Mate Third, USN	Osaka area, Japan
Henry Fabian, Jr.	Machinist's Mate Second, USN	Osaka area, Japan
Philip Earl Saunders	Chief Boatswain's Mate, USN	Osaka area, Japan
Jack Lawrence Wash	Seaman First, USN	Zentsuji, Japan

YP-17

Name	Rating	POW Camp
Lowren Augustus Arnett	Seaman First, USN	Osaka area, Japan
Lawrence Edward Bluma	Boatswain's Mate Second, USN	Zentsuji, Japan
Harold William Dutro	Fireman First, USN	Hirohata, Japan
Arthur Earnest Foote	Machinist's Mate First, USN	
Anthony Joseph Podries	Machinist's Mate First, USN	Hirohata, Japan
Hiram Jefferson Prickett	Quartermaster First, USN	Osaka area, Japan
Homer Lamar Townsend	Chief Boatswain's Mate, USN	Zentsuji, Japan

Twelve of the above individuals were returned to U.S. military control after the end of hostilities in August 1945. Machinist's Mate First Arthur Foote died on 15 July 1945 in an air raid on the Kawasaki Steel Mill.[25]

9

Cutter *McLane* and *YP-251* Sink Submarine in Alaskan Waters

> *Chances of seeing enemy action whilst here seems extremely remote.*
> —Entry made in a Royal Canadian Air Force base log book regarding the perceived likelihood that a unit of the bomber reconnaissance squadrons sent north to Ketchikan at the request of the United States might confront a Japanese submarine[1]

On 9 July 1942, a month after the Battle of Midway, two Alaskan-based patrol vessels, the Coast Guard cutter *McLane* and *YP-251*, were credited with sinking the Japanese submarine *RO-32*. On receipt of orders to search for a submarine reportedly bombed the previous afternoon by a Canadian patrol aircraft, the YP left Section Base, Ketchikan at 0115 for grid "Vernon Nine" south-southeast of Sitka. Spanning a mere seventy-nine feet in length, the wooden-hulled *YP-251* was the former F/V *Foremost* which the Navy had acquired on 31 December 1941; one of many such Pacific Northwest halibut schooners constructed by Scandinavian shipwrights on Ballard beaches in Northwest Seattle, Washington, in the early 1900s to fish the northern waters off Alaska and Bristol Bay. The schooners came in all sizes and shapes but shared some common characteristics: a stepped deck forward over the fo'c'sle; a midships hold; the pilothouse aft of the hold; a bait shed on the rear deck; and two masts, often with twin booms for unloading the hold. The *YP-251* was one of forty Yippies manned by Coast Guard crews under U.S. Navy operational control during the war.[2]

Pacific Northwest halibut schooner *Foremost* before her conversion to *YP-251*. Courtesy of H. E. Lokken, www.fvoa.org/slideshowtest/f/jpg_foremost.htm

After studying a chart of the area, her commanding officer, Lt. Neils P. Thomsen, USCG, had decided to search for the sub in an area to the northwest of where it had been bombed. His decision was based on an assumption that if the submarine were damaged or suspected a search was forthcoming, it would prefer to lie on the bottom in fifty-two fathoms of water, with its engines shut down to avoid detection, rather than continuing to operate in 100-to-50-fathom waters. Five and a half hours after departing Ketchikan, *YP-251* arrived at her destination, where she was met by the *McLane* (WSC-146), which came alongside for orders. The 125-foot steel-hulled cutter had been on the lookout for an enemy submarine since 7 June when, while patrolling in Dixon Entrance between Cape Chacon and Barren Island, she had received a report of one having been sighted in Hidden Inlet. However, a search of the Portland Canal and the bays as far as Hattie Island proved fruitless. The cutter resumed her previous patrol and as the days passed, expanded her search efforts beyond the Dixon Entrance to include waters in the vicinity of Forrester's Island and Cape Muzon. During that period, her crewmen frequently sighted RCAF patrol planes in the area, one of which may have been the Bolingbroke bomber that later caught the submarine on the surface.[3]

Earlier—after receiving a U.S. request for assistance in patrolling Alaskan waters—Canada had dispatched six RCAF units north, including the No. 115 Bomber Reconnaissance Squadron. While the likelihood of detecting a surfaced submarine had seemed remote to the aircrew of bomber No. *9118*, an airman had sighted the silhouette of a sub emitting white smoke, its outline definitely not one of the new American fleet units or older "S-boats." After dropping a single 250-pound bomb in the water forward of the target's conning tower, the submarine disappeared beneath the surface, and the plane reported its last visible position at 55° 20' north, 134° 41' west.[4]

Following the expected arrival of the Canadian minesweeper *Quatsino* (J152), the three ships began their search operation southeast of Annette Island off Dixon Entrance, a strait about fifty miles wide and long that forms the boundary between Alaska and British Columbia. The *McLane* took up its station two miles abeam of the YP and began an "expanding square" search toward the north, while the minesweeper, two miles on her opposite beam, began the eastern leg of her pattern. The *McLane* was to stay inside of *YP-251* on all courses, as she had a listening device. Thomsen believed that if the submarine were between them, his ship's noisy engines would drive it towards the *McLane* to be detected by her sound gear. Conversely, should the sub try to creep slowly away, it would remain contained within the expanding search pattern.[5]

The cutter gained an underwater sound contact at 0800 and immediately put about and, with the contact ahead of her, decreased speed to close in for an attack. She lost contact and launched a depth charge, set to explode at 300 feet, but it failed to detonate. The *McLane* regained sound contact at 0905, and pursued the sub for an hour, its intermittent sound signature indicating that it was running at short intervals and zigzagging the entire time. Once again losing contact, the cutter cruised in the vicinity until 1540 when she "picked up" the sub again. After devoting thirteen minutes to refining her attack criteria, the *McLane* dropped two depth charges, set to explode at 150 and 250 feet, respectively, and three minutes later, two more, set at 200 and 300 feet. Thereafter, air bubbles began rising to the surface in the vicinity, signifying a sunken or gravely damaged submarine, or the purposeful venting of air by the enemy in an attempt to fool its pursuers into giving up the chase. At 1735, as the *McLane* approached the *YP-251* from astern, a torpedo streaked under the cutter's bow, an apparent desperation action by the sub—one that revealed its location.[6]

Chapter 9

Map 9-1

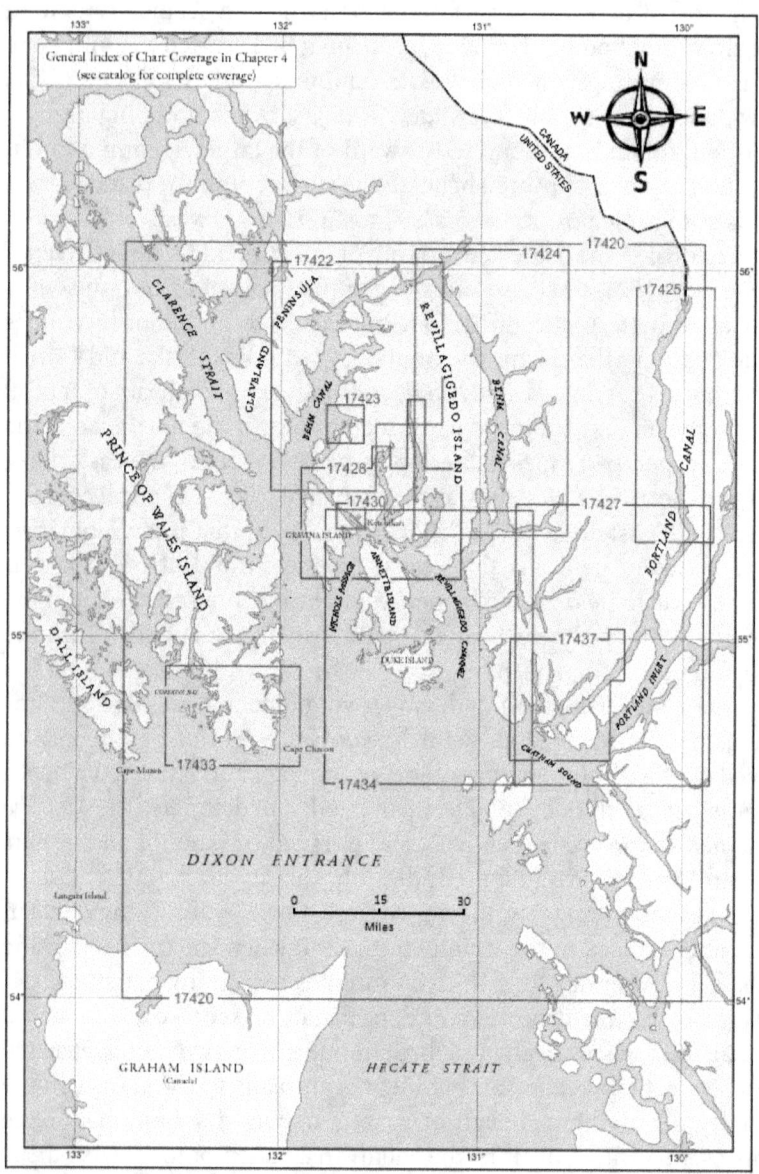

A Royal Canadian Air Force bomber (No. *9118*), Coast Guard cutter *McLane*, and the *YP-251*—a former Pacific Northwest halibut schooner—were credited with sinking an enemy submarine in Southeast Alaskan waters.
Source: http://www.nauticalcharts.noaa.gov/nsd/xml2html.php?xml=coastpilot/ files/cp8/CPB8_E34_C04_20121215_1209_WEB.xml

McLane's commanding officer, Lt. Ralph Burns, USCG, was standing in the bow, saw the torpedo's yellow head and green body, and heard it hiss as it sped toward the cutter, leaving a 125 foot-long feather in the water. As the *McLane* went full ahead in the direction from which the torpedo had come, the *YP-251* sighted a periscope, which just as quickly vanished, and dropped a depth charge over the site. The cutter then proceeded to that spot, by then marked with a smoke bomb, dropped two depth charges, and remained in the vicinity, attempting to regain sound contact. After a large oil slick appeared, the sub, damaged and likely desperate to know what was transpiring above her, chanced a look around. The *YP-251* sighted her periscope at 1935, dropped a depth charge, and after starting a turn to starboard bumped a submerged object, as if riding over a sand bar. The *McLane* dropped explosives, set at 200 and 100 feet, after which air bubbles, large quantities of oil, and a substance resembling rock wool—a mineral fiber universally installed on submarines as an insulator and sound-deadening agent—appeared on the surface. The cutter remained in the area until early morning, monitoring nearby waters for any source of noise, but there was only silence below.[7]

KUDOS FOR A JOB WELL DONE

The *McLane*, *YP-251*, and the RCAF Air Corps were officially credited with sinking the *RO-32* on 9 July 1942 at location 55° 20' north, 134° 40' west. The two vessels were each awarded a battle star and their commanding officers received the Legion of Merit.[8] The associated citation for Lt. Neils P. Thomsen follows:

> For exceptionally meritorious conduct as commanding officer of the *YP-251* during action against a hostile submarine in North Pacific water, July 9, 1942. Although an air driven torpedo passed 28 yards astern of his craft during the engagement, Lieut. Thomsen relentlessly pursued his target until spreading oil slicks and continuous air bubbles gave evidence of the probable destruction of the enemy vessel.[9]

LIKELY DESTRUCTION OF A SOVIET VS. JAPANESE SUBMARINE

Many years after the fact, the sinking of the *RO-32* was called into question. The U.S. Coast Guard District Officer had credited the two ships with sinking a sub soon after the attack, and in February 1947 the Joint Army-Navy Assessment Committee attributed the *RO-32*'s destruction to Allied surface craft and aircraft. However, in 1967 the U.S. Navy determined that the submarine had been inactive at the time of its supposed loss and was, in fact, still afloat at the end of the war.[10]

This finding begs the question: Whose submarine perished in Alaskan waters sixty-nine years ago? It may have been the Soviet *Shch-138*. While technically allied with the West, Soviet leadership was leery of an Allied invasion, and its submarines offered a clandestine means by which to monitor the rapid American buildup of military bases, ports and airfields close to Soviet territory. Russian submarines operated in the area. One, the *L-16*, was torpedoed by the *I-25* off the Pacific Northwest on 11 October 1942, resulting in not only her loss but also the loss of the lives of everyone aboard. The *Shch-138*, operating from a port near Vladivostok (on the Pacific, not far from Russia's borders with China and North Korea), was reported missing on 10 July, the day after a submarine was sunk by the *McLane* and *YP-251*. The Soviet Navy later claimed the *Shch-138* had been lost on 18 July in Nikolaevsk-na-Amure Harbor due to an explosion of four of its torpedoes. Reportedly, the sub was raised immediately, but sank in a storm the next day while under tow, was raised again on 11 July 1943, and thereafter scrapped. While the account might be true, it is unlikely that the Soviet Union would admit to engaging in submarine espionage against an ally.[11]

The theory that the submarine was Soviet is bolstered by a photograph taken by a crewman of the RCAF bomber No. *9118*. It clearly shows a detonation just forward of the sub's conning tower. Experts in Japan, Europe, and the United States were unable to identify the type of submarine, but close examination of the photo revealed the numeral "8" among other indiscernible figures. The sub depicted in the photo is painted gray, the convention of Soviet submarines of the Pacific Fleet, in order to differentiate them from the Japanese submarines which were painted black.[12]

Capt. Neils P. Thomsen, USCG, passed away on 2 January 2007 at the age of ninety-nine. Born in Denmark and the great-grandson of a count, he grew up in Fresno, California. At age 15, he ran away from home, jumped a Pacific freight train headed up the northwest coast, and joined a commercial sailing ship, the *Forest Dream*. During its ensuing fourteen-month voyage from Puget Sound to Mauritius Island in the Indian Ocean, the five-masted barkentine was destroyed in a gale, leaving Thomsen the sole survivor. The young man continued to go to sea in ships, became an officer in the Merchant Marine, and in World War II entered the Coast Guard. After commanding *YP-251*, he received orders to the attack transport *Hunter Liggett* (APA-14) and took part in the occupation and defense of Guadalcanal and Bougainville in the summer and autumn of 1942 as staff navigator and chief pilot to commander, Third Amphibious Force. He later commanded the cargo ship *Menkar* (AK-123). After retiring from the United States Coast Guard in 1952, Thomsen continued his life at sea by operating the USPS mail boat in the Aleutian Islands and founding the Aleutian King Crab processing plant. He retired from the Department of Defense a second time at age eighty, after having piloted a dredge off the coasts of Washington and Oregon.[13]

10

U-boat Attacks in Torpedo Junction

> *The story of the YP-389 personifies the character of the Battle of the Atlantic along the East Coast of the United States, where small poorly armed fishing trawlers were called to defend American waters against one of Germany's most feared vessels. It is one of the most dramatic accounts of an engagement between Axis and Allied warships during the dark days of World War II.*
>
> —David W. Alberg, leader of the National Oceanic and Atmospheric Administration expedition, who, aboard the NOAA ship *Nancy Foster* on 9 September 2009, confirmed that wreckage found on the seafloor off Cape Hatteras, North Carolina, the previous month was the *YP-389*. The shipwreck lies at a depth of about 300 feet in an area known as the "Graveyard of the Atlantic," which contains numerous Allied warships and merchant vessels and German U-boats sunk in "Torpedo Junction" during the Battle of the Atlantic.[1]

Following Germany's declaration of war against the United States on 11 December 1941, Adm. Karl Donitz, commander-in-chief U-boats, immediately initiated a submarine campaign off North America by dispatching five of Germany's Type IX U-boats—*U-66, U-109, U-123, U-125,* and *U 130*—to American waters. Donitz had requested that the *Kriegsmarine* make its twelve newest long-range U-boats available for the operation, but the naval staff in Berlin retained control of six. The remaining one, *U-128*, was in need of urgent repairs and would, upon completion, sail alone for America on 8 January 1942. Packed with fuel, food and ammunition, the five U-boats that would launch Operation *PAUKENSCHLAG* ("Drumbeat") sailed from Lorient, a seaport in Brittany in northwestern France, between 18 and 27

December 1941. Each submarine carried sealed orders, to be opened after passing 20 degrees west longitude, directing them to different destinations. All the boats were to be in position by 13 January 1942 for a fast, surprise attack on the eastern seaboard of the United States. The *U-123* sank the British freighter S.S. *Cyclops* in Canadian waters on the 11th, and two days later the *U-130* sent the Norwegian merchant vessel S.S. *Frisco* to the bottom off Nova Scotia, as well as the Panamanian merchant vessel S.S. *Friar Rock* about 110 miles southwest of Cape Race, Newfoundland. The submarines continued to attack shipping as far south as Cape Hatteras, North Carolina, before low fuel forced an end to operations on 6 February 1942. The subs headed home having sunk twenty-five ships equaling 156,939 tons.[2]

With such easy pickings available, Donitz also began sending Type VII U-boats to the U.S. East Coast. These assignments mandated special preparation due to the shorter range of these submarines. Every conceivable space was crammed full of provisions. Fresh water tanks were used to carry additional diesel oil, and the submarines made the Atlantic crossing at a very low speed on a single engine to conserve fuel. By the time the "drumbeaters" had returned to their French bases, the next wave of submarines had already reached the East Coast, and Donitz continued to send successive groups. Following their arrival, the U-boats normally remained safely submerged by day, surfacing at night to pick off merchant vessels outlined against the lights of the cities. During the first six months of the U-boat offensive, some 397 ships, totaling over two million tons, were sunk.[3]

The primary target area was the North Atlantic Coastal Frontier, extending from Maine to North Carolina (which, following the addition of South Carolina, was renamed the Eastern Sea Frontier on 7 February 1942.) Rear Adm. Adolphus Andrews, USN, the frontier commander, had very few resources available for its defense: seven cutters, four converted yachts, three 1919-vintage patrol boats, two gunboats dating from 1905, and four wooden-hulled submarine chasers. About 100 aircraft were available, but were short-range types suitable only for training. All larger planes were under U.S. Army-Air Force control, and, in any case, the USAAF was at the time neither trained nor equipped for anti-submarine work.[4]

THE EARLY DARK DAYS

> It is submitted that should enemy submarines operate off this coast, this command has no forces available to take adequate action against them, either offensive or defensive.
>
> —Commander, North Atlantic Naval Coastal Frontier, 22 December 1941[5]

In an effort to obtain vessels quickly with which to patrol East Coast waters, as well as men to crew them, the Navy sought out, as it had in San Diego, regional fishermen and their boats. Many of the fishermen who were of an age to serve chose to remain with their own boats as warrant officers or enlisted ratings. Some, however, wanted to serve aboard destroyers or other combatant ships and were disappointed to be ordered to boats similar to those to which they were accustomed. An eighteen-year-old fisherman from Maine, who enlisted after Pearl Harbor, recounted his feelings about learning that he was being sent to the *YP-375* (an ex-fishing vessel employed as a minesweeper before conversion to a YP) and described the shock of seeing the masts of scores of merchant ships that had been sunk off Cape Hatteras:

> Her original name was [*Raymonde*], out of Gloucester, and I went aboard her at Boston. I was very dejected, I thought, "Here I am a fisherman who joined the Navy, and now I'm on a fishing boat again." But that's what they wanted . . . fishing [boat] experience, so we got our ratings really quick. . . . It was a converted fishing vessel, actually a Highliner. She was a two-masted schooner, and the Navy took her over, and put her out on patrol. Our first assignment was clearing mines. . .
>
> We put into Cape Hatteras, and at midnight the captain says to me, "Let me know when you see a lot of poles sticking up out of the water." This was off South Carolina, in the regular freight channels. . . . The Germans would wait at the buoys, about 60 miles off shore [and] they'd [the merchant ships] be sitting ducks. So, we're 65 miles off shore, and around midnight, I see these big poles sticking up out of the water. Boy it's eerie, when you see something like that. There were all the masts of the ships that they had sunk . . . We saw ship after ship as we went down [proceeded south], some awash, others just stacks showing, some with three or four feet of

freeboard. . . . The skippers [of the torpedoed ships] would try to run for shore, and beach them. The ones with the masts sticking out of the water, they didn't make it. From Sandy Hook south, I think there were 167 merchant ships sunk; and nobody knew that they were crucifying us out there.[6]

FIRST NAVAL DISTRICT

The *YP-375* was a unit of the Inshore Patrol of the First Naval District. Its commandant, Rear Adm. William T. Tarrant, USN, was headquartered at Boston, Massachusetts, with district vessels assigned in May 1942 to six different section bases: Boston, and Woods Hole, Massachusetts; Portsmouth, New Hampshire; and Portland, Rockland, and Bar Harbor, Maine. Some of the following vessels were fitted out at the Boston Navy Yard and subsequently assigned elsewhere. Most, including the base minesweepers *AMb-19*, *20*, *21*, and *22*, remained in the First District. They were converted to YPs *377-380* at the yard and assigned to Section Base, Woods Hole to protect an anchorage to the northwest in Buzzards Bay, where shipping formed into convoys.[7]

Ship Name or Designation (Former Type Vessel/Name and Name of Commanding Officer if Known)	Length Feet	Displ Tons	Year Built
Section Base, Boston, Massachusetts: Commissioned 14 April 1941			
Siren PY-13 (ex-steel hulled yacht *Lotosland*)	196' 5"	800	1929
Gallant PYc-29 (ex-*North Star*, Lt. (jg) D. R. Stoneleigh)	177	350	1909
Bold AMc-67 (ex-*Chief*, *Accentor*-class)	97	195	1942
Combat AMc-69 (ex-*Acme*-class, Lt. (jg) David A. Mitchell, USNR)	97	195	1941
Detector AMc-75 (*Accentor*-class)	97	205	1941
Governor AMc-82 (*Accentor*-class, Lt. Alfred F. Page, Jr.)	97	195	1941
Kingbird AMc-56 (ex-fishing trawler *Governor Saltonstall*)	96	206	1940
Skipper AMc-104 (*Acme*-class)	98	195	1942
Trident AMc-107 (*Accentor*-class, Ens. Edmond J. Massello, USNR)	98	195	1941
Vigor AMc-110 (*Accentor*-class)	98	195	1942
AMb-27			
YP-210 (ex-yacht *Sea Sails III*, Jerry, Lochinvar)	78	60	1928
YP-215 (ex-*Verlaine*)	39	35	1940
YP-222 (ex-*Bobolink III*, former Coast Guard vessel)	72' 3"	37	1929
YP-274 (fishing vessel ex-*Onza*)	57	31	1936
YP-375 (ex-*Raymonde/AMb-17*)	84	110	1929

Ship Name or Designation (Former Type Vessel/Name and Name of Commanding Officer if Known)	Length Feet	Displ Tons	Year Built
Section Base, Woods Hole, Massachusetts			
AMb-1			
YP-377 (ex-fishing trawler/*AMb-19*)	79		1941
YP-378 (ex-fishing vessel hull/*AMb-20*)	89	81	1941
YP-379 (ex-fishing vessel hull/*AMb-21*)	85	69	1941
YP-380 (ex-fishing vessel *John E. Murley*/*AMb-22*)	88' 7"		1941
Sub-Section, Portsmouth, New Hampshire			
Puffin AMc-29 (ex-fishing dragger *Mary Jane*, Lt. (jg) Odber R. McClean, Jr.)	90	210	1936
Valor AMc-108 (*Accentor*-class)	98	195	1941
YP-211 (ex-power boat *Radiant*)	57		1926
YP-212 (ex-*Centaur*)	57	35	1929
YP-216 (ex-*Lark III*)	57	38	1939
Section Base, Portland, Maine: Commissioned 22 December 1941			
Accentor AMc-36 (*Accentor*-class, Lt. (jg) Gordon Abbott, USNR)	97	221	1941
Bulwark AMc-68 (*Accentor*-class, Ens. Lawrence Dana, USNR)	97	195	1941
Chimango AMc-42 (*Accentor*-class, Ens. J. T. G. Nichols, USNR)	97	200	1941
Cotinga AMc-43 (*Accentor*-class, Lt. S. W. Carr, USNR)	97	200	1941
Fulmar AMc-46 (*Accentor*-class, Lt. (jg) Allen Russell, USNR, Lt. (jg) Charles W. Logan, USNR)	97	185	1941
YP-210 (ex-yacht *Sea Sails III*, *Jerry*, *Lochinvar*)	78	60	1928
YP-215 (ex-*Verlaine*)	39	35	1940
Section Base, Rockland, Maine			
YP-213 (ex-*Esrom V.*)	50	24	1937
Section Base, Bar Harbor, Maine			
YP-228 (ex-fishing vessel *Voyageur*)	63	39	1937[8]

SEARCH FOR AN ENEMY SUBMARINE

At Boston, two minesweepers worked the swept channel daily, beginning at sunrise, to ensure safe harbor passage for shipping. Other vessels performed guard and escort duty in the harbor's north channel and at Nantasket Roads (the deep water anchorage to seaward), and maintained patrols from Cape Ann (located thirty miles northeast of Boston and forming the northern edge of Massachusetts Bay) to Peaked Hill Bar on Cape Cod; in the Cape Cod Channel connecting Cape Cod Bay in the north to Buzzards Bay in the south; and at Gloucester's Eastern Point.[9]

On 16 May 1942, the patrol yacht *Siren* was ordered to search for an enemy submarine. This assignment followed receipt of a report at 0530 that a fishing boat had sighted a sub on the surface in the vicinity of Cape Ann, heading southeast before it disappeared into fog on the ocean's surface. Two OS2U-3 Kingfisher maritime patrol aircraft were dispatched from Naval Air Station, Squantum (Quincy, Massachusetts), to search the approaches to Massachusetts Bay. At 1315, plane *5563* sighted a submarine on the surface, which had a long conning tower and single gun aft, characteristic of a 740-ton class U-boat. As the submarine crash dived, the plane turned and attacked it from the U-boat's port quarter, releasing two depth charges which hit the water about thirty seconds after the sub had submerged. Plane *5563* then requested assistance from *5560*, which immediately proceeded to the position of the attack, but dropped no depth charges as the appearance of a large oil slick seemed to indicate that the sub had sustained sufficient damage to necessitate its immediate surfacing. However, no further signs of her were detected and the *Siren* returned to port on 20 May, having achieved negative results.[10]

INSHORE PATROL OPERATIONS

Up the coast at Portsmouth, New Hampshire, YPs maintained a 24-hour patrol around the Navy Yard, the docks, waterfront, and lower harbor, and waters up the Piscataqua River, and along the coast to York Harbor, Maine. They also monitored the anti-submarine nets used to keep U-boats out of the port of Portsmouth and the main passage into the Piscataqua River. Coastal minesweepers based at Portland, Maine, swept the channel past Willard Rock and the approaches to Hussey Sound daily, and performed additional sweeping when large fleet units entered or left anchorage. Portland had the closest harbor to Europe, thus making it the site of many naval activities. In addition to performing sweeping duties, AMcs were assigned as guard ships at various points surrounding Casco Bay. The YPs patrolled Chandler Cove inside the bay and in Littlejohn Passage and Hussey Sound outside the bay. If their workload allowed, the sea lanes from Cape Elizabeth to Cape Ann and the shipping lanes into Portland Harbor were also patrolled.[11]

A PARTICULAR HATRED FOR U-BOATS

Aside from patriotism, some fishermen had personal reasons for wanting to serve in the Navy during the war. John O. Johnson, owner/skipper of the fishing vessel F/V *Aeolus*, was fishing in the Gulf of Maine on 3 June 1942 when a German submarine surfaced alongside and gave him and his crew five minutes to get into the dory and away from the *Aeolus* before they shelled it, sending it to the bottom. The six fishermen had a long 36-hour row before reaching land. Johnson, who had an unlimited master's license, immediately joined the U.S. Navy, vowing to get Hitler. However, as a newly commissioned naval officer he never saw sea duty, and instead taught navigation to ensigns at the Great Lakes Naval Training Station. Johnson had wanted to see action and instead, cooled his heels for the remainder of the war.[12]

The submarine that sank the *Aeolus* was the *U-432*, commanded by *Kapitänleutnant* Heinz-Otto Schultze, which earlier on 17 May had found the 324-ton fishing trawler *Foam*, owned by General Seafoods Co. of Boston, en route to the banks off Nova Scotia, and shelled it, sinking the boat and killing one crewman. Two weeks later, on 2 June, the *Aeolus* left Gloucester in company with the *Ben and Josephine*, an otter trawl dragger, bound for the Seal Island fishing grounds off Nova Scotia. Late the following afternoon, the two fishing vessels were 170 miles east of Cape Ann when the *U-432* surfaced near the *Ben and Josephine* and sprayed it with machine gun fire. After the sub allowed the crew to abandon ship in dories, it shelled the *Ben and Josephine* with its deck gun, setting the 102-ton vessel on fire and sinking it. The *U-432* then quickly overhauled the *Aeolus*, which until the attack had been about five miles astern of the dragger steering a parallel course. All efforts by Johnson to evade contact proved futile and, upon closing his boat, the sub fired a warning shot, followed by shouted orders to stop engines and put over dories. After the six men aboard rowed clear, the U-boat reopened fire with its deck gun and sank the fishing vessel. A day and a half later, the survivors landed on the coast of Maine at Mount Desert Rock light, an isolated Coast Guard lighthouse sited on a low-lying, wave-swept rock. They arrived close behind the eight crewmembers of the *Ben and Josephine*, which, like the *Aeolus*, had suffered no personnel casualties.[13]

COAST GUARD CUTTERS PRESSED INTO SERVICE

In addition to the YPs assigned to Inshore Patrol duties in the First Naval District, others were operating farther out to sea as units of the Eastern Sea Frontier Force. When Rear Admiral Andrews received word of the loss of the *Cyclops* to the *U-123* on 11 January, he ordered the few vessels under his command to sea. One of these was the *YP-49*, a 75-foot wooden-hulled former Coast Guard cutter, *CG-182*, built in 1925. Fitted with two depth charges, she was dispatched on 16 January to patrol duty in Barnegat Bay, New Jersey, which, framed by the Barnegat Peninsula and north end of Long Beach Island, was shielded from rough Atlantic seas by barrier islands to the east.[14]

Adm. Ernest J. King, commander-in-chief United States Fleet, had informed Andrews on 1 January 1942 that while he recognized the weakness of the force assigned to the North Atlantic Coastal Frontier, little help would be forthcoming, writing:

> This condition is paralleled in all naval coastal frontiers. A review of the situation indicates that it will be inadvisable to detach any vessels from their present duty with the Fleets, at least until additional new construction destroyers have been commissioned and have joined.[15]

Five weeks later, after thirty-five ships had been sunk and another four damaged by U-boats in American and Canadian waters, King authorized Andrews to employ anywhere within the frontier any or all of the 70-foot and 80-foot cutters of the Coast Guard normally assigned to local defense forces. On 11 February Andrews, in turn, directed that all navy districts within the Frontier and Naval Operating Base, Newport, Rhode Island:

> Arm, equip, and provide with depth charges all 70 to 75 foot and 80 to 83 foot Coast Guard cutters immediately. As many depth charges as practicable should be carried. Guns should be one pounder and machine guns .50 caliber if available, with three inch, 23 caliber on the 83 foot cutters if practicable. Listening gear to be installed as it becomes available. This to be given highest priority. These vessels are to be used on coastal sea lane patrol. Expedite action and report immediately action taken.[16]

This endeavor was neither instantaneous nor easy. An officer assigned to a 75-foot ex-Prohibition era cutter described putting the dilapidated craft back into service, the challenges associated with training its aged crew, and duty aboard the vessel:

> They call[ed] it a "six bit-er," seventy-five feet long. It had been . . . partially submerged in the Cooper River in Camden, [and] they resurrected [it] . . . Once they got the thing ship-shape, as much as they could, then they put the crew aboard. . . . They put a Lewis machine gun on the bow, gave us a bunch of World War One rifles and a Tommy-gun, two depth charges we couldn't outrun, and said, "Go get 'em." . . . these were much older men. These were recalled fleet reserves and they had [in years past] served on huge ships and they didn't know anything about small ships, small arms, or anything like that. . . . our job was anti-submarine warfare and survivor rescue. If a ship was torpedoed in our territory, they would send us a message, and we would go and pick up the dead bodies. That time of the year, no one lasted long in the Atlantic Ocean.

The YP (former cutter) was assigned to the Fourth Naval District under the command of a lieutenant (junior grade) who had been a Merchant Marine officer before the war. The ship's normal routine alternated anti-submarine patrols between Atlantic City and Cape May with time in port to refuel and load provisions, and scramble as necessary to recover survivors. Few crewmen of torpedoed ships remained alive very long in cold Atlantic waters unless they were in a lifeboat or quickly rescued by another vessel in the vicinity. Patrol vessels dispatched in darkness often found, at first light, only deceased mariners, bobbing on the ocean's surface in their old style, cork life jackets.[17]

Eight 75-foot former Coast Guard cutters, all constructed in 1925, were put into service in the Eastern Sea Frontier over the next four months: *YP-8*, *11*, *49*, and *52* in March, YPs *15* and *49* in April; and YPs *19* and *27* in June. On reporting for duty, the *YP-8* was assigned to "Race Patrol" near Race Rock Lighthouse at the entrance to Long Island Sound. The *YP-11* operated out of Atlantic City on Cape May, the southernmost point of the state of New Jersey, separating the Delaware Bay from the Atlantic; and the *YP-49* from Lewes, Delaware, on Cape Henlopen at the southern entrance to the bay. On 1 April, the *YP-52* rescued the forty-one survivors of the American tanker S.S. *Tiger*—which had been torpedoed by the *U-754* the previous day off Cape Henry while the ship waited to embark a pilot to enter port at Norfolk, Virginia—and landed them at Section Base, Little Creek.[18]

In April, two more ex-cutters (*CG-149* and *CG-203*) reported for duty as YPs *15* and *59*, respectively. The *15* was assigned to Naval Operating Base, Newport, Rhode Island, for patrol of the harbor entrance and the waters of the Rhode Island Sound, which run along the coast and stretch from the Narragansett Bay to where the sound opens into the Atlantic between Block Island, Rhode Island, and Martha's Vineyard, Massachusetts. On 10 June, the *YP-15* journeyed to Gay Head, located on the western shore of Martha's Vineyard, and back. Known for its quiet natural serenity, the town and surrounding area boast picturesque 130-foot tall clay cliffs, atop which sits a lighthouse.[19]

The YPs *19* and *27* joined the frontier force in June; the former vessel reported to Naval Operating Base, Newport and the latter to Little Creek, Virginia. The *YP-27* was thereafter assigned inner guard ship duties in Sector Two of the waters of the Fifth Naval District, which, stretching from Maryland to the northern region of North Carolina, were divided into three sectors.[20]

ADDITIONAL PATROL CRAFT SOUGHT

Seventy-nine Allied and neutral vessels were sunk around the world in the month of March, with all but four of the losses occurring in the coastal or offshore waters of North America. There was little change in the method of submarine attacks within the frontier, and no noticeable shift in location. Hatteras remained the favorite area, as the narrow continental shelf enabled the U-boats to operate in deep water close to shore with great effectiveness and comparative impunity. Ship losses might have been even greater had not Admiral King implemented new policies to help ensure greater secrecy as to ship departures and movements. On 5 March 1942 he ordered a halt to the practice of merchant vessels hoisting flags to indicate imminent departure, and within days suggested that whenever possible, ships should leave port after dark. These actions were followed by direction that the naval districts "dim out" coastal lights to reduce the glare that so plainly silhouetted vessels against the sky.[21]

These changes were obviously beneficial, but with 49 percent of the world's losses occurring within the Eastern Sea Frontier, Andrews remained anxious to obtain any vessel he could acquire. On 15 March, he sent all activities under his command a dispatch that revealed the pressing need for almost anything that could float: "Vessels in your district that can be purchased and are capable of carrying depth charges and guns and are fit for sea patrol report at once." Throughout the final few weeks of the month, additional help arrived in the form of twenty-four British trawlers lent by England for "anti-submarine operations under Command on East Coast North America." With two exceptions, they were coal burners, and none of them, Andrews believed, were suitable for operations in southern waters. Following a period of overhaul, fourteen were ready for duty, and Andrews made perceptible gains in other types of vessels as well. By the end of March, his force totaled ninety-four ships, exclusive of destroyers operating within the frontier. He also anticipated additional assistance from the Royal Navy in the form of five corvettes that were expected to arrive the following month.[22]

In April, Andrews implemented a system of patrolled anchorages, segmented voyages, short escorted convoys through endangered areas, and independent daylight sailings along shipping routes patrolled by surface craft and covered by airplanes. Five escort groups were formed from the available U.S. and Royal Navy ships, consisting of nine destroyers, five corvettes, nine patrol craft, two gunboats, and ten trawlers, with an additional eighteen small vessels set aside as a reserve pool. However, his assets were still insufficient to provide adequate protection for merchant ships traveling in convoys or to perform other tasks such as rescue at sea and offensive action against submarines. Accordingly, Andrews extended the existing practice of daylight sailing and convoying ships through only the most dangerous areas. Twenty-four vessels were lost to U-boats during the month, 33 percent of the U.S. and Allied total, making the frontier once again the most dangerous area for merchant shipping in the world.[23]

Having pressed all readily available Coast Guard cutters into service, and still in need of more vessels, Andrews sought to obtain some from the New England fishing fleet. Admiral King had written the commandant of the First Naval District on 12 February requesting that "immediate investigation and report be made as to the feasibility of arming a considerable number of the Cape Cod fishing boats, particularly with depth charges, for anti-submarine operations on the Grand Banks and other fishing grounds in the North Atlantic, and employing them as a volunteer force under Naval control." The commandant's response conveyed, in part, that his district's section of the Joint Merchant Vessel Board had made an extensive search of the district during the past two years to locate vessels that could be acquired and converted into patrol craft, and that the most satisfactory types were fishing boats of the trawler and dragger type. Many of these vessels would come from the Gloucester fishing fleet, including the *Donald Amirault* (YP-438), *Gertrude L. Thebaud* (WPYc-386), *Babe Sears* (YP-445), *Gov. Saltonstall* (AMc-56), *Edith L. Boudreau* (YP-437), *Raymonde* (YP-375), *Theresa M. Boudreau* (YP-430), *Dartmouth, Ida & Joseph,* and *Natalie III*.[24]

Interestingly, some of the trawlers acquired were 110-foot former World War I submarine chasers that had been sold as surplus following the war. Hurriedly built with an expected life span of only four-to-five years, the steel-framed wooden vessels had proved to be unusually durable, as well as exceptionally fast. Constructed with a pilot house a few feet aft of midship, the sub-chasers offered a long, narrow afterdeck to carry seine nets, space for an adequate fish hold, and room below the foc'sle to bunk upwards of twenty fishermen. Those converted to Gloucester "mackerel boats" included the *Mary W., Frank S. Grinnell, Three Sisters,* and *Serafina N*. Two former sub-chasers (most recently the fishing vessels *Whitby II* and *Fidus*) returned to naval service as the *YP-178* and *YP-180*. In March and April they patrolled waters from Watch Hill Light in the westernmost part of Rhode Island, to Montauk Point Lighthouse on New York's Long Island Sound, and to Sandy Point Shoals Light in Maryland. Other duties included assignment to the Race Patrol.[25]

Yachts were also being purchased from builders' yards or from private owners and converted into patrol craft. Examples of stately craft whose gleaming hulls and topside bright work were quickly turned to Navy gray included the *Agawam* (YP-208), *Althea* (YP-249), *Charmaire* (YP-335), *Effort II* (YP-175), *Freba* (YP-204), *Innisfail* (YP-354), *Kikai* (YP-206), and *Sunshine III* (YP-334). These acquisitions helped stem the tide, but in mid-March when Andrews began to escort full convoys through frontier waters, he still had an insufficient number of ships. Accordingly, four 79 to 89 foot private craft, which had been designated as base minesweepers, were converted to YPs, as was a former motor torpedo boat, *PT-8*, and three 110-foot steel-hulled fishing trawlers built by Fore River Shipyard of Quincy, Massachusetts. The Navy had acquired the sister ships *Salem, Lynn,* and *Cohasset* on 6 February 1942 and designated them as coastal minesweepers *AMc-200, 201,* and *202*. With the continued pressing need for patrol craft, the ships were reclassified as YPs in May.[26]

THIRD NAVAL DISTRICT

The headquarters of the Third Naval District was located in the Federal Office Building at 90 Church Street in New York City, as was Capt. H. M. Jensen, USN (Retired), who commanded the Inshore Patrol. The district's patrol yachts, coastal minesweepers, and YPs were distributed among section bases in April/May 1942 as shown below:

Ship Name or Designation (Former Type Vessel/Name and Name of Commanding Officer if Known)	Length Feet	Displ Tons	Year Built
Ambrose Section, Section Base, Tompkinsville, New York			
Zircon PY-16 (ex-yacht *Nakhoda*, Lt. Comdr. Cornelius M. Sullivan)	235' 4"	1,400	1929
Iolite PYc-24 (ex-yacht *Souris*/reclassified *YP-454*)	107	350	1930
Gallant PYc-29 (ex-yacht *North Star*, Lt. (jg) D. R. Stoneleigh)	177	224	1909
Acme AMc-61 (*Accentor*-class, Lt. Marcus L. Whitford)	97	205	1941
Assertive AMc-65 (*Accentor*-class)	97	205	1941
Ideal AMc-85 (*Accentor*-class)	97	205	1942
Limpkin AMc-48 (*Accentor*-class)	97	205	1941
Lorikeet AMc-49 (*Accentor*-class, Ens. Lawrence G. Fitzsimmons, Jr., USNR)	97	205	1941
Victor AMc-109 (*Accentor*-class)	97	205	1942
YP-9 (ex-patrol boat *CG-105*)	75	37	1924
YP-12 (ex-patrol boat *CG-204*)	75	37	1925
YP-47 (ex-patrol boat *CG-152*)	75	37	1925
YP-104 (ex-yacht *Marinette II*)	74		1926
YP-106 (ex-motor torpedo boat *PT-69*, Chief Boatswain's Mate Frank Killian, USN Retired)	72	40	1941
YP-189 (ex-*Ace*)	109	74	1918
YP-249 (ex-yacht *Althea*, Ens. W. R. Herrick, USNR)	106	118	1930
YP-252 (ex-*Wild Duck*)	104	87	1929
YP-253 (ex-*Montauk*)	122' 1"	111	1919
YP-254 (ex-*Norseman*, Lt. (jg) W. E. Paris, USNR)	90		1939
YP-256 (ex-*Phantom*)	68	50	1925
YP-257 (ex-*Alice and Mildred*)	84	78	1928
YP-387 (ex-fishing trawler *Cohasset/AMc-200*)	110	301	1941
Montauk Section, New London, Connecticut: Capt. A. A. Corwin, USN (Ret.)			
Sylph PY-12 (ex-yacht *Intrepid*)	205	858	1929
Sapphire PYc-2 (ex-yacht *Buccaneer*, Lt. A. N. Daniels, USNR)	165' 4"	450	1929
Acme AMc-61 (*Accentor*-class, Lt. Marcus L. Whitford)	97	205	1941
Demand AMc-74 (*Accentor*-class)	97	205	1941
Dominant AMc-76 (*Accentor*-class)	97	205	1941

Ship Name or Designation (Former Type Vessel/Name and Name of Commanding Officer if Known)	Length Feet	Displ Tons	Year Built
YP-8 (ex-patrol boat *CG-191*)	75	37	1925
YP-175 (ex-motor yacht *Effort II*)	80	55	1928
YP-178 (ex-*Whitby II*, former sub-chaser *SC-168*)	110		1918
YP-230 (ex-*Eryholme*)	72		1930
YP-265 (ex-yacht *Go Deo*)	62		1937
YP-388 (ex-fishing trawler *Lynn/AMc-201*)	110	301	1941
YP-389 (ex-fishing trawler *Salem/AMc-202*)	110	301	1941[27]

On 8 April 1942, the patrol yacht *Zircon* rescued sixteen survivors from the American freighter *Otho*, which the *U-754* had sunk five days earlier about two hundred miles east of Cape Henry, Virginia. The Navy was then fitting most merchant vessels with a naval gun, and an officer-in-charge and group of sailors, termed the "U.S. Navy Armed Guard," maintained and employed the gun in defense of the ship. One of the survivors from the *Otho* was an Armed Guard sailor. The *Zircon* and other yachts were usually employed as units of the offshore patrol and as convoy escort ships. Six weeks later, on 26 May, the patrol yacht *Sapphire* rescued the thirty survivors of the U.S. freighter *Plow City*, sunk five days earlier by the *U-588*. The submarine interrogated one crewman on board before returning him to his shipmates with rum and cigarettes; U-boat sailors also helped the Americans right a capsized lifeboat.[28]

The YPs assigned to the Ambrose Section carried out night patrols of the net and boom installed between South Beach, Staten Island, and Norton's Point on Coney Island. Outside New York Harbor, they conducted patrols from Sandy Hook, New Jersey, to the whistle buoy at the entrance to Gedney's Channel (the deep-water entrance to the harbor), and from that buoy to the Rockaway Inlet breakwater on the south coast of Long Island. Vessels on night patrol were under orders to report, upon their return the following morning to Section Base, Tompkinsville (on Staten Island), the existing visibility and sea conditions and any light or glow seen the previous night which might silhouette and threaten the safety of ships. A representative report on 7 May 1942 noted:

> 50 Street lights from Ft. Tilden and East Rockaway Inlet visible more than one mile to seaward. Sky glow over Brooklyn and Manhattan sufficient to silhouette ships in outer harbor and several miles to seaward. Darkening of Coney Island and Staten Island effective.[29]

Commander Inshore Patrol received word on 9 May that the U.S. Navy Blimp *K-6* had made contact with a submarine approximately three miles from Scotland Buoy, which marked a shoal off Sandy Hook called the Outer Middle Ground. The *YP-189* and submarine chaser *PC-64* were ordered from their patrol duties to search the area, and the *YP-9, YP-254*, and sub-chaser *PC-507*, berthed at base, directed to prepare to get underway immediately. All efforts to locate the submarine were unsuccessful.[30]

Lt. (jg) Douglas Elton Fairbanks, Jr., USNR, the American actor, was briefly assigned (20 February to 13 March 1942) to duty with the Inshore Patrol, Ambrose Section.[31]

The YPs based at New London, Connecticut, normally patrolled the waters near Race Rock Light, southwest of Fishers Island at the entrance to New York's Long Island Sound. This routine changed on 8 May when commander, Montauk Section received a report at 0730 of a submarine sighted on an eastbound course five to seven miles west of Weekapaug Point, Rhode Island, and sent the *YP-175* to investigate. Before her arrival, two PT boats dropped depth charges on a contact, twelve miles east of Southeast Light, Block Island, at 0955, and returned to Newport, leaving the *Eagle*-class patrol craft *PE-48* at the scene. The hunt for the submarine continued and mid-afternoon the *Sapphire* launched two depth charges off Great Salt Pond, Block Island, following which the *YP-175* and sub-chaser *PC-826* were ordered to the scene to assist. No anti-submarine attack was forthcoming, however, as the enemy seemingly had eluded all pursuers.[32]

With one or more U-boats at large, the commandant of the First Naval District ordered that all westbound traffic through the Cape Cod Canal be held in Buzzard's Bay anchorage, and commander Inshore Patrol, Montauk Section ordered the *YP-230* to halt all eastbound traffic west of Race. At 1925, a submarine was sighted southwest of Point Judith, and Coast Guard Station, Trumbull (at New London) ordered the cutter *CG-135* to assist *YP-230* in stopping eastbound traffic in Long Island Sound. After anti-submarine efforts came to naught, westbound Cap Code Canal traffic, ships detained in Buzzard's Bay, and eastbound traffic from Long Island Sound, were released.[33]

LOSS OF THE PATROL CRAFT *YP-387* AND *YP-389*

Increased Eastern Sea Frontier requirements—including convoy escort duty, and patrol of defensive minefields (intended to protect anchorages where merchant ships assembled to form convoys) to ensure that friendly vessels did not unknowingly stray into them—was placing an unremitting and increasing strain upon the assets available. Accordingly, YPs assigned to District Inshore Patrols began to be used as escort vessels and in other roles when larger, more heavily-armed ships were not available.[34]

Photo 10-1

Fishing schooner *Cohasset* before her conversion to Coastal Minesweeper *AMc-202* and later *YP-389*.
Courtesy of NavSource, http://www.navsource.org/archives/11/03202.htm

An example was the *YP-389* (assigned to the Montauk Section of the Inshore Patrol), built as the fishing trawler *Cohasset* for R. O'Brien and Co. of 34 Boston Fish Pier. The Navy had acquired and equipped her and her two 110-foot sister ships, *Salem* and *Lynn*, for use as minesweepers before refitting them as patrol vessels, a duty for which they were not particularly well-suited. True sub-chasers had good speed and range, were fitted with sonar to find submarines, and had sufficient armament to dispatch them. The *YP-389*'s top speed was perhaps 10 knots on a good day with a following sea. She had no sound gear and her armament was unimpressive, a single bow-mounted 3-inch deck gun, two .30-caliber machine guns, and four depth charges on racks with two spares. The vessel also had no fresh water storage tank as her designer had believed she would only remain at sea long enough to bring in a full catch. Thus crew quarters had no showers, nor, for that matter, proper ventilation. The trawler, however, was representative of the types of small vessels that were being pressed into service to meet the emergency conditions that existed on the coast.[35]

On May 20, soon after the YPs *387*, *388*, and *389* reported for duty to the Third Naval District, the *387* was heading north from the Delaware Capes to meet a convoy from New York, when she was run down by the 19,250-ton American freighter *Jason* (a former U.S. Navy collier that had entered service in June 1913). The freighter stopped, picked up fifteen survivors, and, after transferring all but one man to the cutter *USCG-477*, proceeded to Delaware Bay. Six members of the ship's complement were lost or unaccounted for. Two days later, the same cutter reported sighting a ship's mast—with ensign (American flag) and call letters of the *YP-387* (signal flag hoist) still flying from it—protruding from the water. The *YP-334* later confirmed finding the mast, as well as a small lifeboat, at 39° 01' north, 74° 39' west. This site, where the ship sank in forty feet of water with all depth charges set on "safe," was marked with a buoy.[36]

On 24 May, the *YP-388* and *389* were ordered out of New London, Connecticut, to investigate wreckage and help search for lifeboats reported adrift south of Long Island, New York. The lifeboats with survivors from the American merchantman S.S. *Plow City* were located in the late afternoon by the *Sapphire*. (The merchant vessel had been sunk by the *U-588* two days earlier about 200 miles off Cape May.) The *388* and *389* entered New York Bay two days later, on 26 May, and proceeded to Section Base, Tompkinville where the commanding officer of the *389*, Lt. Roderick Johnstone Philips, presented a list of repairs and alterations his ship required before transit south to North Carolina. The 43-year old Philips was a naval reserve officer called to active duty the previous January. The *388* and *389* were being sent to the Fifth Naval District, which included the waters of the north coastal region of North Carolina along with those of Maryland and Virginia. The Sullivan Dry Dock and Repair Co. of Brooklyn installed a fresh water tank in the *YP-389*, scraped and painted her bottom, and fitted baffles to prevent light from escaping from the engine room and galley hatches at night. At completion, she stood out of port, bound for Norfolk, Virginia, as an escort for an "eight and one-half knot" convoy, but proved unable to keep up with the merchant vessels.[37]

On arrival, the YP laid over at Naval Operating Base, Norfolk for six days, during which Philips tried to get some work done on his engines and obtain information regarding the ship's operating schedule, both to no avail. At the end of this layover, he was ordered to proceed to Section Base, Morehead City, North Carolina, and to report to the senior officer at the Coast Guard station on Ocracoke Island. While at the Section Base, Philips was able to get his engines overhauled.[38]

Soon thereafter, the *YP-389* put to sea on her first patrol. On 9 June she and the *YP-388* escorted the American cargo ship S.S. *West Lashaway* south to waters off Cape Lookout lighthouse. Philips used this underway period to test fire his 3-inch gun, and found that something was wrong with the firing mechanism. On returning to base for provisioning, further orders, and needed repairs, a chief gunner's mate inspected the gun and found that the firing spring was broken. This information was passed to "operations" at Morehead City, which agreed to obtain the replacement part. However, necessity soon trumped discretion. Provisions were put aboard the ship and with her only credible weapon inoperative, the *YP-389* was ordered back out on patrol.[39]

Philips' orders were for his ship to operate in the vicinity of Hatteras in order to warn friendly shipping away from a defensive minefield laid to protect the area around Diamond Shoals and Cape Hatteras from submarines, but which during the time he had been in port had claimed the S.S. *F. W. Abrams*. Through a combination of unfortunate circumstances, including a lack of proper navigational information and bad weather in which her master lost sight of the cutter providing escort services, the American tanker strayed into the minefield and sank. Sent to prevent any reoccurrence of such a tragedy, the *YP-389* took up her Hatteras patrol on 14 June. In the late evening on the 18th, she was five miles west of Diamond Shoals, steering a northeasterly course at six knots on a warm, quiet night, beneath a dark and nearly moonless sky. Mindful of the need to be vigilant near the field—into which he dare not stray, but also could not operate very far from—Philips had posted lookouts on the bridge wings, as well as on the flying bridge and on the stern. The ship reached the end of her run around midnight, turned, and began the return leg on a southwesterly course.[40]

In the early morning hours, Philips had the deck (was the officer of the deck on the bridge) when a cry from the starboard bridge wing caused him to look in that direction. Stunned to see a U-boat appear out of the gloom to shoreward, he ordered battle stations set. As the executive and engineering officers, Ens. Ray P. Baker, Jr. and Ens. R. M. McKellar, raced topside, having been awakened at 0245 by the alarm, the submarine took the ship under fire with its 20mm anti-aircraft gun fitted on the after part of the conning tower, followed by heavier rounds from the 88mm deck gun. U-boat commanders normally engaged vessels at a fairly close range, because, while their deck gun was capable of a rate of fire of 15 to 18 rounds per minute with a good crew, it had no range finder. Moreover, submarines were poor gun platforms as they rolled a lot in any type of sea.[41]

This submarine, the *U-701*, had left Brest in northwestern France on 19 May and proceeded a short distance down the coast before putting in at Lorient to load mines. She stood out of the German submarine base the next day bound for the Chesapeake Bay to operate with seven other U-boats, dubbed group *Hecht*. Five of the *Hecht* boats, including the *U-701*, were to participate in special operations involving a coordinated submarine assault along America's east coast. Three units were to mine Delaware Bay, Boston Harbor, and the Chesapeake Bay, while the remaining two boats landed *Abwehr* (intelligence) agents ashore on Long Island, New York, and in northern Florida. During the Atlantic crossing, the *701*'s commanding officer, *Kapitänleutnant* Horst Degen, received a radio message from Donitz on 8 June, ordering him to lay the mines as early as possible on the night of 11 June, followed by new guidance the next day: "execute task as long as situation is favorable, no time limitation." Degen reported "execution of fouling" on 12 June, signifying that he had laid the mines off the entrance to the Chesapeake Bay. With this chore completed, he was free to begin hunting shipping in his assigned operational area, which ranged from fifteen miles south of Cape Lookout north to the Chesapeake Light. (Degen's war diary was later lost when the *U-701* sank. References to the following entries are from a U-boat Command Headquarters reconstruction based on information he provided to Donitz.) Degen found that merchant vessels transiting the Cape Hatteras area were moving only during the late afternoon and early evening (when escorts could detect periscopes breaking the surface and attack) and that the shipping off Cape Lookout was particularly well protected. On 16 June he noted:

> Cape Hatteras: traffic only between 1700 and 1900 hours. Cape Lookout: Heavy air, stationary sea patrols, good bombs.

Degen sighted a tanker and freighters in convoy in the latter area, but wisely chose to let them pass, and instead attacked a large freighter sailing alone. The ship was very lucky as both torpedoes inexplicably missed.[42]

A diary entry for 17 June recorded that the *U-701* had been depth-charged that day ("3 destroyers on N-course in formation and a buoy layer. 1 searching destroyer dropping isolated depth charges at position"), which resulted in damage to some gauges and the submarine's main periscope. Degen received a congratulatory message from Donitz the next day, informing him that one ship had already been damaged by the minefield he had laid off Virginia. (The *U-701* would be the only submarine of group *Hecht* to achieve its goals, and the mining operation would be the only one in American waters to achieve any appreciable success during the war.) In a 20 June report, Degen summarized conditions encountered over the previous two days, including a chance meeting with, and ensuing destruction of, the *YP-389*:

> Situation at Cape Hatteras: Traffic in batches, no longer by day, [shipping] recently [began to] set off far from land, [and] rounds Diamond Shoal 10 nm [nautical miles] distant. Sighted 18 June 2 tankers, 1 freighter in line ahead [of] formation without escort, N-course, far out of effective range. Was surprised by [a] guard vessel in the haze. Destroyed in 1-1/2 hourly artillery combat.

Having surfaced off Hatteras and sighted what Degen later indicated he thought was the same cutter that had previously dropped depth charges near the *U-701*, he took it under fire. *YP-389* replied with machinegun fire. Over the next hour and a half, the German raider expended a combination of semi-armor piercing, high explosive, and incendiary rounds, apparently because her gun crew seized every available shell in the ready-use magazine. There were twenty-eight rounds in the magazine, which enabled the gun crew to start firing immediately after surfacing without having to wait for shells to be brought up from the main magazine inside the pressure hull.[43]

As off-watch sailors aboard the YP boiled out of crew's quarters on deck, an 88mm round killed the first to emerge and injured three others, forcing the other crew members to take shelter behind trawling winches. Philips notified the Coast Guard station at Ocracoke that he was under enemy attack and also warned Fifth Naval District ships and aircraft. The Coast Guard replied that help was on the way. With the 3-inch gun broken, Fireman 2nd Class Crabb and 1st Class Wilson returned fire with .30-caliber machine guns mounted in exposed positions on the signal bridge and the boat deck.[44]

Philips had initially turned seaward in order to minimize his ship's cross section by presenting only her stern to the enemy's guns. However, aware that he could neither outgun nor outrun the submarine (which could make nearly 18 knots on the surface), he ordered a westerly course towards shore, from which he thought help would be coming. The U-boat twice approached the YP sufficiently close for Philips to order Fireman 3rd Class Cole to drop depth charges, but they apparently had no effect. For a time, it appeared that the ex-trawler might escape into shallow water nearer shore, where the larger submarine dared not follow lest it run aground. The enemy was finding it difficult to score hits on the *YP-389* due to her low profile. However, the longer the one-sided battle lasted, the more likely it was that even in the gloom, the gunners would find the range. Moreover, the YP was no longer returning fire. Philips had ordered his machine gunners to cease fire because small caliber projectiles were not effective against the U-boat and muzzle flashes were pinpointing their location for the Germans.[45]

Another 88mm round hit, activating the engine room fire extinguishing system, flooding the space with CO_2, and forcing the watch team to evacuate to above deck. Thereafter, the *U-701* closed to within two hundred yards of the besieged vessel and began to fire pointblank into her starboard side. An incendiary round stuck the bridge, setting the chartroom on fire, and a short time later the YP's stern was also in flames.[46]

No further efforts by the officers and men could save the vessel, and the commanding officer thus gave the order to abandon ship. The survivors slipped over the side with only their lifejackets. The life rafts had been shot away and the life boats could not be lowered safely due to persistent enemy fire. Philips stayed at the helm until the last crewman was safely away. With the throttles full ahead, he then abandoned as the *U-701* continued its dogged pursuit of the YP into the distance, continuing to shell it until the ship sank at 0414, five to eight miles northeast of Buoy No. 4. After entering the water, Philips gathered his men around him and helped to keep their spirits up until they were rescued by the cutters *CG-462* and *CG-481* at 0800. All but six of the eighteen survivors were injured or seriously injured. They, as well as the body of a crewmember later found washed up on the beach, were taken to Morehead City, from which four grievously hurt men were transferred to Norfolk Navy Hospital. The remaining five missing sailors had been seen killed, or were assumed dead, with likely some or all of them interned in the hulk of the sunken *YP-389*. (A list of the officers and men assigned to the vessel and their status following the battle is provided in Appendix F.) [47]

THE END OF *U-701*

Horst Degen sank four ships and damaged another five by torpedo, gunfire, or delayed-action mine laid at the entrance to the Chesapeake Bay during what would be *U-701*'s final war patrol. On 15 June, a mine sank the British trawler HMS *Kingston Ceylonite* (FY-214) and on that same day, others damaged the American tankers S.S. *Robert C. Tuttle* and M.V. *Esso Augusta* and the destroyer *Bainbridge* (DD-246). Two days later a mine sank the American merchantman S.S. *Santore* in the same field. After sending the YP to the bottom, an action more challenging and time consuming than he had envisioned, Degen turned to his principal weapons. Between 26 and 28 June 1942, he torpedoed the Norwegian merchant ship *Tamesis* and the U.K. tanker *British Freedom*—damaging both, but not sinking them—and then sank the American tanker S.S. *William Rockefeller*. A week later his luck ran out. On 7 July a USAAF Hudson A29 out of Cherry Point, North Carolina, caught the submarine surfaced and taking in fresh air off Cape Hatteras, and sank it with three 325-pound depth charges. Two days later, a Coast Guard sea plane recovered seven survivors including Degen, 110 miles offshore. The men were first taken to Fort Hunt (an interrogation center for German prisoners at Sheridan Point on the Potomac River in Virginia) and then interned in various POW camps until the end of the war. During interviews, surviving crew members indicated that they considered the destruction of the little ship a wasteful and untidy piece of work, and the captain gave the impression that he was ashamed of it.[48]

AFTERMATH

> *The YP-389 reveals the difficulties involved in converting small vessels for war purposes . . . . She assumed this duty only because no ships adequate to the task were available in the Frontier.*
> —Rear Adm. Adolphus Andrews, Commander, Eastern Sea Frontier, war diary entry, June 1942

Andrews praised Lt. Philips in a war diary entry for "keeping his ship afloat in the face of concentrated enemy fire for one hour coupled with his demonstrations of leadership in keeping his men together in the four hours they waited in the water." He then turned to the key reason for the loss of *YP-389*: "Section bases, operating bases, navy yards are all at the present time overworked and incapable of meeting every demand made upon them but a man of war deprived of her main battery is worse than useless while performing her duties at sea." Andrews, who remained chronically short of ships in the face of a determined adversary, expressed his frustration in a separate entry by quoting Alfred Thayer Mahan, emphasizing the importance of quality personnel: "Historically, iron men in wooden ships are better than wooden men in iron ships," and then observing himself, "Historically the point may be well taken, but it does not apply to the conditions of the present when neither iron men nor iron ships are enough."[49]

On 7 August 2009, a NOAA-led expedition, part of a multi-year effort to study World War II shipwrecks sunk in 1942 off the North Carolina coast, located the wreckage of the *YP-389* in 300 feet of water about eighteen miles off Hatteras Inlet. The small ex-trawler was one of 137 vessels—Allied and German military and merchant ships—lost off North Carolina during World War II, of which about forty have been located to date.[50]

FOURTH NAVAL DISTRICT

Navy Yard Philadelphia was the headquarters of the Fourth Naval District, commanded by Rear Adm. Adolphus E. Watson, USN. Capt. H. B. Mecleary, USN (Retired), who commanded the inshore patrol, was located at Section Base, Cape May, New Jersey, as were the following vessels in April/May 1942:

Section Base, Cape May, New Jersey

Ship Name or Designation (Former Type Vessel/Name and Name of Commanding Officer if Known)	Length Feet	Displ Tons	Year Built
Alabaster PYc-21 (ex-yacht *Alamo, Rellimpa, Ranley, Ronaele*, Lt. Comdr. Adolph F. Edel, USNR)	148	385	1932
Blue Jay AMc-23 (ex-fishing dragger *Charles S. Ashley*, Lt. Hiram S. Walker, Jr., USNR)	93	185	1936
Canary AMc-25 (ex-fishing vessel *John G. Murley*)	80	165	1940
Egret AMc-24 (ex-fishing vessel *Julia-Eleanor*)	90	110	1937
Flamingo AMc-22 (ex-fishing dragger *Harriet N. Eldridge*)	93	199	1940
Roller AMc-52 (*Accentor*-class, Lt. (jg) H. E. Ferrill, USNR)	97	201	1941
Skimmer AMc-53 (*Accentor*-class)	97	201	1941
YP-11 (ex-patrol boat *CG-196*)	75	37	1925
YP-49 (ex-patrol boat *CG-182*)	75	37	1925
YP-110 (ex-motor torpedo boat *PT-8*)	81	52	1940
YP-221 (ex-*Marmot*)	92	108	1936
YP-259 (ex-wooden motor yacht *Selma, Consort III, Scout VI*)	70.5	69	1928
YP-334 (ex-yacht *Sunshine III*)	100	120	1930[51]

The YPs based at Cape May carried out patrols in area waters, usually in the vicinity of a defensive minefield and Overfills Shoal in Delaware Bay. Occasionally, one might be assigned to assist the Station Ship positioned at the Harbor Entrance Control Point. This routine changed following implementation of a system of patrolled anchorages, segmented voyages, and short escorted convoys. Requirements to accompany merchant ships north to New York and south to the Virginia Capes, resulted in YPs making the Delaware Capes-south-to-Winter Quarter Shoal portion of the run, and the return transit, with northbound convoys. Due to the war, the lightship that had been stationed at the shoal off Virginia to warn mariners had been replaced by a buoy which also served as a reference point for coastal traffic and for the approach to Chesapeake Bay from the north.[52]

The newly enacted measures were only partially successful against the German submarines, which continued to sink shipping and elude pursuers. On 1 May, thirty-six survivors of the Norwegian merchant ship S.S. *Bidevind* were landed at the Coast Guard Station near Toms River in New Jersey. The *U-752* had torpedoed her at 0543 the previous morning about seventy-five miles southeast of Ambrose

Lightship. The ship's confidential publications in a weighted bag went down with her at 40° 13' north, 73° 46' west. On 2 May 1942, a Navy blimp made a submarine contact about ten miles off Rehoboth Beach, following which the cutters *CG-471* and *CG-477* dropped depth charges with undetermined results. Six days later, the fishing vessel *Irene and May* brought in a lifeboat and ten survivors from the torpedoed S.S. *Pipestone County*. The American freighter had been bound from Trinidad to Boston when sunk by the *U-576* about 475 miles east of Cape Henry, Virginia. The submarines continued to operate with seeming impunity. On 10 May, the *YP-259* reported sighting a periscope 250 yards away at 38° 47' north, 74° 54' west. She dropped one depth charge over the spot where it had quickly disappeared, and noted a slight oil slick, not indicative of a kill. Blimps and planes also searched the area without results.[53]

FIFTH NAVAL DISTRICT

Rear Adm. Manley H. Simons, USN, headquartered at Naval Operating Base, Norfolk, Virginia, commanded the Fifth Naval District. The inshore patrol in March 1942 was comprised of eight old Navy destroyers—*Cole, Dallas, Dickerson, Dupont, Hamilton, Herbert, Roper*, and *Upshur*, five Coast Guard cutters—*Calypso, Cuyahoga, Dione, Legare*, and *Rush*, and the patrol yacht *Tourmaline*. These vessels patrolled Sections I, II, and III, and, as need dictated, the destroyers rotated to other duties or entered Norfolk Naval Shipyard for repairs. The British trawlers HMS *Hertfordshire, Norwich City*, and *Duhamel* reported for duty to the inshore patrol on 27 March, and were joined by the *St. Zero* the following day. In April 1942, additional destroyers rotated in and out and the USC&GS Ship *Oceanographer* joined the inshore patrol. To the south at Section Base, Morehead City, North Carolina, the inshore patrol under Comdr. E. J. Estess included the minesweeper *Kestrel* (AMc-5)—a former fishing boat named the *Chanco*—and several Coast Guard cutters.[54]

On 18 March, the *Tourmaline* and *Cuyahoga* rescued eight survivors from the British tanker *San Demetrio*, sunk by the *U-404* on 16 March. Two and a half weeks later, on 6 April, the *U-552* torpedoed the British tanker S.S. *Splendour* and the Norwegian whale factory ship S.S. *Lancing* about fourteen miles from the Hatteras Light in the Outer Banks of North Carolina. The *St. Zero*, assigned as an escort for the *Splendour*, delivered an unsuccessful attack on the submarine, and picked up the master, thirty-five crew members, and five U.S. Navy Armed Guard gunners and landed them at Norfolk.⁵⁵

LOSS OF THE PATROL YACHT *CYTHERA*

The patrol yacht *Cythera* (PY-26) left Norfolk at 0300 on 1 May 1942 en route to Pearl Harbor via the Panama Canal, but was never seen or heard from again. After she failed to arrive at Christobal on 8 May as expected, commander, Offshore Patrol Atlantic of the Panama Sea Frontier received orders to search for the yacht. The resulting hunt for the thirty-five-year-old vessel in waters of the Panama and Eastern Sea Frontiers produced negative results, as succinctly noted in a 30 May Eastern Sea Frontier patrol log entry:

> Nothing has been heard from *Cythera* (PY-26) which departed Hampton Roads 1 May [1942] to arrive Canal Zone May 8. Ship considered lost.⁵⁶

Following an unsuccessful search, a lack of communications with the *Cythera*, and her failure to appear in the Canal Zone, the Navy was forced to announce formally that the ship was lost "due to suspected enemy action." On 2 June notices were sent to family members advising them that their husbands/sons had been placed in a "missing status." It was policy to hold missing personnel in this status for one year before declaring them dead. However, although the Navy assumed that all seventy-one officers and men aboard the yacht had perished at sea, this presumption was not the case for two crew members. A few weeks later an article appeared in the German newspaper, *Deutsche Zeitung* in Den Niederland, announcing that two American sailors "Charles and James" had been brought back from Atlantic coastal waters.⁵⁷

The *Cythera* was a product of Ramage & Ferguson, a shipbuilding yard in Leith, Scotland. Built as the *Agawa* for William L. Harkness, an oil baron with investments in Standard Oil, newspaper articles about her launching on 20 September 1906 described the yacht's cabins as elegant and her hull lines as graceful. Shortly after America entered World War I, the ex-*Agawa*, then named *Cythera*, was leased to the United States Navy by the Harkness family, and her once gleaming white hull soon sported a black and white camouflage pattern. Following refitting, the patrol yacht was commissioned on 20 October 1917 and, ordered overseas, operated from Gibraltar on escort and patrol duty in the Mediterranean. Two officers who commanded her, Capt. Raymond L. Jack, USCG, and Comdr. Walter Gordon Roper, USN, received the Navy Cross for transporting and escorting troops and supplies through "waters infested with enemy submarines and mines." Following the war, the *Cythera* arrived at New York City on 5 February 1919, was decommissioned, and returned to her owners.[58]

Photo 10-2

Patrol yacht *Cythera* (PY-26) in port, March 1942.
Photo # NH 83392 courtesy of the Naval History and Heritage Command

The Navy bought the yacht from the Harkness family in 1942, three weeks after the attack on Pearl Harbor. Following its delivery to the Philadelphia Navy Yard, she once again underwent refitting for naval service, receiving three 3-inch/50 gun mounts and two stern depth charge racks. The *Cythera* was placed in commission on 3 March under the command of fifty-six-year-old Lt. Comdr. Thomas W. Rudderow. After being commissioned an ensign in the Naval Militia of Pennsylvania on 14 July 1916, Rudderow had served during World War I aboard the transport *De Kalb* (ID# 3010), and destroyers *Allen* (DD-66) and *McCall* (DD-28) of the Destroyer Forces at Queenstown, Ireland. Discharged from active duty on 25 June 1919, he remained in the Naval Reserve until he was transferred to the Honorary Retired List on 1 September 1939. When recalled to active duty on 3 January 1942, he was serving as the superintendent and commanding officer of the Pennsylvania Nautical School ship *Seneca*. Filling out the wardroom of the *Cythera* were four reserve officers: Lt. Casper L. Zacharias, and Ensigns Robert Earl Brister, William Logan Bunker, Jr., and Stratton Christensen.[59]

After departing Norfolk, bound for Pearl Harbor and duty with the Pacific Fleet, the *Cythera* had been at sea for less than twenty-four hours when she was torpedoed by the *U-402*. She quickly slid beneath the waters of the cold North Atlantic. The submarine, commanded by Baron Siegfried von Forstner, had been cruising on the surface some 115 miles off Cape Fear, North Carolina, when around midnight, on 1 May, the bridge lookout spotted a small warship zigzagging on a southerly course. The submarine submerged and launched a torpedo attack. Two torpedoes struck the *Cythera*, splitting her in half. As she sank, depth charges on her stern exploded resulting in additional crew casualties. The *U-402* surfaced and plucked the only survivors, Seaman 2nd Class James Monroe Brown and Pharmacist's Mate 1st Class Charles Harold Carter, from the sea.[60]

The submarine turned on its search light to inspect debris floating in the large oil slick from the ship. Brown and Carter were found covered in oil and clinging to a small raft. Taken aboard as prisoners, they requested to be returned to the water, to which Von Forstner replied: "No, boys, the war's over for you." During the return voyage to France, the two Americans were treated well, given cigarettes and allowed to go topside for fresh air every day. In the almost three-week trip to the submarine base at St. Nazaire, the U-boat crew and prisoners formed a bond and the Americans invited the Germans to visit them in the United States after the war. On reaching port, the captives were transported to *Marlag und Milag Nord*, a POW camp for Navy and Merchant Marine personnel located near Westertimke, Germany. Brown was sent to a POW camp in Upper Silezia, Poland, until finally liberated in April 1945 by forward units of Patton's Third Army. He was later returned to America, along with Carter, who was released in May.[61]

SIXTH NAVAL DISTRICT

The commandant of the Sixth Naval District was Rear Adm. William H. Allen, USN. Among his forces in spring 1942, he had the patrol yacht *Ruby* (PY-21) which was employed in anti-submarine offshore patrols, and inshore patrol units based at Charleston, South Carolina, and Mayport, Florida. Section Base, Southport, North Carolina, under Lt. Comdr. S. B. Haskell, and Section Base, Savannah, Georgia, on Cockspur Island, commanded by Comdr. W. H. Stiles, Jr., USN (Retired), had Coast Guard cutters and small craft (H.P. #2, 5, and 6) for guard ship duty and patrol of their area waters.

Ship Name or Designation (Former Type Vessel/Name and Name of Commanding Officer if Known)	Length Feet	Displ Tons	Year Built
Section Base, Charleston, South Carolina:			
Exultant AMc-79 (*Accentor*-class)	97	219	1942
Fearless AMc-80 (*Accentor*-class)	97	219	1941
YP-24 (ex-cutter *CG-106*, Lt. Harry C. Warmington, USNR)	75	37	1924
YP-216 (ex-*Lark III*)	57	38	1939
YP-217 (ex-yacht *Zapala*)	111	158	1927
YP-218 (ex-yacht *Consort IV*)	86	87	1936
YP-219 (ex-yacht *Nancy D.*)	71' 1"		1924
YP-241 (ex-ketch *Morning Star*)	80' 5"	62	1938
Section Base, Mayport, Florida: Lt. Comdr. M. R. Sanders, USNR			
Turaco AMc-55 (*Accentor*-class, Lt. (jg) Allard B. Heyward, USNR)	98	275	1941
Emerald PYc-1 (ex-yacht *Tamarack IV*, *Savitar*, Lt. (jg) Robert W. Graham, USNR)	96	104	1922
YP-31 (ex-patrol boat *CG-167*)	75	37	1925
YP-32 (ex-patrol boat *CG-208*)	75	37	1925[62]

Assignments for the Charleston-based YPs included guard ship duty at Station No. 1, patrol and convoy duty, and escorting inbound or outbound ships entering or leaving harbor. In the Mayport-Jacksonville area, the *Turaco* swept waters around St. Johns Lightship (located five miles offshore, marking the approach for the St Johns River), and conducted patrols from St. Johns River jetty to Ponte Vedra Beach. The YPs patrolled waters between St. Johns Lightship and Brunswick, Georgia, while the yacht *Emerald* operated off the Florida coast or served as a harbor entrance control ship in the St. Johns River. Unlike other areas, where lightships were removed during the war to prevent them from becoming easy kills for enemy submarines, the 135-foot St. Johns Lightship (LV-84) remained on station, with no armament.[63]

On 8 April, the *YP-32* was patrolling along the northeast Florida coast from Ponte Vedra (a part of the Jacksonville beaches area) to Fernandina, below the Georgia border, when at 0408 it was ordered to investigate flares and explosions ten miles east-northeast of San Simons Island, Georgia. In late morning, the YP picked up forty-seven survivors from the American tankers S.S. *Oklahoma* and S.S. *Esso Baton Rouge*, torpedoed by the *U-123*. After arriving with the men at the Coast Guard dock on San Simons Island at 1605 they turned them over to the Coast Guard.[64]

The *Turaco* left Section Base, Mayport at 0236 the following day en route to the position of the torpedoed American merchantman S.S. *Esparta*, sunk by the *U-123*. Following her arrival at a little past dawn, the minesweeper searched for survivors, who had apparently already been picked up. The *YP-31* had also proceeded to the *Esparta* from her patrol area in the vicinity of St. Johns Lightship. She made contact at 0655 with a suspected sub a few miles to the north and, after using her sound gear to refine its course, dropped a depth charge forty-five minutes later, although it failed to explode due to shallow water. The YP lost contact at 0835, and, after regaining the submarine on sound gear thirty minutes later, dropped a second depth charge at 0947. It also failed to explode and contact was again lost. The patrol craft returned to Mayport at 1752.[65]

U-BOAT OFFENSIVE SHIFTS TO THE GULF OF MEXICO AND CARIBBEAN

Two days later, on 11 April, the *U-123* sank the American tanker S.S. *Gulfamerica* about five miles off Jacksonville in full view of people on shore. At age 85, *Kapitänleutnant* Reinhard Hardegan recalled that night in 1942 off Jacksonville, on Florida's northeast coast, during which his U-boat sank the *Gulfamerica*:

> There was moonshine, how you say, moonlight. There were lights on the shore. And many people. Bars were open. People were on the beaches.

He could see a roller coaster, all lit up, and streams of car headlights heading toward the shore. To avoid hitting civilians near the shore with the gun rounds often used to finish off torpedoed vessels, he positioned the *U-123* between the coast and the tanker so that he could shoot out to sea. Over the course of the war, Hardengan, one of Germany's top U-boat aces, sent twenty-one merchant ships to the bottom and damaged four more, sank an auxiliary warship and damaged a converted Cunard-White Star Limited steam passenger ship, the British armed merchant cruiser HMS *Aurania*.[66]

Despite Hardegan's successes and those of other U-boat commanders, full convoy protection resulted in an immediate reduction of shipping losses off the East Coast, and Donitz directed more U-boats to the Gulf of Mexico where pickings were easier. By the end of 1942, the number of merchant vessels sunk by U-boats had dropped dramatically, due to several measures, including requiring coastal towns and cities to extinguish their lights at night, instituting a convoy system, and increasing the number of escort and patrol vessels. Continuously increasing aircraft patrols also made east coast waters more dangerous for the U-boats and convoys more difficult to attack.

11

Gulf, Panama, and Caribbean Sea Frontiers

> *All survivors picked up. Proceeding Venice, Louisiana, full speed to arrive about 0130 EWT [local time]. Clear docks for landing. Most serious injured aboard. PC-519 and Pilot Boat UNDERWRITER, following with other survivors.*
>
> —Message sent by the submarine chaser *PC-566* following the sinking of the S.S. *Robert E. Lee*, with 266 passengers aboard, forty-five miles south of the Mississippi River mouth while en route from Key West to New Orleans, by the *U-166*. Following the discovery in late May 2001 of the wreck of the U-boat on the ocean floor less than a mile from that of the passenger ship, the sub-chaser received long overdue credit for sinking the only submarine lost by Germany in the Gulf of Mexico.[1]

The highest number of the ships sunk or damaged by U-boats in the Gulf, Caribbean, and Panama Sea Frontiers occurred in 1942 and 1943, although there were ship losses in 1944 as well. The losses were greatest in the Caribbean Sea Frontier, followed by the Gulf and Panama Sea Frontiers.

GULF SEA FRONTIER

The Navy established the Gulf Sea Frontier in February 1942, with headquarters at Key West, Florida. Its first commander, Capt. Russell S. Crenshaw, was also commandant of the Seventh Naval District. Although responsible for the protection of the Florida Gulf Coast and Straits, most of the Bahamas, the Gulf of Mexico, the Yucatan Channel (a strait connecting the Caribbean with the Gulf of Mexico), and most of Cuba, the only ships available to him were ones drawn from the Seventh and Eighth Naval Districts. In an emergency, Crenshaw could use craft from the Key West Sound School (which supported instruction of Navymen in the use of sonar) in the Florida Straits and Yucatan Channel. Due to this shortage of naval assets, merchant vessels operating in the Gulf Sea Frontier were defended against U-boats in only rudimentary fashion during the early months of the war. The Seventh Naval District was responsible for the coastal and inshore waters of Florida, except for those to the west of the Apalachicola River. This area, and the waters of the states bordering the Gulf to the west of Florida—Alabama, Mississippi, Louisiana, and Texas—were under the Eighth Naval District.[2]

SEVENTH NAVAL DISTRICT

When war broke out on 7 December 1941, Rear Adm. William H. Allen was commandant of both the Sixth and Seventh Naval Districts, with headquarters co-located at Navy Yard, Charleston, South Carolina. Captain Crenshaw, then assistant commandant, was physically located at Key West, Florida, to oversee the day-to-day operations of the Seventh Naval District, whose local defenses included three section bases as well as Coast Guard air bases at Miami and St. Petersburg, Florida. As a part of the Navy's reorganization of naval coastal frontiers as sea frontiers on 6 February 1942, the headquarters of the Seventh Naval District relocated to Key West, and Crenshaw became the acting commander of the sea frontier and commandant of the Seventh Naval District. The adjustment of district boundaries to conform to those of the new Gulf Sea Frontier, resulted in the transfer of some activities, including Section Base, Mayport, to the Sixth Naval District.[3]

The Inshore Patrol was an activity of the Gulf Sea Frontier and the Seventh Naval District. Its patrol area was to seaward from the coasts of Florida out to and including the sea lanes. The Key West Section extended from Fowey Rocks to Sanibel Island, and as far west as the Dry Tortugas (a small group of islands located at the end of the Florida Keys, about sixty-seven miles west of Key West); the Port Everglades Section from Cape Canaveral to Fowey Rocks; and the St. Petersburg Section from Sanibel Island to Cape St. George. Vessels assigned to these sections operated from bases at Key West, Port Everglades (the deep water port of Ft. Lauderdale), and St. Petersburg, respectively. A listing of the patrol yachts, YPs, and coastal minesweepers that comprised the patrol in July 1942 is provided below, as well as the names of commanding officers, if known:

Seventh Naval District Inshore Patrol:
Comdr. A. M. Steckel, USN (Ret.)

Ship Name or Designation (Former Type Vessel/Name and Name of Commanding Officer if Known)	Length Feet	Displ Tons	Year Built
Key West Section: Lt. Comdr. A. W. Long, USNR			
Summit AMc-106 (Acme-class, Lt. Comdr. George L. Hoffman, USNR)	98	195	1942
Governor AMc-82 (Accentor-class, Lt. Alfred F. Page, Jr.)	97	195	1941
Guide AMc-83 (Accentor-class, Lt. (jg) Alvin Hero)	97	195	1941
Ideal AMc-85 (Accentor-class)	97	195	1941
YP-231 (ex-Janirve)	54	38	1941
YP-232 (ex-Encore)	55	16	1940
YP-271 (ex-Carol Anne)	55	40	1941
YP-331 (ex-Recco III)	55	20	1939
YP-332 (ex-Atlantis)	92	85	1928
YP-340 (ex-yacht Sovereign, Barbara, Kalolah)	83	84	1927
YP-352 (ex-yacht Annette R.)	90	88	1929
YP-356 (ex-From Now On)	67	35	1940
*YP-357 (ex-Mystic)	85	84	1939
*YP-358 (ex-yacht Mercury IV)	63	32	1936
YP-359 (ex-Done Gone)	55	27	1941
YP-392 (ex-ketch-rigged motor yacht Trade Wind)	62	52	1938
YP-393 (ex-Bismallah III)	57	31	1939
YP-394 (ex-yacht Pan-Che)	72	56	1929
YP-398 (ex-Lady Alberta)	62	46	1940
YP-403 (ex-yacht Chanticleer)	60' 1"	16	1941
*YP-405 (ex-Blue Jacket)	60	43	1942
*YP-408 (ex-yacht Sea Dream)	90	82	1925
YP-451 (ex-yacht Idalia)	62' 1"		1927
YP-452 (ex-Marileen)	74	40	1927
Port Everglades Section: Lt. Comdr. Warren C. Ives, USNR			
*Carnelian PY-19 (ex-Seventeen, Lt. Comdr. G. L. Hoffman, USNR)	190	609	1930
*Emerald PYc-1 (ex-Savitar, Lt. (jg) Robert W. Graham, USNR)	96	104	1922
Tapacola AMc-54 (Accentor-class, Lt. (jg) Russell E. Fitzpatrick, USNR)	98	275	1941
Turaco AMc-55 (Accentor-class, Lt. (jg) Allard B. Heyward, USNR)	98	275	1941
*YP-218 (ex-yacht Consort IV)	86	87	1936
YP-248 (ex-Chris Craft Benmar)	57		1940
YP-272 (ex-yacht Lone Wolf)	62	50	1939

Ship Name or Designation (Former Type Vessel/Name and Name of Commanding Officer if Known)	Length Feet	Displ Tons	Year Built
*YP-395 (ex-yacht *Rosewill III*)	77	74	1937
YP-453 (ex-yacht *Pleiades*)	79	51	1928
St. Petersburg Section: Lt. Comdr. C. F. Dege, USCG			
Stalwart AMc-105 (*Acme*-class, Lt. (jg) F. W. Dieht, USNR)	98	195	1941

Vessels identified by asterisks were assigned to the Inshore Patrol for operations, but were available to commander, Gulf Sea Frontier, for escort or other duty as needed.[4]

INITIAL OPERATIONS

The most important duty of the Key West Inshore Patrol was to protect the anchorage where merchant ships assembled, and the approaches to it, with patrols and minesweeping. District vessels assigned to the anchorage patrol detachment—the coastal patrol yacht *Emerald*, and YPs *231, 232, 271, 331, 332,* and *340*—were charged with guarding the anchorage area, continuously patrolling the channel to the anchorage, and maintaining a patrol in the Rebecca Shoals-Dry Tortugas area. As a part of the Navy's recently enacted practice of escorting merchant convoys, Key West was the southern terminus of the Gulf Coast route. Merchant vessels sailed at about 0200 to arrive off Rebecca Shoal about daylight. After rounding the shoal, a treacherous coral bank located forty-three miles west of Key West, convoys formed for passage through the Florida Straits.[5]

Coastal minesweepers were responsible for sweeping the principal harbors of the Seventh Naval District, and the approaches to them, for contact, magnetic, acoustic, and combination mines in order to protect naval forces and merchant shipping. Since Key West was an assembly point, AMcs swept the main ship channel daily as well as the channel to the convoy anchorage. They also "led out" (swept ahead of) outbound and inbound convoys. In the Port Everglades area, minesweepers worked the channels and approaches to Fort Pierce, Lake Worth Inlet, Port Everglades, and Miami. At St. Petersburg, on Florida's gulf coast, the AMcs swept the Tampa Bay ship channels daily except when periodically engaged in sweeping at Boca Grande.[6]

The first day of April 1942 found the YPs *232, 248, 271,* and *272* patrolling sea lanes from Fowey Rocks (south-southeast of Key Biscayne on Florida's southeast coast) north to Lake Worth, bordering

West Palm Beach. Over the course of the month, YPs performed other tasks as well, including guard ship duty at Lake Worth and Fort Piece Inlets, and off the entrance to Key West. The *Emerald* was on station as Examination Boat at the Key West main ship channel, scrutinizing inbound and outboard shipping, while the larger yacht *Carnelian* patrolled the 110-mile stretch of water from Cape Canaveral north to Lake Worth.[7]

As additional vessels reported to the district they were allocated either to the inshore patrol or to captains of the port at Key West, Miami, Tampa, and St. Augustine, who were responsible for both the control and protection of shipping and the security of waterfront facilities within their respective ports. The inshore patrol was responsible for keeping local waters safe and providing protection and escorts for shipping, in addition to other duties:

- ensure safe entrance to, and exit from, harbors, by sweeping channels, and by providing escorts and patrols when circumstances warrant;
- patrol Defensive Sea Areas and Defensive Coastal Areas, extending patrols seaward to cover swept channels and other areas as necessary;
- provide timely information of enemy forces, vessels or aircraft;
- visit and search suspicious merchant vessels;
- patrol the areas of obstacles positioned for defensive measures, especially during thick weather or darkness, to protect the obstacles and prevent light craft from going over them;
- emphasize training and development of anti-submarine warfare.[8]

To ensure their readiness to carry out emergent requirements, district vessels loaded to capacity with fuels and stores upon return to port. When operating out of the area, they had access to Bahaman, Cuban, and Mexican harbors, bases, and facilities to replenish if necessary.[9]

EIGHTH NAVAL DISTRICT INSHORE PATROL

When word of the attack on Pearl Harbor reached the headquarters of the Inshore Patrol of the Eighth Naval District at New Orleans, Louisiana, all officers and men on shore leave were ordered to return to their units immediately. Just eight vessels then comprised the inshore patrol: YPs *14*, *19*, *45*, and *98*; the patrol yacht *Onyx* (PYc-5); and coastal minesweepers *Courlan*, *Develin*, and *Ostrich*. The YPs *14* and *45* were assigned to patrol duty; *YP-19* was at Naval Air Station,

Corpus Christi, Texas; and the *YP-98* en route there for duty as a plane guard ship. The following is a summary of the inshore patrol craft, as well as units that reported for duty relatively soon thereafter, and names of commanding officers or officers in charge:

Eighth Naval District Inshore Patrol:
Comdr. H. B. Broadfoot, USN

Ship Name or Designation (Former Type Vessel/Name and Name of Commanding Officer if Known)	Length Feet	Displ Tons	Year Built
Section Base Mobile, Alabama (two units)			
Fort Morgan: Lt. T. B. Hendley, USNR			
Choctaw Point: Lt. H. P. Benton, Jr., USNR			
YP-45 (ex-*CG-133*)	75	37	1925
YP-160 (ex-*Sea Rebel*, Ens. Ernest O. Saltmarsh)	77	47	1930
YP-161 (ex-fishing vessel *Yes Sir*)	67	31	1934
Section Base Sabine Pass, Texas: Lt. Comdr. E. E. Kerr, USNR			
Develin AMc-45 (*Accentor*-class, Lt. (jg) M. J. Blancq, USNR)	97	205	1941
YP-14 (ex-*CG-181*, Ens. Parris)	75	37	1924
YP-162 (ex-*Cajun*, Ens. H. P. Swayze)	70		1939
Section Base Galveston, Texas: Lt. Comdr. J. D. Moore, USN (Ret.)			
Ostrich AMc-51 (*Accentor*-class, Lt. W. H. Harrison, USNR)	97	213	1941
YP-19 (ex-*CG-177*, Ens. W. W. Tarleton, USNR)	75	37	1924
YP-158 (ex-*Southern Breeze*, Ens. Eli B. Roth, USN)	99	63	1911
YP-188 (ex-*Adroit II*, Ens. Richard L. Hudson, USNR)	104	60	1920
Section Base Corpus Christi, Texas: Lt. Comdr. William F. Warms			
YP-156 (ex-*Bonne Fortune*, Ens. Wright)	78		1937
Section Base Burrwood, Louisiana: Lt. Comdr. W. J. Ashley, USNR			
Onyx PYc-5 (ex-*Janey III*, *Rene* and *Pegasus*)	119	190	1924
Courlan AMc-44 (*Accentor*-class)	97	205	1941
YP-159 (ex-*Lysistrata III*)	74	43	1939
YP-196 (ex-FWS *Tijenta*)	53		1938
YP-157 (ex-*Lev III*)	77	40	1935[10]

INSHORE PATROL ACTIVITIES

On 16 December 1941, *YP-45*, a 75-foot former Prohibition-era Coast Guard cutter, received orders to maintain a continuous patrol of the Mobile, Alabama Harbor entrance and to be alert, following the district's receipt of a report about an unidentified submarine sighted in Chochawachee Bay (an inlet of the Gulf of Mexico on the Florida Panhandle). She was, however, unable to find any evidence of an enemy submarine. The following day, the inshore patrol received YPs *56*, *157*, *158*, *159*, *160*, *161*, and *162* from the Maritime Commission. On reporting for duty, *YP-161* was assigned to Naval Air Station, Pensacola and the others were allocated among the section bases of the district.[11]

On 22 December, the *YP-45* was on station off Fort Morgan, carrying out examination ship duties involving monitoring and occasionally boarding and inspecting shipping entering or leaving Mobile Bay. Two separate units comprised Section Base, Mobile—one at Fort Morgan on Mobile Point at the entrance to the bay, and the other at Choctaw Point in the city of Mobile. At that time, district YPs had little or no armament to defend themselves or to conduct attacks on enemy submarines. This shortcoming was partially alleviated by the December delivery of two railcars of munitions (100 Mark VI depth charges and assemblies). The *YP-45* and *YP-160* received four depth charges apiece in January 1942 and two .50-caliber machine guns the following month. Subsequently, other inshore patrol craft were similarly armed. Following relief by the *YP-160*, the *YP-45* returned to base on Christmas Eve for fuel, supplies and crew rest. Three days later, she relieved her sister ship on station. Other section bases implemented similar patterns of alternate periods of patrol, which included the employment of coastal yachts or minesweepers for such duties if they were not otherwise employed.[12]

On 13 January, the *YP-158* (which had reported to Section Base, Galveston, on Pelican Spit, just two week earlier) was condemned as unfit for duty. Formerly the yacht *Southern Breeze*, she was admittedly a bit elderly, having been built by Nilson Yachts of Baltimore, Maryland, in 1911. She would, however, return to duty, following overhaul of her machinery. In the interim, her loss was offset by the arrival of the *YP-188* at Galveston ten days later.[13]

REPORTS OF ENEMY SUBMARINES IN GULF WATERS

On 28 January, following the district's receipt of a report of a submarine sighting near Corpus Christi, the *YP-188* was ordered to get underway from Section Base, Galveston and proceed southwest along the Texas coast to Section Base, Sabine Pass, where she was to load depth charges. On completion, she was to rendezvous with the *YP-156* and cutter *Boutwell* (WSC-130) in the vicinity of Aransas Pass near Ingleside, to furnish them with depth charges. Once the ordnance was aboard the vessels, all three were to begin a search for the submarine. The *YP-188* stood out of Sabine Pass in the early evening with fourteen depth charges, as well as a Thompson machine gun and 120 rounds of ammunition for good measure, and joined up with the *156* and the cutter. At 2100 the following evening, a Canadian vessel reported sighting a submarine, and headquarters dispatched the cutter *CG-466* to investigate. All efforts proved futile, however, and on 31 January searching vessels received orders to return to their respective bases.[14]

At 2027 on 8 February, Captain of the Port, Galveston reported that a submarine had been sighted off Baytown in the Houston ship channel. The port was closed to ship traffic, and the *YP-188* and cutter *Dorothy* were dispatched up the channel to conduct a search. The coastal minesweeper *Ostrich*, then assigned to guard ship duty in Bolivar Roads off Galveston, received orders to patrol off the harbor entrance. A search of the channel proved fruitless, but efforts continued nonetheless. A subsequent sighting of a submarine to the southeast resulted in orders from commander, Inshore Patrol to "intensify the patrol and be on alert." However, he determined the following morning that reports were unfounded and directed the vessels to secure.[15]

U-BOAT ATTACKS COMMENCE

German U-boats began offensive operations in the Gulf of Mexico in late spring. At a little past noon on 6 May 1942, commander, Inshore Patrol notified the CGC *Boutwell* of a sub sighting, and ordered the cutter to proceed at full speed, attack, and report action. Three minutes later commanding officer, Section Base, Burrwood received similar orders to send his best available craft to attack and report. A flurry of related orders followed these dispatches. All section bases, and Harbor Entrance Control Post, Pensacola were instructed to establish offensive patrols, be alert, and report any action. Section Base, Burrwood and the Coast Guard tug *Tuckahoe* (WYT-89) received orders to allow no shipping to pass out of Burrwood, Louisiana until further notice. Other section bases received the same guidance to hold shipping in port. The purpose of the base at Burrwood, situated at the south end of the Mississippi River delta in the Southwest Pass, and its assigned units was to deter the presence of enemy submarines in the Gulf of Mexico and to monitor traffic entering the river's mouth.[16]

Burrwood reported to commander, Inshore Patrol at 1435 that patrol yacht *Onyx* and minesweeper *Courlan* had orders to investigate the submarine sighting and attack, if opportunity allowed, and that *YP-157* was patrolling off the South and Southwest Passes of the Mississippi. From Head of Passes, located eighteen miles below Fort Jackson and just south of the town of Venice, the river branched out into Southwest Pass, South Pass, and Pass a l'Outre before emptying into the gulf. Commander, Inshore Patrol ordered the *Courlan* recalled for patrol duty, and informed the cutter *Boutwell* of an aircraft sighting of fifty survivors on a raft to the east of the reported position of the submarine. In the early evening, the *Boutwell* recovered forty-one survivors from the torpedoed American merchant ship S.S. *Alcoa Puritan*, sixty miles southeast of South Pass.[17]

At 2318, Naval Air Station, Pensacola reported an aircraft sighting of a ship on fire. The *Onyx* and *Boutwell* confirmed that a large merchant ship was burning fiercely at the specified location, and while the patrol yacht worked to recover survivors, the cutter searched for a submarine. Around dawn, commander, Inshore Patrol ordered the cutter to continue the search in the direction of the Southwest Pass, and a little before noon dispatched the tug *Tuckahoe* to proceed to the scene of the burning vessel and attempt salvage.[18]

The *Onyx* returned to Burrwood during the early evening of 7 May and reported that the ship that had been shelled and set ablaze was the Honduran merchant vessel *Ontario*, and that her entire crew of forty-five had been rescued. At the time of the attack, the unescorted and unarmed ship had been making twelve knots trying desperately to reach safe haven in the nearest port. Her master was well aware that there was an enemy submarine in the area, having received a distress signal the previous day from the *Alcoa Puritan*. The U-boat currently stalking his ship had attacked the freighter fifteen miles off the mouth of the Mississippi. (After the *Alcoa Puritan* plunged to the bottom, the submarine approached the survivors and a German officer with a megaphone shouted, "Sorry we can't help you, hope you get ashore," and then waved as it moved away.) Despite the *Ontario*'s evasive zigzag course, the *U-507* easily closed on her port quarter and opened fire, destroying the bridge, wheelhouse and mainmast, and setting the ship ablaze. Thirty-two American, eleven Honduran, one Dane and one British crew members were forced to abandon ship in three lifeboats. The burning vessel was last seen afloat at 0440. A salvage crew aboard the *Boutwell* later returned to the site to find the ship had gone down.[19]

To avoid attack by aircraft or patrol vessels, German submarines often remained submerged by day, surfacing at night to hunt under the cover of darkness. At 0945 on 9 May, the American tanker S.S. *Gulf King* reported that it had sighted a submarine lying on the bottom. Commander, Inshore Patrol informed Section Base, Sabine Pass that Army bombers had been dispatched to cover the sub, and ordered the base commander to take immediate offensive action with its best available patrol vessels and to keep him informed. In response, the Section Base reported at 1147 that the coastal minesweeper *Develin* and *YP-162* had proceeded and that Army shore artillery was standing by. Much later, following an unsuccessful ten-hour search, a second report conveyed "nothing sighted by patrol vessels."[20]

U-BOAT ATTACKS ESCALATE

During the late morning of 10 May 1942, the *U-506* torpedoed the American tanker M.V. *Aurora* about forty miles off Southwest Pass, Louisiana. Hit on the starboard side, aft of the bridge, the ship began to list to starboard but, with a shift in ballast, was able to return to an even keel and proceed. Ninety minutes later, she was hit by a second torpedo, and then a third, after which the submarine surfaced and began firing, forcing the nine officers, twenty-nine men and twelve armed guards to abandon ship. *Kapitänleutnant* Erich Würdemann, believing the sinking tanker was finished, departed. In the early evening, at 1700, the coastal patrol yacht *Onyx* and *YP-157* rescued all fifty survivors, one of whom later died of his wounds. The Coast Guard tug *Tuckahoe* arrived on scene, sent a rescue party on board with a fire hose and extinguishers, and took the damaged vessel under tow for Southwest Pass. The *Aurora* drifted onto a shoal at the entrance. Initially judged to be a total loss, she was later salvaged and returned to service as the *Jamestown*.[21]

DESTRUCTION OF *U-166*

The only German submarine destroyed by American forces in the Gulf Sea Frontier was the *U-166*, which the sub-chaser *PC-566* dispatched on 30 July 1942, after the U-boat torpedoed and sank the American passenger ship S.S. *Robert E. Lee*, with 266 passengers aboard, south of the mouth of the Mississippi River. The officers and men of the sub-chaser did not receive credit for this action until nearly fifty-nine years later, following discovery of the wreck of the submarine less than a mile from that of the *Robert E. Lee* during seafloor survey work for BP Amoco PLC and Shell Oil Company.[22]

During the late afternoon of 29 July 1942, the passenger ship was en route from Key West to New Orleans with the *PC-566* positioned 800-1,000 yards ahead, ten degrees on her starboard bow, conducting a sound search with no contacts made. The first indication of danger was a torpedo wake sighted 150 yards from the starboard bow of the *Robert E. Lee*, and closing. The master ordered general quarters set, and the rudder hard right to point his ship's bow at the torpedo, in the hopes that by this maneuver it would pass harmlessly down her port or starboard side. Such was not to be. The torpedo struck abaft the starboard beam, causing a terrific explosion, and the passenger ship began to settle rapidly by the stern, her bow coming clear of the water.[23]

The sub-chaser immediately attacked the previously undetected U-boat. Built by Brown Shipbuilding Co. of Houston, Texas, and commissioned only two weeks earlier, the 173-foot ship had been designed for just such a task. Two Fairbanks Morse diesel engines gave her a top speed of 20 knots, and she was well armed with one 3-inch dual purpose gun mount, one 40mm mount, three 20mm guns, two rocket launchers, four depth charge projectiles, and two depth charge tracks.[24]

As Lt. H. G. Claudius, USNR, commanding officer of *PC-566*, closed on the sub's suspected position, her wake became visible because she was operating near the surface. Her periscope then appeared, protruding about three feet out of the water and moving to the right at 3 or 4 knots across the bow of the sub-chaser toward the sinking ship. As he drew closer, Claudius endeavored to keep the periscope fine on his starboard bow, believing the sub was watching the *Robert E. Lee*, and unaware that the *PC-566* was off her starboard quarter. At 260 yards, the sub-chaser gained initial sound sonar contact. The periscope disappeared; however, the submarine's wake was still visible, with sound contact maintained to about 120 yards as the ship closed. Claudius described the ensuing events in his after action report:

Upon the loss of the sound contact the ship was brought to the right still following the wake and when directly over the established position of the submarine a five charge pattern of depth charges was laid. The first charge from the starboard rack was [set to detonate at a depth of] 250 feet, second charge from the port rack was 100 feet, and at the same time two "K" guns were fired set at 150 feet, and the final charge was laid by the starboard rack at 250 feet.

Following the attack, the sub-chaser steadied on the same heading for about a thousand yards before reversing course in an effort to re-establish sound contact, which provided Claudius a visual opportunity to check the status of the *Robert E. Lee*. He discovered that she had slipped beneath the surface, with only life boats, rafts and debris marking the spot where she had been hit.[25]

Approaching the position of the first depth charge attack, the *PC-566* regained sound contact about ten degrees off her port bow and 360 yards ahead, and maintained contact to a distance of about 200 yards. Claudius then came left, over the estimated position of the U-boat, and fired a second pattern of five depth charges. He repeated the previous maneuver, continuing along the apparent heading of the U-boat before reversing course in an effort to again establish contact, but without success.[26]

The first of four planes (an A29, OS2U, and two PBYs) ordered to the scene in response to a report sent by the sub-chaser, appeared and received instructions to aid in the search for the U-boat. The *PC-566* made a complete search of the area in which it had lost contact with the sub, followed by the area in which survivors were adrift, but did not regain sound contact. After a second plane arrived overhead, Claudius decided it was relatively safe to begin rescue operations as the U-boat was apparently either sunk or in no condition to attack, and he was now supported by two aircraft making a careful search of the entire area.[27]

During rescue operations, the *PC-566* took aboard approximately 275 survivors from the *Robert E. Lee*, including all the injured. At 2035, the sub-chaser *PC-519* and the tug *Underwriter* (belonging to the New Orleans Bar Pilots Association) arrived on scene and picked up all survivors who remained in lifeboats. Although under the conditions it was impossible to determine the total number rescued, Claudius reported that he believed 383 passengers and crew members were landed at Venice, Louisiana, leaving twenty-three missing, undoubtedly lost with the ship.[28]

Despite strong evidence of the U-boat's destruction, in his report the commanding officer of the *PC-566* modestly took credit only for damaging the enemy submarine:

> The area of the attack developed a large oil slick at least 200 feet in diameter, and the oil appeared to be a slick of light clean oil which gave a brownish gray tint to the very deep blue water which was over 1,000 fathoms in depth. This oil had a definite odor of diesel oil, but no debris was noticed in the area in which the submarine attacked.
>
> While I cannot positively state that the submarine was sunk, it is my opinion based on the definiteness of the attack as to the submarine's position when firing depth charges which was confirmed by sound search and sight that the submarine was sunk or so mortally wounded that she would never return to her base.[29]

Not only was the *PC-566* not given credit for sinking the submarine, the Navy's Anti-Submarine Warfare Assessment Committee admonished the sub-chaser for a poorly executed attack. Three days later, a Coast Guard J4F twin-engine amphibious aircraft was patrolling about 100 miles south of Houma, Louisiana, at an altitude of 1,500 feet. Spotting a U-boat on the surface, it quickly dove on the target and dropped a single depth charge, the only weapon carried by the small plane, slightly ahead of the wake of the now submerged submarine. The depth charge exploded, and following the appearance of an oil slick on the surface, the aircraft returned to its field and reported the attack. After the war, German naval records confirmed that the *U-166* was reported lost in the area, and as her loss coincided with the J4F attack, the Navy gave credit to the aircraft's pilot and single crewman. The *U-166* is now correctly credited to the *PC-556*. The Coast Guard patrol plane is believed to have made an unsuccessful attack against the *U-171*.[30]

PANAMA SEA FRONTIER

Commander, Panama Sea Frontier was responsible for the defense of the Pacific and Atlantic sea approaches to the Panama Canal, a thoroughfare vital to both commercial shipping and to the Navy's ability to move ships rapidly between the Atlantic and Pacific Fleets. To the west, the sea frontier encompassed an ocean area stretching from the Mexico-Guatemala border and out around the Galapagos Islands to latitude 5° south. On the eastern side of Panama, the frontier spanned the waters from the Mexico-British Honduras boundary on the Yucatán Peninsula eastward along latitude 18° 5' north to longitude 80° 27' west, and then south-southeast to Punta de Gallinas, a headland in northern Colombia and the northernmost point on the mainland of South America. The headquarters of Rear Adm. Frank H. Sadler, who commanded the sea frontier as well as the Fifteenth Naval District, was located at Balboa at the Pacific entrance to the Canal.[31]

FIFTEENTH NAVAL DISTRICT INSHORE PATROL

Section Base, Cristobal, provided facilities for the units of Inshore Patrol, Atlantic, under the command of Lieutenant Commander Perdue, and Section Base, Balboa for Inshore Patrol, Pacific under Lieutenant Commander Harris. Guayaquil, a seaport in Ecuador, and the Galapagos Islands, which lay 525 miles to the west and a part of that country, were available to U.S. Navy ships for liberty, upkeep, fuel, supplies and fresh provisions.

Fifteenth Naval District Inshore Patrol—Pacific
Section Base, Balboa, Canal Zone

Ship Name or Designation (Former Type Vessel/Name and Name of Commanding Officer if Known)	Length Feet	Displ Tons	Year Built
Agate PYc-4 (ex-yacht *Armina, Stella Polaris*)	110	185	1930
Topaz PYc-10 (ex-yacht *Doromar, Topaz*)	112	160	1931
Pipit AMc-1 (ex-fishing vessel *Spartan*)	76.8	126	1936
Longspur AMc-10 (ex-fishing vessel *New Ambassador*)	74.8	107	1935
YP-209 (ex-yacht *All Alone*)	95	78	1928
YP-241 (ex-ketch *Morning Star*)	80'5"	62	1938
YP-364 (ex-purse seiner *New Hope/AMb-6*)	75.5	107	1940[32]

Three 75-foot ex-Coast Guard cutters—YPs *26, 46,* and *48*—were based at Cristobal for duty as inner harbor patrol craft. Normally, one vessel was on patrol, one on standby moored at the barracks, and one undergoing upkeep, repair, or overhaul. The YP on duty patrolled the harbor between the anti-submarine net at the entrance and buoys No. 1 and 2 in a crisscross pattern, pulling a drag astern. It also crossed the channel directly astern of each and every vessel entering the harbor, to ensure that an enemy submarine was not in trail, and was responsible for controlling all outgoing small boat traffic.

Section Base, Cristobal, Canal Zone

Ship Name or Designation (Former Type Vessel/Name and Name of Commanding Officer if Known)	Length Feet	Displ Tons	Year Built
Jade PY-17 (ex-yacht Athero II, Caroline, Dr. Brinkley)	171	562	1926
Moonstone PYc-9 (ex-yacht Nancy Baker, Mona, Lone Star)	172	645	1929
Barbet AMc-38 (Accentor-class, Ens. Stuart T. Hotchkiss, USNR)	97	221	1941
Brambling AMc-39 (Accentor-class, Ens. John E. Johansen, USNR)	97	205	1941
YP-26 (ex-CG-252)	75	37	1925
YP-46 (ex-CG-146)	75	37	1925
YP-48 (ex-CG-103)	75	37	1924[33]

ACQUISITION OF TUNA CLIPPERS

When the United States declared war on Japan on 8 December 1941, the government ordered the California tuna fleet (some ninety vessels, of which about eighty were at sea) to make port in California or, if fishing off the Galapagos, the Panama Canal Zone. Four days later, commander, Offshore Patrol Pacific ordered the 328-foot gunboat *Erie* (PG-50) to proceed immediately to Calders near Puntarenas, and to seize the fishing boat *Alert*, which was reported to have Japanese crew members aboard. Less than an hour later orders came to seize or sink on sight the fishing boats *Alert, Navigator, Seaboy, America,* and *Prospect*. Japanese nationals found aboard apprehended tuna clippers were removed and interned. On 16 December, the Fifteenth Naval District notified the Eleventh Naval District that two San Diego-based fishing vessels—the *Conte Bianco* and *San Salvador*—were to be taken over by the Navy. However, the number of ex-tuna clippers deemed necessary to help protect the Panama Canal Zone quickly expanded. Two days later the *Erie* proceeded to Balboa, escorting the *Navigator, Conte Bianco, Shasta,* and *Invader*, which had been taken that day. The Fifteenth Naval District sent a request to the Navy's Bureau of Navigation later that day for personnel to man the tuna clippers "mustered" into the Navy:

> Acquired 7 tuna boats and expect 30 more. No personnel to operate same. Request seven officers or petty officers; quartermasters, cooks,

diesel engineers, engine crews of 3 men, radio operators, deck crews of 3 men. Also, large contingents of recruits and Jr. officers.[34]

The skippers of some boats, or their owners, were reluctant to lose to the Navy their means of making a living from the sea. In recognition of that reality, and as a result of an agreement between the United States and Costa Rica, local authorities at Puntarenas denied clearance to all fishing vessels then in port, as well as any entering Puntarenas in the future. Per Navy direction, six fishing vessels—the *Felice, White Star, Santa Margarita, Normandie, Theodore Foss,* and *Daiho II*—made port by 16 December, and were joined by the *Chicken of the Seas, San Salvador,* and *City of San Pedro* two days later. On 18 December, the *Erie* reported to the Fifteenth Naval District that it had seized or detained twelve fishing vessels, and requested that the transfer of thirty-two prisoners (Japanese subjects) on four tuna boats be arranged on her arrival at Balboa.[35]

On 29 December 1941, in response to a Chief of Naval Operations message requesting the names of the tuna boats which the Fifteenth Naval District wished to charter, Sadler identified twelve vessels: the *Conte Bianco, Invader, Anna M., Emma R., Sao Joao, Patria, Cape Horn, Madeirense, California, Europa, Challenger,* and *Saint Therese.* After only receiving authorization for eight, Sadler informed the Eleventh Naval District in San Diego on 5 January that the *Conte Bianco, Anna M., Sao Joao, Patria, Madeirense, California, Europa,* and *Challenger* had been taken over by the Navy, the *Theo Foss* and *Daiho II* detained under suspicion, and the balance of the boats released. The Fifteenth Naval District requisitioned the eight tuna clippers under Bare Boat Charter arrangements and provided copies of the charter to the skippers for their signatures. Four tuna boats were permitted to return to California to transport the catches of the eight detained boats, as well as their own. The U.S. Army requisitioned the *Shasta* and *Cape Horn* for use as tugs in the Canal area, and employed the *Invader* to resupply military forces at Isla Seymour Island, as well as other Galapagos Islands, and Cocos Island, Costa Rica.[36]

WARNINGS OF JAPANESE AND GERMAN SUBMARINES

The Fourteenth Naval District (headquartered at Pearl Harbor) informed the Thirteenth Naval District (at Seattle, Washington) via naval message on 29 December 1941 that an estimated fourteen Japanese submarines were operating in the Eastern Pacific, including Hawaii. By that date, Japanese submarines had already attacked a dozen merchant ships off American's West Coast. The following day, the navy staff in Washington, D.C., sent a message to commander, Panama Coastal Frontier warning of the discovery of pre-staged fuel supplies which appeared to be intended for the support of enemy submarines:

> Report from Mexico that a canvas fuel tank discovered submerged about 20 feet off Manzanillo [a port city on the Pacific in southwest Mexico]. Similar reports concerning San Nicolas [the most remote of California's Channel Islands], about 70 miles S.W. of San Pedro, California.[37]

Concurrent with the warnings that Japanese submarines were, or might soon be, operating in the Pacific approaches to the Panama Canal, Sadler received a report of the presence of German submarines off the Atlantic side. A message sent 30 December 1941 by British Intelligence at Barranquilla, Colombia conveyed in part:

> Germans have 4 subs off Colombia coast to be increased to 10 or more by January 15 when Colombia will decide it will participate in war. If South America as a whole declares war in January, Panama Canal will be attacked immediately. E. Broller is German Naval Chief in Cartagena who will issue orders for the attack.[38]

Verification of submarines operating off the Americas came on 1 January 1942, when the U.S. Army transport ship S.S. *Copiapo* reported being stopped by a Japanese sub off the coast of Peru, and then allowed to proceed. Two weeks later, the American merchant vessel S.S. *Andrew Jackson* reported sighting a submarine in Pacific waters south of Panama.[39]

PANAMA SEA FRONTIER FORCES BOLSTERED

On 13 January 1942, Presidential Proclamation #2536 established the Cristobal and Gulf of Panama Maritime Control Areas and by month's end the Fifteenth Naval District had created separate inshore patrols, operating from Cristobal and Balboa, respectively, to safeguard the approaches to the Canal. In related actions, the district also established both Army and Navy advanced bases on Seymour Island, in the Galapagos, and at Salinas, Ecuador, and a Navy seaplane base in the Gulf of Fonseca (on the Pacific bordering El Salvador, Honduras and Nicaragua), and began conversion of tuna boats acquired for naval use.[40]

The *Erie* reported to commander, Panama Sea Frontier on 8 February 1942 that several persons aboard the gunboat had sighted a periscope 1,000 yards distant toward the sun, after which three depth charge attacks were made with no indication of success. Two days later, Admiral King assigned the following forces (some reallocated from the Fifteenth Naval District) to the Panama Sea Frontier:

- Destroyer Squadron 33 (minus one destroyer division that was to remain on temporary duty with the Atlantic Fleet;
- Gunboat *Erie* (PG-50);
- Submarine chasers *PC-454, 456, 458, 460,* and *509*;
- Patrol yacht *Jade* (PY-17), and coastal patrol yachts *Agate* (PYc-4), *Moonstone* (PYc-9), and *Topaz* (PYc-10);
- Motor Torpedo Boat Squadron 2;
- Naval aircraft as made available by commander-in-chief Atlantic Fleet;
- All inshore patrols within the limits of the frontier, as formed.[41]

Sadler also recommended to King, the addition of fifteen ex-tuna boats to the Panama Sea Frontier Force. These included the eight—*Conti Bianco, Anna M., Sao Joao, Patria, California, Madeirense, Europa,* and *Challenger*—operating as part of the frontier forces, as well as another seven—*Invader, Cape Horn, Shasta, St. Therese, Alert,* and *Emma R. S.* at Balboa, and *Amano* at San Jose—not under Navy charter. However, in lieu of the extra seven tuna clippers that Sadler desired, the Navy decided to acquire additional West Coast boats for the Canal Zone, and directed the Eleventh and Twelfth Naval Districts to get them ready for military service:

> 16 purse seiners from the 11th and thirty-four from 12th being requisitioned under bare boat charter for the Canal Zone. Urgently required. Desirable that they be armed with .50 caliber machine guns and depth charges.[42]

Sadler received word on 21 February that twenty purse seiner boats with Navy crews would leave San Diego for Panama in two days. At month's end, he formed the tuna boats in his sea frontier into a squadron, which, although temporarily allocated to commander Inshore Patrol, was permanently assigned to the offshore patrol.[43]

ALLEGED AID TO AXIS SUBMARINES BY VICHY FRANCE AND SPAIN

On 19 February 1942, King sent a message to commander-in-chief Atlantic Fleet, with information copy to commander, Panama Sea Frontier concerning the possible provision of aid to Axis submarines by a Spanish vessel. Such an action, in retrospect, would not have been surprising as, although Spain officially remained neutral throughout World War II, it was ideologically aligned with Nazi Germany and Fascist Italy.

> Strong possibility that Spanish tanker *Zorossai*, anchored since February 3 about 8 miles northwest of Punta Macolla [Venezuela], working with Axis submarines. Immediate boarding and investigation recommended.[44]

That same day the American freighter S.S. *Thompson Lykes* accidently rammed and sank an unidentified vessel, which the master believed to be a submarine, about seventy nautical miles north of Cristobal. He reported that no survivors had been located, but that there was oil visible over a considerable area, and recommended an air search. The destroyers *Tattnall* (DD-125) and *Barry* (DD-248) subsequently searched the area but found no survivors or debris. A determination that the vessel sunk by the *Lykes* was the French submarine *Surcouf* (NN3), then en route to Tahiti via the Panama Canal, was not universally accepted.[45]

In the decades since the war, the loss of the *Surcouf* has long been the subject of controversy and conspiracy theories. Named after an eighteenth-century French pirate (hated by the British) and launched in 1929, the 361-foot submarine was at the time the largest ever constructed. The *Surcouf* carried a floatplane in a hangar abaft the conning tower, and was heavily armed with twelve torpedo tubes, and twin 8-inch guns mounted in a turret forward of the conning tower. However, despite the sub's formidable size and capabilities, she proved to be plagued by mechanical problems. She also rolled badly when on the surface in rough seas, and it was difficult to adjust her trim during a dive, resulting in her taking over two minutes to dive to a depth of only forty feet, making her vulnerable to aircraft.[46]

When Germany invaded France, the *Surcouf* was being refitted in Brest, France, but managed to escape across the English Channel to Britain despite having only a single usable engine. She travelled across the Atlantic and made her way southward, calling at the Naval

Dockyard in Halifax, Nova Scotia; the Portsmouth Naval Shipyard in Kittery on the southern boundary of Maine; the Navy Submarine Base in New London, Connecticut, and the Naval Annex in Bermuda. While in Bermuda, the Free French submarine became the subject of widespread speculation and rumor among Royal Navy and American forces stationed on the island, who feared she might go rogue and torpedo convoys en route to Europe, or defect to the "Vichy" French territory in the West Indies or Central America. The French State was the formal title of France's puppet Vichy administration installed by the Nazis after they conquered France in 1940, but "Vichy France," "Vichy Regime," "Vichy Government," or "Vichy" were commonly used to describe the government, which, officially neutral, collaborated with the Axis powers from July 1940 to August 1944.[47]

After standing out of Bermuda on 12 February 1942, the *Surcouf* vanished. She was not in the best condition according to those who had worked on her at the Portsmouth Naval Shipyard four months earlier, and during a previous visit to Bermuda she had suffered from both a large fuel leak and a seawater leak in her battery compartment that caused a chlorine gas problem. Contributing to the submarine's maintenance-related problems were a relatively untrained crew and a lack of repair parts needed for her French-built equipment, France being under German control.[48]

Despite official acceptance on both sides of the Atlantic that the *Surcouf*'s loss resulted from a night-time collision with an American freighter, unsubstantiated rumors about her demise persist. The most enduring story is that Royal Navy divers, acting on the instructions of British espionage chiefs, secretly mined the submarine's hull while she was in Bermuda's Royal Naval Dockyard. Allegedly, time-delayed mines were set to detonate after the *Surcouf* had left Bermuda and were intended to send her to the bottom. Skeptics of both this scenario and the supposed collision with the *Thompson Lykes* north of the Panama Canal entrance—who believed the latter was not possible based on the position of submarine at that time—conjectured that she may have been depth-charged by an American aircraft that mistook her for a German submarine. In any event, the *Surcouf* became known as the mystery submarine of World War II. In remembrance of her loss, and that of the 130 men aboard her, former Free French leader and future French president General Charles de Gaulle unveiled a memorial on 23 September 1951 at Cherbourg, *Surcouf*'s home port.[49]

Three days after the loss of *Surcouf*, a War Department telegram to any or all U.S. Navy ships and to commander, Task Force 2 conveyed the following guidance regarding Vichy naval forces in the French West Indies:

> Orders issued to destroy or capture French Naval vessels which may leave port in French West Indies, [auxiliary cruiser] *Barfluer* with Admiral Robert and small number of French seaplanes on usual flights excepted. French territorial waters to be disregarded if necessary to destroy enemy ships or submarines.[50]

Vice Adm. Georges A. M. J. Robert, who had arrived at Martinique in 1939 aboard the French cruiser *Jeanne d'Arc*, was Vichy High Commissioner for the Antilles (Martinique and Guadeloupe), Guiana, and Saint Pierre et Miquelon. Martinique was officially pro-Vichy, and America and Great Britain wanted to limit any impact of its stance on the war. After the United States prepared plans to capture the island, Robert agreed in late 1941 to keep the French naval vessels immobilized in return for the Allies not invading the French Antilles. Allied fears that the French naval vessels in Martinique might try to slip away to Europe persisted, however, until mid-1943, when Robert returned to France and Free French sympathizers took control of the French fleet.[51]

SUBMARINE SIGHTINGS CONTINUE

During the early evening of 19 February 1942, the American submarine *S-21* sighted an unidentified submarine in Pacific waters south of Panama. In the coming days other sightings and detections of submarines were reported including one of a vessel operating in a dubious manner. On 23 February, the patrol yacht *Jade* reported sighting a ship which did not answer her challenge. When pursued, it escaped beyond the horizon on a northwesterly course. Believing the movement may have been a possible feint to draw out patrol vessels, commander Offshore Patrol, Atlantic ordered the *Jade* to remain alert for action, but not to abandon her area or leave the vicinity of the Canal except in the case of hot pursuit.[52]

There was a periscope sighting at 0611 on 25 February, and later that morning the destroyer *Goff* (DD-247) reported being attacked by two submarines in the same vicinity, twelve miles due north of Station Ship, Cristobal. The submarines concurrently fired one torpedo each from different angles. Fortunately both missed. Informed of the attack, the American submarine *Drum* (SS-228), which was on the surface in the area, detected the faint sound of propellers with its sound gear, and after submerging, was able to reacquire the screw beats, but lost contact because the bearing of her adversary changed rapidly.[53]

March brought several more sightings and detections of submarines by planes and surface vessels. Sea Frontier Forces had been strengthened at the expense of the Fifteenth Naval District. This shortfall would soon be remedied, however, as additional YPs reported to the district.[54]

EMPLOYMENT OF PATROL CRAFT

In April 1942 the YPs assigned to the inshore patrol of the Fifteenth Naval District were organized into two squadrons: YP Squadron One (ex-tuna boats) and YP Squadron Two (ex-purse seiners), based at Balboa on the Pacific side of the Panama Canal, except for YPs *26*, *46*, and *48*, which were assigned to Section Base, Cristobal for inner harbor patrol. Located on the east bank of the French Canal, the base at Cristobal hosted the vessels of the inshore patrol and the transit group with the latter responsible for the escort of shipping. Two other patrol craft at Cristobal, the *YP-13* and *YP-10*, lay submerged alongside the dock until raised on 27 April and beached. Formerly the cutters *CG-123* and *CG-194*, they had been transferred to the Navy in 1933 and 1934, respectively, and when or why they sank pierside is unknown. At least one, the *YP-10*, returned to duty as a district craft.[55]

The district acquired twenty-two additional patrol craft in May and April 1942. The YPs *3*, *8*, *18*, *287*, and *301* reported for duty on 18 March; a group of fifteen from San Diego—YPs *294*, *295*, *299*, *302*, *305*, *310*, *311*, *312*, *313*, *314*, *315*, *317*, *321*, *322*, and *326*—arrived in mid-April; and *YP-209* and *YP-241* arrived on 26 April. There were, not surprisingly, growing pains associated with the Navy's use of so many ex-fishing boats (whose modifications were limited to being fitted with machine guns and depth charge racks) for patrol duties. Commander, Inshore Patrol highlighted some early operational limitations of the vessels, and that of associated shore support, in his war diary entry for 1 April 1942:

> Five ships were erroneously reported sunk off Cape Mala. This error arose from a garbled message. Great difficulty is being experienced with operating YP vessels because of lack of shore personnel,

untrained crews, and inadequate communication facilities. Radio equipment of ex-purse seiners and ex-tuna boats assigned to this command is entirely inadequate to provide reliable communications. The equipment of these vessels is being overhauled to make the best of what is available.[56]

Despite these challenges, the availability of the vessels enabled commander, Panama Sea Frontier to establish a picket line of YPs off the Pacific side of the Panama Canal in late April. Stretching across the Gulf of Panama, from Cape Mala, Panama, to Pinas Point, Columbia, the patrol would help protect the canal and its shipping from Japanese submarines. A summary of new acquisitions, including four minesweepers that would be reclassified as YPs, is provided below:

Ship Name or Designation (Former Type Vessel/Name and Name of Commanding Officer if Known)	Length Feet	Displ Tons	Year Built
AMb-6 (ex-purse seiner *New Hope*/reclassified YP-364)	75.5	107	1940
AMb-10 (ex-purse seiner *Ardito*/reclassified YP-368)	73.7	101	1939
AMb-16 (ex-purse seiner *Belvidere*/reclassified YP-374)	71.2	95	1939
Barbet AMc-38 (*Accentor*-class, Ens. Stuart T. Hotchkiss, USNR)	97	221	1941
Brambling AMc-39 (*Accentor*-class, Ens. John E. Johansen, USNR)	97	205	1941
AMc-145 (ex-purse seiner *J. DiMaggio*/reclassified YP-383)	87.3	160	1940
YP-3 (ex-*M.V.H.*/*Sandra*)	36	9	1917
YP-8 (ex-CG-191)	75	37	1925
YP-10 (ex-CG-194)	75	37	1924
YP-13 (ex-CG-123)	75	37	1925
YP-18 (ex-CG-263)	75	37	1925
YP-209 (ex-yacht *All Alone*)	95	78	1928
YP-241 (ex-ketch *Morning Star*)	80' 5"	62	1938
YP-287 (ex-tuna clipper *American Voyager*, Lt. (jg) J. W. Rhea)	96.8	263	1937
YP-294 (ex-purse seiner *Vivian A.*)	73.6	103	1938
YP-295 (ex-purse seiner *Jackie Boy*)	73.8	103	1938
YP-299 (ex-purse seiner *Dux*)	75	124	1936
YP-301 (ex-purse seiner *El Rey*)	75.9	108	1939
YP-302 (ex-purse seiner *California Star*)	73.9	103	1936
YP-305 (ex-purse seiner *Phyllis*)	69.3	82	1939
YP-310 (ex-purse seiner *Sea Star*)	74.8	107	1935
YP-311 (ex-purse seiner *San Vito*)	70.7	85	1939
YP-312 (ex-purse seiner *Sea Giant*)	79	125	1936
YP-313 (ex-purse seiner *Mineo Bros.*)	73	102	1939
YP-314 (ex-purse seiner *Virginia II*)	72.2	110	1937

Ship Name or Designation (Former Type Vessel/Name and Name of Commanding Officer if Known)	Length Feet	Displ Tons	Year Built
YP-315 (ex-purse seiner *Santa Lucia*)	72.8	109	1937
YP-317 (ex-purse seiner *California Rose*)	72.2	106	1936
YP-321 (ex-tuna clipper *Belle of Portugal*)	127.9	393	1937
YP-322 (ex-purse seiner *El Padre*)	71.4	107	1937
YP-326 (ex-purse seiner *Marettimo*)	72.6	107	1936[57]

PATROL YACHTS AND YPS ORDERED TO HAWAII

The acquisition of the vessels in March/April was partially offset by the Bureau of Ships' reassignment of nine former tuna clippers to the Hawaiian Sea Frontier. The YPs *277* (ex-*Triunfo*), *284* (ex-*Endeavor*), *289* (ex-*Paramount*), *290* (ex-*Picaroto*), and *292* (ex-*Azoreana*) departed the Canal Zone on 8 April 1942 en route to Honolulu via San Diego. A second group—YPs *237* (ex-*Anna M.*), *239* (ex-*Challenger*), and *240* (ex-*Conte Bianco*)—sailed a week later. The YP-238 (ex-*Madeirense*), scheduled to depart with these three ships, was detained in order to undergo extensive repairs and ultimately stood out of Balboa for Pearl Harbor on 14 July. Continuing this movement of vessels between commands, two patrol yachts and a coastal patrol yacht left Balboa on 28 April bound for Pearl Harbor via San Diego.[58]

DISTRICT CRAFT BOLSTER SEA FRONTIER FORCES

On 23 May, King directed all commandants to make a vigorous selection of craft from local defense forces for transfer to sea frontier forces. Commander, Panama Sea Frontier recommended changes within his frontier to King (who since 12 March had been Chief of Naval Operations as well as Commander-in-Chief United States Fleet). He suggested bolstering the offshore patrol with the fleet tug *Woodcock* (AT-145) and eleven YPs, and having as many YPs on the Atlantic side of the Canal as possible without interfering with the YP patrol in the Pacific. There had been a sharp increase in submarine activity in the Caribbean in May. Accordingly, after receiving concurrence, all available units suitable for the task were used for intense patrol duty and escort work on the Atlantic side.[59]

SURVIVORS BROUGHT TO CRISTOBAL

German submarines sank nearly fifty American merchant ships in the Caribbean and Gulf of Mexico in June 1942, with the resultant loss of many mariners and U.S. Navy Armed Guard members. Some of the vessels that plucked survivors from the sea were themselves sunk before reaching port. Some seafarers were rescued more than once, or perished at sea after seemingly having found a haven safer than a lifeboat or raft.[60]

In the Canal Zone, YPs and Higgins boats were kept busy in mid-June receiving survivors transferred to them by merchant ships offshore, including thirty-eight from the freighter S.S. *American*, which had been torpedoed in the early evening of 11 June by the *U-504* off Honduras. The British steamship *Kent* picked up the survivors and landed them at Cristobal on 15 June. Other survivors came from the American passenger ship S.S. *Sixaola* and the merchant vessel S.S. *Solon Turman*, which the *U-159* had torpedoed on 13 June.[61]

The submarine found and sank the *Sixaola* about fifty miles off Bocas del Toro, Panama, killing twenty-nine crewmembers, most asleep in crew quarters in the bow. The 58 surviving crewmen, 6 Armed Guards, and 108 passengers took to five boats and six rafts, with the *U-159* administering the coup de grace at 0431 after the master and chief mate abandoned ship. The *Sixaola*, however, stubbornly remained afloat for another two hours. The Germans questioned the survivors, offered medical aid, gave exact course and distance to the nearest land, as well as two packages of German cigarettes, and then departed. The American merchantman S.S. *Carolinian* rescued thirty-two survivors, the patrol gunboat *Niagara* (PG-52) seventy-five more, and the Army tug *Shasta* (a former tuna clipper) picked up twenty-three. Three days later, the submarine chaser *PC-460* rescued the final forty-two survivors and delivered them to Cristobal on 18 June 1942.[62]

After sinking the *Sixaola*, the *U-159* sank the *Solon Turman* in the early evening, a hundred miles north of Cristobal. Two torpedoes split her gun deck, snapped her after mast, brought down the radio antenna, and sent deck cargo into the air. Almost everyone aboard abandoned ship in two lifeboats; the one exception, a Navy Armed Guard blown overboard, was picked up by one of the boats. The ship sank by the stern, after which, as he had done earlier, *Kapitänleutnant* Helmut Witte surfaced and offered food, water, medical supplies and cigarettes after questioning the survivors. The men in the boats were picked up by two Colombian schooners, *Envoy* and *Zaroma*, twenty-eight hours later, transferred to the sub-chaser *PC-458*, and landed at Cristobal.⁶³

Section Base, Cristobal received Navy Armed Guard survivors on 16 June and over the next four days. On 21 June, the *YP-26* and two Higgins boats were dispatched outside the anti-submarine nets guarding the harbor to rescue the crew of a ship that had wandered into a defensive minefield, hit a mine and sank. Survivors were brought to the Section Base, given first aid, and sent to Fort Davis. The fort, sited on Gatun Lake near the Atlantic entrance of the Panama Canal, was the headquarters of the U.S. Army's 14th Infantry Regiment, assigned to protect the Panama Canal Zone.⁶⁴

Four former San Diego tuna clippers—YPs *280* (ex-*Cape San Vincent*), *281* (ex-*San Salvador*), *288* (ex-*Western Pacific*), and *291* (ex-*Normandie*)—reported to the base for duty on 23 June. Their presence eased the work load of the other district vessels and was timely, as survivors from yet another torpedoed ship arrived the next day.⁶⁵

CARIBBEAN SEA FRONTIER

The main coastal shipping route along the eastern seaboard, which conveyed vessels to and from the Caribbean, began at the St. Lawrence River. Connecting the Great Lakes with the Atlantic, the river traversed the Canadian provinces of Quebec and Ontario and formed part of the international boundary between Ontario and New York. After passing into the Atlantic at Cabot Strait, shipping proceeded along the coast of Nova Scotia and then outside the Georges and Nantucket Shoals to New York, where they were joined by ships from New England ports that had passed through the Cape Cod Canal and Long Island Sound. From New York Harbor, ships proceeded southward to Cape Hatteras on the North Carolina coast (a transit in which vessels might join the shipping route from, or depart to, the Chesapeake and Delaware Bays) and down the Atlantic seaboard to Florida. From Florida, shipping passed through the Straits of Florida bound for the Gulf of Mexico, or took the Old Bahama Channel to the Windward Passage between the islands of Cuba and Hispaniola, joined by ships proceeding directly from New York to the Panama Canal. Many vessels bound for the Lesser Antilles, Trinidad, the Guianas in the northeastern area of South America, and the oil distilleries of the Dutch West Indies passed into the Caribbean through the Mona Passage separating Puerto Rico and Hispaniola. In addition considerable traffic moved from New York to Cape San Roque, Brazil, and the River Plate (estuary of the Rio de la Plata) off the coast of Argentina and Uruguay.⁶⁶

Map 11-1

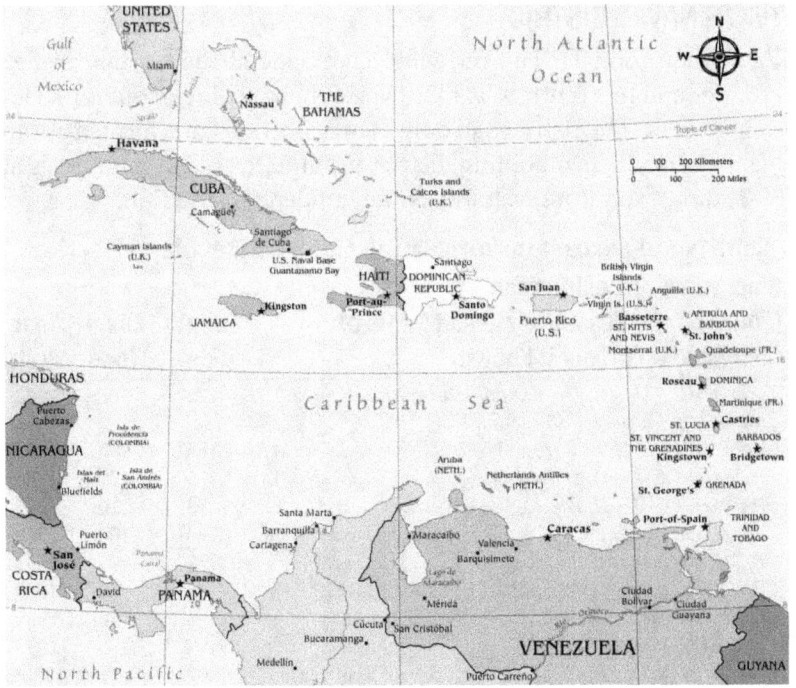

Caribbean Sea.
Source: http://www.lib.utexas.edu/maps/americas/txu-oclc-123908752-caribbean_2006.jpg

The Atlantic and Gulf Coasts of the United States, where on average over a ship a day had been sunk during the first half of 1942, were relatively free from U-boat attacks after July. This condition was not true of the Caribbean where submarines attacks, begun as a part of Operation *NEULAND* ("New Territory") on 16 February, continued throughout the summer. In July, August, and September alone, U-boats sank seventy-five ships. The frequency of attacks decreased significantly after this period, but continued through the summer of 1944. The principal trouble spots were:
- the Dutch islands of Curacao and Aruba, where over a half million barrels of gasoline and oil derivatives were produced daily;

- Trinidad, through which most of the Allied shipping to and from South America, and all of the bauxite trade, had to pass; and,
- The Windward Passage, a strait in the West Indies and a direct shipping route from the East Coast of the United States to the Panama Canal.[67]

TENTH NAVAL DISTRICT

Vice Adm. John H. Hoover, USN commanded the Caribbean Sea Frontier and the Tenth Naval District. When war broke out on 7 December 1941, the district had only a single section base, located at San Juan, Puerto Rico, adjoining district headquarters, although bases at St. Thomas, and Roosevelt Roads were under construction.

Tenth Naval District Inshore Patrol: Capt. J. M. Ashley, USN (Ret.)

Ship Name or Designation (Former Type Vessel/Name and Name of Commanding Officer if Known)	Length Feet	Displ Tons	Year Built
Turquoise PY-18 (ex-yacht *Ohio*, *Maramichi*, *Walucia III*, *Kallisto* and *Entropy*, Lt. Clusman)	172	565	1922
Opal PYc-8 (ex-yacht *Coronet*)	185	590	1928
YP-28 (ex-*CG-225*, Ens. Beckerleg)	75	37	1924
YP-64 (ex-USCGC *Eagle*, Lt. (jg) Whitney)	98	210	1925
YP-202 (ex-*Almina*, Lt. (jg) Erickson, Lt. (jg) J. A. Barnett)	120	104	1930
YP-203 (ex-motor yacht *Genzam*, Lt. A. Hessberg)	97' 7"	97	1931
YP-205 (ex-motor yacht *Sabiha III*, Lt. Schumann)	96	50	1930
YP-208 (ex-yacht *Agawam*, Lt. (jg) W. C. Beatie)	102	150	1920
YP-224 (ex-*Vigilant*)	54' 4"	78	1939
YP-454 (ex-yacht *Souris*, *Iolite* PYc-24, Ens. Symington)	107		1930[68]

"Inshore patrol" was a bit of a misnomer with regard to the Tenth Naval District, as the patrol area stretched 600 miles from latitude 25° north, southward to 15° north, and eastward roughly along Santo Domingo-Haiti, with no end boundary. This area included Santo Domingo; Puerto Rico; the Virgin Islands; the Lesser Antilles, as far south as Dominica Channel; and all pertinent channels and land approaches. By April 1942, inshore patrols had expanded to include San Juan, Mayaguez, Ponce, and Roosevelt Roads, Puerto Rico, as well as the waters of St. Thomas, Antigua, Guantanamo, and Trinidad. Capt. J. M. Ashley was singularly responsible for all patrol operations until, following the establishment of Section Base, St. Thomas, the Virgin Islands Sector came under Comdr. H. W. Neely. The *YP-28* was reassigned to St. Thomas to patrol the harbor entrance and approaches, and other patrol craft joined her at the section base.[69]

Ship Name or Designation (Former Type Vessel/Name and Name of Commanding Officer if Known)	Length Feet	Displ Tons	Year Built
Section Base, St. Thomas, Virgin Islands: Comdr. H. W. Neely, USNR			
YP-28 (ex-CG-225, Ens. Beckerleg)	75	37	1924
YP-436 (ex-*Philip and Grace*)	89		1942
YP-442 (ex-fishing dragger *Gloucester*)	88		1929
YP-445 (ex-fishing dragger *Babe Sears*)	87		1929
Section Base, Teteron Bay, Trinidad, British West Indies			
YP-63 (ex-USCGC *Dexter*)	98	210	1925
YP-219 (ex-yacht *Nancy D.*, Ens. Collins)	71'1"		1924
YP-610 (ex-*E. R. Stuart*)	100[70]		

VAST AREA AND INSUFFICIENT ASSETS

Vice Admiral Hoover had fewer assets at his disposal than other frontier commanders, as those nearer the United States had first priority for available planes, vessels, and mines. He was also burdened with keeping an eye on the Vichy French in Martinique and Guadeloupe. Because the frontier was so decentralized, subordinate commanders at Guantanamo, Curacao, and Trinidad were given almost complete responsibility for their respective areas. As part of a "Destroyers for Bases" deal on 2 September 1940, Britain received fifty aged destroyers, and the United States received the right to construct bases in eight British possessions. However, when war broke out on 7 December 1941, Naval Operating Base, Trinidad had not yet been commissioned and had few ships for defense. There were only the patrol yachts *Opal* and *Turquoise*, YPs 63 and 64, a seaplane tender supporting four Catalinas of Squadron VP-31, and one utility transport. Despite a shortage of escort vessels, the commander of the Trinidad base and the equally poverty-stricken base at Curacao joined in establishing convoys between these two critical areas.[71]

Located off the coast of Venezuela, Trinidad commanded a vulnerable approach to the Panama Canal and the South American trade routes. The island measures roughly thirty-five by fifty-five miles, with two long, narrow peninsulas extending westward toward the continent to form the Gulf of Paria. Because of the proximity of the Venezuela coastline, the gulf is landlocked except for two channels, the "dragon's mouth" to the north and the "serpent's mouth" to the south. Vessels arriving at the base on Teteron Bay for the first time normally were met by a patrol boat for escort through the Boca de Navios, one of the straits comprising the Dragon's Mouth, into the Gulf of Paria and then to Teteron Bay.[72]

The island of Curacao, however, was of even greater importance than Trinidad. As one of the largest oil-refining centers in the world, it supplied desperately needed oil and high octane gasoline without which the Allied campaigns in Europe and the Pacific would have become difficult almost to the point of impossibility. Moreover, Curacao also served as a defensive base for the protection of principal shipping routes to all the war theaters from northern South America, the Caribbean, and Panama.[73]

Map 11-2

Commander, Caribbean Sea Frontier had few vessels to escort oil tankers proceeding from Curacao and Trinidad through U-boat infested waters or to monitor the activities of "Vichy" French in Martinique and Guadeloupe.
Source: http://www.lib.utexas.edu/maps/americas/txu-oclc-123908752-caribbean_2006.jpg

OPERATIONS IN TRINIDAD WATERS

Until the Navy organized formal Key West-Trinidad convoys in July 1942, with escort provided by combatant ships, the efforts of the few planes and vessels based at Trinidad were largely devoted to rescue operations. Sea planes were often forced to jettison bombs in order to be sufficiently light enough to land on the water to rescue seamen from torpedoed ships. Patrol yachts and YPs were similarly kept busy rescuing survivors, returning to Port-of-Spain, Trinidad, landing them and, after taking on fuel and water, immediately departing on the next patrol. Continuous operations were particularly hard on the YPs; at one time the *YP-219* had been stripped of all her engine parts, except the blocks, to repair other craft.[74]

U-BOAT ATTACK ON CONVOY TAG-18

More than 200 Allied convoy-routes existed during the war. Each convoy was identified by two or more letters, which normally designated the departure and destination harbors; H or O were used for some convoys, meaning homeward bound to or outbound from a particular port. The number following the letters was the convoy's sequence in leaving the port of origin. Thus, TAG-18 was the eighteenth convoy to depart Trinidad on the Trinidad-to-Aruba-and Guantanamo route. On the eve of her departure, the masters and commanding officers of merchantmen and escort ships were likely concerned about the possibility of U-boats along their route. None of them could know that *Kapitänleutnant* Georg Lassen would execute one of the most successful series of attacks by a single sub on a convoy—theirs.[75]

The "slow convoy," so designated due to the best speed that its members could make, stood out of Port-of-Spain on 2 November 1942 under escort of the patrol yacht *Siren* and four submarine chasers, *PC-469*, *495*, *559*, and *561*. As the ships proceeded northwest, the weather was fine and clear, and the sea smooth. The night sky, although absent a visible moon, was bright with starlight. In the very early hours after midnight, the convoy was making 8 knots as it passed northwest of Grenada. The *Siren*, commanded by Lt. Comdr. H. G. White, was patrolling at a speed of 10 knots ahead of the formation, while the PCs, which were much faster, moved about more vigorously on the flanks. They had to cover large sectors due to the enormous size of the merchant convoy, which stretched out for miles. None of the escort ships were fitted with radar, but all had sound gear and were listening intently for any sign that an enemy submarine might be nearby, when, at 0202, an explosion shattered the tranquil darkness.[76]

The 2,260-ton Canadian merchant vessel *Christian J. Kampmann*, hit by two torpedoes from the *U-160*, sank by the stern with the loss of seventeen crewmen, and two sailors of the Navy Armed Guard. The convoy proceeded on in orderly fashion with all vessels entirely blacked out. Just as the moon appeared on the horizon, Lassen fired

Patrol yacht *Siren* (PY-13) under way.
Source: http://www.navymemorial.org

two torpedoes at the convoy, now sailing north of Margarita Island off the northeastern coast of Venezuela. Both hit the 11,015-ton Norwegian tanker *Thorshavet*—positioned in the middle of the formation—on her starboard side. It exploded, killing two men on watch in the engine room. The ship slowed and fell out astern of the formation; survivors abandoned ship in four lifeboats.[77]

Not satisfied after having put one ship down, with a second settling by the stern, Lassen sought other opportunities. The *U-160* attacked TAG-18 a little before noon on 3 November, sinking the 4,034-ton British merchant vessel *Gypsum Empress* and damaging the 8,546-ton Panamanian tanker M.V. *Leda*. In a running attack that had begun when the convoy was approximately ninety miles northwest of Trinidad, the *Leda* torpedoed and set on fire the fourth victim within eleven hours. Everyone aboard abandoned ship; the master, Jens P. Michelsen, was so badly injured that he died aboard the *PC-495*, which, commanded by Lt. Charles W. Frey, USNR, rescued the crew from lifeboats and a life raft. The *Leda* was subsequently taken in tow, but foundered in shallow waters thirty miles northwest of Trinidad on 5 November and was lost. Frey described the attacks on the *Gypsum Express* and *Leda*:

> After a tough night I had gone below at about 5 a.m. [to get some rest]. At about 6:30 the officer of the deck called me and said, "Captain, I think they have just hit another one". At the same time he sounded the general alarm. I went up to the bridge and saw the torpedoed ship, an ore carrier, several columns to starboard of the *Leda*, in the first line of the convoy. She started to settle by the stern and drifted back toward the rear of the column. It was broad daylight. The sun had been up an hour.
>
> Just as all hands got on deck, there was another explosion and a huge flash of flame appeared over the *Leda*. The flame was followed by a column of smoke that rose about 1,000 feet into the air and then settled down, covering the torpedoed and burning tanker.

It was a spectacular sight. We were within 500 yards of the *Leda* and thought we would never see the vessel after that, but as the rest of the convoy moved on and the smoke cleared away, we saw that the *Leda* was still afloat. We made an intensive patrol of our sector and then received word to drop aft and pick up survivors.

Georg Lassen, who over the course of the war was credited with sinking twenty-six ships, was finished with TAG-18. However, the *U-129* was also nearby.[78]

Having already lost four of his charges, the convoy commander was desperate for additional escorts, but received just one, the destroyer *Lea* (DD-118), a World War I-vintage "four piper" commissioned on 2 October 1918. Ordered to join the convoy, she left her moorage off Naval Operating Base, Trinidad around dawn on 3 November, stood out, and, after passing Chacachacare Island light, set course 312 true and increased speed to 25 knots. At 1119, having left the Venezuelan Testigos Islands to port, she changed to an east-northeast heading, and a little over an hour later, began sighting survivors on rafts. The *Lea* picked up eight men from the *Christian J. Kampman* and then proceeded north-northwest. At 1430, a wreck came into view eight miles distant, and as the *Lea* closed, four lifeboats. The destroyer recovered all forty-three survivors of the *Thorshavet*, and then unsuccessfully attempted to sink the derelict with depth charges before continuing on to join convoy TAG-18. A salvage ship arriving on scene three days later found that the motor tanker had sunk.[79]

The *Lea* joined the convoy at 2207 and was assigned a patrol station 7,000 yards astern of TAG-18. (Asked whether he had experienced any trouble finding the group of ships, the DD's commanding officer replied, "No, I just followed the wreckage from one point to another".) The convoy now consisted of nineteen merchant vessels and various escorts. Steering south-southwest on 4 November, at 0920 the destroyer sighted Bonaire Island off her starboard bow, and in mid-afternoon, Little Curacao Island on the horizon. Located about fifty miles north of Venezuela, Bonaire, Curacao, and Aruba comprised the "ABC islands" of the Dutch Caribbean. During early evening, the cutter *Colfax* came alongside the *Lea* and embarked the survivors who were aboard. The destroyer then resumed her station, amid calm seas and good visibility.[80]

That same evening, a subsidiary convoy joined TAG-18, forcing the *Lea*, *Siren* and four sub-chasers, already spread thin, to try to shield thirty-seven merchant vessels. There were gaps in the anti-submarine screen and the *U-129* found one. At 0310 on 5 November, the lead ship in the right hand column, the American tanker *Melton*, blew up, as did the Norwegian tanker M.V. *Astrell*, further back in the same column, three minutes later. The *U-129* hit the *Melton* with three torpedoes fired from her bow tubes plus one from her stern tubes, and the *Astrell* with both torpedoes fired from her stern tubes. At 0330 the convoy commander ordered the ships to execute an emergency turn to port, and fifteen minutes later an emergency turn to starboard, while the escorts searched for the submarine. The *PC-469* fired a starshell at 0347, hoping perhaps to unveil a U-boat in the gloom, but to no avail. During the late morning, the sub-chaser gained sound contact and dropped a pattern of depth charges, followed nine minutes later by a second attack by the *PC-495*, results unknown. After regaining contact later in the afternoon, the *469* lobbed 300-pound depth charges over the side with her K-guns, again with no evidence of any harm done to a submarine. The survivors of the *Melton* and *Astrell* were picked up by the Dutch motor torpedo boat *TM-23* and the *CG-475* and landed at Curacao and Aruba.[81]

A little before noon on 6 November 1942, the *PC-561* made two attacks on doubtful contacts. That evening, two ships left the formation for their ports of destination. TAG-18 arrived at Guantanamo Bay two day later, minus the *Christian J. Kampmann, Thorshavet, Gypsum Empress, Leda, Meton*, and *Astrell*.[82]

The Navy awarded battle stars to just fifty-eight ships in the American Theater over the course of the war. Twenty-three stars were associated with Convoy TAG-18. Every officer and man aboard the *Siren, Lea*, submarine chasers *PC-469, PC-495, PC-559* and *PC-561*, minesweeper *Hamilton* (DMS-18), and cutters *CG-6, Colfax*, and *Rush* received a battle star to place on their American Theater ribbon. Navy Armed Guard units aboard the *Ardmore, F. H. Bedford, Jr., Benjamin Bourn, City Service Kansas, Edward L. Doheny, Domino, Eagle, Gulfpride, Peter Hurll, Leda, Meton, Moldova, Nishmaha, Pan Gulf, Paulsboro*, and *Felix Taussig* were likewise recognized.[83]

12

Additional Tuna Clippers Sent to the South Pacific

> *Get your men on those machine guns; there will be an aerial attack any minute.*
>
> —Advice offered by Lt. Christian Rasmussen (who had lost his ship, the *YP-284*, to Japanese destroyer fire off Guadalcanal on 25 October 1942) to CWO Kenneth G. Adams, after boarding the *YP-347*, upon her arrival at Guadalcanal. Rasmussen then asked for a drink of whiskey, but there was none aboard, and he declared that the worst thing that could happen to anyone was to get stuck ashore.[1]

The *YP-347* (ex-*Star of the Sea*) was one of the fourteen former San Diego tuna clippers that had made passage from San Diego to Pearl Harbor, arriving on 17 May 1942. On 30 July 1942, she and the *YP-237* (ex-*Anna M.*) and *YP-348* (ex-*Cabrillo*) left Hawaii bound for the South Pacific in company with the oiler *Kaloli* (AOG-13) for the first leg to Palmyra. Adams kept a diary in which he described the transit to the island, and visits to South Pacific islands, likely representatively of those made by other ships:

> That old skipper of the freighter assigned me the task of staying out in the lead to portray a destroyer to discourage a submarine attack. So all during daylight hours we zigged and zagged out front.
>
> From Palmyra the three of us (YPs) continued on to Tutuila, Samoa. Two days before arrival a hurricane struck. That night a sea hit us on the port side and stove in a section of the storm boards that served to keep the main deck from flooding. We took enough water to give a list. Luckily, I was on the bridge and grabbed the wheel and put it hard to port . . . to bring her upright, then straightened her out

with the weather [seas] astern and slowed down to facilitate making necessary repairs.

> Landfall, at the opposite side of the island from the harbor, was made at night. . . . There were mine fields to protect the harbor at Pago Pago, making it necessary to follow closely a swept channel to the entrance. Dawn had arrived to make the task easier and safer. . . . Not until we reached the entrance could the bay be seen, as the final leg of the run was in close along the beach.[2]

A Navy launch came out to meet the ships and led them to a mooring buoy in mid channel. Sailors scanning the shore through binoculars sighted natives who appeared to be women wearing skirts. A trip ashore quickly disproved this belief. What they had observed were males wearing a lava lava, a knee-length piece of cloth wrapped around the waist and tucked in at the belly. Ashore Adams encountered native members of the island defense force as well as other Samoans, whom he described thus:

> One day as I strolled along the waterfront, two Samoans in kaki lava lavas and Marine caps gave me a snappy salute, which I returned, thinking all the while they were playing soldier. Actually they were members of the Feta Feta Guard, a branch of the Marine Corps, all of whom are natives to guard the island, but never to be sent elsewhere. They receive regular Marine pay and have all the military privileges. . . .
>
> All the male Samoans are heavily tattooed especially their thighs and waist. I couldn't distinguish any design. To me it appeared as a multitude of small ink dots close together. There must be a punishment of blinding an eye for some infraction of native law, for there are quite a number of men with the use of only one eye. The men are all powerfully built. . . .
>
> Contrary to the general opinion about South Seas beauties, the Samoan girls are not what I would call pretty, and they all look alike as peas in a pod.[3]

Following a four-day stay at Pago Pago Harbor, Tutuila, Samoa, the YPs left port for New Zealand, with Virgil Pash, the oldest of the skippers, selected by the others as group commander. He relinquished this duty, and the position of his YP as lead boat, to Adams after finding that Adams was obtaining the best navigational fixes. The ships approached land at Cape Bret on the northern North Island coast in New Zealand, and entered a swept channel that extended all the way to Auckland. With many islands to avoid, and the need to make many course changes, the vessels anchored as night fell, lest one or more end up aground on a rocky point. In the morning, they weighed anchor and proceeded into Auckland harbor and their designated berths. Thereafter, the three YPs operated independently. The *347* left Auckland on 10 September for Bora Bora in the Society Islands. Encountering huge swells en route, Adams frequently had to turn his ship's head into the seas to keep from foundering. The challenges endured were quickly forgotten, however, on arrival at the beautiful island.

> Our first task was to take a load of meat to Bora Bora, traveling alone. It took us twelve days to get there, of which ten were spent wallowing along in the trough of tremendous swells rolling up from the Antarctic. Day and night Leon, Johnny the engineer, and I took turns keeping our eyes on the oncoming seas, and when we would spot a comber approaching, over to starboard went the wheel and speed reduced in order to meet the dangerous sea head on. That went on day and night for ten days until reaching a latitude of decent weather. We three were bushed by that time. Virgil Pash [skipper of the *YP-348*] left port two days behind us and had the starboard bow bulwarks [of his ship] bashed in.
>
> Bora Bora is a beautiful island encircled by a reef with deep water in the lagoon. At the center rises a craggy mountain with cliffs and spires all covered in green growth and palm trees.
>
> That night I attended the outdoor theatre with the usual palm log seats. The screen became forgotten when a full moon rose to silhouette that beautiful, picturesque mountain. I sat there spellbound, wondering if it might not all be a dream that my eyes were beholding such a spectacular act of nature. Surely there could be no possibility of my ever witnessing a sight more breathtaking and stunning.
>
> The weather was clear on the day of the ship's departure, with the tip of a mountain on Tahiti visible off to eastward. The return trip to Auckland was easy, the seas having subsided to normal.[4]

The *YP-347* left Auckland on 4 November 1942 bound for Noumea, New Caledonia. Seventy-five miles from the reef entrance, the vessel's main engine developed a problem requiring repair, and for

Beautiful Bora Bora in the Society Islands.
Source: http://www.ibiblio.org/hyperwar/USN/Building_Bases/img/bases2-p193.jpg

three days Adams and crew drifted on a calm sea before they were able to resume their journey. After entering the lagoon, the YP came upon two small islands with a deep channel between them. Adams' orders included information that the waters between them were mined, and to steer clear by going around the eastern one and then anchor to await a pilot. After waiting several hours without a response to his signal flag requesting a pilot, Adams proceeded into port on his own. There, unlike at Bora Bora, the Americans did not receive a warm welcome. Adams explained:

> Noumea is a French city whose citizens acted unfriendly in the extreme. I might go so far as to say that they glared at we Yanks. The reason, we were to learn, was that they were Vichy French and Nazi sympathizers. It is a strange feeling to be hated, seemingly, for no reason at all. One trip ashore was enough for all of us.[5]

The *YP-347* left Noumea en route to Espiritu Santo, New Hebrides, via Efate as it had come in, minus a pilot, with the captain himself steering around the aforementioned island and steadying on a course for the reef entrance before turning the wheel over to a crewman in his fifties. After instructing him how to proceed, Adams left the bridge to attend to another matter. On his return a few minutes later, he noted that the ship was too close to the island and, glancing over the side, saw a round object twice the size of a basketball not more than thirty feet away and about ten feet below the surface. Adams grabbed the wheel and steered the YP away from the lethal area, all the while expecting to be blown skyward at any moment. After arriving at the harbor at Efate, a lovely island on which the United States had constructed a base and airfields to support its offensive in the Solomons, Adams reported to military headquarters. On his way, he passed a number of stretchers containing dead men with pale, waxen faces who he believed to be casualties of war flown in from Guadalcanal.[6]

The next working port was Espiritu Santo. On arrival, the *347* anchored in a deep channel between two islands near where a troop transport (the converted passenger liner S.S. *President Coolidge*) had stuck a mine in a defensive field a few days earlier, sinking close to shore. As she was loaded with beer and whiskey, divers expended much effort in retrieving her cargo. The YP departed Espiritu Santo for Guadalcanal on 7 November escorted by the destroyer-minesweeper *Hopkins* (DMS-13). She arrived at Aola Bay on 26 November with special food for Thanksgiving dinner for the troops in the Aola Bay, Kukum, and Tulagi area. Following a decision to build an airstrip thirty-three miles east-southeast of Henderson Field on Lunga Point, a force of U.S. Army soldiers and Marines had three weeks earlier landed unopposed at Aola Bay on 4 November 1942.[7]

Adams described the transit to Aola Bay, and noted that after the *YP-347* arrived at Guadalcanal everything went smoothly:

> Most of our run in the Solomons took place at night. And a spooky experience it was, approaching a place where death and destruction was taking place. The sea, protected by islands, was flat calm. A haziness cut [the] visibility to cause apprehension for course changes. My imagination caused the air to smell of death. Off in the distance ahead came the sound of gunfire to drive home the fact that war lay close at hand. It all seemed so unreal and fantastic that I should soon be exposed to the danger of a hateful enemy.

As it happened, the day ended quietly with the unloading accomplished in peace. Leaving Guadalcanal, the *YP-347* transited across the channel to Florida Island, at which the motor torpedo (PT) boats were based, to unload her remaining cargo.[8]

DELIVERY OF THANKSGIVING TURKEYS

As Thanksgiving approached in the autumn of 1942, the Navy decided that Marines fighting on Guadalcanal would have their turkey dinner just like everyone else. Thus, YPs 289 and 290, in addition to the 347, received orders to deliver the makings to Guadalcanal. Ex-tuna clippers *Paramount* and *Picaroto* commanded by Ed Madruga and Victor Rosa, the 289 and 290, loaded 160 tons of frozen turkeys at Havannah Harbor, Efate Island. The southernmost island of the New Hebrides, Efate lay along the Bora Bora-Australia supply line between Fiji, 600 miles to the east, and New Caledonia, 300 miles farther southwest toward Guadalcanal. Escorted by a destroyer, in the darkness they neared a designated beach off Guadalcanal, where the YPs encountered shellfire from Lunga Point. While transferring their cargo to Higgins boats, they were informed that an aircraft had dropped depth charges on a contact about two miles to their starboard. Departing the island for Noumea, New Caledonia during a heavy rainsquall, Joe Madruga, a crewman aboard his brother's ship, thanked the Lord for nature's assistance in making detection by the enemy more difficult. As the YPs entered port at Noumea and passed anchored battleships, cruisers, destroyers and other vessels, each warship in turn lowered her flag, a gesture crewmen believed to be a salute to naval units returning from the Solomons Island Campaign. Around this time, Edward Madruga conveyed his thoughts and those of his crew in a letter received in November 1942 by the American Tuna Association of San Diego. He wrote, "I like my job very well and I know all the boys from the tuna fleet now in the navy don't for a moment regret joining up. They like the service very much indeed."[9]

OVERVIEW OF THE PACIFIC FLEET SERVICE FORCE

At the time of the Japanese attack on Pearl Harbor, Rear Adm. William L. Calhoun, USN, was the commander of the Pacific Fleet's Service Force. Overnight these duties increased enormously and, soon promoted to vice admiral, he remained in this position until 1945. The Service Force was comprised of Squadrons Two, Four, Six, and Eight, with the latter responsible for the supply and distribution to the fleet of all fuels, food, and ammunition. (Squadron Four was subsequently deleted as part of reorganization, was later reconstituted,

Map 12-1

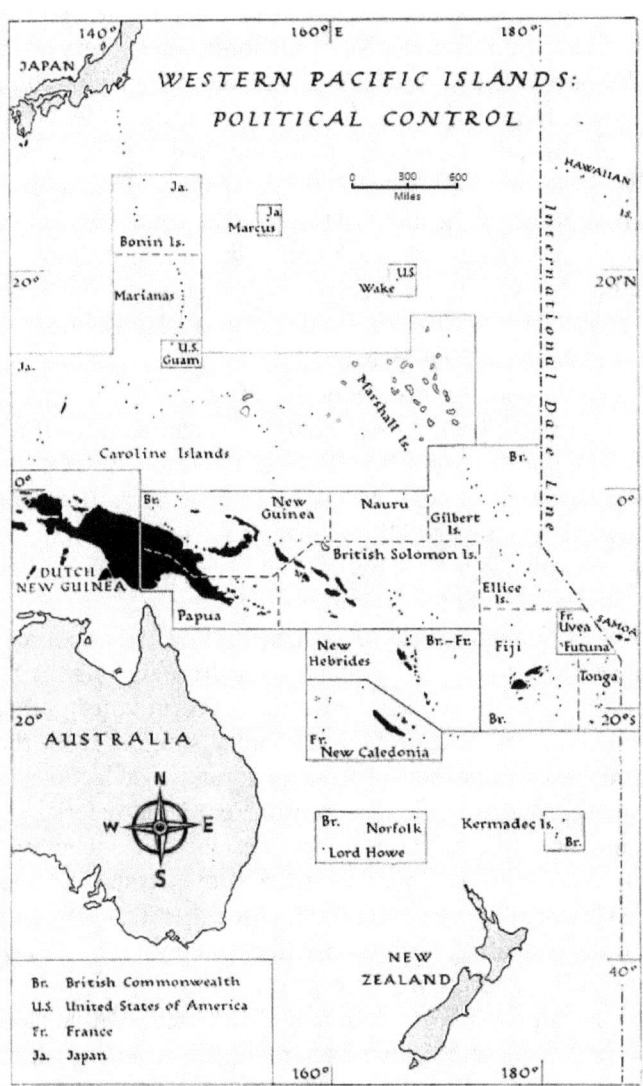

Political Control of Western Pacific Islands in 1939.
Source: http://www.lib.utexas.edu/maps/historical/pacific_islands_1943_1945/western_pacific_political_control.jpg

and Squadrons Ten and Twelve added.) As complaints about a lack of fresh provisions began to come from the fleet, Commander Service Squadron, South Pacific at Nouma, New Caledonia, made every effort to alleviate this shortage by requesting additional refrigerator ships and making efforts to procure more fresh provisions from New Zealand. In the meantime, tinned and dry provisions had to make up the difference. By the summer of 1942, with the campaign at Guadalcanal about to begin, support for the military forces in the South Pacific was critical. However, in late July there were only fifteen logistic ships in theater, including four ex-tuna boats hurriedly deployed from Pearl Harbor: the YPs *284* and *290* at Tongatabu, Tonga Islands, and YPs *239* and *346* at Efate in the New Hebrides.[10]

As the war continued, the number of ships assigned to the Service Force steadily increased. Each new campaign brought additional requirements for supply and support and associated ships. By September 1943, the Service Force had 324 vessels. A new Squadron Four was commissioned in October 1943 and dispatched to Funafuti in the Ellice Islands to furnish logistic support to the fleet and, in February 1944, Squadron Ten was sent to Majuro in the Marshalls. Squadron Six had the duty of remaining near or close behind the striking forces as they advanced towards Japan. As such, Squadron Six was the final link in service support between the United States and the fighting forces on the front lines. Squadron Eight hauled supplies from the West Coast and Caribbean areas to bases, anchorages, and lagoons in the forward area. Squadron Ten then transported these materials to the intended units or, in some cases, to newly established anchorages in what had been enemy territory a short time before. To support task units unable to break away from operations, Squadron Ten passed its supply ships on to Squadron Six still loaded with ammunition, fuel, and provisions. After discharging the cargo at sea to combat groups, the empty supply ships were passed back by Squadron Six to Squadron Ten to be refilled, or still farther back to Squadron Eight, which resupplied them from the West Coast, Hawaiian, or other areas. By the end of July 1945, a few weeks before the war in the Pacific ended, there were 2,930 ships assigned to the Service Force.[11]

The continual and expanding requirements for logistical support for the fighting forces in the Pacific would result in many additional YPs being sent to the South Pacific. Five of these vessels—YPs *514*,

516, *517*, *518*, and *519*—left San Diego on 2 November 1942 for Tutuila. The *514* and *516* had orders to report on arrival to the commanding general of the defense forces in Samoa. The ships were the ex-tuna clippers *American Beauty, Queen Amelia, St. Ann, Commodore,* and *Queen Elizabeth,* respectively.[12]

13

Consolidation of the Southern Solomon Islands

> *KILL OR BE KILLED*
> —Declaration in the name of Vice Adm. William Halsey, USN, posted on a sign at Tulagi in 1943, reminding Navy servicemen of the realities of war.[1]

"Consolidation of Southern Solomons" is a phrase used to describe the period from 8 February to 20 June 1943, following the completion of the enemy's evacuation of all its forces from Guadalcanal on 7 February 1943. Thereafter, the Japanese strengthened their positions in the upper Solomons, while still carrying out air raids and submarine attacks on shipping in the southern islands. In the late winter and spring of 1943, a total of 141 Navy ships would earn 225 battle stars for combat in those waters. Three, YPs *417*, *YP-516*, and *YP-517*, were assigned to the Guadalcanal-Tulagi area as small supply ships.[2]

The *YP-516* and *YP-517* were the former San Diego tuna clippers *Queen Amelia* and *St. Ann*, while the *YP-417* was an ex-New England trawler recently arrived in South Pacific waters. The Navy had acquired the latter steel-hulled vessel and her sister ship *416*, formerly the *Calm* and *Drift*, in 1941 for use as anti-submarine patrol vessels along the eastern seaboard. However, a pressing need for service ships in the South Pacific found them far from New England waters in 1943.[3]

VOYAGE TO THE SOUTH PACIFIC

Lt. (jg) James B. O'Donnell brought the *417* from the East Coast to the South Pacific. After departing Charleston, South Carolina, the ship passed through the net gate at Port Everglades, Florida, during the late afternoon of 15 December 1942 and moored at the Section Base. The following day, she made the short transit down the coast to Miami, remaining there until 19 February 1943, when she stood out of the harbor in company with the dredge *Mindi*, tugs *Ed Moran* and *Theo Moran*, and sub-chasers *SC-749* and *PC-627* bound for Guantanamo Bay, Cuba.[4]

While transiting the Old Bahama Channel between the northern coast of Cuba and Great Bahama Bank, a sudden squall reduced visibility to zero, causing the *YP-417* to lose contact with the group. Unable to contact any of the other units by radio, she continued on and rejoined the group a day and a half later. After a Christmas Day spent at sea, the vessels passed through the Guantanamo Bay net gate at 1307 on 26 December and moored at the U.S. Naval Station, the YP remaining only long enough to receive fuel and provisions before standing out.[5]

On the morning of 30 December, the *417* passed the unlite gas buoy marking the entrance to the swept channel leading to the Panama Canal and entered the channel, arriving two hours later at Navy Base, Coco Solo, whereupon fueling ship began. In mid-afternoon, she proceeded to Section Base, Cristobal for a nearly two-week interlude. On the morning of 10 January 1943, a pilot boarded to take the ship through the canal. Crossing the forty-eight-mile-wide Isthmus of Panama took almost ten hours because vessels had to negotiate Gatum Locks Number 1 and 2, pass through Gatum Lake, then Pedro Miguel Locks North and South, and Miraflores Lake and its north and south locks before arriving at Balboa Harbor on the Pacific side of the canal.[6]

Ships bound for the South Pacific were normally held in the Canal Zone until a sufficient number had been assembled to form a transit group. Time spent awaiting departure was devoted to final voyage preparations. The *YP-417* cleared her berth at 0805 on 21 January 1943, and lay off Taboquilla Island, Panama, awaiting the other vessels of which the oiler *Sepulga* (AO-20) was in charge as her captain was the "Senior Officer Present Afloat." Eight submarine chasers— SCs *521*, *700*, *738*, *740*, *749*, and *750*, and PCs *1119* and *1121*—the yard minesweepers YMS-10 and YMS-70, and YPs *414*, *418*, and *421* comprised the remainder of the group.[7]

Steering a south-southwest course the *417* traversed the equator on 28 January, marking the occasion with the customary Crossing the Line ceremony. On the last day of the month, she stood off the *Sepulga*'s starboard side at a twenty-five foot distance, with the captain conning (giving speed and rudder orders), while receiving fuel and provisions. After clearing the oiler's side, she fired two .50-caliber machine guns (No. 4 and 5 atop the pilot house) and the starboard .30-cal. machine gun before resuming her position in the group. The *YP-417* arrived at Bora Bora on 10 February, proceeded through the net gate, and anchored in Teavanui Harbor. Preparations for combat duty continued in port with the removal of large awnings rigged aft to provide crewmen relief from the hot sun. If left in place, the shade covering would have impeded sailors on lookout duty in sighting and giving warning of enemy aircraft.[8]

After a six-day stay, *YP-417* got under way and rendezvoused off the island with the escort group, now minus the oiler, for passage to Tutuila, Samoa. Arriving during the late morning of 23 February, she entered Pago Pago Harbor and made up to Mooring Buoy D, her starboard side to the portside of *YP-421*. At a little past noon the following day, the *417* went alongside the oil dock at the naval station to take fuel, and thereafter stood out to join the escort group, now bound for Suva, the capital city of Fiji on Viti Levu Island. Leaving Fiji as part of a group of ships, the YP made New Caledonia, the New Hebrides, and finally the Solomon Islands.[9]

CONTINUED DANGER IN THE SOLOMONS

In the spring and summer of 1943 *YP-417* make trips across the twenty-mile-stretch of Iron Bottom Sound separating Tulagi and Guadalcanal, hauling whatever was needed. There were frequent enemy air raids against Guadalcanal, the worse occurring on 7 April when 177 Japanese planes raided the Guadalcanal-Tulagi area; twenty-five were shot down. Luckily, the *417* was not in the harbor at the time. Nicholas J. Lavnikevich, a pharmacist's mate second when he reported aboard on 1 October 1942, described at age eighty-three the period from 13 April to 20 June 1943 for which the YP was awarded a battle star:

> We were almost daily under Japanese air attacks. Not our boat, but the island of Tulagi and the island of Guadalcanal. . . . Guadalcanal was of course where the Henderson Air Field was and that's where

the aircraft were that took off and were bombing the other islands that were Japanese held. So, we saw a lot of anti-aircraft not from our boat as such, although there were a few times . . . We weren't supposed to fire on any Japanese aircraft because we would give our position away, or so that was the theory anyway . . . [On one occasion] every ship, every gun, every pistol on the place was firing. It was really unbelievable. [The sky] was just lit up like [the] Fourth of July with all the tracers and bombs going off.[10]

SUPPORT FOR PT BOAT SQUADRONS

The former Massachusetts fishing trawler *YP-417* (which, unlike the ex-San Diego tuna clippers, did not have a refrigerated cargo hold) was often employed as a small oiler to carry deck-loaded drums of fuel to PT boats. Lavnikevich recalled providing fuel to Motor Torpedo Boat Squadron 2 to which Lt. (jg) John F. Kennedy's *PT-109* was assigned:

> We refueled the PT boat squadron of Jack Kennedy. He wasn't with the group at that time he was off somewhere in a meeting or whatever, but we got to meet the fellows on the boats. . . . We loaded our decks with the large 55-gallon drums of high octane gasoline. That's what they used. And of course we would have been a great target. But, at any rate these were loaded on the deck of our ship and then we would rendezvous with some of these PT boats and refuel them.

(Kennedy arrived at Tulagi on 14 April and took command of his boat nine days later. On 30 May 1943, several PT boats, including his, were ordered to a new motor torpedo boat base in the Russell Islands in preparation for an invasion of New Georgia.)[11]

The *417* left Espiritu Santo on 18 April for Star Harbor on San Cristobal Island's north coast (one of the southern Solomon Islands), to refuel five PT boats—*56*, *157*, *159*, *160*, and *162*—from Motor Torpedo Boat Squadron Nine in transit to Guadalcanal from Noumea, New Caledonia. The engineers aboard the boats used hand pumps to draw the gasoline out of the drums and force it through a "shammy" (chamois leather) to filter out any impurities before it reached the storage tanks. At completion of the fuel transfer, the YP made Guadalcanal.[12]

THE PRACTICE OF "CUMSHAW" ALIVE AND WELL

As their ship was not a frozen food supply vessel, the forty officers and men of the *YP-417*, like those aboard other fleet units, received limited fare. This situation led enterprising sailors to find other ways to augment their subsistence via "cumshaw." This term refers to acquisition of something through unofficial means, whether deviously or ingeniously. Lavnikevich described the food and his efforts, along with those of his shipmates, to acquire chow by other means. In addition, he discussed their conversion of the ship's salt water ballast tanks (which when filled were designed to provide greater stability during storms) for the storage of fresh water which could then be traded for food.

> Well, it [the food] was pretty awful. When we first got out to the Solomon Islands it was canned and powered. . . . And Spam . . . [which] was called luncheon loaf and it was a little too salty. . . . Any time there was a large vessel that was unloading food, we never had any trouble getting a group of men to go . . . to help unload—it was mostly canned food but once in a while we'd actually get some fresh meat. . . . We'd go down the ladders and all through the hold and we would come out with a case of something. And that lasted for quite a while, so we were sort of beggars.
>
> And then we found that we could load [fresh water]—we had converted our ballast tanks which held salt water. We had some pretty ingenious people on the ship. They pumped all the [salt] water out and used some kind of chrome paint to paint the inside of these tanks and we'd fill them with fresh water. And then some of the small craft that came with the fresh food from New Zealand and Australia, we would make a deal with them. We'd give them fresh water if maybe we could get a little fresh food. And . . . fresh eggs, for example, you know, that was really something. So we got to bargain pretty well, cause . . . we'd go back and forth between Guadalcanal and Tulagi and there was a place where we got water. I think it was Florida Island that had water coming down off the hills, pure clean water and we would fill our tanks when we could . . . And so that's how we managed to survive, but believe me nobody cared for powered eggs or Spam for many, many, many years to come after that.[13]

ARRIVAL OF OTHER FORMER NEW ENGLAND TRAWLERS

In addition to YPs *414*, *418*, and *421* that made the Pacific crossing with the *417*, six other former New England fishing trawlers arrived in the South Pacific in 1943. YPs *415*, *416*, *419*, *420*, *422*, and *423* departed San Diego on 5 April, bound for Tutuila, and then Noumea, New Caledonia. The *YP-422*, which L. Ron Hubbard, the founder of Scientology, had briefly commanded following its acquisition by the Navy, grounded on Tumbo Reef off New Caledonia on 23 April 1943. She was declared a total loss on 13 June 1944, following the removal of all salvageable equipment and material.[14]

Ship Name or Designation (Former Type Vessel/Name and Name of Commanding Officer if Known)	Length Feet	Displ Tons	Year Built
YP-414 (ex-beam trawler *Squall*)	131' 2"	369	1937
YP-415 (ex-beam trawler *Swell*, Lt. (jg) H. Baker, USNR)	131' 2"	369	1936
YP-416 (ex-fishing trawler *Drift*)	147	310	1941
YP-417 (ex-fishing trawler *Calm*, Lt. (jg) James B. O'Donnell)	147	310	1941
YP-418 (ex-fishing trawler *Crest*)	147	310	1938
YP-419 (ex-fishing trawler *Illinois*)	118' 4"	300	1941
YP-420 (ex-beam trawler *Arlington*, Ens. E. J. Masselo, USNR)	131' 2"	369	1936
YP-421 (ex-beam trawler *Surf*, Paul C. Huelsenbeck)	145	310	1936
YP-422 (ex-fishing trawler *Mist*)	133' 3"	310	1941
YP-423 (ex-beam trawler *Storm*)	145	310	1936[15]

JAPANESE AIR THREAT

Following completion of the Japanese evacuation from Guadalcanal on 7 February 1943, there was a lull in the fighting in the Solomon Islands, as both sides wanted a breather. This interlude did not last long as Halsey's admonition "Keep pushing the Japs around" epitomized the prevailing attitude.[16]

The Americans had the advantage in quality of aircraft, and sometimes in numbers as well, while the Japanese had superior position. The only Allied airbase was Henderson Field on Guadalcanal, augmented by a fighter strip at Aola Bay and in the Russell Islands to the northwest. The Japanese had Rabaul and, progressing southwest through the Solomons toward Guadalcanal, facilities at Buka, Kahili, Vila, Munda, and Rekata Bay. The latter served only seaplanes. Bombers were able to stage at Rabaul or Bougainville for raids on

Tulagi-Guadalcanal, refuel en route, strike their targets, and return to Rabaul beyond the range of fliers from Henderson Field.[17]

The principal duty of YPs was to provide logistics support to the U.S. Army's XIV Corps in the Guadalcanal-Tulagi area, which included the American Division, the first Army unit sent to Guadalcanal. As it had arrived piecemeal during the summer and early autumn of 1942, its soldiers had been fed into combat beside the battle-hardened Marines. Between landing on Guadalcanal on 7 August and early December 1942 the Marines had lost over 600 men and suffered an additional 10,635 casualties, of which only 1,472 resulted from gunshot wounds. Decimated by malaria and malnutrition over the course of the Battle for Guadalcanal, the 1st Marines were relieved by the American Division on 9 December 1942, and were sent to Australia to rebuild their strength, rest, and refit for future combat. The XIV Corps would continue operations in the Guadalcanal area until all Japanese resistance had ended.[18]

Map 13-1

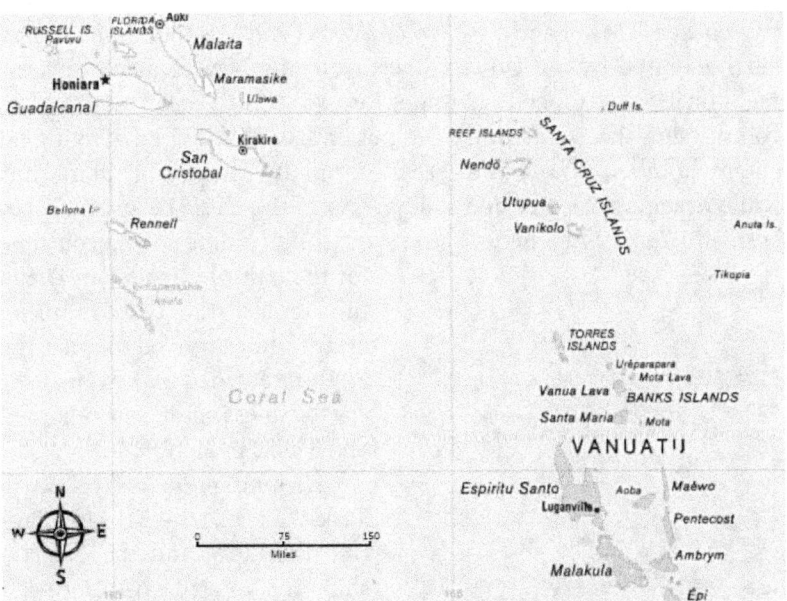

Small groups of YPs—former tuna clippers and fishing trawlers—made repeated runs through dangerous waters between Espiritu Santo and Guadalcanal to provide vital food and other supplies to Marine Corps and Army ground forces.
Source: http://www.lib.utexas.edu/maps/islands_oceans_poles/solomonislands.jpg

In order to resupply the Army troops on Guadalcanal, pairs of YPs, sometimes accompanied by other vessels, made frequent trips to Espiritu Santo, New Hebrides, to obtain refrigerated cargo from larger Navy supply ships. Returning to Guadalcanal, YPs would typically anchor at Lunga Point to discharge a portion of their cargo, and then spend the night anchored or moored to a buoy off Kukum Beach. The following morning, they would proceed across the channel to Tulagi Harbor, moor at Government Wharf or Sturgis Dock and deliver the rest of their stores.[19]

This shuttle duty was not without risk because passage through South Pacific waters remained dangerous. A brush with the enemy occurred on 31 March when Task Unit 32.4.3—YPs *516* and *517*—were attacked by a twin-engine Mitsubishi 96 bomber about seventy miles east of San Cristobal Island. No damage resulted from several dropped bombs. A week later, during the late morning of 5 April, Task Unit 32.4.7 came under air attack off Ulawa Island in the southern Solomons. The task unit included the net laying ship *Locust* (YN-17), with the auxiliary service craft *Taupata* (YAG-26) in tow astern, the sub-chaser *SC-640*, and YPs *516* and *517*. (The 118-foot *Taupata* had been acquired by the United States from the New Zealand government on 10 November 1942 under Reverse Lend-Lease and placed in commission that same day.) The net layer succeeded in dodging an enemy bomber, as well as a torpedo from an undetected submarine, while dragging the wooden sailing vessel. The YPs *516* and *517*, *Locust*, and *Taupata* earned a battle star. Good fortune would continue for the pair of former San Diego tuna boats. The *Queen Amelia* and *St. Ann* survived the war; the *St. Ann* returned to the tuna fishery business and was renamed *Sun Venus* in 1949.[20]

Around noon on 18 April, Task Unit 32.4.3—*YP-515* (flagship), *YP-518*, and the Liberty-ship S.S. *Peter Sylvester*—left Guadalcanal for Espiritu Santo. The following day, a Japanese bomber found the *YP-518* and, from approximately 30,000 feet,

Photo 13-1

YP-516, the former tuna clipper *Queen Amelia*, under way.
Source: http://www.navymemorial.org/

dropped two bombs that landed 400 yards off the starboard quarter of the ship. The *518* was not able to answer the attack because the plane was so high overhead that it was out of range of her thee 20mm guns. Having attempted and failed to destroy the small ship, the aircraft then disappeared into the clouds and was not seen again. Mindful of the possibility that there might be other enemy aircraft in the area, the commanding officer, Lt. (jg) Richard G. Savidge, USNR, kept all hands at their battle stations until 1345. The *YP-518*, however, did not meet *Navy and Marine Corps Awards Manual* criteria for a battle star, defined thus:

> The prerequisite to the wearing of a star on an area service ribbon shall be honorable service in a ship, aircraft unit or shore-based force at the time it participated in actual combat with the enemy. In instances in which the duty performed did not result in actual combat with the enemy but is considered equally hazardous, the Chief of Naval Operations may award an operation of engagement star to the units concerned.[21]

AIR ATTACK ON SHIPPING AT GUADALCANAL

In the early afternoon of 16 June 1943, a large group of Japanese aircraft arrived over Guadalcanal and, as bombers attacked ships unloading cargo, Zeros engaged in dog fights with American planes over Henderson Field. The cargo ship *Aludra* (AK-72) and the destroyer-transport *Schley* (APD-14) were off Togama Point discharging cargo, and the *Celeno* (AK-76), *Deimus* (AK-78), and *Liberty*-ship S.S. *Nathaniel Currier* were unloading between Lunga Point and the Tenaru River. There were also several tank landing ships and many small craft in the area; most likely the YPs *516* and *517* were discharging cargo at Lunga Point or across the channel at Tulagi. Each patrol craft received a battle star for the period from 5 April to 16 June 1943 for "Consolidation of Southern Solomons." Navy ships could only receive a single star for any one operation, no matter how many engagements with the enemy. At a minimum, the YPs were likely involved in combat on 5 April and 16 June, the beginning and end dates of the award period for the battle star they earned.[22]

The objective of the big Japanese air offensive on 16 June was shipping in the Guadalcanal area. Vessels off Lunga Point were attacked by eighteen to twenty-four dive bombers, with several Zeros coming in to strafe. Friendly fighters engaged enemy planes as they cleared, and few escaped. Some fighters closed the formation and were fired at by friendly vessels. There were many ships present at Guadalcanal due to a training exercise and the offloading of men and materials for the establishment of a headquarters for Rear Adm. Richmond K. Turner, commander Amphibious Force South Pacific. The commander of a group of infantry landing craft, located near Kokumbona Beach, Guadalcanal, witnessed simultaneous bombings at Tulagi and Guadalcanal. Off Lunga Point, heavy smoke rose from a ship, three aircraft fell in flames, and about twenty planes engaged in dog-fights. Across Iron Bottom Sound, he also sighted two planes on fire and falling near Tulagi Harbor, a parachute descending in the same area; to the northwest, a parachute descended over Savo Island. Near the end of the action, another plane fell in flames and a parachute came down toward the sea off Lunga Point.[23]

JAPANESE SUBMARINE SINKS THE *ALUDRA* AND *DEIMOS*

The *Aludra* and *Deimos* survived the air attack only to be torpedoed a week later by the Japanese submarine *RO-103*. The *YP-514* and *518* were en route to Espiritu Santo from Guadalcanal on the morning of 23 June when the destroyer *O'Bannon* came up astern and signaled a request that they turn around to pick up survivors. Arriving at the scene of the disaster at 0720, they found *Deimos* and *Aludra* sinking, the former from two torpedo hits in the stern and the latter from one torpedo hit in the bow. While the *O'Bannon* screened the ships from any additional attacks, the *Skylark* and YPs searched for and recovered survivors. All survivors from the *Aludra* were picked up by the *Skylark* and *YP-514*, and those of the *Deimos* by the *YP-518*. Crowded aboard the latter 128-foot ship were 113 survivors—13 officers and 100 enlisted. The *YP-514* picked up two dead and seventy wounded men.[24]

With the recovery of all visible survivors completed, the *YP-518* went alongside the *O'Bannon* and transferred to her the commanding officer of the *Deimos* as well as seven other officers and forty-one men. The *Skylark* and the YPs continued their search until about 1112, and then set a course for Espiritu Santo. The following day the *Skylark* conducted a burial at sea for two *Aludra* crewmen and three army and one navy service members killed while taking passage aboard her. The *YP-514* performed a service for one unknown soldier, who had also been aboard the cargo ship, but having no identification tag, could not receive final rites by name.[25]

Four of the five YPs highlighted in the preceding few pages had been built in San Diego yards for the local fishing community, as traditional diesel-powered wooden bait boats, with deckhouse forward and bait tank aft. The other former tuna clipper, the steel-hulled *YP-515*, was unique, having begun her naval service in 1919 as the fleet tug *Chimo* (No. 22).

Ship Name or Designation (Former Type Vessel/Name and Name of Commanding Officer if Known)	Length Feet	Displ Tons	Year Built
YP-514 (ex-tuna clipper *American Beauty*, Bos'n Charles E. Kaufman, USNR, Lt. (jg) George P. Paine, USNR)	129.1	456	1938
YP-515 (ex-fleet tug *Chimo*, tuna clipper *Falcon*)	157	512	1919
YP-516 (ex-tuna clipper *Queen Amelia*)	112	268	1941
YP-517 (ex-tuna clipper *St. Ann*)	94.8	248	1941
YP-518 (ex-tuna clipper *Commodore*, Lt. (jg) Richard G. Savidge)	128	300	1942

In addition to the battle star garnered by the *517* for her actions during the air attack off Ulawa Island, she would receive a second star eight months later for what the Japanese termed the "Sixth Air Battle over Bougainville."

14

Occupation and Defense of Cape Torokina

There were centipedes three fingers wide whose bite caused excruciating pain for a day, butterflies as big as little birds, thick and nearly impenetrable jungles, bottomless mangrove swamps, man-eating-crocodile-infested rivers, millions of insects, four types of rats larger than house cats, and heavy torrents of rain bringing enervating humidity. And sacred skull shrines, reminders of days of cannibalism and head-hunting.

—James Bradley and Ron Powers, describing in the book *Flags of Our Fathers* the conditions encountered by U.S. Marines on Bougainville in the Solomons

In 1943, the American military strategy in the Southwest Pacific was simple: advance northwest through the Solomon Islands and capture the powerful Japanese military base at Rabaul, New Guinea. This action would make it possible to open a direct route to the Philippines, and retake the islands as General MacArthur had promised. (The strategy would create successfully one of the two roads to Tokyo later used by the Allies: the New Guinea-Leyte-Luzon-Okinawa and the Marshalls-Marianas-Iwo Jima routes.) By late autumn 1942, the 1st Marines had crushed the Japanese on Guadalcanal and, relieved of their duties by the American Division, had left for Australia. However, while the Allies had the use of Henderson Airfield on Guadalcanal, the enemy stronghold at Rabaul was well-buttressed by airdromes (sites from which aircraft flight operations take place) located at Bougainville, the Shortland Islands, and New Guinea.[1]

As a part of the plan to take Rabaul, the Marine 4th Raider Battalion, with Army reinforcements, made an amphibious landing at Segi Point on the southeast cape of New Georgia, Solomon Islands, on 21-22 June 1943 to begin the New Georgia offensive. By 25 August, this force had pushed through impenetrable jungles across a portion of the forty-five-mile-long island, swept the last Japanese defenders into the sea, and captured Munda airfield as well as Bairoko Harbor along the northwestern shore of New Georgia. The next objective was to seize an area on Bougainville, in order to build an airstrip from which bombers could fly airstrikes against Rabaul.[2]

BOUGAINVILLE

Bougainville, the largest island of the Solomons, lay near the northwestern end of the island chain, some 190 miles east of Rabaul. The mountainous island is dominated by the Emperor and Crown Prince Ranges, which include two active volcanoes, the largest of which, Mt. Balbi, rises to 10,171 feet. The dense jungle on the lower mountain slopes and coastal plains and the swamp areas immediately inland from the beaches are due to an annual average precipitation of 100 inches. These conditions made the island, as one Marine termed it, "a wet hell;" malaria and other tropical diseases were prevalent. There were approximately 54,000 natives, and Bougainville was one of the few places in the South Pacific with credible reports of headhunting still taking place. The Japanese had invaded the island and the adjacent smaller Buka in early 1942 when fewer than twenty Australian troops and a few naval coast watchers were based there. The soldiers withdrew into the jungle to observe the enemy until evacuated, while the coast watchers remained to report enemy air and sea movements. Their warnings of convoys and air raids coming down the slot had helped the Marines to achieve victory on Guadalcanal.[3]

On 1 November 1943, the 3rd Marine Division (Reinforced) of the I Marine Amphibious Corps launched Operation CHERRY BLOSSOM with an amphibious assault landing at Cape Torokina, Bougainville. The division's orders were to seize an initial beachhead and to occupy and defend the area between the Laruma and Torokina Rivers to a distance of 2,250 yards back from the water's edge. The Marines were to prepare to continue the attack in coordination with the U.S. Army's 37th Infantry Division upon the latter's arrival subsequent to D-Day, in order to extend the beachhead sufficiently to establish naval facilities and an airfield in the Torokina area.[4]

The Japanese opposed the landing with airstrikes from Rabaul. American forces countered with fighters launched from airfields at

Map 14-1

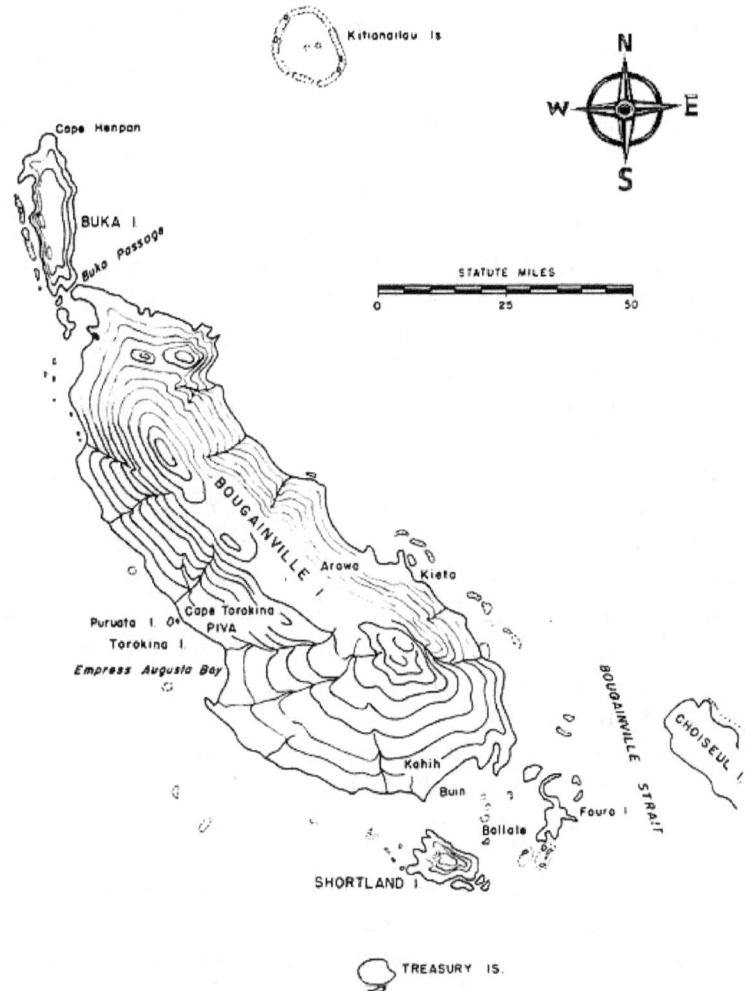

Marine Corps and Army assault forces landed at Torokina on Bougainville to seize the deep water port at Empress Augusta Bay and an adjacent area upon which to construct a major airfield. American bombers could then fly airstrikes against the Japanese base at Rabaul, and range over the South Pacific to protect Allied convoys and task forces during the forthcoming invasion of the Philippines.
Source: http://www.ibiblio.org/hyperwar/USN/Building_Bases/maps/bases2-p271.jpg

Munda, New Georgia, and Vella Lavella. Located west of New Georgia, the latter island was home base for Marine Fighter Squadron

VMF-214 (the "Black Sheep" led by Maj. Gregory Boyington), which at the time was enjoying some rest and relaxation in Sydney, Australia, before returning to a second combat tour on 27 November 1943. A Japanese task group, dispatched from Rabaul to Empress Augusta Bay to attack U.S. Navy transport ships in an effort to break up the landing, found on nearing the bay that Rear Adm. Anson Merrill's Task Force 39 was blocking the entrance. The task force included Destroyer Squadron 23, commanded by Capt. Arleigh Burke. After covering the initial landing at Bougainville, the "Little Beaver" squadron would participate in twenty-two separate engagements over the next four months, destroying one enemy cruiser, nine destroyers, one submarine, several smaller ships, and approximately thirty aircraft. During that period, the future Chief of Naval Operations received his nickname "31-knot Burke" for pushing his destroyers to just under boiler-bursting speed when in battle.[5]

From 6 to 19 November 1943, the remaining regiment of the 3rd Marine Division and the Army 37th Infantry Division landed at Torokina to strengthen the force already ashore and expand the beachhead. There was no thought of pushing across the 250 square-mile island to eliminate the 25,000 Japanese in what would be a brutal, costly, slow action. Instead, the Allies planned to take only a small piece of Bougainville, perhaps six square miles, including the deep port at Empress Augusta Bay, to build a major airfield from which American planes would range over the South Pacific to help provide security for the Allied convoys and task forces which would invade the Philippines in October 1944.[6]

Following the 3rd Marines' initial assault on the Torokina beachhead, the Navy began lifting additional occupational forces from Guadalcanal, termed reinforcement echelons. Each echelon, numbered successively, embarked in the ships of a naval task group for movement to Bougainville, and by 14 November, 33,861 men and 23,137 tons of supplies had been landed at Empress Augusta Bay. On their arrival, many task groups found air battles in progress over Bougainville and/or fighting by Marines ashore. The Japanese, wishing to squash the continued strengthening of the naval advanced base, also attacked task groups in transit to or departing from the bay.[7]

Marines engaged the enemy at Piva Trail and Coconut Grove in mid-November. However, the first encounter of Japanese resistance of any strength occurred on 20 November and developed into the Battle of Pivot Forks, fought through 25 November by the 3rd Marines, the 2d Raider Regiment, and the 9th and 21st Marines. Artillery was employed with increasing fire power until 24 November, when an attack by the 3rd Marines destroyed a majority of the enemy force, estimated as a reinforced regiment. Leaving some 11,000 dead, most of the remaining Japanese fled west towards the Torokina River. The following day, the 1st Battalion 9th Marines and six companies of the 2d Raiders passed through the 3d Marines, against light retiring resistance, to occupy the hill east of the Piva River. During the protracted and often bitter jungle warfare in which the Marines suffered many casualties to malaria and other tropical diseases as well as to combat, YPs *514* and *415* arrived at Torokina to ensure the hard-fighting leathernecks a turkey dinner on Thanksgiving Day.[8]

"TURKEY SHIPS" DELIVER THE FIXINGS

YPs *514* and *415* (the former tuna clipper *American Beauty* and beam trawler *Swell*) left Guadalcanal on 17 November 1943, loaded with turkey and other fresh provisions for Segi Point, New Georgia, and other recently seized areas. After unloading food at anchor off Signal Tower, Segi, the following day, the two YPs next made Sasevele Bay, New Georgia, and then Vella Lavella. Following their arrival at the Balioa anchorage on the morning of 21 November, the YPs alternately moored to Pier 1 to offload. In early evening, they stood out to sea bound for the Treasury Islands as units of a convoy of eight tank landing craft, one infantry landing craft and two submarine chasers. In the darkness, the officer of the deck aboard *YP-514* sighted anti-aircraft fire and a searchlight dead ahead and he called the captain, but all was quiet by the time the skipper arrived on the bridge.[9]

The refrigerated *YP-514* was well-suited for duty as a small service force vessel. Spanning 129 feet with a 30-foot beam and a 15-foot draft, she had the capacity to carry 300 tons of cargo, 35,000 gallons of fuel, and 8,000 gallons of water. Her single heavy duty diesel coupled to a single propeller could only push the ship to a speed of 11 knots, but allowed a 10,000-mile cruising radius. She had both an IFF radar and echo-ranging anti-submarine sound gear, and for self-defense, three 20mm anti-aircraft guns, two .50-caliber machine guns, one six-pounder gun, and depth charges, which afforded her three officers and twenty-five men some measure of comfort.[10]

The *YP-514* had sailed from San Diego for Tutuila a year earlier on 2 November 1942 in company with four other YPs. Following her arrival she had been assigned to transport fresh provisions to British Samoa; Funafuti, Ellice Islands; and Wallis, Samoan Islands. The latter, a French possession, was the site of a landplane and seaplane base for use by U.S. Navy and Marine Corps aircraft. Ordered to Efate, the YP conducted station-ship and submarine listening-post duty there. She reported to Espiritu Santo on 23 April 1943, and over the next seven months made fourteen trips to Guadalcanal, transporting nearly three million pounds of frozen foodstuffs to an area still under enemy attack.[11]

In November, following Guadalcanal resupply duty, the *415* and *514* made the first YP run to Treasury Island, a few kilometers south of Bougainville, and then to Empress Augusta Bay, with mostly Thanksgiving turkeys and cranberry sauce as their cargos. The ships arrived at Treasury Island to unload on the morning of 22 November, and while anchored in Blanche Harbor, transferred 1,200 gallons of water to seven PT boats before departing for Bougainville in the late afternoon. The "Turkey ships" rendezvoused with Task Group 31.6 (transporting the Seventh Echelon) south of the island. The task group included eight tank landing ships—LSTs *334, 390, 397, 398, 446, 447, 449,* and *472*; six infantry landing craft—LCIs *61, 63, 328, 332, 335,* and *336*; and the fleet tug *Sioux* (AT-75). Destroyer Squadron 22—*Bennett* (DD-473), *Conway* (DD-507), *Renshaw* (DD-499), *Saufley* (DD-465), *Sigourney* (DD-643), and *Waller* (DD-466)—accompanied the group to provide protection. As she approached the task group, *YP-514* received the convoy's base course and speed by flashing light message in addition to instructions to take station on the port quarter of the formation.[12]

The two islands, Mono and Stirling, which comprise the Treasury Islands (often referred to in the singular), were separated by a harbor from which a few palm tree-dotted coral islets protruded. Although the island group was a part of the British protectorate of the Solomon Islands' Shortland District, the Japanese had held it until less than a month before. Lying just seventy-five miles from Cape Torokina, the islands were an ideal site for a support base for the planned Marine amphibious assault on Bougainville Island as well as the Solomons and Bismarcks Campaigns into 1944. The 8th Brigade Group of the 3d New Zealand Division came ashore at Treasury on 27 October and,

Photo 14-1

YP-415, the former beam trawler *Swell*, under way in 1942 near Boston. Navy Yard Boston photo # 4473-42 25 September 1942; Boston National Historical Park Collection NPS Cat. No. BOSTS-14817; NavSource, www.navsource.org/archives/14/31415.htm

after several days of fighting on the beachhead and areas inland, declared the islands secure on 12 November. Navy Seabees then began construction of a motor torpedo boat base, a supply dump, and an airfield on Stirling Island to create U.S. Naval Advanced Base, Treasury Islands. From this site, PT boats would patrol area waters and fighter planes would participate in the campaign to neutralize Japanese air power at Rabaul.[13]

During the morning of 23 November, the two YPs arrived at Bougainville to deliver their food stores. At 0730 *YP-514* anchored in Empress Augusta Bay in four fathoms of water. Within minutes, the threat warning changed from green to red and she weighed anchor, moved a safer distance offshore, and dropped the hook in fifteen-fathom water. Because they needed more time to unload, the tank landing ships had been the first units to enter port. Enemy shore batteries took the beached "amphibs" under fire at 0820 and shelled them for about ten minutes with 77mm mortar fire. The *LST-447* suffered three dead and nine wounded, two base personnel were also killed.[14]

The YPs stood out of the bay in the early afternoon, bound for Guadalcanal with Task Group 31.6. Shortly after midnight, the destroyer *Bennett* detected a group of ships bearing 120 degrees true at 35,000 yards. These ships proved to be Destroyer Squadron 23. A few hours later the destroyer *Sigourney* notified the YPs that they were to divert to Vella Lavella with two tank landing ships, and at 0536 the *Sigourney*, with the YPs *415* and *514* escorting LSTs *447* and *449*, detached from the task group. On arrival at the island, the tank landing ships stood into the beach at the Juno River to offload Torokina ground force casualties. (Within the task force, ships' colors were ordered to half-mast in honor of the sailors killed in action aboard the *LST-447*; a burial at sea from the *LST-398* followed.) As the casualties were brought ashore, the destroyer and YPs patrolled nearby. Following retraction of the LSTs from the beach, the group reformed and set a course for Guadalcanal.[15]

The YPs received a battle star for delivering the turkey and fixings on 23 November 1943; the *YP-514*'s war diary noted "survived enemy air raids on their [the task group's] approach to Cape Torokina."[16]

BATTLE OF CAPE ST. GEORGE

> *An almost perfect action that may be considered a classic.*
> —Vice Adm. William S. Pye, president, U.S. Naval War College[17]

In the early hours of 25 November, as the YPs were in transit to Guadalcanal, a Japanese destroyer force, that had just landed 920 men at Buka to reinforce a garrison on the island the enemy now considered at risk due to its proximity to Bougainville, was intercepted by Destroyer Squadron 23. The enemy force split into a screening column of two destroyers and a transport column of three destroyers, while Arleigh Burke in turn divided his force into three destroyers under his direct command, and two destroyers under Comdr. B. L. Austin. Under heavy cloud cover on the dark, moonless night, Burke raced west to get between the Japanese and their base at Rabaul. After gaining radar contact with the two enemy screening destroyers, he turned his division directly toward them and launched fifteen torpedoes, before turning sharply away to avoid counter-attack. Austin was eager to attack from the opposite side, but was ordered off by Burke. Having sighted the American DDs just thirty seconds before the torpedoes arrived and with scant time to maneuver, the *Onami* was obliterated in a massive explosion and *Makinami* crippled by a hit amidships. Austin sighted the remaining destroyer-transports, and after making a report to Burke, received orders to finish off the *Makinami*, while the destroyer squadron commander pursued the second column. Following a long stern chase while maneuvering to avoid a brace of enemy torpedoes, Burke closed with the Japanese ships at 0215. With dawn fast approaching and Rabaul all too near he sank the *Yugiri* with gunfire before racing back east. The battle was over with the Little Beavers sinking three Japanese destroyers without suffering a single hit.[18]

AIR ATTACK OFF THE TREASURY ISLANDS

> *The most persistent, prolonged and confusing attack by well-trained, Japanese pilots we have observed.*
> —Statement by Capt. Arleigh Burke, USN, commander Destroyer 23, concerning the enemy air attack against Task Group 31.6, which the Japanese military command at Rabaul called the "Sixth Air Battle of Bougainville"[19]

As convoys continued to transport echelons of the landing and occupation forces to the Bougainville beachhead, the Ninth Echelon, Northern Force formed at Guadalcanal on the morning of 2 December. Comprising (the Guadalcanal section of) Task Group 31.6 were eight tank landing ships—LSTs *334, 390, 397, 398, 446, 447, 449,* and *472*—and *YP-517*, escorted by units of Destroyer Squadron 45—*Fullam* (DD-474), *Guest* (DD-472), *Bennett* (DD-473), and *Terry* (DD-513). Spanning a mere ninety-five feet, the *YP-517* had only two years earlier sported a coat of bright white paint as the tuna clipper *St. Ann*.[20]

After leaving the Kukum area, the group proceeded toward Cape Torokina via a route south of the Russell Islands. The following morning it was joined by the fleet tug *Sioux* (AT-75), and that afternoon by five infantry landing craft—LCIs *62, 64, 222, 335,* and *336*. Comprising the Vella LaVella section of the task group, they were escorted by *Braine* (DD-630) and *Renshaw* (DD-499), the balance of Destroyer Squadron 45. A Marine Parachute Battalion and Headquarters Company were embarked aboard the LCIs, while the LSTs carried equipment, supplies and troops of the 251st Coastal Artillery, 62nd New Zealand Radar Squadron, I Marine Amphibious Corps, and other units of the echelon.[21]

That night, as the group passed the Treasury Islands twenty-two miles to the east, it was attacked at 1955 by a force of enemy torpedo and horizontal and/or dive bombers. During the nearly hour-long action, the convoy was under almost continuous harassment. Fortunately, in the darkness the enemy planes were unable to distinguish their targets until near the termination of their attack runs. However, these conditions also prevented ships from sighting and taking the fast moving aircraft under fire until they appeared suddenly in a dive out of the gloom. The northern horizon was obscured by a dark band of cloud cover extending northwest to northeast, and a crescent moon—shining through a light haze of cirrus clouds almost directly overhead—was partially obscured at times by broken cumulus. Surface visibility was fair, and the sea smooth with little wind.[22]

At the time of the attack, the tank landing ships were in an open sea formation of three columns, with the infantry landing craft, the fleet tug *Sioux* (AT-75) and *YP-517* in a line across the rear of the group. The six destroyers were initially disposed in an anti-submarine screen around the convoy. As the attack developed, they moved in closer to the formation to provide better anti-aircraft protection. The tank landing ships stationed in the first and last positions in the left and right columns, and the second one in the center column, had barrage balloons aloft at 2,000-3,000 feet to form a protective "X" pattern. Each dirigible-shaped balloon was tethered to a tending ship with metal cables intended to defend against low-level aircraft attacks by damaging the offending plane on collision with the cables. At the very least the cables made an attacker's approach more difficult. The devices were carried aboard the LSTs because they each had a deck sufficiently large to bed down one inflatable, and a winch to ease out and recover it. The task group was steering course 310 true at 9 knots. Ten to twenty miles northwest of its location, Destroyer Squadron 23 was providing cover along the routes of both the Ninth Echelon, en route to Bougainville, and the Eight Echelon bound for the Treasury Islands.[23]

The executive officer of the destroyer *Guest* described in his report of the action how the battle unfolded:

> Initial radar contact with the enemy was made by the Task Group at 1850, almost simultaneously in the west and in the southwest at a distance of 24 and 29 miles respectively. Twenty-five minutes later the task force contacted [on radar] enemy planes to the north at a

distance of 20 miles and, immediately prior to the development of the attack, enemy planes were contacted in the northwest and in the northeast, 15 to 20 miles distant.

These planes approached and at 1955 one of more passed over the task group and a red flare which burned approximately 3 minutes was dropped dead ahead of the group.

At 2000 . . . a large group of enemy planes bearing 265° at a distance of 30 miles split into two groups, one group circling to come in from the northwest and the other from the southwest. A third group was also approaching from the southeast and was first picked up at a distance of about 12 miles bearing 120°. The group to the northwest further divided into smaller groups of planes while the third group approaching from the southeast continued to close the task group and at approximately 2020 launched torpedoes on the starboard quarter. At 2027 from the *Braine*, *Terry*, and this vessel, torpedoes were sighted in the water to starboard.

By this time, the LST group had made an emergency turn to port of 60° and had returned to base course . . . successfully avoiding the torpedo attack. It is believed that three or four planes came in from the port quarter [of the formation] at the same time the larger group approached from the starboard quarter.

Other enemy planes were contacted orbiting at about 10 to 12 miles in the southeast and southwest even as the torpedo attack was being pressed home. At 2032 enemy planes came in from 310° and the *Bennett* reported shooting down one of these at 2033 and a second at 2036. At the same time planes were approaching from 230° and enemy planes were contacted in all quadrants at a distance of 12 to 25 miles. At 2042 planes approached from the northwest and from the north. . . . From 2100 until 2157 contacts were made on enemy planes at various ranges and bearings to the northwest but none were threatening.[24]

At that point in the war, the enemy was concentrating on night air attacks and, as was standard practice prior to such attacks, one or more dropped-flares and white float lights helped guide attack groups. As the action began, an inexperienced gunner aboard the *Fullam* took under fire a plane well beyond range, resulting in an immediate attack against the destroyer by a dive bomber in a flat dive dead ahead. This "one-two" tactic "teased" a ship into disclosing its position to a nearer aircraft poised for an attack. In the *Fullam*'s case, however, the destroyer increased speed causing the bombs to land astern. Over the course of the lengthy air attack, every ship fired at aircraft coming in low and fast, as they appeared suddenly within the range of their guns. Many of the attacks originated from "down moon" and were made against the starboard side of the formation. The final tally was four planes shot down—one each by the *Fullam* and *LST-334*, and two by the *Bennett*—with several other aircraft hit, but not seen to crash.[25]

The units of Task Group 31.6 escaped unscathed. Despite several torpedo and bomb near misses during the lengthy and almost continuous attack by the group of aircraft—some visually identified as "Bettys" (twin-engine torpedo-bombers) and others as "Vals" (single-engine dive bombers)—none of the ships suffered any material damage. To the northwest, a second group of aircraft had simultaneously attacked Destroyer Squadron 23. Comdr. B. L. Austin described the action:

> The enemy planes, estimated to have numbered from fifteen to twenty-five, made contact shortly after dark as if informed of the general location of our forces. One major group attacked the ninth echelon about ten miles to the southeast while the other delivered its attack on Squadron Twenty-three. The attack was businesslike and developed quickly after short feeling out period and placing of flares. Some planes were identified as Betty's. Some carried torpedoes and some bombs. Attacks were by several groups from different directions and were pressed home. At least five of the planes were shot down by Destroyer Squadron Twenty-three.

The only damage inflicted on the Little Beaver squadron by the enemy was to the destroyer *Converse* (DD-509), which suffered some hull damage and minor personnel casualties from the near miss of a five-hundred pound bomb.[26]

The following morning, the Ninth Echelon embarked in Task Group 31.6 arrived in the vicinity of Cape Torokina and at 0500 was met by pilots who would guide the vessels to their unloading areas. Four of the LSTs beached to the east of the cape and the remaining four at Puruata Island, while the destroyers took stations seaward as screening ships. As tank landing ships unloaded, the LSIs discharged their troops and cargo, and *YP-517* delivered its cargo of frozen food to help feed the several thousand combat and support personnel then on the island. After embarking litter and ambulatory patients from base medical aboard the LSTs, the task group left Bougainville in late afternoon for return transit to Guadalcanal. The *517* subsequently received a battle star for her actions during the air attack.[27]

FALL OF RABAUL APPEARS INEVITABLE

Christmas 1943 was a big day for Bougainville. The Thirteenth Echelon arrived with the *YP-415* and *514*'s cargo of turkey and fresh provisions. Embarked in the amphibious ships, the 164th Regimental Combat Team, American Division arrived as relief of the 9th Marine Regiment. However, the biggest gift to the greater war effort at year's end was completion of the large bomber airstrip above the forks of the Piva River. Admiral Halsey sent congratulations to Maj. Gen. Oscar W. Griswold (commanding XIV Army Corps, which relieved the 3rd Marines on 15 December) on completing this very difficult and significant accomplishment via a humorous message:

> In smashing Jungle and Japs to build that strip there had been neither bull nor dozing at Torokina [meaning no bulldozers were available to assist with work by the Navy Seabees in the abysmal terrain]. Well done and Merry Christmas to all!

With the airstrip completed, it now seemed inevitable that Rabaul would fall.[28]

15

Breaking the Bismarck Islands Barrier

> *The heroes of the Arawe operation were the little fellows of the "spit-kits" [sub-chasers] and the "splinter fleet [other types of wooden vessels]," faithfully landing their cargos despite vicious air attacks and lack of protection from their own air force.*
> —Samuel Eliot Morison in History of United States Naval Operations in World War II, Volume VI, Breaking the Bismarcks Barrier

While the occupation and defense of Torokina was in progress, the Allies took another step along MacArthur's New Guinea-to-the-Philippines invasion route with amphibious landings on New Britain, a part of the Bismarck Archipelago located to the immediate west of Bougainville. The goal of Operation DEXTERITY was to gain control of the Vitiaz and Dampier Straits on the southwest side of the island. Allied forces had fought their way up the southeast coast of New Guinea to the Huon Peninsula located opposite the straits. In the process, they had recaptured Japanese-held Australian bases and other areas from which American and Australia forces were then operating in support of the New Guinea Campaign. However, MacArthur also wanted control of New Britain, which lay across the straits, to deny the enemy continued use of these waterways. The Japanese had been moving men and supplies by barge south through the Bismarcks to the Solomons. Control of both sides of the straits would also ensure a safer and more direct route for Allied forces during their impending push towards the Philippines.[1]

To break the Bismarcks barrier, the Allies planned to capture Cape Gloucester on the northwestern point of New Britain, commanding Dampier Strait. The 7,500 Japanese troops based there to defend an airdrome and other areas could expect no land or sea reinforcements from Rabaul, located 250 miles away on the northeastern coast of the mountainous New Britain. Rapid movement of troops over land was not possible and Allied forces would control the waters adjacent to the landing beaches. The enemy, however, had potent "air reach," and amphibious and support ships would have to battle waves of planes arriving overhead from Rabaul airfields.[2]

Map 15-1

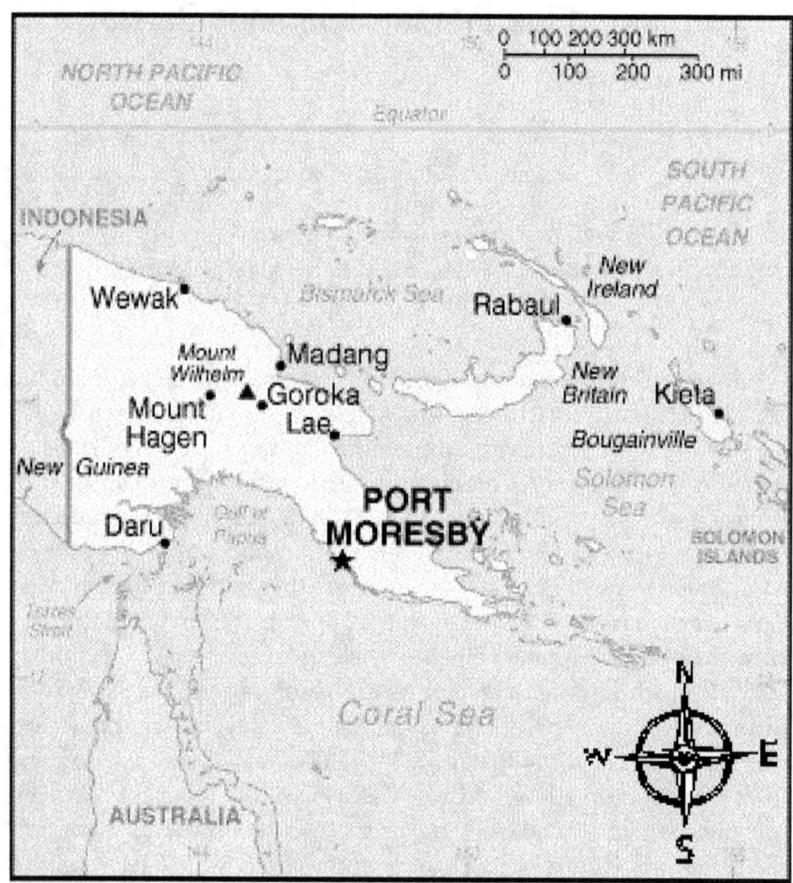

Amphibious landings on New Britain—a part of the Bismarck Archipelago located to the west of Bougainville—was another step along the Allies' New Guinea-to-the-Philippines invasion route.
Source: http://www.lib.utexas.edu/maps/cia12/papua_new_guinea_sm_2012.gif

GEOGRAPHY

The operation by the New Britain Force was to take place in two sequential phases: first, overwater movement and landing of a task force at Arawe, intended as a precursor to the second phase at Cape Gloucester, with the troops hitting the beach charged to seize, occupy and defend those areas. During the assembling and staging of naval forces, task units arrived first at Milne Bay on the eastern tip of New Guinea where Rear Adm. Daniel E. Barbey, USN, was embarked in the repair ship *Rigel* (AR-11). Barbey, who was in charge of the operation, was commander of the 7th Amphibious Force (Task Force 76). The sheltered bay was deep enough for large ships to enter and was the site of a forward Allied base with a bomber strip that permitted air operations against Japanese shipping and positions on the north coast. Allied ships arriving at Milne Bay were fueled, watered, and provisioned before proceeding through Ward Hunt Strait up the coast to Buna, Morobe, and forward areas.[3]

The Buna area on the northern coastal plain of New Guinea hosted an advanced base and airstrips; seventy-five miles further up the coast at Morobe Bay was a safe anchorage and staging point for Allied forces during the New Guinea Campaign. The forward-most naval base in friendly hands was Finschhafen on the Huon peninsula, which the Allied had taken on 2 October 1943. The Navy desired an advanced PT boat base further north than the one at Morobe, and believed that Finschhafen Harbor would be suitable. However, it proved to be rather shallow and had considerable fringing reef. Accordingly, Dreger Harbor, some three miles south, was selected, with the added bonus that the harbor also provided for greater dispersal of the boats when in the harbor. Enemy air activity was still fairly active, particularly at night, and mooring the boats apart from one another helped ensure their survival. Separating the harbors was Cape Cretin, a bold headland that, rising from the shoreline, was very picturesque. Off this point, assault groups and resupply echelons would assemble prior to departure for New Britain lying across the straits. Approximately six miles below Dreger Harbor was Hanisch Harbor from which landing craft (LCT) would embark, transport and land elements of the Arawe Task Force.[4]

Chapter 15
OPERATION DEXTERITY

The 112th U.S. Army Cavalry Regiment (Reinforced), which comprised the landing force, was withdrawn from garrison duty at Woodlark Island in Milne Bay and concentrated at Goodenough Island to the east of mainland New Guinea two weeks before the operation. The invasion force boarded transport ships during the afternoon of 13 December, and the convoy sailed at midnight. It proceeded to Buna in New Guinea to rendezvous with most of the escorting destroyers and, after making a deceptive feint north towards Finschhafen, turned toward Arawe after dusk the following day.[5]

The naval force off Arawe was subjected to a heavy air raid on 15 December shortly after the landing. At 0841 the destroyer *Reid* (DD-369) detected two groups of enemy aircraft bearing 052 true at fifty-nine miles. Nine minutes later, she and the *Shaw* (DD-373) had the planes at thirty-four miles, and *Shaw* vectored fighters to intercept the high flyers. Commander Task Force 76 described the action:

> [At 0857] our planes reported contact. 4 P-38's attacked 15 Zeros at 25,000 feet 15 miles NE of Arawe. 12 P-38's saw Betty bombers and 20 Oscar fighters heading east having approached from the direction of Rein Bay. This is believed to be the enemy formation on Shaw's screen. This formation was not attacked because the fighters were recalled to stop the Val dive bombers which suddenly appeared over Arawe undetected.
>
> Shaw reported enemy planes 335°—14 miles [at 0901]. This was the Val dive bombers over Arawe starting the attack. There were two groups, approximately 30 aircraft—at least 18 were Vals, one Val released 3 bombs on [the destroyer] *Conyngham* [DD-371]. Skillful maneuvering caused bombs to miss [by] 50 yards. Slight damage and several casualties to personnel were caused at the landing beach.[6]

The Japanese Aichi D3A ("Val") dive bombers escorted by A6M5 ("Zero") fighters evaded the USAAF combat air patrol of sixteen P38 Lightnings, and attacked the recently arrived first supply echelon of five tank landing craft (LCT) and fourteen medium landing craft (LCM). These ships managed to evade the bombs; the first wave of attackers, in turn, suffered no losses. Shortly before noon, P38s shot down a Zero and at 1800 drove off a force of Zeros, and Mitsubishi G4M3 ("Betty") and Mitsubishi Ki-21-II ("Sally") bombers.[7]

The *YP-236*, which would receive a battle star for the period from 15 to 31 December, may have been operating in the vicinity of the dive bomber attack, perhaps near Cape Cretin or at or near Hanisch Harbor where a separate enemy attack occurred that same day. Planners had specified that provisions would be provided at Buna from the HMAS *Merkur*, an Australian victualing stores and supply vessel, repair ship *LST-453*, landing craft repair ship *Amycus* (ARL-2), or a YP, and by a YP at Dreger Harbor. However, *LST-453* was staged at Hanisch Harbor, with the *YP-236* likely nearby. The LST was providing repairs and the YP was provisioning the landing craft in the supply echelons. A formation of twin-engine bombers struck Hanisch Harbor in the early evening of 15 December while, above and astern of the group, a dog-fight between six fighters was in progress. At least twenty bombs rained down, straddling LCTs in the harbor. While ships were hit by bomb fragments, they suffered no serious damage, and the casualties were limited to minor injuries to two personnel.[8]

Map 15-2

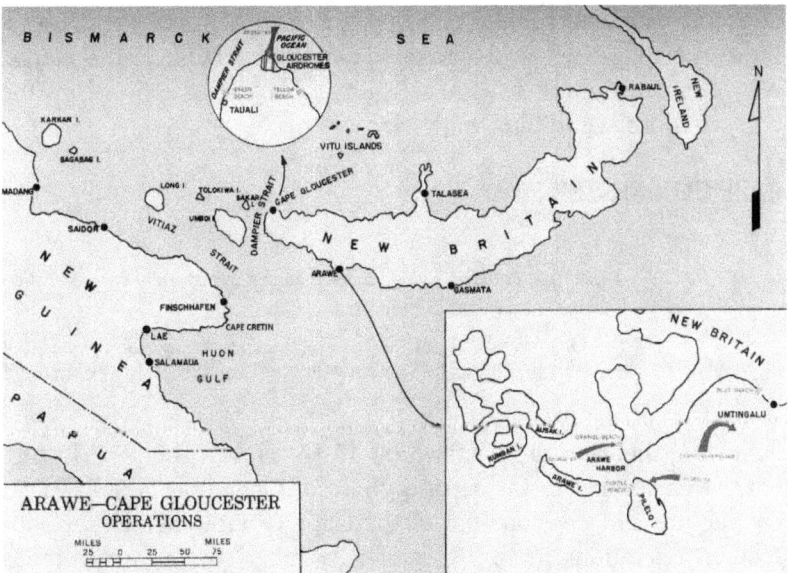

The *YP-236* was positioned near Cape Cretin, New Guinea, to provide provisions for assault groups and resupply echelons during landings across the Vitiaz and Dampier Straits at Arawe, New Britain.
Source: http://www.lib.utexas.edu/maps/historical/engineers_v1_1947/arawe_cape_gloucester_1947.jpg

In addition to the *YP-236*, three other former tuna clippers supported the operation by transporting provisions and supplies from Milne Bay to Buna and other forward areas:

Ship Name or Designation (Former Type Vessel/Name and Name of Commanding Officer if Known)	Length Feet	Displ Tons	Year Built
YP-233 (ex-tuna clipper *San Joao*)	113.6	281	1929
YP-236 (ex-tuna clipper *Europa*)	109	267	1931
YP-278 (ex-tuna clipper *Liberty*, Lt. Swartz)	117.4	334	1937
YP-283 (ex-tuna clipper *City of San Diego*, Lt. Marden)	116.2	311	1931

The *YP-233* left Milne Bay at 1300 on 7 December 1943 to provision naval vessels in the Buna area, followed five days later, by the *YP-278*, similarly bound for Buna and forward areas. Both ships were warned in their movement orders, "Enemy aircraft are active northward from Oro Bay and enemy submarines are reported north of Cape Ward Hunt." The *YP-283* was dispatched from Milne Bay on 19 December to provision ships in the ports north of Buna. However, due to Japanese air raids then in progress, Lt. Marden, on arrival at Buna, was to join an escort provided by the Naval Officer-in-Charge, New Guinea, Comdr. G. Branson, Royal Navy, and proceed up the coast to Morobe and the Dreger Harbor area.[9]

CAPE GLOUCESTER

> *A tall man could lie with his head under the cover of the vegetation line and his feet out in the water.*
>
> —Observation about the landing beaches at Cape Gloucester that were so shallow as to warrant the title "beach" mainly by courtesy[10]

Following the capture of Arawe on 15 December, the New Britain Force transitioned to the second phase of Operation DEXTERITY, the capture and development of the Cape Gloucester area for subsequent operations in the Bismarck Archipelago. The amphibious landing at Cape Gloucester presented special challenges, because the waters en route to it were narrow, shallow, and treacherous. Additionally, since Japanese aircraft were still a threat, the Navy was reluctant to risk ships larger than LSTs in the approach straits and the reef-filled waters off the assault beaches.[11]

On 26 December, the 1st Marine Division, commanded by Maj. Gen. William H. Rupertus, covered and supported by heavy naval and air bombardment, landed on the beaches southeast and southwest of Cape Gloucester against minor opposition. The narrow beach, which heavy rains had converted into a sea of mud, and the thick swamp and jungle beyond, presented the major difficulties. Marine forces took Target Hill-Silimati Point on the first day, and against stiffening resistance, captured the airdrome area on 30 December. Enemy air reaction was initially strong and determined but after continued successful interception by Allied fighters, had virtually ceased by the end of December. With both flanks of the vital Vitiaz Straits now secured, and the waters between the Solomon and Bismarck Seas open for future unrestricted use by the Allies, naval forces withdrew.[12]

Earlier, on 16 December, commander, Task Force 76 had ordered the *LST-453* to "proceed to Cape Cretin area and anchor in best berth inside reefs." Following arrival at Dreger Harbor, the ship reported that there was insufficient room for LCTs at Cretin-Dreger, and that she was investigating the possibility of Langemak Bay, north of Finschhafen, as a suitable anchorage for herself. The operation plan specified that provisions would be provided at Cape Cretin from the *LST-453* and a YP (the *236*). Commander, Task Force 76 noted in a war diary entry that at 1920 on 31 December:

> *SC 743*, *YP 236*, APcs *2* and *15* arrived and departed Cape Sudest for Milne Bay. These units came from Cape Cretin area. *APc 2* and *APc 15* had sustained battle damage and *YP 236* had grounded at Cape Cretin, all will require overhaul.

The submarine chaser *SC-743* left Buna on 31 December 1943, escorting *YP-236* with *APc-2* towing *APc-15* to Milne Bay, where the group arrived the following night. The *YP-236* and *APc-2* then departed Milne Bay for Cairns, Australia, for repairs.[13]

16

Tarawa

> *The capture of Tarawa knocked down the front door to the Japanese defenses in the Central Pacific.*
> —Observation by Adm. Chester Nimitz regarding the acquisition of the Gilbert Islands, which came at a high cost in terms of lives lost

Operation GALVANIC, the code word for the planned assault and capture of Tarawa and Makin in the Gilbert Islands in November 1943, was a part of the overall American strategy of conducting an offensive through Micronesia—the Gilbert, Marshall, and Carolina Islands—at the same time as MacArthur's New Guinea-Mindanao approach to Japan. In order to set up forward air bases capable of supporting operations across the Central Pacific to the Philippines and on to Japan, the U.S. needed to take the heavily defended Marianas Islands. The use of land-based aircraft to weaken enemy defenses and provide some measure of protection for the invasion forces necessitated capturing the Marshall Islands, northeast of Guadalcanal. However, an enemy garrison and air base on the island of Betio, at Tarawa Atoll in the Gilbert Islands, guarded against the arrival of invasion forces from Hawaii. Thus, the starting point for the planned invasion of the Marianas lay far to the east, at Tarawa.[1]

SERVICE SQUADRON FOUR

During the preparatory period for GALVANIC, Nimitz approved use of floating mobile bases to provide logistic support, and on 1 November 1943, Service Squadron Four was commissioned. Based at Funafuti, Ellice Islands, and under the command of Capt. H. M. Scull, the

Map 16-1

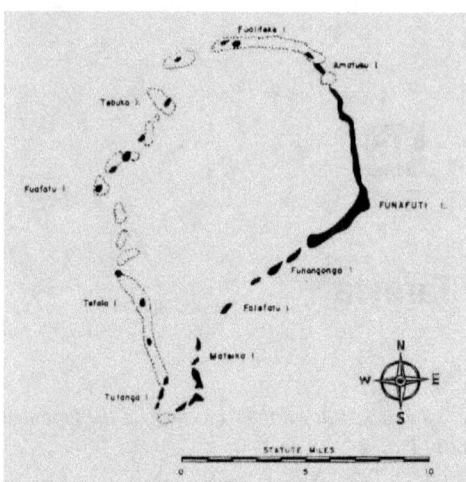

Service Squadron 4 ships based at Funafuti Atoll, Ellice Islands, which including the patrol yacht *Southern Seas*, provided forward logistic support for assault forces that landed at Makin and Tarawa in the Gilbert Islands.
Source: http://www.ibiblio.org/hyperwar/USN/Building_Bases/maps/bases2-p233.jpg

squadron consisted of the destroyer tender *Cascade* (AD-16) and twenty-three other vessels ranging from the repair ships *Phaon* (ARB-3) and *Vestal* (AR-4) through tugs and patrol craft to fuel-oil barges and 500-ton lighters.[2]

Three of the ships joining the squadron—the gasoline tanker *Patapsco* (AOG-1), the minesweeper *Sheldrake* (AM-62), and the patrol yacht *Southern Seas* (PY-32)—left Espiritu Santo, New Hebrides, during the late afternoon of 12 November 1943, bound for Funafuti. The ships set a course east-northeast to pass near the Santa Cruz Islands en route to their destination, the patrol yacht taking station behind the tanker in the column formation and the minesweeper making anti-submarine sweeps

Photo 16-1

Patrol yacht *Southern Seas* (PY-32) under way.
National Archives Photo 80-G-266771, http://www.navymemorial.org

ahead. At 0800 on 16 November, Funafuti Atoll came into view dead ahead, and the group entered the lagoon by way of the Southeast passage and anchored in the Ellice Islands.³

ENEMY AIR RAID ON FUNAFUTI

In the early hours of the following day, Japanese aircraft—nine single planes and a three-plane formation—attacked the base at Funafuti. The planes were believed to be twin-engine medium bombers; one plane, illuminated by a searchlight, was reported to be a "Sally," Type 97. The first of the aircraft, approaching singly from the northwest, was picked up on radar at 0337. The air raid warning sounded at 0400, enabling all hands to take cover before the first of ten bombing runs began at 0416. The island's Marine Corp anti-aircraft batteries—two 90mm batteries, three 40mm guns, and one .50-caliber machine gun—opened fire at 0420. Some ships in the lagoon were able to deliver 3-inch and 40mm fire as well. A total of seventy-two to eighty-two bombs were dropped, killing two Navy personnel, destroying a B24 bomber and a C47 cargo plane, and damaging additional aircraft. Four of the bombs landed in the water, close aboard the *Patapsco*.⁴

Map 16-2

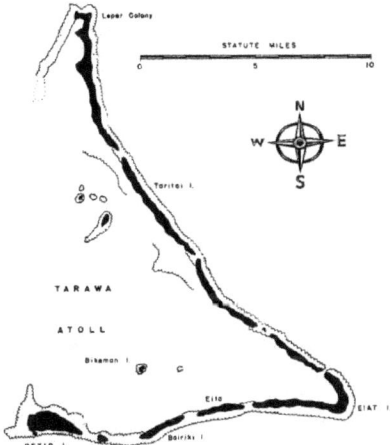

The 2nd Marine Division encountered heavy opposition after coming ashore on the lagoon side of Betio Island at Tarawa Atoll.
Source: http://www.ibiblio.org/hyperwar/USN/Building_Bases/maps/bases2-p315.jpg

Chapter 16
CAPTURE OF TARAWA AND MAKIN

Two regiments from the 27th Infantry Division landed at Butaritari Island Makin Atoll, on 20 November and, following light Army losses—64 killed and 150 wounded, signaled "Makin taken," three days later. The 2nd Marine Division, facing a much larger enemy force on Tarawa, suffered heavy casualties—871 killed, an additional 124 men who would succumb to their wounds, and 2,306 wounded or missing in action. Nearly all of these casualties were suffered in the seventy-six hours between the landing on 20 November and the island of Betio being declared secure during the early afternoon of 23 November.[5]

SERVICE SQUADRON FOUR UNITS MOVE FORWARD

At 0645 on 3 December, submarine chaser *SC-1317*, tank landing ships *LST-240* and *LST-268*, minesweeper *YMS-290*, and patrol yacht *Southern Seas* departed Funafuti for Tarawa and Makin. The task unit was scheduled to arrive at Tarawa Atoll on 7 December. The *LST-240* arrived at Bititu anchorage on 8 December; at year's end the *SC-1317*, *LST-240*, and *Southern Seas* were still at Tarawa. The *Southern Seas* and *YMS-290* received battle stars for the Gilbert Islands operation for the period from 13 November to 8 December 1943.[6]

17

The Marianas—Saipan, Guam, and Tinian

> *Hell is on us.*
>
> Mamoru Shigemitsu, Japan's Minister of Foreign Affairs, remarking on the invasion of Saipan, June 1944

In the short span of the two months between 15 June and 12 August 1944, the Japanese lost their last chance for victory in the Pacific after one U.S. Army division and two Marine Corps divisions captured Saipan, Guam and Tinian. Termed Operation FORAGER, the successful offensive had been undertaken to obtain a site from which Army Air Force B29s could conduct a strategic bombing campaign of Japan. The outlook for the Japanese had already been bleak. As a part of Nimitz's island leapfrogging strategy, amphibious forces had seized Kwajalein, Majuro and Eniwetok atolls in the Marshalls in February, tightening the noose around the Japanese homeland's outer zone of defense. In March and April, landings in the South and Southwest Pacific added the Admiralties, Emirau in the Bismarcks, and Hollandia and Atipae, New Guinea, to the rapidly growing numbers of breaches in the Japanese defensive perimeter. Shore-based Army, Navy and Marine air squadrons neutralized bypassed enemy strong points, while the planes of Task Force 58 repeatedly struck Truk in the Caroline Islands, the operating base for the Combined Fleet, akin to the U.S. Navy's Pearl Harbor. Japanese leaders were well aware that the most decisive actions of the war were at hand. Adm. Soemu Toyoda, commander-in-chief Combined Fleet, in a message to all of his commanding officers on 4 May 1944 warned:

The war is drawing close to the lines vital to our national defense. The issue of our national existence is unprecedentedly serious; an unprecedented opportunity exists for deciding who shall be victorious and who defeated.[1]

Throughout the summer of 1944, all but one of the battle stars earned by Yippies was for actions in the South and Southwest Pacific. This tally changed with actions of YPs *41*, *42*, and *56* at Saipan, and later at Iwo Jima and Okinawa.

SERVICE SQUADRON TWELVE

It might seem curious that YPs were in the Marianas as it would make no sense to employ small, slow vessels to haul groceries from Pearl Harbor when larger vessels could perform such duties easily. These three YPs, however, were survey ships and units of Service Squadron Twelve. The squadron, dubbed "the harbor stretchers," was a harbor development and salvage unit charged with clearing harbors in forward areas, making it possible to berth ships and bring vital supplies to the frontlines.[2]

PRIOR DUTY IN THE 1930S

The YPs *41*, *42*, and *56* were former Coast Guard cutters that had been built in 1926 by Defoe Boat and Motor Works of Bay City, Michigan. Propelled by diesel engines coupled to two shafts, the 98-foot vessels could at best make 12 knots; their armament in 1930 was a single 3-inch/23 gun mount. (The single gun was undoubtedly augmented with machine guns during the war.) Although of modest outfit, the survey ships were very economical to operate and their shallow 4 ½-foot draft allowed them to work waters denied larger vessels.[3]

The Navy assigned the three sister ships to duty with the survey ship *Hannibal* (AG-1), the former British collier S.S. *Joseph Holland*, said to have been acquired in 1898 by Commodore George Dewey in the South China Sea prior to the Battle of Manila Bay, when he had to buy ship and cargo to get the coal she carried. Adm. Richard G. Visser, a former commanding officer of the *YP-42*, recalled duty aboard her as both fulfilling and enjoyable:

> The *YP 42* was my first command, and I learned the basics of ship handling and seamanship from this experience. We had loads of fun in Panama; all of us together when the ship was in port, going

Photo 17-1

YP-56—one of three same type vessels that would earn battle stars in World War II performing survey ship duties in forward areas—moored at Coco Solo, Panama Canal Zone, in 1937.
Source: http://www.navsource.org/archives/14/143105601.jpg

to the several swank beer gardens in the evenings and to the Union Club on Saturday nights for dinner and dancing, a most romantic spot where you drink and dance under the moon and stars and where you and your money are soon separated. On Sunday afternoon there were the horse races which were fun to attend.

The *YP 42* operated independently away from the *Hannibal* much of the time. For example I was in charge of the survey of the Gulf of Nicoya on the west coast of Costa Rica. The entrance of this gulf is about as wide as the English Channel. It took us three months to do the job, and I didn't see the *Hannibal* during all this time. The *YP 41* brought us supplies and mail.[4]

The *41* was equipped with one the Navy's first depth finders, and her captain, Lt. (jg) Richard Halstead, had an unusual mascot aboard ship, a spectacled bear, native to Central and South America, named Oscar. One officer had a special dislike for Oscar, having been bitten by the bear, and believed the commanding officer should get rid of it. Decades later, Halstead fondly recalled his former duty:

> The *YP 41* was painted white, with yellow superstructure. It had two Winton air injection engines, carried 1,500 gallons of drinking water and sometimes as many as fifty men. It was very wide and made the trip from Norfolk to Panama easily. It had a wooden deck and one half inch thick steel hull.

> These boats [YPs] ran survey lines as many miles as possible from "can't see to can't see" eight a.m. to dark; as many as thirty thousand miles per year in glossy water, teeming with sharks, barracudas and crocodiles.
>
> I found the largest scorpion in the world one day on the east coast of Panama. He is in Smithsonian [Institute] now. Big as a crab. I chopped down a manzanilla tree [one of the most deadly in the world] and got poisoned as Lord Nelson had done a century before. Almost lost my eyes. We spent October, November, and December in Norfolk Naval Shipyard each year.[5]

The survey ships operated off the coast of Panama for eight months each year. They spent the remaining four months in Norfolk, Virginia, for repairs, time needed for the hydrographic engineers to get their temporary charts and sounding records in shape to turn over to the Hydrographic Office, and provide leave and liberty for the crew. During transits to and from the Canal Zone, crewmen took "dynamic soundings" to obtain samples of water at different depths. Their findings were sent either to Woods Hole, Massachusetts, or to the Scripps Institute of Oceanography at La Jolla, California. Visser described an experience during her duty:

> We would probably take soundings at six locations on each trip. There was one rather protected anchorage behind one large island and only about one half mile from another with a good swimming beach. At first we liked to go in swimming until someone started fishing for sharks over the stern. After one was hooked we would shoot him. There were as many as six or seven ten-or-twelve-foot sharks on lines over the stern at one time. Most of us lost our interest in swimming after that.[6]

Aboard a survey ship such as the *Hannibal*, the duty of the officers, hydrographic engineers, and crew was to obtain information needed to construct nautical charts showing the contour of the ocean floor. Before the survey ship and its sounding boats went into an area, a control system first had to be established to determine the exact latitude and longitude of the area of water to be surveyed. Generally, the ship's commanding officer, executive officer, and senior hydrographic engineer first visited port authority officers to discuss matters such as right-of-way at tower and signal sites, clearing or cutting of timber on the top of high hills and mountain peaks, the use of lighthouses as triangulation stations, and procurement of materials and food.[7]

Where it was difficult to locate signals on land, the survey ships sometimes used square "floaters" made of four steel drums and 2 x 12 timbers about fifteen feet long. These structures were moored in comparatively shallow water and had signal flags mounted on them. Prior to the commencement of each day's survey operations, hydrographic engineers created rough charts depicting the location of the signals (towers or floaters) on them. *Hannibal*, her motor launches, and the two YPs took thousands of individual depth soundings in the course of charting a particular area of the ocean floor. Crewmen aboard the motor launches heaved lead lines from platforms to take depth soundings; a platform or "chains" performed the same function from the ships. In deeper waters, vessels ran lines of soundings. Visser described how data was obtained and provided to the Naval Hydrographic Office (renamed the Oceanographic Office in 1962) for chart creation:

> The officers taking the soundings record the information on the boat sheets. Quartermasters simultaneously read angles with sextants between these stations, thus determining the position of the boats. Periodically small changes in the course steered have to be made to stay on the sounding lines drawn on the boat sheets. The location of the sounding lines and the distance between them are designated by the engineers after a study is made of the nature of the terrain of the ocean floor. Fathometers are used to periodically measure the depth of the water. From the bottom of the sounding boat the signal of the fathometer sends a sound wave to the ocean floor. The time of the returning echo gives the depth of the water.
>
> [During this process] the senior hydrographic engineer spends about ninety per cent of his time aboard the mother ship joining with the captain and executive officer in formulating plans and procedures for the work, and they review the progress made and the accuracy of the results obtained.
>
> The boat sheet material is worked up onto smooth sheets when the ship is in Norfolk or Philadelphia. The completed sheets are sent to the Oceanographic Office and are the basic material for the making of the new charts.[8]

PACIFIC BOUND

1 December 1943 found the survey ship *Bowditch* (AGS-4), *YP-41*, *YP-42*, and *YP-56* undergoing a navy yard overhaul in Drydock No.

1 at Balboa, Canal Zone, to ready the ships for duty in the Pacific. *Bowditch*, the former motor vessel M.V. *Santa Inez*, built by Burmeister and Wain of Copenhagen, Denmark, in 1929, had been purchased by the Navy on 4 March 1940. She and the three YPs were assigned to Hydrographic Office survey duty, operating directly under the Vice Chief of Naval Operations, but had been ordered to duty under commander, Service Force, Pacific Fleet. The *Hannibal* remained behind to complete her service as a station ship at Norfolk, Virginia, before decommissioning eight months later on 20 August 1944.[9]

After leaving the Canal Zone, the YPs arrived at San Diego on 13 January 1944 to undergo conversion and repair, while the *Bowditch* made San Pedro, a little further up the coast, to load necessary materials, before she proceeded to Hawaii. On 24 January, five Marine Corps officers and seventy men boarded her for transportation and the *Bowditch* departed Pearl Harbor for Tarawa, Gilbert Islands, in company with the net cargo ship *Keokuk* (AKN-4) and submarine chaser *PC-1127* as escorts.[10]

MAJURO ATOLL, MARSHALL ISLANDS

En route to the Marshall Islands, the ship held general quarters, conducted emergency drills, and expended 240 rounds of high explosive, incendiary 20mm shells in target practice at target balloons. The *Bowditch* arrived at Tarawa in the mid-morning of 2 February 1944 and reported to commander, Service Squadron Four before discharging her passengers and departing for Majuro Atoll. As a first step in Nimitz's planned offensive through the Gilbert, Marshall, and Caroline Islands, the 2nd Marines had taken Tarawa in the Gilberts a little over two months earlier.[11]

Having prevailed in the Battle of Tarawa and gained the Japanese airfield on the atoll, and well as Makin, which lay 105 miles northwestward, and Abemama seventy-five miles to the southeast, American forces moved into the Marshall Islands. The first goal of the Marshalls operation was achieved when an attack group under Rear Adm. Harry W. Hill took unoccupied Majuro on 31 January 1944. Desired for its deep, protected harbor, the atoll soon hosted a base that soldiers, sailors, and Marines accustomed to battle-ravaged islands considered a paradise. Shortly after its occupation, the largest fleet of tankers the Pacific Fleet had ever assembled arrived at the lagoon. Formed into a mobile supply force under Capt. Worrall R.

Carter, they would support the armada of ships needed for the Battle for Kwajalein, codenamed Operation FLINTLOCK. The conquest of Kwajalein, the hub of the enemy's defense system, would be the next step in the Marshalls operation, followed by the capture of Eniwetok as soon as possible thereafter.[12]

Preparation for the Battle of Kwajalein began with raids by planes of the Central Pacific's Fast Carrier Force (Task Force 58)—*Enterprise, Saratoga, Essex* and three more of her class, and six light carriers of the *Independence* class—against one or more atolls in the Marshalls every day from 29 January to 6 February 1944. Their mission was to destroy enemy air and sea power in the archipelago. Kwajalein, in the heart of the Marshall Islands, was the world's largest coral atoll as measured by its area of enclosed water, 324 square miles. Comprising its land mass were ninety-seven islets, with the largest being the linked islands of Roi-Namur in the north and Kwajalein Island to the south, the objectives of the 4th Marine Division and U.S. Army 7th Infantry Division's assault. Three days of air and naval bombardment by four battleships, three heavy cruisers, eleven destroyers, three

Map 17-1

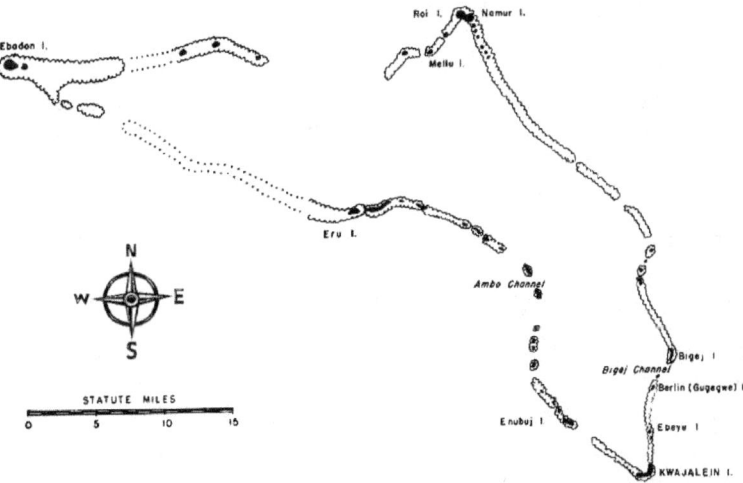

As the 4th Marines came ashore on the linked islands of Roi-Namur in the north, the 7th Infantry Division simultaneously landed at Kwajalein Island on the southeast corner of Kwajalein Atoll.

Source: http://www.ibiblio.org/hyperwar/USN/Building_Bases/maps/bases2-p323.jpg

escort carriers, and bombers from Tarawa preceded the landings at Kwajalein on 2 February by the 7th Division. Getting ashore proved much easier than taking the island, but five days later the atoll was entirely in American hands.[13]

ENIWETOK ATOLL

The *Bowditch*, anchored at Eniwetok Atoll, Marshall Islands, with YPs *41* and *42* alongside, was engaged in survey and charting duty for Service Squadron Twelve on 1 July 1944. Since 25 June, the *YP-56* had been maintaining an armed guard on the *IX-22*, the former *Oregon* (BB-3) commissioned on 15 July 1896. The old battleship had been sold for scrap and was later, despite being stripped to the main deck, reacquired by the Navy for service as an ammunition barge. The characteristics of the little survey ships, and the identities of their commanding officers on 1 May 1945, follow:

Ship Name or Designation (Former Type Vessel/Name and Name of Commanding Officer if Known)	Length Feet	Displ Tons	Year Built
YP-41 (ex-cutter *Mahoning*, Lt. J. C. Bunn, USNR)	98	210	1926
YP-42 (ex-cutter *Gallatin*, Lt. (jg) W. J. Goodheart, USNR)	98	210	1926
YP-56 (ex-*Naugatuck*, Ens. J. P. Kowski, USNR)	98	210	1926[14]

The YPs departed Eniwetok during the late morning of 17 July in company with the salvage ship *Gear* (ARS-34), with repair dock *ARD-16* in tow, and fleet tug *Zuni* (ATF-95), bound for Tanapag Harbor, Saipan. The other two members of the task unit—the destroyer *Edwards* (DD-619) and cutter *Woodbine* (WAGL-289)—served as escorts. The *Bowditch* followed that afternoon in another task unit.[15]

SAIPAN, TINIAN AND GUAM TAKEN

The fifteen Mariana Islands are orientated in an arc stretching from Farallon de Pajaros south to Guam, with the four largest islands—Saipan, Tinian, Rota, and Guam—at the southernmost end. The Allied invasion of Saipan began on 15 June, with landings by the 2nd and 4th Marine Divisions opposed by the Japanese Army's 43rd Division. The ensuing fierce fighting led to the decision to commit at once the Allies reserve force, the U.S. Army 27th Infantry Division. By the time the island was secured three weeks later on 6 July, the American casualties were the highest suffered to date in the Pacific War—2,949 killed and 10,464 wounded. Because of the Bushido Code, the Japanese had been determined to fight to the death; enemy losses totaled 21,000 killed in action, 8,000 suicides and 921 prisoners.[16]

With Saipan taken, U.S. forces moved down the island chain. The 3rd Marine Division and the 77th Infantry Division came ashore on Guam on 21 July and drove the 18,500 Japanese defenders north until the island was secured on 8 August. As fighting continued on Guam, the 2nd and 4th Marine Divisions landed on Tinian on 24 July and took the island after six days of combat.[17]

SURVEY SHIPS SUPPORT "HARBOR STRETCHING"

During the fighting on Tinian and in the skies above it, the YPs *41*, *42*, and *56* were three miles to the north at recently captured Saipan where they earned battle stars for the period from 24 July to 10 August. The ships had arrived at Saipan from Eniwetok at 1345 on 24 July. As the *Bowditch*'s motor launches conducted wire drags and took soundings of the harbor bottom, the YPs built survey signals along the southeast coast of Saipan, and planted buoys. On 29 July, the YPs took soundings of the Saipan anchorage as the MLs sounded the channel and seaplane landing areas. Shortly after midnight on the 30th a tremendous explosion rocked the area caused by the detonation of a cache of eighty-four tons of dynamite ashore—believed due to enemy infiltrators—resulting in slight damage to the superstructures of motor launch No. *3* and the *YP-41*.[18]

DUTY AT GUAM

Ordered to duty at Guam, the *YP-56* left Tanapag Harbor on 1 August. That night she came under fire, not from the enemy, but from the destroyer *Bryant* (DD-665) on radar picket duty. A war diary entry described the incident:

> Attempted to identify by TBS and MN [communicate by VHF and FM radio] without success. At 2120 fired two star shells, but were unable to see contact. After further attempts to identify contact, by flashing light, opened fire at 2154. After three salvos had been fired, target identified himself by light as YP 56 en route Guam. He sustained no damage. Expended 14 rounds 5"/38 AA common and 6 star shells.[19]

The YP arrived at Apra Harbor, Guam, the following day, and on 4 August began survey work with the *Hydrographer* (AGS-2). Acquired by the Navy from the Coast and Geodetic Survey on 15 April 1942, the ship had been classified as a patrol yacht (PY-30) prior to commissioning. Its duties over the next few days included installation of a tide gauge, reconnaissance for triangulation, and marking of triangulation and hydrographic stations. On 8 August the *YP-56* began a large-scale survey of Calalan Bank to obtain the underwater topographical information needed to place an emergency breakwater of sunken barges along the axis of the bank. Survey parties from the *Hydrographer* were engaged in performing special surveys and other tasks required for the development of Apra Harbor. Activities by other units included the removal of coral heads and dredging prior to the construction of docks and piers.[20]

The capture of the Marianas enabled continued movement forward in the Central Pacific. In the Southwest Pacific, MacArthur was in control of Biak—a small island near the north coast of Papua on which a strategically sited Japanese Army airfield had served as a base for operations in the Pacific theater—as well as western New Guinea, and was poised to cross the Celebes Sea to fulfill his promise to return and liberate the Philippines.[20]

18

The Leyte Landings and Aftermath

> *Should we lose in the Philippines operations, even though the fleet should be left, the shipping lane to the south would be completely cut off so that the fleet, if it should come back to Japanese waters, could not obtain its fuel supply. If it should remain in southern waters, it could not receive supplies of ammunition and arms. There would be no sense in saving the fleet at the expense of the loss of the Philippines.*
>
> —Adm. Soemu Toyoda, Imperial Japanese Navy, discussing Vice Adm. Takeo Kurita's mission to destroy completely the transports in Leyte Bay following the American invasion of the Philippines, and why there were no restrictions as to the damage that his force might take.[1]

By early 1944 the Allies had driven Japanese forces from many of their island bases in the south and central Pacific, while isolating many of their other bases (most notably in the Solomon Islands, Bismarck Archipelago, Admiralty Islands, New Guinea, Marshall Islands, and Wake Island). In June, a series of American amphibious landings captured most of the Mariana Islands (bypassing Rota). That offensive breached Japan's strategic inner defense ring and gave the Americans a base from which B29 bombers could attack the Japanese home islands. The Japanese counterattacked in the Battle of the Philippine Sea, fought between the First Mobile Fleet and American Fifth Fleet from 19 to 21 June. In what one American aviator termed "The Great Marianas Turkey Shoot," the U.S. Navy destroyed three enemy aircraft carriers—*Hijo*, *Shokaku*, and *Taiho*—some 480 planes, and almost that number of aviators, leaving the Japanese Navy with virtually no carrier-based aircraft or experienced pilots for the forthcoming Battle of Leyte Gulf.[2]

THE BATTLE FOR LEYTE GULF

The Battle of Leyte Gulf is generally considered to be the largest naval battle of World War II. It was fought in waters near the Philippine islands of Leyte and Samar from 23 to 26 October 1944, between U.S. and Australian forces and the Japanese Navy. Only days earlier, two corps of two divisions each of the U.S. Sixth Army had landed on 20 October at Tacloban and Dulag, Leyte. That same morning, President Roosevelt broadcast a message to the Philippine people about the Allied effort to restore their freedom:

> On this occasion of the return of General MacArthur to Philippine soil with our airmen, our soldiers and our sailors, we renew our pledge. We and our Philippine brothers in arms—with the help of Almighty God—we will drive out the invader; we will destroy his power to wage war again, and we will restore a world of dignity and freedom—a world of confidence and honesty and peace.[3]

The capture of Leyte was part of a strategy to isolate Japan from the countries it had occupied in Southeast Asia, and in particular, to deprive its forces and industries of vital oil supplies. The Battle of Leyte Gulf secured the beachheads that the Sixth Army had established on Leyte from attack from the sea. However, hard fighting would be required before the island was completely in Allied hands at the end of December 1944. The Battle of Leyte on land was fought in parallel with an air and sea campaign in which the Japanese reinforced and resupplied their troops on Leyte while the Allies attempted to interdict them and establish air-sea superiority in preparation for amphibious landings at Ormoc Bay, located on the opposite, western side of the island.[4]

JAPANESE AIR ATTACKS AGAINST TACLOBAN HARBOR

Nine days after army troops landed at Leyte, the Navy established Naval Operating Base, Leyte at Tacloban on 29 October 1944. The port of Tacloban could accommodate twelve to fifteen vessels of 20-foot draft. There were no other major port facilities on Leyte Island, although numerous indentations along the west coast afforded anchorage except during the southwest monsoon. Ormoc Bay, on the west coast, had unlimited anchorage for a large number of vessels, but was also vulnerable to the southwest monsoons.[5]

Map 18-1

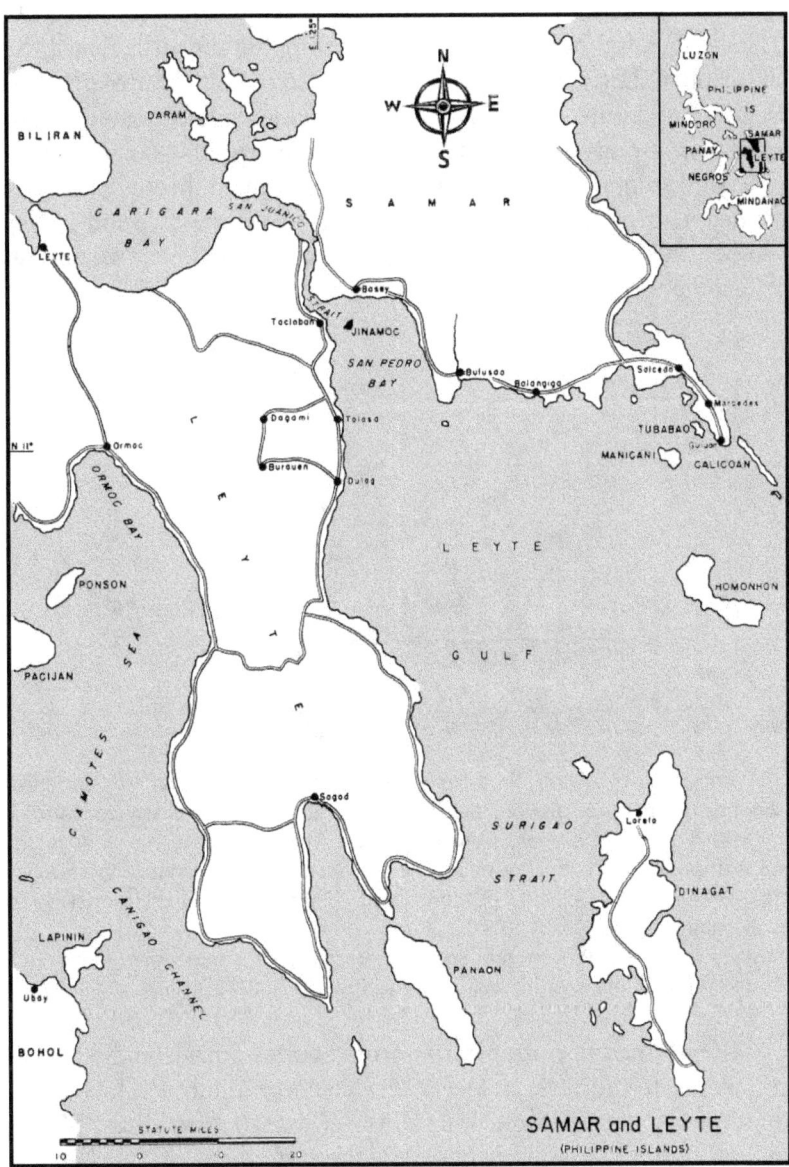

Leyte Island, Philippines.
Source: http://www.ibiblio.org/hyperwar/USN/Building_Bases/maps/bases2-p379.jpg

The Battle of Leyte Gulf was the first battle in which Japanese aircraft carried out organized kamikaze attacks. Their efforts to defeat the Allies through the use of suicide planes, essentially pilot-guided explosive missiles, as well as conventional aircraft would continue. On 3 November, Japanese planes raided the shipping and airfield facilities at Tacloban, Leyte. A kamikaze crashed into the freighter *Matthew P. Deady*, setting the ship's cargo on fire and killing two Armed Guard sailors and twenty-six troops on board. Kamikaze attacks against fleet units and shipping in Leyte Gulf waters continued through mid-December. During air strikes by conventional bombers on 23 and 24 November, the *YP-421*, a former fishing trawler, shot down two aircraft at Tacloban.[6]

Photo 18-1

The war service of *YP-421*, the former Massachusetts beam trawler *Surf*, included shooting down enemy dive bombers at Leyte, Philippines, and subsequently working with Lt. Comdr. Leonard Goldsworthy, the Royal Australian Navy's premiere mine disposal expert and, not surprisingly, its most highly decorated officer. Navy Yard Boston photo # 4284-42 14 September 1942, Boston National Historical Park Collection NPS Cat. No. BOSTS-14828
Stephen P. Carlson, Preservation Specialist, Boston NHP, Charlestown Navy Yard, Boston, Mass., http://www.navsource.org/archives/14/143142101.jpg

The *421* had been transferred from Service Squadron, South Pacific Force, to the Seventh Fleet's Service Force in July 1944. Ordered to join other service force units at Leyte, she left Naval Base, Manus in the Admiralty Islands just north of the eastern end of New Guinea, for Kossol Roads, Palau, on 28 October 1944. Service Force, Seventh Fleet was tasked with re-provisioning Leyte by thirty days after the assault on 20 October. The YP stood out of Palau the morning of 12 November as a part of the Kossol Roads – Leyte Convoy No. 1, comprised of the destroyer *Deede* (DE-263), S.S. *Yochow*, a merchant ship of British registry, and *YP-421*. The commander of Escort Division 16, who was embarked in the destroyer, was not impressed with the latter ship, noting:

> The convoy order describes the *YP 421* as an escort; however, in view of the fact that this vessel, while equipped with sonar gear, has neither depth charges to attack a submarine nor voice radio to quickly inform *DEEDE* of any contacts developed, and due to the additional fact that she has only one knot reserve speed for this movement, I have reclassified *YP 421* as a member of the convoy and stationed that vessel 500 yds. astern of *YOCHOW*.[7]

Any indignation the commanding officer of the YP must have felt as "tail end Charlie" at the back of a 9-knot convoy was probably surpassed by the welcome presence of the destroyer's guns. The convoy reached its destination during the early afternoon of 15 November 1944, whereupon the convoy commander directed the vessels to proceed independently. The *Deede* anchored in the northern transport anchorage, Leyte Gulf, off Tacloban.[8]

WARNING RED, ENEMY AIRCRAFT INBOUND

On 23 November enemy aircraft attacked Tacloban Harbor where the *YP-421* lay at anchor near a group of Army tugs. Her lookouts first sighted the group of seven "Sally" bombers when they were less than five miles away. As two planes approaching off her port bow crossed her starboard bow at a height of about 800 feet, she took them under fire at a distance of 1,000 yards with two .50-caliber machine guns, one 20mm gun, and her single 3-inch/50 mount. Despite limitations imposed by visual sighting and manual elevation and train of guns, her gunners hit one of the two bombers. It burst into flame and crashed off the ship's starboard quarter. There had been little time to engage the targets, as at a speed of about 200 knots the planes were covering over 100 yards per second.[9]

Another group of bombers—this time six "Vals"—struck the following day, once again detected visually at less than five miles off the port bow of the *YP-421*. Two of the planes approaching the ship split apart, one passing down her port side and the other her starboard. As they roared by, the *421* opened with all her guns at the enemy, who closed to about 100 feet distant at a height of 150 feet. Her four .50-caliber machine guns expended a total of 1,100 rounds; the two

20mms, 410 rounds; and the larger, slower 3-inch mount, two rounds at their targets. After passing through this barrage, the Val off her port side lost control and crashed well astern of the ship. The *YP-421* claimed "Sure Assist" for the single aircraft she shot down in each of the two attacks, meaning that other vessels had been firing as well.[10]

ENEMY EFFORTS UNSUCCESSFUL

The Japanese Navy suffered very heavy losses at the hands of the U.S. Navy's Third and Seventh Fleets during its efforts to thwart the Allied invasion of the Philippines. Thereafter, with fuel supplies severely curtailed, the majority of Japan's surviving large ships remained in port for the remainder of the war.[11]

19

The Assault and Occupation of Iwo Jima and Okinawa

> *It is very evident that survey operations will be carried out under adverse conditions as the island is not secured and there is continuous fire between the forces on the island and from our own fighting ships in the surrounding areas.*
>
> —USS *Sumner* (AGS-5) war diary entry for 4 March 1945 regarding conditions at Iwo Jima on the arrival of the survey ship, minesweeper *YMS-357*, tank landing craft *LCT-1061*, and survey ship *YP-42*.

The Battles of Iwo Jima and Okinawa were fought by Allied forces between February and August 1945 to secure island bases for a final B29 bomber assault on Japan. The Iwo Jima operation was conducted first because it was expected to be easier than an assault on Okinawa. Due to the enemy's prolonged and bitter defense of Leyte and Luzon, the planned dates for both actions had slipped, and the Pacific Fleet had to cover and support both invasions, while the Seventh Fleet and its amphibious forces were concurrently engaged in liberating the Southern Philippines.[1]

On 19 February as naval gunfire pounded the island, more than 450 ships massed off Iwo Jima. Marines of the 4th and 5th Divisions hit the four assault beaches shortly after 0900, initially finding little enemy resistance. Coarse volcanic sand hampered their movement as they struggled to move up the beach from the surf zone. As the protective naval gunfire subsided to allow for advancement, the Japanese emerged from fortified underground positions to begin a heavy barrage of fire against the invading force. The 4th Marines continued

Map 19-1

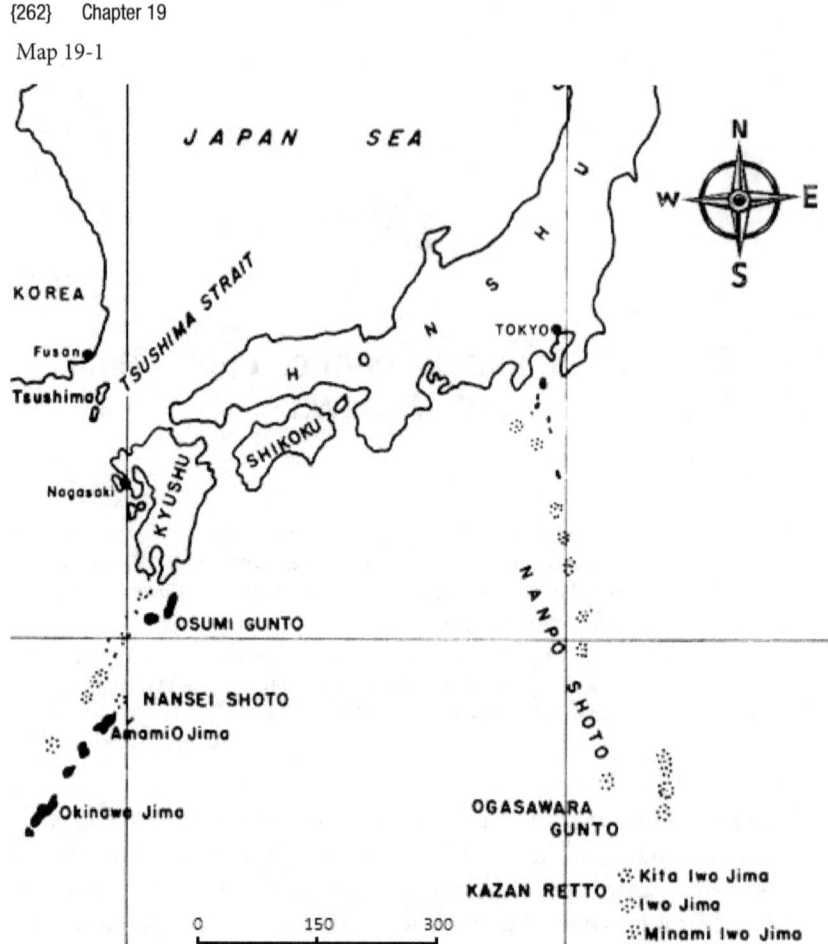

Marine Corps and Army assault forces, and Navy ships offshore, suffered heavy losses at Iwo Jima and Okinawa to gain strategically located island airfields for an assault by B29 bombers on the Japanese homeland.
Source: http://www.ibiblio.org/hyperwar/USN/Building_Bases/maps/bases2-p338.jpg

to push forward against heavy opposition to take the Quarry, a Japanese strong point, while the 5th Marine Division's 28th Marines isolated Mount Suribachi that same day. The 3rd Marine Division joined the fighting on the fifth day, charged with securing the center sector of the island. The fortified enemy defenses linked miles of interlocking caves, concrete blockhouses and pillboxes, which required frontal assaults to gain nearly every inch of ground. Maj. Gen. Harry

Schmidt, commanding the Fifth Amphibious Corps—of which the 3rd, 4th, and 5th Marines were a part—declared Iwo Jima secured on 16 March. Ground fighting, however, continued between then and the official completion of the operation on 26 March 1945.[2]

SURVEY SHIP WORK

The *YP-42* arrived at Iwo Jima on 4 March as one of the three vessels in Echelon No. 1. The group had departed Guam under secret orders on 27 February with the *Sumner* towing the tank landing craft *LCT-1061* which was loaded with heavy lift and general utility equipment necessary to construct an advanced camp. Embarked aboard the survey ship were two officers and seventy construction battalion (Seabee) personnel who would identify a site and construct a camp. The *YP-42*, which was to assist the *Sumner* with a special survey of island waters, carried neither passengers nor cargo.[3]

The survey group arrived to find the unloading of equipment and supplies to the beach continuing from amphibious ships in the transport area, supported by ships of the Gunfire and Covering Force. The *Sumner* and *YP-42* began survey work, handicapped initially by enemy action. The *Sumner* was hit by an enemy round on 8 March, killing one crewman and wounding three others. Over the next several weeks, the hydrographic engineers and their survey teams from the *Sumner* constructed towers and beacons for the triangulation of Iwo Jima, while the *YP-42* took soundings as another preliminary step to chart production. The ships also performed other tasks necessary for development of the harbor, including laying buoys to mark the boundaries of anchorages and boat harbors, and assisting in placing a pipe line in the northeastern tanker mooring.[4]

Following the completion of this work, the *Sumner* left Iwo Jima for Guam on 3 May. During the early evening of 14 May the fleet units at Iwo Jima received warning of a storm approaching from the southwest. The area was hit the following morning, with Force 11 winds and extremely rough seas. Twelve-to-twenty foot waves breaking over the salvage ship *Valve* (ARS-28) washed a motor machinist's mate second class who was trying to place canvas over the engine room blower intakes over the side. Since the condition of the sea precluded rescue, the *Valve* sent a message to units ashore requesting that they pick up the man, and later received word that he had been rescued and was in good condition.[5]

Other ships chose to get underway to ride out the storm at sea. The tank landing ship *LST-847* left the anchorage and cleared Iwo Jima to avoid the heavy debris and drifting dredging pipe line rafts being washed out to sea. At 0910, she was about five miles due west of Iwo Jima, when a lookout sighted a man on one of the rafts. After maneuvering as near the raft as the violent, storm-heavy seas permitted, the LST used a line-throwing gun to fire a shot line over the raft, allowing the survivor to retrieve a messenger line to which a life ring was attached. The man, who turned out to be Seaman First K. I. Cogger from the *YP-42*, was brought aboard, given first aid and put to bed. His ship departed Iwo Jima on 20 May and arrived five days later at Apra Harbor. Both she and the *Sumner* received a battle star for the period from 4 to 16 March 1945.[6]

Iwo Jima—which would be strategically important as an air base for fighters escorting the B29s flying long-range bombing missions against mainland Japan, and as an emergency landing strip for crippled B29s unable to make it back to their base in the Mariana Islands—came at a high cost. The vital link in the chain of bases was gained through the individual and collective courage of fighting Marines over a thirty-six day period. The brutal fighting resulted in 26,000 American casualties, including 6,800 dead. Only 1,083 of the 20,000 Japanese defenders survived.[7]

OKINAWA

> *Enemy forces encountered were limited to shore batteries, submarines, planes, baka (human-piloted rocket-powered aircraft-dropped) bombs, mines and suicide boats, rafts and swimmers.*
>
> —Rear Adm. Alexander Sharp, USN, wryly describing the challenges faced by ships at Okinawa

The eighty-two-day-long Battle of Okinawa was fought on the Ryukyu Islands of Okinawa, and was the largest amphibious assault in the Pacific. Four divisions of the U.S. Tenth Army (the 7th, 27th, 77th, and 96th) and two Marine divisions (the 1st and 6th) fought on the island, supported by naval, amphibious, and air forces. The purpose of the operation, which lasted from 1 April through mid-June 1945, was to capture the large island—located only 340 miles from mainland

Japan—for use as a base for air operations during the planned invasion of Japan.[8]

Japanese accounts of the battle have referred to it as *tetsu no ame* or *kou no kaze*, "iron rain" or "steel wind," respectively, due to the ferocity of the fighting, the intensity of kamikaze attacks from the Japanese defenders, and the sheer numbers of ships and armored vehicles that assaulted the island. The battle resulted in the highest number of casualties in the Pacific Theater during World War II. Japan lost over 100,000 soldiers, either killed, captured or committed suicide, and the Allies suffered more than 65,000 casualties of all kinds.[9]

Two of the ships present, the YPs *41* and *56*, were a long way from home, having been delivered by the Defoe Boat & Motor Works of Bay City, Michigan, to the Coast Guard in 1926 as the patrol craft *Mahoning* and *Naugatuck*. They arrived at Okinawa in time for the last three massed single or multi-day kamikaze attacks (*kikusui*) of the enemy's Operation TEN-GO. Prior to and between the first of these kikusui on 6 April and the last one on 22 June were individual kamikaze assaults on Navy ships. Attack number seven lasted from 23 to 25 May, during which 165 kamikaze and 150 other planes sank three U.S. ships and damaged another six. Due to the losses of kamikaze and other type planes to U.S. naval guns and fighters, there were progressively fewer aircraft available for ensuing kikusui. One hundred ten kamikaze and 110 other type planes sank one ship and damaged seven others in the eighth attack between 27 and 29 May. The enemy mustered fewer (fifty kamikaze/forty other) planes for a strike between 3-7 June, and damaged only three ships. In the final kikusui on 21 and 22 June forty-five kamikaze joined forty other planes to sink one ship and damage four others. The final TEN-GO tally was twenty-one U.S. ships sunk, forty-three scrapped or decommissioned either as a result of damage or repairs not finished by the end of the war, and twenty-three ships put out of action for more than thirty days.[10]

Upon reaching Iwo Jima from Guam on 20 May, the YPs *41* and *56* had reported for duty to the *Bowditch* at Nakagusuku Wan, a bay off the southeast coast of Okinawa. The *56* remained in Nakagusuku Wan to build signal towers, while the *41* transited up the east coast to Chimu Wan—which was to be used as a seaplane base—to join *Bowditch*'s four launches in sounding and signal-building work. Four days later, in the late night darkness on 24 May, the YP and launches fired on a low-flying twin-engine enemy aircraft, expending twenty-six

Photo 19-1

The 98-foot Coast Guard cutter *Gallatin*, later *YP-42*, at Defoe Boat & Motor Works in Bay City, Michigan, after being launched in 1926. In 1945, she was at Iwo Jima and later, with sister ships YPs *41* and *56*, at Okinawa as well.
Photo courtesy of the Bowling Green University Historical Collection of the Great Lakes, http://www.navsource.org/archives/14/143104201.jpg

rounds of 20mm and forty rounds of .30-caliber. There were no casualties, and it was believed that the plane suffered numerous hits.[11]

Two days later at about 1530 the *YP-41* and launches witnessed a kamikaze attack on the submarine chaser *PC-1603*, which was then lying at anchor in the wan while conducting a sound search, and assisted in survivor rescue. The commanding officer of the PC described the sudden appearance of two Kawasaki "Tony" kamikaze aircraft on a gray, overcast day characterized by intermittent rain and many low cloud banks, and the deadly aftermath:

> The two enemy planes, which crash dived the ship, came in out of the overcast on the ship's port side. . . . It was only a fraction of a minute from the time that they were identified as enemy by their red balls until the first plane peeled off and struck the ship on the port side forward of the pilot house near the waterline.
>
> The impact of this first plane hitting the ship was terrific and as a result officers and men were in a stunned condition. Men in the

water, many with bloody faces, added to the confusion. Several men were blown overboard and others who were in the forward compartment, had crawled through the hole made by the plane in the port side of the ship.

General quarters were sounded immediately after the first plane hit. The second plane banked back circling around our bow and then came in from starboard striking at the main deck near the base of the forward bulkhead of the pilot house.... Immediately after the second plane hit the entire area in the vicinity of the pilot house was a mass of flames; the heat was intense....

After the second plane crashed the life rafts were lowered and several men were sent overboard to aid men in the water.... The USS *LCI 1078*, as well as small boats from the USS *BOWDITCH*, came to our aid.... The order was given to abandon ship at about 1620.

Three crewmen were reported missing in action and presumed killed, and thirteen others wounded in the attack. (The *PC-1603* was decommissioned on 21 June and towed to the ship graveyard at Kerama Retto, a small island located southwest of Okinawa; the hulk was ordered destroyed on 24 October 1945.)[12]

Enemy action in Chimu Wan continued on 27 May, when the YP and sounding boats witnessed a battle between a U.S. Navy destroyer, minesweeper, sub-chaser, and three Japanese "Vals." The *Fletcher*-class DD shot down one plane, but the other two crashed the destroyer-minesweeper *Forrest* (DMS-24) and submarine chaser *PC-1396*. Assistance was provided to the *Forrest* until she was inside Nakagusuku Wan. The PC suffered topside damage, but was still seaworthy and able to proceed from Chimu Wan to Nakagusuku Wan under her own power.[13]

A month later, as the *Bowditch* and YPs continued their surveys of the Okinawa Shima Area, the *YP-41* shot down an unidentified Japanese plane at Chimu Wan on 26 June. This attack followed the tenth and final kikusui massed attack, which coincided with the Allied announcement of the end of organized enemy resistance on the island, and the ritual suicide of Generals Mitsuru Ushijima and Isamu Cho, the commanding general and chief of staff of the Japanese Thirty-second Army.[14]

Chapter 19
CONGRATULATIONS FROM THE BRITISH PRIME MINISTER

> *The strength of will-power, devotion and technical resources applied by the United States to this task, joined with the death struggle of the enemy of whom 90,000 are reported to be killed, places this battle amongst the most intense and famous of military history.*
>
> *It is with profound admiration of American valor and resolve to conquer at whatever cost might be necessary that I send you this tribute from your faithful ally and all your British comrades in arms who watch these memorable victories from this island and all its camps aboard. We make our salute to all your troops and their commanders engaged.*
>
> Winston Churchill in a message to President Harry Truman on 22 June 1945

The *YP-41* and *YP-56* received a battle star for the period from 20 May to 30 June 1945, as did the *YP-42*, which was designated, along with the others, as a part of the Hydrographic Survey Unit. She did not actually report for duty at Okinawa until July, having, after arrival at Guam from Iwo Jima on 25 May, undergone needed repairs. The three diminutive "harbor stretchers" collectively garnered eight battle stars during the war.[15]

20

Mine Clearance at Balikpapan, Borneo

> *To date no specific evidence of controlled harbor minefields have been discovered. Several false leads have been checked in an effort to locate a shore control station without results. It is planned that the location vessel YP 421 search suspected areas for mines and connection cables.*
>
> —A preliminary report statement made by Mobile Explosives Investigation Unit One regarding the identification and clearance of enemy-emplaced beach obstacles, land mines, and booby traps at Balikpapan, Borneo.[1]

Considering the contributions made throughout the war by patrol yachts and YPs, it is fitting that the *YP-421* participated in the final amphibious operation in the Pacific at Balikpapan, Borneo, for which she received a battle star for the period 26 June to 7 July 1945. The *421* was chosen, perhaps, due to the mettle she had shown the previous autumn at Leyte in shooting down two Japanese bombers, or for her recent efforts as a member of the Seventh Fleet Service Force's Ship Salvage, Firefighting and Rescue Unit. The citation for a Navy Unit Commendation she received for the period from 3 March to 10 June 1945 reads:

> Accompanying the preliminary bombardment groups and working under continuous enemy attack throughout the assault phase of nine major landings, the Ship Salvage Fire-Fighting and Rescue Unit, Service Force, Seventh Fleet, fought and extinguished 10 major fires, completed emergency battle damage repairs on 69 vessels including combat fleet units, refloated and salvaged 146 badly damaged ships, towed 13 major vessels to safety, and recovered one sunken submarine under heavy mortar fire. In 3 months, the Unit

completed the emergency clearing of Manila Harbor, opening the port fully to Allied use. During the operation, over 350 vessels of all sizes were raised, removed or disposed of along with large quantities of enemy underwater ordnance. The teamwork, professional skill and unselfish devotion to duty of the entire Unit resulted in accomplishment beyond the highest expectations and contributed immeasurably to the successful liberation of the Philippine Islands.

At Balikpapan, the *YP-421*—a former Massachusetts beam trawler commanded by Walter E. Baker, USN—was assigned to support the U.S. Navy's Mobile Explosives Investigation Unit (MEIU) One, based in Australia on the southern side of the Brisbane River. The Unit's duties included supplying mine and bomb disposal teams for the Southwest Pacific Area, collecting captured Japanese explosive ordnance in order to disassemble and analyze it, and furnishing the intelligence information to the disposal personnel in forward areas. The MEIU worked with Royal Australian Navy Rendering Safe Mines officers in addition to U.S. Navy EOD personnel.[2]

The Royal Australian Navy's premiere mine disposal expert, Lt. Comdr. Leonard Goldsworthy, RAN, boarded the *YP-421* at Nalunga—a small Philippine island, across the Sulu Sea from Borneo—on 9 May 1945. Goldsworthy was the RAN's most highly decorated officer, having been awarded the George Medal, the George Cross, and the Distinguished Service Cross, as well as a "Mention in Despatches" for the incredible courage and proficiency he had displayed in carrying out an extremely dangerous vocation. A "mention in despatches" signified that one's name had appeared in an official report written by a superior officer and sent to the high command, describing gallant or meritorious action in the face of the enemy. In World War II, honored recipients were authorized to affix a small oak leaf device to their War Medal ribbon. Following his service in Europe defusing German mines of various types, Goldsworthy had been posted to the Southwest Pacific for duty with the MEIU. His work there involved rendering safe Japanese mines and booby-traps in the Philippines and in connection with the landings in the Borneo area.[3]

BALIKPAPAN

The objectives of the Allied Borneo Campaign of 1945 were to deny Japan the continued fruits of its conquests in the Netherlands East Indies, present-day Indonesia, and use of the approaches to those areas.

Map 20-1

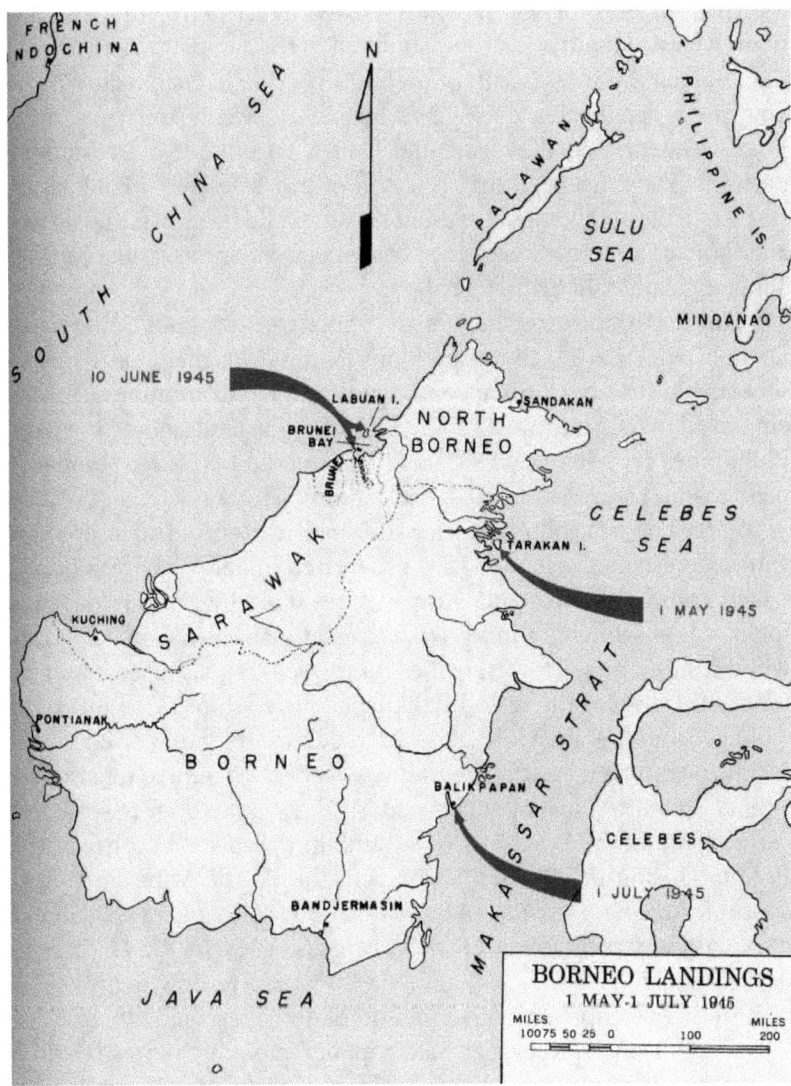

Movement of Australian assault forces en route to landings at Tarakan Island, at Labuan Island in Brunei Bay, and at Balikpapan during the 1945 Borneo Campaign. Source: http://www.lib.utexas.edu/maps/historical/engineers_v1_1947/borneo_landings_1945.jpg

To achieve these aims, an Australian-led force captured Tarakan Island to provide an airfield for support of an assault on Balikpapan, and seized Brunei Bay for an advanced fleet base that could protect resources in the area. The final phase was to occupy Balikpapan for its naval air and logistic facilities as well as its petroleum installations. Many sea mines were encountered in the campaign, and during the final amphibious assault of the last major Allied campaign in the Southwest Pacific area during World War II, twenty-four American minesweepers earned Presidential Unit Citations for extraordinary heroism. The bravery of the crewmen of the "sweeps" at Balikpapan was particularly notable because it came on the heels of heavy losses and damage to minesweepers by mines and Japanese artillery fire at Tarakan Island and Brunei Bay.[4]

Due to the perseverance of the minesweepers and Underwater Demolition Team 11, the amphibious landing was made on 1 July as scheduled. The attack force consisted of the largest number of ships employed in the Southwest Pacific area since the landings at Lingayen, Philippines on 1 January 1945. After an intense two-hour bombardment, assault waves moved ashore, landing without a single casualty in spite of enemy artillery, mortar and small arms fire. The troops met with increased resistance as they progressed inland and fire support, which continued through 7 July, was provided by cruisers day and night. A subsequent landing was made at Cape Penajam on 2 July without casualties. However, the minesweepers paid a heavy price for the freedom of the sea off Balikpapan: three ships sunk and eight damaged and fifty men killed or wounded for fifty mines swept. During the next fifteen days, some twenty sweepers accounted for another twenty-six mines, one of which sent *YMS-84* to the bottom—the last surface ship of the U.S. Navy to be sunk in that distant corner of the Pacific. During the Borneo Campaign, the Pacific Mine Force lost six minesweepers—*Salute* (AM-294) and *YMS-39, 50, 84, 365*, and *481*—and suffered damage to twelve others—*YMS-10, 47, 49, 51, 314, 329, 334, 335, 339, 363, 364*, and *368*. It is unclear how many mines waiting in nearshore and offshore waters were disarmed by explosive ordnance disposal experts at Balikpapan. Goldsworthy was credited with rendering safe more than 300 German and Japanese mines during the war.[5]

Postscript

Anytime, anyone wanted something special delivered along our route, they said "send it by YP." They could always count on it being delivered.
—Anthony Mascarenhas, USNR, the first of the tuna boat skippers to be promoted to lieutenant, remarking on his YP service[1]

Following Japan's surrender on 10 August 1945, the YPs still in service overseas returned home to the United States. The Navy returned the vessels it had loaned, chartered or leased to their former owners, and sold or otherwise disposed of the rest. Many patrol yachts and YPs had left naval service prior to the end of the war. As more recently-constructed sub-chasers and other types of patrol craft had joined the fleet, the Navy began offering the smaller, less seaworthy—or simply worn out—vessels to their original owners.

Up until 1944, the law required all military surplus to be sold at action, and thus the patrol yachts and patrol craft that had been acquired by the Navy were auctioned. A Congressman from Berkeley, at Don Owen's request, introduced a bill that required the boats to be offered first to the prewar owner. Under the new law, Owen, the previous owner of the *Pat Pending, YP-119*, received a letter from the War Shipping Administration, Washington, D.C., on 29 August 1944 informing him:

> The above-named vessel is now available for disposal as surplus property. Consideration may be given to the return of vessel, as is, where is, to the former owner, in accordance with the provisions of Public Law No. 305, 78th Congress, Chapter 199, Second Session, (H. R. 3261), a copy of which is enclosed herewith.
>
> The vessel is now lying at Coast Guard Base, Alameda, Calif. and may be inspected at that port. If you are interested in re-acquiring the above-mentioned vessel, you are requested to make inspection and submit an offer for the Administrator's consideration, in time

to reach the addressee, as shown below on or before September 26, 1944.[2]

Don Owen thereafter made an offer of $10 along with photographs showing the condition of the boat. The Navy raised the price to $100 and the *Pat Pending* was returned to him on October 12, 1944, the first YP returned under Public Law 305.

A few months later Owen received a letter from the Secretary of the Navy, James Forrestal, on 6 March 1945, which conveyed in part:

> Soon after the outbreak of hostilities, and at a time when the menace to national defense and vital interests was most critical, your yacht *PAT PENDING* was made available to the Navy and became a contributing factor toward the furtherance of the war effort.
>
> In recognition of the war service rendered by the *PAT PENDING*, you are authorized to place on the stack or in the vicinity of the bridge five chevrons, or one for each six months of service with the Navy.

(A copy of this letter is displayed in Appendix H.)[3]

The return of a yacht to its former owner signified the long-awaited homecoming of a prized possession, albeit perhaps a little scarred or weary from its service. Reuniting fishing boats with their owners enabled families and other community members involved with fisheries to earn a living from the sea once again. A summary of the eighteen patrol yachts and 259 YPs struck prior to war's end follows. Thirty-three were relatively small former West Coast sardine seiners, mostly from the Monterey and San Francisco areas. Only three were from among the forty-six former San Diego tuna clippers: YPs *262* (ex-*Theodore Foss*), *263* (ex-*Emma R. S.*), and *503* (ex-*St. Therese*). All three had old hulls—the *Foss* was built in 1900, the other two in 1928. Nine tuna clippers taken by the Navy for service as YPs—*235, 269, 277, 279, 280, 281, 284, 345,* and *346*—had been lost by May 1945, leaving thirty-four of the versatile workhorses still plying waters for the Navy. Two of these ships, *YP-289* and *YP-520*, were subsequently lost to a typhoon off Okinawa on 7 October 1945. *YP-239* survived the typhoon but was damaged beyond repair and ordered destroyed in August 1946. The YPs still in service at war's end were subsequently disposed of via sale. The ex-fishing trawler F/V *Surf* (*YP-421*), which earned battle stars for the Leyte and Balikpapan landings, was sold in 1946.

Photo Postscript

YP-520 (ex-tuna clipper *Conte Grande*) was lost due to grounding during Typhoon LOUISE at Buckner Bay, Okinawa, on 9 October 1945.
US Navy photo # NH 105659 from the collections of the U.S. Naval History and Heritage Command, NavSource, http://www.navsource.org/archives/14/31520.htm

Date Struck Patrol Yachts (PY/PYc) and Patrol Craft (YP)

Date Struck	
12 Feb 1944	YP-88, 428, 430, 431, 432, 433
6 Mar 1944	YP-11, 391, 435
8 Apr 1944	YP-300, 302, 311, 331
21 Apr 1944	YP-176, 177, 190, 442
16 May 1944	YP-95, 436, 437, 441, 443, 445
9 June 1944	YP-199
28 Jun 1944	YP-136, 212, 247, 250, 260, 272, 273, 275, 335, 390, 412, 413, 422, 534, 566
18 Jul 1944	Carolita (PYc-38); YP-84, 86, 160, 194, 196, 333, 502, 527, 535, 538, 540, 544
29 Jul 1944	Paragon (PYc-36); YP-111, 191, 200, 202, 204, 206, 207, 231, 232, 248, 261, 271, 352, 356, 358, 359, 379, 392, 393, 394, 396, 398, 447, 452, 506, 507, 524, 536, 542, 549, 558, 568, 572, 573, 574, 579, 603, 612
22 Aug 1944	YP-189, 254, 293, 295, 297, 298, 304, 312, 313, 318, 322, 329, 434, 543
16 Sep 1944	YP-70, 187, 210, 213, 218, 221, 228, 249, 263, 317, 332, 334, 355, 378, 408, 409, 454, 456, 457, 458, 459, 460, 461, 462, 463, 464, 466, 467, 468, 469, 470, 471, 473, 474, 475, 476, 477, 478, 479, 480, 482, 483, 484, 487, 499, 500, 501, 508, 509, 510, 526, 600

Date Struck Patrol Yachts (PY/PYc) and Patrol Craft (YP)

23 Sep 1944	YP-156, 157, 159, 161, 163, 164, 165, 184, 188, 215, 274, 376, 377, 406, 489, 490, 491, 493, 494, 495, 496, 497, 498, 511, 570, 609
11 Oct 1944	Captor (PYc-40)
14 Oct 1944	Agate (PYc-4), Black Douglas (PYc-45), Impetuous (PYc-46), Marcasite (PY-28), Patriot (PYc-47), Persistent (PYc-48), Retort (PYc-49), Sea Scout (PYc-43), Topaz (PYc-10); YP-96, 132, 166, 180, 211, 216, 217, 229, 230, 257, 353, 357, 362, 364, 370, 373, 410, 485, 486, 503, 521, 529, 530, 531, 546, 547, 548, 601, 613
13 Nov 1944	Amber (PYc-6), Olivin (PYc-22); YP-75, 114, 131, 168, 192, 220, 259, 301, 315, 339, 340, 488, 505, 565
27 Nov 1944	Emerald (PYc-1); YP-133, 154, 382, 384, 385, 386, 418
11 Dec 1944	YP-83, 416, 417, 420
22 Dec 1944	YP-383
19 Jan 1945	Jade (PY-17), YP-338
20 Jan 1945	YP-265, 423
8 Feb 1945	Gallant (PYc-29), Onyx (PYc-5); YP-4, 537, 608
23 Feb 1945	YP-73, 175, 582, 593, 594
10 Mar 1945	YP-35, 402
30 Mar 1945	YP-262
19 May 1945	YP-27, 37, 43, 563, 602, 606
28 Apr 1945	YP-5, 33, 39, 55, 58
10 Mar 1945	YP-94
30 Mar 1945	YP-108
19 May 1945	YP-305[4]

Appendix A: Yard Patrol Craft (YP)

ANONYMS USED

AMb: Base minesweeper
AMc: Coastal minesweeper
CG: Coast Guard, followed by numerical portion of hull number
Cruiser: Cabin (or open) cruiser
DD: Diesel dragger (a type of fishing vessel propelled by diesel engine)
F/V: Fishing vessel (generic term)
FWS: U.S. Fish & Wildlife Service
PS: Purse seiner (a type of fishing vessel)
PT: Motor torpedo boat
RB: Recreational boat
SC: Submarine chaser
SP: U.S. Navy Section craft, followed by numerical portion of hull number
TC: Tuna clipper (a type of fishing vessel)
Trawler: Generic fishing trawler or fishing beam trawler
USCG: U.S. Coast Guard, followed by name of patrol boat or cutter

Note: To save space, only the names of commanding officers not identified in the text of the book are included in this table.

Ship	Former Vessel Type/Name	Length Feet	Displ Tons	Year Built	Builder or Location Built
YP-2	yacht *Relief*	35	10	1910	Yarmouth, Maine
YP-3	M.V.H., *Sunda*	36	9	1917	W. E. Huff
YP-4	yacht *Stephanotis*, CG-975	66		1909	Nova Scotia, Canada
YP-5	CG-102	74'11"	37	1924	Mathis Yachts
YP-6	CG-209	74'11"	37	1925	Kingston Dry Dock
YP-7	CG-272	74'11"	37	1925	Lake Union Dry Dock
YP-8	CG-191	74'11"	37	1925	Portsmouth Naval Shipyard
YP-9	CG-105	74'11"	37	1924	Mathis Yachts
YP-10	CG-194	74'11"	37	1924	Chance Marine
YP-11	CG-196	74'11"	37	1925	Chance Marine
YP-12	CG-204	74'11"	37	1925	Kingston Dry Dock
YP-13	CG-123	74'11"	37	1925	Defoe Boat & Motor Works
YP-14	CG-181	74'11"	37	1924	Southern Shipyard

Appendix A

Ship	Former Vessel Type/Name	Length Feet	Displ Tons	Year Built	Builder or Location Built
YP-15	CG-149	74'11"	37	1925	Dachel-Carter Shipbuilding
YP-16	CG-267	74'11"	37	1925	Lake Union Dry Dock
YP-17	CG-275	74'11"	37	1925	Lake Union Dry Dock
YP-18	CG-263	74'11"	37	1925	Lake Union Dry Dock
YP-19	CG-177	74'11"	37	1924	Rice Brothers Corp.
YP-20	CG-163	74'11"	37	1924	New York Yacht, Launch
YP-21	CG-199	74'11"	37	1925	Chance Marine
YP-22	CG-221	74'11"	37	1925	Vinyard Shipbuilding
YP-23	CG-286	74'11"	37	1925	Mathis Yachts
YP-24	CG-106	74'11"	37	1924	Mathis Yachts
YP-25	CG-142	74'11"	37	1924	Dachel-Carter Shipbuilding
YP-26	CG-252	74'11"	37	1925	Gibbs Gas Engine Co.
YP-27	CG-301	74'11"	37	1925	Gibbs Gas Engine Co.
YP-28	CG-225	74'11"	37	1924	Colonna's Shipyard
YP-29	CG-116	74'11"	37	1924	Rice Brothers Corp.
YP-30	CG-251	74'11"	37	1925	Gibbs Gas Engine Co.
YP-31	CG-167	74'11"	37	1925	New York Yacht, Launch
YP-32	CG-208	74'11"	37	1925	Kingston Dry Dock
YP-33	CG-253	74'11"	37	1925	A.W. DeYoung
YP-34	CG-258	74'11"	37	1925	A.W. DeYoung
YP-35	CG-222	74'11"	37	1925	Vinyard Shipbuilding
YP-36	CG-280	74'11"	37	1924	Mathis Yachts
YP-37	CG-273, Q-173	74'11"	37	1925	Seattle, Washington
YP-38	CG-269	74'11"	37	1924	Lake Union Dry Dock
YP-39	CG-276	74'11"	37	1925	Lake Union Dry Dock
YP-40	CG-175	74'11"	37	1925	Rice Brothers Corp.
YP-41	USCG Mahoning	98'0"	210	1926	Defoe Boat & Motor Works
YP-42	USCG Gallatin	98'0"	210	1926	Defoe Boat & Motor Works
YP-43	Daraga, SP-43			1915	Camden Anchor
YP-44	USCG Winnie	65			
YP-45	CG-133	74'11"	37	1924	Crowninshield Shipbuilding
YP-46	CG-146	74'11"	37	1925	Dachel-Carter Shipbuilding
YP-47	CG-152	74'11"	37	1925	Soule Steel
YP-48	CG-143	74'11"	37	1924	Mathis Yachts
YP-49	CG-182	74'11"	37	1925	Southern Shipyard
YP-50	CG-1278	74'11"	37	1924	Mathis Yachts
YP-51	CG-261	74'11"	37	1926	A.W. DeYoung
YP-52	CG-160	74'11"	37	1924	New York Yacht, Launch
YP-53	CG-101	74'11"	37	1924	Mathis Yachts
YP-54	CG-168	74'11"	37	1925	New York Yacht, Launch
YP-55	CG-169	74'11"	37	1925	New York Yacht, Launch
YP-56	USCG Naugatuck	98'0"	210	1926	Defoe Boat & Motor Works
YP-57	CG-169	74'11"	37	1924	Mathis Yachts
YP-58	CG-183	74'11"	37	1924	Southern Shipyard
YP-59	CG-203	74'11"	37	1924	Kingston Dry Dock
YP-60	CG-207	74'11"	37	1925	Kingston Dry Dock
YP-61	USCG Dallas	98'0"	210	1925	Defoe Boat & Motor Works
YP-62	USCG Corwin	98'0"	210	1925	Defoe Boat & Motor Works
YP-63	USCG Dexter	98'0"	210	1925	Defoe Boat & Motor Works
YP-64	USCG Eagle	98'0"	210	1925	Defoe Boat & Motor Works

Yard Patrol Craft (YP) {279}

Ship	Former Vessel Type/Name	Length Feet	Displ Tons	Year Built	Builder or Location Built
YP-65	USCG *Pronto*	71			
YP-66	yacht, patrol boat *C-252*	67'4"		1917	Luders Marine
YP-67	*CG-100*	74'11"	37	1924	Mathis Yachts
YP-68	*Psyche V.*, SP-9	65		1911	Nock Shipyard
YP-69	USCG tug *Patriot*	98'0"	210	1926	Defoe Boat & Motor Works
YP-70	gas yacht *Gypsy*	101	108	1928	George Lawley & Sons
YP-71	barkentine *Intrepid*	205	596	1930	George Lawley & Sons
YP-72	PS *Calvacade*	87.0	152	1940	Martinac Shipbuilding Co.
YP-73	PS *Corsair*	84.5	114	1937	
YP-74	PS *Endeavor*	72.1	101	1937	
YP-75	yacht *Kooyong III*	75	29	1929	Consolidated Shipbuilding
YP-76	cruiser *Now Listen*	44'0"		1926	
YP-77	yacht *Pamnorm*	79'4"		1931	Consolidated Shipbuilding
YP-78	Naval Academy YP	75	50	1941	Hutchinson Boat Works
YP-79	Naval Academy YP	75	50	1941	Hutchinson Boat Works
YP-80	Naval Academy YP	75	51	1941	Elscot Boats, Inc.
YP-81	Naval Academy YP	75	51	1942	Elscot Boats, Inc.
YP-82	Naval Academy YP	75	51	1942	Elscot Boats, Inc.
YP-83	PS *Rio Del Mar*	71.2	94	1937	Tacoma, Washington
YP-84	PS *Ketchikan*	69.6	94	1937	
YP-85	PS *Nick C. II*	72.1	97	1939	Western Boat Builders
YP-86	PS *Pacific Fisher*	73.6	113	1937	Martinolich Shipbuilding
YP-87	PS *Valiant*	70.4	102	1937	Seattle, Washington
YP-88	PS *Adventure*	74.6	101	1937	
YP-89	PS *Challenger*	69.1	91	1937	Seattle, Washington
YP-90	PS *Montara*	71.3	99	1937	
YP-91	*Lucivee*	75		1928	George Lawley & Sons
YP-92	PS *Helen B.*	72.3	102	1938	Tacoma, Washington
YP-93	PS *Margaret F.*	69.0	98	1937	Seattle, Washington
YP-94	PS *Western Chief*	76.4	115	1936	Western Boat Builders
YP-95	PS *Nordic Pride*	74.8	114	1940	
YP-96	*Midnight Sun*	78'1"	107	1922	Tacoma Boatbuilding
YP-97		66		1941	
YP-98	*Caroline*	112		1929	
YP-99	Naval Academy YP	75	51	1942	Elscot Boats, Inc.
YP-100	cancelled	75			Elscot Boats, Inc.
YP-101	cancelled	75			Elscot Boats, Inc.
YP-102	motor yacht *Kura*	77	81	1930	Lake Washington Shipyard
YP-103	*Nippon Maru*	72		1938	
YP-104	yacht *Marinette II*	74		1926	Consolidated Shipbuilding
YP-105	yacht *Sybarita*	85		1927	Consolidated Shipbuilding
YP-106	*PT-69*	72	40	1941	Huckens Yacht Corp.
YP-107	*PT-70*	72	40	1941	Higgins Industries
YP-108	yacht *Joyita*	69	51	1931	Wilmington Boat Works
YP-109	yacht *Elvida*	107'5"	86	1923	
YP-110	*PT-8*	81	52	1940	Philadelphia Naval Shipyard
YP-111	yacht *Blue Moon*	56	27	1927	Fellows & Stewart
YP-112	*Pez Espada II*	44'10"	42	1934	
YP-113	motor yacht *Elogrier*		20	1929	Nunes Brothers, Sausalito, California

Appendix A

Ship	Former Vessel Type/Name	Length Feet	Displ Tons	Year Built	Builder or Location Built
YP-114	motor yacht *Adventuress*	45	32	1940	Colberg Boat Works, Stockton, California
YP-115	motor yacht *Bee, Kennylee*	48		1930	Stephens Brothers, Stockton, California
YP-116	*Balboa*			1928	
YP-117	motor yacht *Xanadu*	59'6"	37	1935	Peterson Boat Building Co.
YP-118	motor yacht *Jasmine, Skeeter*	30	23	1930	Harold R. Fish & Company, Oakland, California
YP-119	motor yacht *Lightnin, Pat Pending*	50	17	1929	Lake Union Dry Dock
YP-120	yacht *Grathea II, Borenna II*	57	30	1928	Defoe Boat & Motor Works, Bay City, Michigan
YP-121	cruiser *Bobanet*	43		1929	Stephens Brothers
YP-122	wooden motor yacht *Mary Kay*	45		1929	Harbor Boat Building Co., Los Angeles, California
YP-123	*Seamonger*			1924	Malmo, Sweden
YP-124	*Intrepid*			1927	Leung Yee
YP-125	*Spinster*			1926	
YP-126	cruiser *Mabi II*	43		1931	Stephens Brothers
YP-127	gas yacht *Lila M., Alma R., Elizabeth, Bounty*	44		1929	Stephens Brothers, Stockton, California
YP-128	*Bonnie Dundee III*	66		1935	
YP-129	*Felica*	67		1922	Kahn
YP-130	gas yacht *Junemma*	44		1931	Matthews Boat Company
YP-131	wooden motor yacht *Sobre las Olas*	105	122	1929	Wilmington Boat Works, Wilmington, California
YP-132	wooden motor yacht *K'Thanga*	92		1926	John Twigg and sons, San Francisco, California
YP-133	cruiser *Cherie*	52		1928	Stephens Brothers
YP-134	RB *Cherie II*			1930	Lake Union Dry Dock
YP-135	cruiser *Armador II*	40	28	1931	Stephens Brothers
YP-136	yacht *Memory*	66		1919	Herreshoff Mfg.
YP-137	RB *Motap*	57		1914	Matthews Boat Company
YP-138	*Sadye Lynn*			1924	
YP-139	*Beautyrest*			1919	Skarsatra, Sweden
YP-140	wooden motor yacht *Thor, Cormorant*	52	27	1925	Campbell Machine Co., San Diego, California
YP-141	cruiser *Folderal*	48		1931	Stephens Brothers
YP-142	motor yacht *Hermit*	68	44	1927	American Car & Foundry
YP-143	motor yacht *Indolence*	50	26	1926	William Cryer, Oakland, California
YP-144	yacht *Folly II*	63		1931	Stephens Brothers
YP-145	yacht *Ballyhoo fourth*	40		1927	Consolidated Shipbuilding
YP-146	gas yacht *Amida, Denali*	81	51	1926	Luders Marine Construction, Stamford, Connecticut
YP-147	*Celia*			1937	Los Angeles, California
YP-148	PS *Western Queen*	85	168	1940	Western Boat Builders
YP-149	PS *Farallon*	79.9	137	1931	Martinac Shipbuilding Co.
YP-150	PS *St. Francis*	85.3	168	1940	Western Boat Builders

Yard Patrol Craft (YP) {281}

Ship	Former Vessel Type/Name	Length Feet	Displ Tons	Year Built	Builder or Location Built
YP-151	PS *Sunrise*	80.2	129	1931	Western Boat Builders
YP-152	PS *Western Traveler*	78.8	129	1937	Western Boat Builders
YP-153	PS *Waldero*	78.1	130	1936	Anderson & Cristofani
YP-154	PS *Alleta B.*	85.1	154	1936	Martinac Shipbuilding Co.
YP-155	PS *Storm*	74.7	114	1939	
YP-156	*Bonne Fortune*	78		1937	Jahncke Shipyard
YP-157	*Lev III*	77	40	1935	Annapolis, Maryland
YP-158	*Southern Breeze*	99	63	1911	Nilson Yachts
YP-159	*Lysistrata III*	74	43	1939	Mobile, Alabama
YP-160	*Sea Rebel*	77	47	1930	Annapolis, Maryland
YP-161	F/V *Yes Sir*	67	31	1934	Covacevich Shipyard
YP-162	*Cajun*	70		1939	Cox & Stevens Inc.
YP-163	*Jackie Jo*	74	30	1941	
YP-164	yacht *Saxon III*	69	33	1929	Henry B. Nevins Yachts
YP-165	wooden motor yacht *Chiro, Norwester*	75	67	1932	Willis J. Reid Boat Yard, Winthrop, Massachusetts
YP-166	PS *Majestic*	74.1	93	1934	Al Larson Boat Building
YP-167	*Yamato Maru*	75		1931	Honolulu, Hawaii
YP-168	*American Maru*	64	33	1930	
YP-169	*Kasuga Maru*	82	71	1930	Seattle, Washington
YP-170	*Kiyo Maru*	71'6"		1938	Honolulu, Hawaii
YP-171	*Taihei Maru*	68	51	1930	
YP-172	*Kiyo Maru*	72	66	1928	Honolulu, Hawaii
YP-173	*Kasuga Maru*	70		1935	
YP-174	*Nachi Maru*	59'3"	34	1928	Honolulu, Hawaii
YP-175	motor yacht *Effort II*	80	55	1928	Julius Petersen Inc.
YP-176	returned to owners				
YP-177	returned to owners				
YP-178	SC-168, *Whitby II*	110		1918	Wheeler Yachts
YP-179	yacht *Privateer* SP-179	108		1917	Consolidated Shipbuilding
YP-180	SC-101, *Fidus*	110		1918	Electric Launch Company
YP-181	*Helori* SP-181	92	90	1911	Johnson & Blanchard
YP-182	returned to owners				
YP-183	*Fuji Maru*	71	58	1930	Honolulu, Hawaii
YP-184	*Tenjin Maru*	73	39	1926	Honolulu, Hawaii
YP-185	RB *Clarinda* SP-185	98	76	1913	Matthews Boat Company
YP-186	*Tenjin Maru*	61	36	1926	Honolulu, Hawaii
YP-187	*Scout*	79	55	1925	Lurssen Werft
YP-188	*Adroit II*	104	60	1920	Great Lakes Boatbuilding
YP-189	*Ace*	109	74	1918	
YP-190	cancelled				
YP-191	*Usona*	110		1917	Gibbs Gas Engine Co.
YP-192	*Braeburn*	105	173	1918	
YP-193	cancelled				
YP-194	FWS *Sandpiper*	46		1928	Matthews Boat Company
YP-195	FWS *Ibis*				
YP-196	FWS *Tijenta*	53		1938	
YP-197	FWS *Brown Bear*	114'10"	216	1934	Windlow Marine Railway
YP-198	FWS *Eider*	78'3"	152	1913	

Appendix A

Ship	Former Vessel Type/Name	Length Feet	Displ Tons	Year Built	Builder or Location Built
YP-199	FWS *Kittiwake*	73	30	1908	City Island Shipbuilding
YP-200	yacht, FWS *Widgeon*	75	38	1913	Consolidated Shipbuilding
YP-201	returned to owners				
YP-202	*Almina*	120	104	1930	
YP-203	motor yacht *Genzam*	97'7"	97	1931	Nyack, New York
YP-204	yacht *Freba*	104		1930	New York Yacht, Launch
YP-205	yacht *Sabiha III*	96	50	1930	Julius Petersen Inc.
YP-206	yacht *Kikai*	100	73	1926	Consolidated Shipbuilding
YP-207	*Firefly*	90		1928	Boston, Massachusetts
YP-208	yacht *Agawam*	102	150	1920	George Lawley & Sons
YP-209	yacht *All Alone*	95	78	1928	Mathis Yachts
YP-210	yacht *Lochivar*	78	60	1928	Defoe Boat & Motor Works
YP-211	power boat *Radiant*	57		1926	Luders Marine
YP-212	*Centaur*	57	35	1929	Gibbs Gas Engine Co.
YP-213	*Estrom V*	50	24	1937	East Boothbay, Maine
YP-214	*Alfredine IV, SP-214*	99	36	1909	C. L. Seabury Co.
YP-215	*Verlaine*	39	35	1940	Fairhaven, Massachusetts
YP-216	*Lark III*	57	38	1939	St. Simon Island, Georgia
YP-217	yacht *Zapala*	111	158	1927	Luders Marine
YP-218	yacht *Consort IV*	86	87	1936	Mathis Yachts
YP-219	yacht *Nancy D.*	71'1"		1924	Mathis Yachts
YP-220	yacht *Skylark III*	99	67	1920	Herreshoff Mfg.
YP-221	*Marmot*	92	108	1936	American Car & Foundry
YP-222	*Bobolink III*	72'3"	37	1929	George Lawley & Sons
YP-223	returned to owners				
YP-224	*Vigilant*	54'4"	78	1939	Shelbourne, Vermont
YP-225	*Kiyo Maru*	60	42	1930	Honolulu, Hawaii
YP-226	*Tenjin Maru*	72	41	1930	Honolulu, Hawaii
YP-227	motor yacht *Mary C.*	70	33	1939	A. F. Stubenberg, Co., Honolulu, Hawaii
YP-228	F/V vessel *Voyageur*	63	39	1937	East Boothbay, Maine
YP-229	*Chelebark*	67	52	1930	Humphreys Shipbuilding
YP-230	*Eryholme*	72		1930	George Lawley & Sons
YP-231	*Janirve*	54	38	1941	Chance Marine
YP-232	*Encore*	55	16	1940	Electric Launch Company
YP-233	TC *Sao Joao*	113.6	281	1929	
YP-234	TC *Patria*	106.5	229	1928	Campbell Machine
YP-235	TC *California*	106.5	191	1928	Campbell Machine
YP-236	TC *Europa*	109	267	1931	Campbell Machine
YP-237	TC *Anna M.*	101.2	268	1941	Western Boat Builders
YP-238	TC *Madeirense*	131.3	307	1940	Harbor Boat Building Co.
YP-239	TC *Challenger*	113.7	325	1940	
YP-240	TC *Conte Bianco*	111.7	278	1934	Campbell Machine
YP-241	ketch *Morning Star*	80'5"	62	1938	Mathis Yachts
YP-242	Naval Academy YP	75	51	1941	Hutchinson Boat Works
YP-243	Naval Academy YP	75	51	1941	Hutchinson Boat Works
YP-244	Naval Academy YP	75	51	1941	Hutchinson Boat Works
YP-245	Naval Academy YP	75	51	1941	Hutchinson Boat Works
YP-246	Naval Academy YP	75	51	1941	Hutchinson Boat Works

Yard Patrol Craft (YP)   {283}

Ship	Former Vessel Type/Name	Length Feet	Displ Tons	Year Built	Builder or Location Built
YP-247	yacht *Tannis*	108	168	1929	Burger Boat Company
YP-248	*Benmar*	57		1940	Chris Craft
YP-249	yacht *Althea*	106	118	1930	Bath Iron Works
YP-250	gas fishing boat *Spencer*	64	61	1913	Ward & Sons, Seattle, Washington
YP-251	halibut boat *Foremost*	79'8"	66	1924	Seattle, Washington
YP-252	*Wild Duck*	104	87	1929	George Lawley & Sons
YP-253	*Montauk*	122'1"	111	1919	Electric Launch Company
YP-254	*Norseman*	90		1939	Cape May, New Jersey
YP-255	yacht *Stevana*	124'3"	189	1930	Consolidated Shipbuilding
YP-256	*Phantom*	68	50	1925	George Lawley & Sons
YP-257	*Alice and Mildred*	84	78	1928	George Lawley & Sons
YP-258	yacht *Vagrant* PYc-30	117'6"	425	1941	Bath Iron Works
YP-259	wooden motor yacht *Selma, Consort III, Scout VI*	70.5	69	1928	Stockholms, batbyggeri, Saltsjobaden, Sweden
YP-260	wooden motor yacht *Grey Gull*	66		1934	Consolidated Shipbuilding, Morris Heights, New York
YP-261	yacht *Navigation*	135	220	1922	San Diego Marine
YP-262	TC *Theodore Foss*	113.6	229	1900	Risdon Iron Works
YP-263	TC *Emma R.S.*	89.1	148	1928	San Diego, CA
YP-264	TC *Alert*	90.5	180	1930	San Diego Marine
YP-265	yacht *Go Deo*	62		1937	Consolidated Shipbuilding
YP-266	*Roamer*	91		1928	Britt Brothers Boat Builders
YP-267	PS *Democracy*	81	151	1940	Harbor Boat Building Co.
YP-268	PS *John B.*	73	96	1940	Los Angeles, California
YP-269	TC/PC *Sea Tern*	95	184	1930	San Pedro Boat Works
YP-270	PS *Pioneer*	83.5	175	1939	
YP-271	*Carol Anne*	55	40	1941	Electric Launch Company
YP-272	yacht *Lone Wolf*	62	50	1939	Fisher Boat Works, Inc.
YP-273	*Korana*	72		1928	Annapolis, Maryland
YP-274	fishing vessel *Onza*	57	31	1936	George Lawley & Sons
YP-275	*Segelen*	100	154	1929	Vancouver Shipyard
YP-276	*Antares*	96		1930	James Lyman
YP-277	TC *Triunfo*	116	321	1937	
YP-278	TC *Liberty*	117.4	334	1937	Campbell Machine
YP-279	TC *Navigator*	113.1	306	1929	Campbell Machine
YP-280	TC *Cape San Vicente*	116.4	302	1935	Campbell Machine
YP-281	TC *San Salvador*	112.8	280	1931	Al Larson Boat Building
YP-282	TC *Yvonne Louise*	93	201	1937	San Diego, California
YP-283	TC *City of San Diego*	116.2	311	1931	San Diego Marine
YP-284	TC *Endeavor*	131.3	469	1940	Campbell Machine
YP-285	TC *Northwestern*	117	364	1930	Western Boat Builders
YP-286	TC *St. George*	90.4	214	1941	Harbor Boat Building Co.
YP-287	TC *American Voyager*	96.8	263	1937	Al Larson Boat Building
YP-288	TC *Western Pacific*	92.7	215	1940	Western Boat Builders
YP-289	TC *Paramount*	110.1	333	1937	Houghton, Washington
YP-290	TC *Picaroto*	127.9	393	1937	Campbell Machine
YP-291	TC *Normandie*	139.2	522	1938	Campbell Machine
YP-292	TC *Azoreana*	130.4	467	1937	Campbell Machine

Appendix A

Ship	Former Vessel Type/Name	Length Feet	Displ Tons	Year Built	Builder or Location Built
YP-293	PS *Santa Rita*	75.1	110	1939	Tacoma, Washington
YP-294	PS *Vivian A.*	73.6	103	1938	Martinolich Shipbuilding
YP-295	PS *Jackie Boy*	73.8	103	1938	Tacoma, Washington
YP-296	PS *American Rose*	71.3	98	1937	Tacoma, Washington
YP-297	PS *City of Monterey*	73.2	105	1937	Anderson & Cristofani
YP-298	PS *Vittoria*	75.5	119	1936	Al Larson Boat Building
YP-299	PS *Dux*	75	124	1936	Martinolich Shipbuilding
YP-300	PS *Little Flower*	71.3	98	1937	Tacoma, Washington
YP-301	PS *El Rey*	75.9	108	1939	Tacoma, Washington
YP-302	PS *California Star*	73.9	103	1936	Anderson & Cristofani
YP-303	PS *Juanita*	75.2	104	1939	Martinolich Shipbuilding
YP-304	PS *El Capitan*	75.3	107	1937	Martinolich Shipbuilding
YP-305	PS *Phyllis*	69.3	82	1939	Tacoma, Washington
YP-306	PS *Sea Lion*	71.9	89	1935	San Francisco, California
YP-307	PS *Cavaleri*	79.7	125	1935	Fulton Shipyard
YP-308	PS *New St. Joseph*	70	98	1937	San Francisco, California
YP-309	PS *Anna B.*	74.8	105	1939	Tacoma, Washington
YP-310	PS *Sea Star*	74.8	107	1935	Martinac Shipbuilding Co.
YP-311	PS *San Vito*	70.7	85	1939	Western Boat Builders
YP-312	PS *Sea Giant*	79	125	1936	Kruse & Banks Shipbuilding
YP-313	PS *Mineo Bros.*	73	102	1939	Kruse & Banks Shipbuilding
YP-314	PS *Virginia II*	72.2	110	1937	Western Boat Builders
YP-315	PS *Santa Lucia*	72.8	109	1937	Western Boat Builders
YP-316	PS *Sherman Rose*	70	70	1935	Tacoma, Washington
YP-317	PS *California Rose*	72.2	106	1936	Martinolich Shipbuilding
YP-318	PS *New Rex*	76.1	113	1936	Anderson & Cristofani
YP-319	PS *Sea Maid*	70.7	98	1937	Sausalito, California
YP-320	PS *St. Anthony*	69.3	80	1934	San Francisco, California
YP-321	TC *Belle of Portugal*	127.9	393	1937	Campbell Machine
YP-322	PS *El Padre*	71.4	107	1937	Tacoma, Washington
YP-323	PS *Diana*	71	78	1935	Al Larson Boat Building
YP-324	PS *New Roma*	70.0	102	1937	Tregoning & Carlson
YP-325	PS *Star of Monterey*	72.9	104	1935	Harbor Boat Building Co.
YP-326	PS *Marettimo*	72.6	107	1936	
YP-327	*Islander*	75'5"	60	1931	Sampson Fishing Boat Co.
YP-328	*Taihei Maru*	61'9"	33	1934	Honolulu, Hawaii
YP-329	*Miyojin Maru*	56'7"		1927	Honolulu, Hawaii
YP-330	*Kasuga Maru*	57'9"	22	1927	Seichi Funai, Honolulu
YP-331	*Recco III*	55	20	1939	Chicago, Illinois
YP-332	*Atlantis*	92	85	1928	Chicago, Illinois
YP-333	*Amelia*	85	78	1925	
YP-334	yacht *Sunshine III*	100	120	1930	Consolidated Shipbuilding
YP-335	wooden gas yacht *Sea Spray, Charmarie*	76	53	1936	Consolidated Shipbuilding
YP-336	*Orithia*	72	49	1930	M. M. Davis and Sons
YP-337	PS *San Juan*	71.9	72	1930	Seattle, Washington
YP-338	*Discoverer*	91		1933	Seattle, Washington
YP-339	steel motor yacht *Wanderer, Lotosland*	115	195	1929	George Lawley & Sons, Neponset, Massachusetts

Yard Patrol Craft (YP) {285}

Ship	Former Vessel Type/Name	Length Feet	Displ Tons	Year Built	Builder or Location Built
YP-340	Sovereign	83	84	1927	Aladdin
YP-341	wooden gas yacht La Gonave	70	34	1937	American Car & Foundry Co., Wilmington, Delaware
YP-342	Mary M.	63	35	1930	Hemelingen, Germany
YP-343	Konpira Maru	65		1928	Walakoa, Hawaii
YP-344	Tenjin Maru II			1919	Walakoa, Hawaii
YP-345	TC Yankee	105.9	294	1939	
YP-346	TC Prospect	108.7	259	1938	San Diego, California
YP-347	TC Star of the Sea	107	232	1930	Campbell Machine
YP-348	TC Cabrillo	126	427	1935	Campbell Machine
YP-349	TC Queen Mary	134	510	1938	Campbell Machine
YP-350	TC Victoria	129	434	1937	Campbell Machine
YP-351	Yoreda	97'2"		1929	Bay City, Michigan
YP-352	yacht Annette R.	90	88	1929	Luders Marine
YP-353	Gypsy	71	69	1921	
YP-354	yacht Innisfail	80'1"	89	1939	Mathis Yachts
YP-355	Hiwal	104	86	1918	Newcomb Lifeboat
YP-356	From Now On	67	35	1940	Annapolis, Maryland
YP-357	Mystic	85	84	1939	East Boothbay, Maine
YP-358	yacht Mercury IV	63	32	1936	Luders Marine
YP-359	Done Gone	55	27	1941	Electric Launch Company
YP-360	PS Aurora	79.3	122	1940	Tacoma, Washington
YP-361	PS Exposition King	75.4	105	1939	Tacoma, Washington
YP-362	PS Western Star, AMb-4	74.8	118	1939	Western Boat Builders
YP-363	PS Santa Rosa	75.9	106	1940	Tacoma, Washington
YP-364	PS New Hope, AMb-6	75.5	107	1940	Martinolich Shipbuilding
YP-365	PS Cutino Brothers	78.1	114	1940	Tacoma, Washington
YP-366	PS San Jose	71.5	96	1940	Fernandina, Florida
YP-367	PS Belle Haven	70	98	1939	San Francisco, California
YP-368	PS Ardito	73.7	101	1939	Tacoma, Washington
YP-369	PS Stella Maris	71.2	105	1939	Tacoma, Washington
YP-370	PS Dante Alighiere	75.3	105	1939	Tacoma, Washington
YP-371	PS Redeemer	78	114	1940	Tacoma, Washington
YP-372	PS San Giovanni	75.2	106	1939	Tacoma, Washington
YP-373	PS Leslie J. Fulton	70.2	110	1939	Tacoma, Washington
YP-374	PS Belvedere	71.2	95	1939	Tacoma, Washington
YP-375	Raymonde, AMb-17	84	110	1929	Storey Shipbuilding
YP-376	AMb-18	78	72	1941	Kennebunkport, Maine
YP-377	trawler AMb-19	79		1941	Fairhaven, Massachusetts
YP-378	F/V hull AMb-20	89	81	1941	Morse Shipyard
YP-379	F/V hull AMb-21	85	69	1941	Morse Shipyard
YP-380	F/V John E. Murley	88'7"		1941	Morse Shipyard
YP-381	PS St. James	87.9	149	1940	San Francisco, California
YP-382	PS Twin Brothers	75.5	106	1940	Tacoma, Washington
YP-383	PS J. Di Maggio	87.3	160	1940	Tacoma, Washington
YP-384	PS Lina V.	79.3	108	1940	Tacoma, Washington
YP-385	PS Pacific Star	81.3	144	1940	Martinac Shipbuilding Co.
YP-386	PS Lina B.	79.3	134	1936	Martinac Shipbuilding Co.
YP-387	trawler Cohasset	110	301	1941	Fore River Shipyard
YP-388	trawler Lynn	110	301	1941	Fore River Shipyard

Appendix A

Ship	Former Vessel Type/Name	Length Feet	Displ Tons	Year Built	Builder or Location Built
YP-389	trawler *Salem*	110	301	1941	Fore River Shipyard
YP-390	yacht *Alcy*	61	39	1940	Mathis Yachts
YP-391	*Blue Bird*	115		1938	Bay City, Michigan
YP-392	ketch-rigged motor yacht *Trade Wind*	62	35	1938	Robert Jacob Shipyard, City Island, Bronx, New York
YP-393	*Bismallah III*	57	31	1939	Detroit, Michigan
YP-394	yacht *Pan Che*	72	56	1929	Defoe Boat & Motor Works
YP-395	yacht *Rosewill III*	77	74	1937	Consolidated Shipbuilding
YP-396	*Umatilla* LV-88	135'5"	683	1907	New York Shipbuilding Co.
YP-397	*Swiftsure* LV-113, Ens. Richard E. Walker, USCG	133'3"	630	1929	Albina Marine Works
YP-398	*Lady Alberta*	62	46	1940	Chance Marine
YP-399	PS *Big Dipper*	79.4	127	1942	Peterson Boat Building Co.
YP-400	PS hull No. 43, Lt. Albert H. Nienau, USNR	93	187	1942	Tacoma Boat Building Co., Tacoma, Washington
YP-401	*Monterey*	110	65	1917	Puget Sound Naval Shipyard
YP-402	*Messenger*	71		1924	Seattle, Washington
YP-403	yacht *Chanticleer*	60'1"	16	1941	Mathis Yachts
YP-404	F/V *Thomas C. McNeal*	127	219	1923	M. M. Davis and Sons
YP-405	*Blue Jacket*	60	43	1932	
YP-406	yacht *Alma F.*	82	88	1928	Defoe Boat & Motor Works
YP-407	yacht *Maid Marian II*	101'8"	94	1931	Consolidated Shipbuilding
YP-408	yacht *Sea Dream*	90	82	1925	Luders Marine
YP-409	*Katy D.*	88	100	1939	Morse Shipyard
YP-410	yacht *Hermana*	69	46	1929	Harbor Boat Building Co.
YP-411	TC *Sea Wolf*	103	170	1942	Martinolich Shipbuilding
YP-412	yacht *Charmarie*	72	70	1940	Mathis Yachts
YP-413	yacht *Toddywax*	73	70	1931	New York Yacht, Launch
YP-414	beam trawler *Squall*	131'2"	369	1937	Bath Iron Works
YP-415	beam trawler *Swell*	131'2"	369	1936	Bath Iron Works
YP-416	fishing trawler *Drift*	147	310	1941	American Ship Lorain
YP-417	fishing trawler *Calm*	147	310	1941	American Ship Lorain
YP-418	fishing trawler *Crest*	147	310	1938	Fore River Shipyard
YP-419	trawler *Illinois*	118'4"	300	1941	George Lawley & Sons
YP-420	trawler *Arlington*	131'2"	369	1936	Bath Iron Works
YP-421	beam trawler *Surf*	145	310	1936	Bath Iron Works
YP-422	fishing trawler *Mist*	133'3"	310	1941	American Ship Cleveland
YP-423	beam trawler *Storm*	145	310	1936	Bath Iron Works
YP-424	yacht *Reynard*	72'5"	46	1929	Consolidated Shipbuilding
YP-425	*Rose B.*, *Brave* PYc-34	126'7"	163	1930	Defoe Boat & Motor Works
YP-426	DD *Katherine F. Saunders*	93	100	1929	Morse Shipyard
YP-427	DD *Newfoundland*	99	100	1930	Morse Shipyard
YP-428	DD *St. Anthony*	95	100	1929	James Lyman
YP-429	DD *Elvira Gaspat*	96	72	1929	Storey Shipbuilding
YP-430	DD *Theresa Boudreau*	103		1929	Essex, Massachusetts
YP-431	*Viking*	77		1931	Morse Shipyard
YP-432	DD *Columbo*	87	65	1929	Marr

Yard Patrol Craft (YP) {287}

Ship	Former Vessel Type/Name	Length Feet	Displ Tons	Year Built	Builder or Location Built
YP-433	DD *Superior*	100	103	1929	Essex, Massachusetts
YP-434	DD *William H. Killegrew*	80	30	1929	Essex, Massachusetts
YP-435	DD *New Bedford*	84		1929	Morse Shipyard
YP-436	*Philip and Grace*	89		1942	Morse Shipyard
YP-437	*Edith L. Boudreau*	94		1930	Essex, Massachusetts
YP-438	*Donald Amirault*	100		1929	Essex, Massachusetts
YP-439	DD *Rainbow*	89		1929	James Lyman
YP-440	DD *Wamsutta*	84		1929	Morse Shipyard
YP-441	*Leretha*	99		1929	Storey Shipbuilding
YP-442	DD *Gloucester*	85		1929	Warner SB
YP-443	DD *Magellan*	88		1929	Storey Shipbuilding
YP-444	DD *Vagabond*	86		1929	Morse Shipyard
YP-445	DD *Babe Sears*	88		1929	Storey Shipbuilding
YP-446	*Alvan T. Fuller*	89	100	1931	Storey Shipbuilding
YP-447	DD *Venture II*	100	118	1929	Marr
YP-448	schooner-rigged motor fishing vessel *Virginia*	130	75	1941	Mueller Boat Works Inc., Brooklyn, New York
YP-449	F/V *Beatrice & Ida*	88	110	1939	Fred W. Schultz
YP-450	*Ronald & Mary Jane*	91	100	1941	James Lyman
YP-451	yacht *Idalia*	62'1"		1927	Luders Marine
YP-452	*Marileen*	74	40	1927	Chance Marine
YP-453	yacht *Pleiades*	79	51	1928	Consolidated Shipbuilding
YP-454	yacht *Iolite* PYc-24	107		1930	Henry B. Nevins Yachts
YP-455	yacht *Alura*	120'3"	124	1922	Consolidated Shipbuilding
YP-456	*Victory*	50		1942	
YP-457	yacht ex-*Kelble*	63	22	1932	Consolidated Shipbuilding
YP-458	yacht *Bangalore*	76		1929	Mathis Yachts
YP-459	*Northeaster*	43		1936	Fernandina, Florida
YP-460	*Leon*	45		1941	St. Augustine, Florida
YP-461	*Gigi*	44	25	1935	Fernandina, Florida
YP-462	*Wawa*	50	31	1937	Fernandina, Florida
YP-463	*Maud and Mabel*	45	19	1931	Heislerville, New Jersey
YP-464	*Ave Maria*	42	23	1941	St. Augustine, Florida
YP-465	*American Kid*	48	24	1941	St. Augustine, Florida
YP-466	*Huckleberry Finn*	45	26	1942	
YP-467	*Dutchess*	51	27	1942	
YP-468	*Madonna*	42	41	1935	Fernandina, Florida
YP-469	*Red Snapper*	50	33	1938	Fernandina, Florida
YP-470	*Helen C.*	47	28	1937	Fernandina, Florida
YP-471	*F.W. Scheper*	51	32	1941	St. Augustine, Florida
YP-472	*San Antonio*	50		1917	Fernandina, Florida
YP-473	*Captain Fred*	44	30	1941	
YP-474	*Bella*	44		1941	St. Augustine, Florida
YP-475	*Ottis*	55	29	1942	St. Augustine, Florida
YP-476	*Romie*	48	26	1941	St. Augustine, Florida
YP-477	*Howard*	44	27	1942	St. Augustine, Florida
YP-478	*Roseina II*	44	25	1941	St. Augustine, Florida
YP-479	*Gen. Douglas MacArthur*	49	29	1942	St. Augustine, Florida
YP-480	*Miss America*	44	28	1937	Fernandina, Florida

Appendix A

Ship	Former Vessel Type/Name	Length Feet	Displ Tons	Year Built	Builder or Location Built
YP-481	Princess Mary	48	21	1939	Fernandina, Florida
YP-482	Chippewa	55			
YP-483	Hitide	44	26	1937	Fernandina, Florida
YP-484	Cavandago	45	26	1940	
YP-485	Mary-Jo	50		1942	
YP-486	Portugal	44	25	1941	St. Augustine, Florida
YP-487	Uncle Sam	50	27	1940	St. Augustine, Florida
YP-488	M.A. Santos	44	24	1941	St. Augustine, Florida
YP-489	Western I	50	40	1942	
YP-490	Western II	50	40	1942	
YP-491	Lady Mary	50	27	1941	St. Augustine, Florida
YP-492	Marco Polo	43	24	1941	St. Augustine, Florida
YP-493	Riverside	46	28	1939	Fernandina, Florida
YP-494	Mary T.	50	28		
YP-495	Thunderbolt	50		1942	St. Augustine, Florida
YP-496	Little Junior	42	25	1936	Fernandina, Florida
YP-497	Westwind	51		1928	
YP-498	Promised Land	131	137	1938	Smith
YP-499	Mary Ellen	113	144	1937	Fernandina, Florida
YP-500	Charles Mason	113	144	1937	
YP-501	Mellani	53	33		
YP-502	yacht Lauxmont	106	105	1929	Consolidated Shipbuilding
YP-503	TC St. Therese	113	164	1928	Rask
YP-504	TC Cipango	128	177	1929	San Pedro Boat Works
YP-505	Peace	42	24	1938	St. Augustine, Florida
YP-506	yacht Fleet SP-1217	81	41	1917	George Lawley & Sons
YP-507	Clara L. Hudgins	104	91	1917	Pensacola, Florida
YP-508	Felix Salvadore	48		1942	
YP-509		50		1942	Burgman Tractor
YP-510		56		1942	Burgman Tractor
YP-511		56		1942	Burgman Tractor
YP-512	motor yacht Libra II	61'8"		1936	Julius Petersen Inc.
YP-513	yacht Seer	66'9"	48	1938	Hodgdon-Greene
YP-514	TC American Beauty	129.1	456	1938	Campbell Machine
YP-515	PS/TC Falcon	157	512	1919	Ferguson Steel & Iron Co.
YP-516	TC Queen Amelia	112	268	1941	Campbell Machine
YP-517	TC St. Ann	94.8	248	1941	Martinolich Shipbuilding
YP-518	TC Commodore	128	300	1942	Campbell Machine
YP-519	TC Queen Elizabeth	105.1	217	1928	Los Angeles, California
YP-520	TC Conte Grande	135	296	1942	Lynch Shipbuilding
YP-521	Mettamar	89	115	1930	New York, New York
YP-522	TC Chicken of the Sea	113.3	295	1930	Parke & Kibele
YP-523	Malibu	92	87	1926	Seattle, Washington
YP-524	Diana III	47	30		
YP-525	cruiser Marie S.	51'2"	32	1941	Matthews Boat Company
YP-526	American Beauty	50		1942	St. Augustine, Florida
YP-527	Sayon	97	59	1926	Boston, Massachusetts
YP-528	freighter Santa Monica	166	318	1902	W. F. Stone & Son
YP-529	Alicia II	60	32	1929	Red Bank Yacht

Yard Patrol Craft (YP) {289}

Ship	Former Vessel Type/Name	Length Feet	Displ Tons	Year Built	Builder or Location Built
YP-530	One Forty Four	51	20	1942	
YP-531	Paola	65	58	1938	Dachel-Carter Shipbuilding
YP-532	yacht Souris	81'7"		1931	Henry B. Nevins Yachts
YP-533	yacht Rumba	81	43	1930	Consolidated Shipbuilding
YP-534	Whitecap II	73	50	1921	George Lawley & Sons
YP-535	Freda	65	34	1937	Wilmington, Delaware
YP-536	motor yacht Wego	57	37	1941	Julius Petersen, Inc.
YP-537	Witrose	63		1940	Chance Marine
YP-538	Bolo	55	30	1932	Anderson & Cristofani
YP-539	Iroquois	50		1939	Electric Launch Company
YP-540	Miramar	65		1934	American Car & Foundry
YP-541	yacht Jinia III	65'4"	57	1939	Mathis Yachts
YP-542	Hallmar III	58	33	1938	Brooklyn, New York
YP-543	yacht Lev-Lou	53		1936	Consolidated Shipbuilding
YP-544	Wanda D.	53	23	1934	Brooklyn, New York
YP-545	yacht Glenmar			1928	Robert Jacob Shipyard
YP-546	yacht Elgra	73	58	1929	Consolidated Shipbuilding
YP-547	Rocket	82		1932	
YP-548	Dolphin	73	43	1928	Los Angeles, California
YP-549	Edith L. Hudgins	105	94	1938	Norfolk, Virginia
YP-550	Serene II	57'7"	27	1926	Electric Launch Company
YP-551	Eloise III	75	44	1926	
YP-552	yacht Taormina	113'4"	178	1924	George Lawley & Sons
YP-553	yacht Martha N.	97'4"	98	1930	Luders Marine
YP-554	Pirate	72'6"	53	1928	George Lawley & Sons
YP-555	Carthage	66	52	1904	Miami, Florida
YP-556	yacht Fantasy	98'8"	97	1920	Robert Jacob Shipyard
YP-557	yacht Pomander III	81'7"	51	1927	George Lawley & Sons
YP-558	So Dor Ot II	55		1940	Electric Launch Company
YP-559	yacht Kyma	99'9"	66	1928	Lurssen Werft
YP-560	Minnie B.	75		1917	Seattle, Washington
YP-561	Karluk	77		1929	Tacoma, Washington
YP-562	Royo Marie	70		1929	Honolulu, Hawaii
YP-563	yacht Cossack	72	31	1930	Consolidated Shipbuilding
YP-564	motor yacht Navajo	72'8"		1927	Julius Petersen Inc.
YP-565	Corky II	77	63	1926	City Island, New York
YP-566	gas yacht Ensign II, Mariner	85	57	1920	George Lawley & Sons, Neponset, Massachusetts
YP-567	Ruth Ann			1936	Wilmington, Delaware
YP-568	yacht Emrose	77		1938	New York, New York
YP-569	Semloh	87'5"		1936	Nevins B. Nevins Yachts
YP-570	yacht Kittiwake	76		1929	Consolidated Shipbuilding
YP-571	Apache	75		1918	
YP-572	yacht Luneta, Carolyn	90	100	1929	Mathis Yachts
YP-573	yacht Heavy Moon	85		1926	Mathis Yachts
YP-574	yacht Mary Belle	86	100	1929	Mathis Yachts
YP-575	Katmai	83		1915	Seattle, Washington
YP-576	Minnehaha	100	150	1919	Pacific American
YP-577	yacht Annio	89		1926	Luders Marine

Appendix A

Ship	Former Vessel Type/Name	Length Feet	Displ Tons	Year Built	Builder or Location Built
YP-578	yacht *Yorel II*	69'2"		1940	Luders Marine
YP-579	yacht *Saunterer*	90	118	1928	Mathis Yachts
YP-580	*Mystery*	67'7"		1927	New York, New York
YP-581	*Acushnet*	79'7"	35	1929	George Lawley & Sons
YP-582	yacht *Pippin*	55	20	1942	Consolidated Shipbuilding
YP-583	Naval Academy YP	75	50	1943	Hutchinson Boat Works
YP-584	Naval Academy YP	75	50	1943	Hutchinson Boat Works
YP-585	Naval Academy YP	75	50	1943	Hutchinson Boat Works
YP-586	Naval Academy YP	75	50	1943	Hutchinson Boat Works
YP-587	Naval Academy YP	75	50	1943	Hutchinson Boat Works
YP-588	Naval Academy YP	75	50	1943	Hutchinson Boat Works
YP-589	Naval Academy YP	75	50	1943	Hutchinson Boat Works
YP-590	Naval Academy YP	75	50	1943	Hutchinson Boat Works
YP-591	Naval Academy YP	75	50	1943	Hutchinson Boat Works
YP-592	*Judy*	60		1920	New York, New York
YP-593	*Melinda*	105	120	1919	Puget Sound Naval Shipyard
YP-594	*Stranger*	104	120	1917	Mare Island Naval Shipyard
YP-595	yacht *Vellron*	87'2"	62	1918	Consolidated Shipbuilding
YP-596	*Steanline*			1938	
YP-597	F/V *Petrel*	54'8"	39	1929	Columbia City, Oregon
YP-598	*Gitana*	63'6"	49	1931	Dickman
YP-599	*Cordova*	79		1935	Seattle, Washington
YP-600		78	92	1943	Bristol Yachts
YP-601		78	92	1944	Bristol Yachts
YP-602	yacht *Carita*	96	139	1930	Mathis Yachts
YP-603	*Shiawassee*	105		1933	
YP-604	yacht *Little Stranger*	62		1928	Consolidated Shipbuilding
YP-605	cruiser *Panacea*	50'5"		1931	Stephens Brothers
YP-606	yacht *Jean III*	80		1929	New York Yacht, Launch
YP-607	yacht *Flohema II*	72	53	1926	
YP-608	yacht *Solana*	106		1929	Consolidated Shipbuilding
YP-609	*Retreat*	63	24		
YP-610	*E.R. Stuart*	100			
YP-611	*Jodaro*	60		1936	
YP-612	*Maroc*	93		1926	
YP-613	yacht *Cheerio*	65	35	1926	New York Yacht, Launch
YP-614	*Lark*	75		1929	Lurssen Werft
YP-615	*Peregrine*	71	28	1926	
YP-616	cancelled				
YP-617	tuna clipper design, Lt. Leonard K. Lobred, USNR	128	403	1945	Harbor Boat Building Co., Terminal Island, California
YP-618	Lt. Clarence W. Armstrong, USNR	128	403	1945	Harbor Boat Building Co.
YP-619	Lt. (jg) Edward B. Sauvain, USNR	128	403	1945	Fulton Shipyard, Antioch, California
YP-620	Lt. (jg) Robert D. Creighton, USNR	128	403	1945	Fulton Shipyard

Yard Patrol Craft (YP) {291}

Ship	Former Vessel Type/Name	Length Feet	Displ Tons	Year Built	Builder or Location Built
YP-621	Lt. Robert L. Linder, USNR	128	403	1945	Hodgson-Greene
YP-622	Lt. (jg) Floyd E. Eckert, Jr., USNR	128	403	1945	Hodgson-Greene
YP-623		128	403	1945	Astoria Marine
YP-624		128	403	1945	Astoria Marine
YP-625	Lt. Raphael M. Nicola, USNR	128	403	1945	Tacoma Boatbuilding
YP-626	Lt. (jg) Arnold W. Welker, USNR	128	403	1945	Tacoma Boatbuilding
YP-627	Lt. Herbert H. Coe, USNR	128	403	1945	Western Boat Builders
YP-628	Lt. Robert R. Barr, USNR	128	403	1945	Western Boat Builders
YP-629		128	403	1945	Seattle SB & DD
YP-630	Lt. (jg) Everett W. Lampson, USNR	128	403	1945	Seattle SB & DD
YP-631	Lt. John R. Olds, USNR	128	403	1945	Sagstad Shipyard
YP-632	Lt. George A. Cary, USNR	128	403	1945	Sagstad Shipyard
YP-633	Lt. (jg) Frederick Altman, USNR	128	403	1945	Chilman Shipyard
YP-634	Lt. (jg) William W. Williams, Jr., USNR	128	403	1945	Chilman Shipyard
YP-635		128	403	1945	Ballard Marine Railway
YP-636		128	403	1945	Ballard Marine Railway
YP-637	Lt. (jg) Benjamin J. Barlage, USNR	128	403	1945	Martinac Shipbuilding Co.
YP-638	Lt. Arthur D. Jones, USNR	128	403	1945	Martinac Shipbuilding Co.
YP-639	Lt. (jg) Charles L. LecLuyse, USNR	128	403	1945	South Coast Shipbuilding
YP-640	Lt. Roger C. Cahoon, USNR	128	403	1945	South Coast Shipbuilding
YP-641	Lt. Keith L. Davey, USNR	128	403	1945	Bellingham Marine Railway
YP-642	Lt. Donald F. Bohn, USNR	128	403	1945	Bellingham Marine Railway
YP-643	Lt. Burrows Barston, Jr., USNR	128	403	1945	Everett-Pacific SB
YP-644	Lt. (jg) E. B. Moore, USN	128	403	1945	Everett-Pacific SB
YP-645	Lt. Josiah B. Chandler, USNR	128	403	1945	Colberg Boat Works
YP-646	Lt. (jg) Robert L. Philip, USNR	128	403	1945	Colberg Boat Works

Appendix B: Patrol Yachts (PY)

Ship Name and Commanding Officer if Known	Former Yacht	Length Feet	Displ Tons	Year Built	Builder
Isabel PY-10	*Isabel*	245'3"	1,045	1917	Bath Iron Works
Wenonah PY-11	*Wenonah*	163	470	1915	George Lawley
Sylph PY-12	*Intrepid*	205	858	1929	George Lawley
Siren PY-13	*Lotosland*	196'5"	800	1929	Pusey & Jones Co.
Argus PY-14	*Haida*	207'6"	1,072	1929	Germania Werft
Coral PY-15	*Sialia*	207	558	1914	Pusey & Jones Co.
Zircon PY-16, Lt. Comdr. Cornelius M. Sullivan, USNR	*Nakhoda*	235'4"	1,400	1930	Pusey & Jones Co.
Jade PY-17	*Athero II*	171	562	1926	George Lawley
Turquoise PY-18	*Ohio*	172	565	1922	Newport News SB
Carnelian PY-19	*Seventeen*	190	609	1930	Bath Iron Works
Tourmaline PY-20	*Sylvia*	189'7"	750	1928	Bath Iron Works
Ruby PY-21	*Placida*	190	640	1929	Bath Iron Works
Azurlite PY-22	*Vagabondia*	210'11"	1,080	1928	Krupp Iron Works
Beryl PY-23	*Rene*	225	1,400	1929	Pusey & Jones Co.
Almandite PY-24	*Happy Days*	185'4"	705	1927	Krupp Iron Works
Crystal PY-25	*Vida*	225	1,400	1929	Pusey & Jones Co.
Cythera PY-26	*Agawa*	215	1,000	1906	Ramage & Ferguson
Girasol PY-27	*Firenze*	170	700	1926	Krupp Iron Works
Marcasite PY-28	*Camargo*	225'2"	1,130	1928	George Lawley
Mizpah PY-29	*Mizpah*	181	771	1926	Newport News SB
Hydrographer PY-30	*Hydrographer*	165	1,135	1928	Spear Engine Works
Cythera PY-31	*Abril*	205'7"	800	1930	Germania Werft
Southern Seas PY-32	*Lyndonia*	228	1,116	1920	Consolidated Shipbuilding

Appendix C: Coastal Patrol Yachts (PYc)

Ship Name and Commanding Officer if Known	Former Yacht	Length Feet	Displ Tons	Year Built	Builder
Emerald PYc-1	Tamarack IV, Savitar	96	104	1922	Consolidated SB
Sapphire PYc-2	Buccaneer	165'4"	450	1929	George Lawley & Sons
Amethyst PYc-3	Samona II	147	525	1931	Craig Shipbuilding Co.
Agate PYc-4	Arminia	110	185	1930	Mathis Yachts
Onyx PYc-5	Janey III	119	190	1924	Consolidated SB
Amber PYc-6	Infanta, Polaris	120	260	1930	Lake Union Dry Dock
Aquamarine PYc-7, Lt. George A. Lange, USNR	Siele, Seawolf	124	215	1926	Pusey & Jones Co.
Opal PYc-8	Coronet	185	590	1928	Krupp Germania Werft
Moonstone PYc-9	Nancy Baker	172	645	1929	Krupp Germania Werft
Topaz PYc-10	Topaz	112	160	1931	Luders Marine
Andradite PYc-11, Lt. (jg) Anderson J. Crabb, USNR	Comoco, Caronia	140'2"	395	1927	Defoe Boat Works
Sardonyx PYc-12	Queen Anne	175'4"	765	1928	Germania Werft
Jasper PYc-13	Stranger	134	395	1938	Lake Union Dry Dock
Truant PYc-14	Truant	138	375	1892	Herreshoff Mfg.
Garnet PYc-15	Caritas	156'9"	490	1925	Krupp Iron Works
Chalcedony PYc-16, Lt. (jg) Erwin E. Smith, USNR	Velero III	195'1"	1,000	1931	Craig Shipbuilding Co.
Pyrope PYc-17, Lt. (jg) John A. Gorham, USNR	Oceanus, Oceania	156'4"	460	1923	Germania Werft
Peridot PYc-18, Lt. Philip J. Rasch, USNR	Bymar	144'7"	300	1938	Defoe Boat Works
Rhodolite PYc-19	Sea Pine	158	588	1931	Bath Iron Works
Jet PYc-20	Thalia	160	472	1930	Defoe Boat Works
Alabaster PYc-21	Alamo, Rellimpa, Ranley, Ronaele	148	385	1932	Mathis Yachts
Olivin PYc-22, Lt. Albert R. Bryon, USNR	Bidou	124	120	1930	Bath Iron Works
Sard PYc-23	Navigation	90		1922	San Diego Marine
Iolite PYc-24	Souris	107		1930	Henry B. Nevins Yachts
Phenakite PYc-25	Sachem	183	360	1902	Pusey & Jones Co.
Cymophane PYc-26, Lt. Raymond M. Hull, USNR	Robador, Seaforth	161	523	1926	Newport News SB
Colleen PYc-27	Colleen	150	250	1928	Pusey & Jones Co.
Ability PYc-28	Reomar IV	133	280	1926	Defoe Boat Works
Gallant PYc-29	North Star	177	350	1909	Pusey & Jones
Vagrant PYc-30, Lt. (jg) George T. Elliman, USNR	Vagrant	117'6"	425	1941	Bath Iron Works

Appendix C

Name	Former names	Length	Tons	Year	Builder
Lash PYc-31	Caroline	188	339	1914	Robert Jacob Shipyard
Tourist PYc-32	Kehtoh, Dixie, Tourist	150	185	1906	George Lawley & Sons
Palace PYc-33	Idalia, Maylay II, Palace	163	195	1899	John Roach & Co.
Brave PYc-34	Rose B.	126'7"	163	1930	Defoe Boat Works
Felicia PYc-35, Lt. Francis G. Crane, USNR	Felicia	147'9"	447	1931	Bath Iron Works
Paragon PYc-36, Lt. Edward E. Adams, USNR	Paragon	138	176	1929	Bath Iron Works
Mentor PYc-37, Lt. William C. Hayes, USNR	Haida	127	182	1941	Robert Jacob Shipyard
Carolita PYc-38	Ripple	133	236	1923	Krupp Germania Werft
Marnell PYc-39, Lt. Griswold S. Hayward, Jr., USNR	Marnell	135	180	1930	Defoe Boat Works
Captor PYc-40	Harvard	134	520	1938	Bethlehem Steel
Iolite PYc-41	Florence D.	154	200	1914	George Lawley & Sons
Leader PYc-42, Lt. (jg) Clifton R. Anderson, USNR	Curlew	117	230	1927	Whites Yacht Building & Engineering Co., Ltd.
Sea Scout PYc-43, Lt. (jg) Malcolm L. Wood, USNR	Velero II	125	195	1922	William Mueller
Perseverance PYc-44, Lt. Comdr. Charles E. Priolean, USNR	Gem, Athero, Gipsy Jo, Condor, Bedford WPYc-346	164'5"	190	1913	George Lawley & Sons
Black Douglas PYc-45	Black Douglas	150	371	1930	Bath Iron Works
Impetuous PYc-46	Paragon	120	103	1915	Robert Jacob Shipyard
Patriot PYc-47	Katoora	96	83	1930	Herreshoff Mfg.
Persistent PYc-48	Onwego	120	110	1931	Consolidated SB
Retort PYc-49	Enaj IV	120	150	1923	George Lawley & Sons
Sturdy PYc-50	Elda	154	380	1930	Consolidated SB
Valiant PYc-51	Vara	150	190	1929	Herreshoff Mfg.
Venture PYc-52	Vixon	110	138	1913	Consolidated SB

Appendix D: Vaughn, Murphy, and Nevle Navy Cross Medal Citations

CHIEF MACHINIST'S MATE CHARLES HENRY VAUGHN, JR., USNR
The President of the United States of America takes pleasure in presenting the Navy Cross to Chief Machinist's Mate Charles Henry Vaughn, Jr., United States Naval Reserve, for extraordinary heroism and devotion to duty while serving aboard the *YP-346*, in action on 9 September 1942, when that vessel was attacked by enemy surface craft off the coast of Tulagi in the Solomon Islands. During the attack Chief Machinist's Mate Vaughn was on duty in the engine room as Chief Engineer of that vessel and she received a hit in the engine room. He went on deck to report to the bridge and upon his arrival there learned that the bridge was shot away and was informed that the Commanding Officer had been killed. He summarized the situation and remarked that the only thing to do was to beach the vessel. As he made this remark, Private First Class Gerard B. Nevle, USMC, immediately went to the remains of the bridge upon his own initiative and assumed charge of the wheel, bringing the ship under control and steered a course for the beach. Private First Class Nevle left the bridge and went below to minister to the injuries of the second Gunner's Mate. The ship again lost its course; Private First Class Nevle returned to the bridge and although the wheel contained only three broken spokes he brought the ship back under control and steered her onto the beach. He then swam ashore with the injured sailor, left the sailor on the beach and swam back to the ship and assisted in removing the remainder of the personnel of the ship. During the time of the above attack, Private First Class John J. Murphy, USMC, went to the engine room of the *YP-346* and although the regular members of the crew had left the engine room after the hit received therein, Private First Class Murphy worked with Chief Machinist's Mate Vaughn, assisting invaluably in securing the ammonia system and assisting him

as directed. The above important factors were reported because it was felt by Chief Machinist's Mate Vaughn that the action of these two Marines in taking over duties of the sailors during this attack, made possible the beaching of the *YP-346* and the saving of the lives of the majority of the crew thereon. Their action was entirely upon their own initiative and at great risk of their own lives. The Commanding Officer of the *YP-346* was evacuated from the area as a casualty. Chief Machinist's Mate Vaughn's conduct throughout was in keeping with the highest traditions of the Navy of the United States.

PRIVATE FIRST CLASS JOHN J. MURPHY, JR., USMC

The President of the United States of America takes pleasure in presenting the Navy Cross to Private First Class John J. Murphy, Jr., United States Marine Corps, for extraordinary heroism and conspicuous devotion to duty while serving as a member of a Rifle Company of the Second Marines (Reinforced), SECOND Marine Division, aboard the *YP-346* during action against enemy Japanese forces off the coast of Tulagi, Solomon Islands, on the night of 9 September 1942. With his ship illuminated by the enemy and hostile gunfire causing violent explosion of shells inside the magazine directly beneath his battle station, Private First Class Murphy voluntarily remained on board, despite devastating Japanese shellfire, to assist in repairing damage to the engine room until that compartment also became untenable. Although wounded by a shell fragment shortly afterward, he gallantly disregarded his own condition to help evacuate other injured shipmates to a dressing station ashore, following the beaching of the vessel. His conspicuous courage in a situation of grave peril was in keeping with the highest traditions of the United States Naval Service.

PRIVATE FIRST CLASS GERARD B. NEVLE, USMCR

The President of the United States of America takes pleasure in presenting the Navy Cross to Private First Class Gerard B. Nevle, United States Marine Corps Reserve, for extraordinary heroism and conspicuous devotion to duty while serving as a member of a Rifle Company of the Second Marines (Reinforced), SECOND Marine Division, aboard the *YP-346*, during action against enemy Japanese forces off the coast of Tulagi, Solomon Islands, on the night of 9 September 1942. With his ship illuminated by the enemy and hostile gunfire causing violent explosion of shells inside the magazine directly beneath his battle station, Private First Class Nevle voluntarily remained on board despite devastating enemy shellfire, manned the practically demolished bridge and set the vessel on a beaching course. Later, he again risked his life to administer first aid to his wounded shipmates, assisting in their evacuation to protected areas. His conspicuous gallantry and courage in a situation of grave peril were in keeping with the highest traditions of the United States Naval Service.

Appendix E: Raymond, Petritz, and Strand Navy Cross Medal Citations

LIEUTENANT FRED LUMAN RAYMOND, USNR

The President of the United States of America takes pride in presenting the Navy Cross (Posthumously) to Lieutenant Fred Luman Raymond, United States Naval Reserve, for extraordinary heroism in combat while serving on board the U.S.S. *MARYANNE* of the Inshore Patrol, Philippine Islands, during the period from 4 January to 29 April 1942, in organizing, administering and directing forces while exposed to the same hazards as vessels mentioned above. Most of these officers, with their crews, were engaged from 12 April 1942 in missions of major strategic importance and of most hazardous nature involving night sweeping of safe passage through contact mine fields south of Corregidor and distant night patrols for intercepting enemy landing parties. Lieutenant Raymond's conduct throughout this period was in keeping with the highest traditions of the United States Naval Service.

ENSIGN GEORGE KARL PETRITZ, USNR

The President of the United States of America takes pleasure in presenting the Navy Cross to Ensign George Karl Petritz, United States Naval Reserve, for extraordinary heroism in combat with the enemy during the period 7 December 1941 to 7 March 1942, while on board the U.S.S. *FISHERIES TWO*, in the Philippine Islands. While exposed to frequent horizontal and dive bombing attacks by enemy Japanese air forces, Ensign Petritz directed the fire of his anti-aircraft battery and participated in operations of strategic importance in the Manila Bay area involving hazardous missions such as to reflect great credit upon himself and the United States Naval Service.

ENSIGN LOWELL HALL STRAND, USNR

The President of the United States of America takes pleasure in presenting the Navy Cross to Ensign Lowell Hall Strand, United States Naval Reserve, for extraordinary heroism and devotion to duty in action against the enemy while serving at *Fisheries TWO* in the Philippine Islands, in combat against the enemy, directing and operating anti-aircraft from his vessel while exposed to frequent attacks from the enemy and dive bombers during the period from 7 March 1942 to 19 April 1942. His conduct throughout was in keeping with the highest traditions of the Navy of the United States.

Appendix F: *YP-389* Crew List
(3 officers, 22 enlisted)

Name	Rank or Rating	Title or Rating	Status following Attack
Officers			
Roderick J. Philips	Lieutenant	Officer in Charge	all right
Ray P. Baker, Jr.	Ensign	Executive Officer	seriously injured
R. M. McKellar	Ensign	Engineering Officer	injured
Deck Force			
G. L. MacPherson	SM2/c	Signalman Second	all right
C. F. MacLean	Sea1/c	Seaman First	missing
D. L. Anotil	Sea2/c	Seaman Second	all right
M. Hia	Sea1/c	Seaman First	missing
A. T. Battisti	Sea2/c	Seaman Second	all right
G. Behrman	Sea2/c	Seaman Second	all right
C. F. Hensley	Sea2/c	Seaman Second	missing
N. H. Holt	Sea2/c	Seaman Second	injured
R. J. Long	Sea2/c	Seaman Second	seriously injured
R. L. Murch	Sea2/c	Seaman Second	seriously injured
W. W. Nazarsky	Sea2/c	Seaman Second	injured
L. A. White	Sea2/c	Seaman Second	all right
J. A. Milot	Sea2/c	Seaman Second	shifted to *YP-388* at 0800 on 12 June 1942
Engine Room			
G. Tunmer	MM1/c	Machinist's Mate First	injured
C. P. Harris	MoMM1/c	Motor Machine's Mate First	injured
R. Wilson	F1/c	Fireman First	seriously injured
V. W. Crabb	F2/c	Fireman Second	missing
E. C. Bonsall	F3/c	Fireman Third	injured
W. B. Cole	F3/c	Fireman Third	missing
J. C. Doucette	F3/c	Fireman Third	dead
W. J. Sesselman	F3/c	Fireman Third	injured
Other			
W. A. Smith	SC3/c	Ships Cook Third	injured

The crewmembers listed as missing were either seen killed or assumed dead. The body of the crewman listed as dead washed up on the beach, and was removed to Morehead City, North Carolina. Crewman Seaman Second J. A. Milot was not aboard the *YP-389* at the time of the attack.

Appendix G: Patrol Yacht, Converted Yacht, and YP Unit Awards

ANONYMS USED TO IDENTIFY TYPE VESSELS BEFORE CONVERSION TO PATROL CRAFT (YP):
BT: Massachusetts Beam Trawler
TC: San Diego Tuna Boat ("Clipper")
FT: Massachusetts Fishing Trawler
USCGC: Prohibition-era Coast Guard Cutter
HB: Pacific Northwest Halibut Boat

Ship/Former Vessel	Unit Award	Award Period
Patrol Yachts (PY)		
Isabel (PY-10)	Battle Star	8 Dec 1941 – 7 Mar 1942
Siren (PY-13)	Battle Star	1–6 Nov 1942
Southern Seas (PY-32)	Battle Star	13 Nov 1943 – 8 Dec 1943
Converted Yachts		
Fisheries Two	Battle Star	8 Dec 1941 – 6 May 1942
Maryanne	Battle Star	8 Dec 1941 – 6 May 1942
Yard Patrol Craft (YP)		
YP-41 (USCGC *Mahoning*)	Battle Star	24 Jul 1944 – 10 Aug 1944
		20 May 1945 – 30 Jun 1945
YP-42 (USCGC *Gallatin*)	Battle Star	24 Jul 1944 – 10 Aug 1944
		4–16 Mar 1945
		20 May 1945 – 30 Jun 1945
YP-56 (USCGC *Naugatuck*)	Battle Star	24 Jul 1944 – 10 Aug 1944
		20 May 1945 – 30 Jun 1945
YP-236 (TC *Europa*)	Battle Star	15 31 Dec 1943
YP-239 (TC *Challenger*)	Presidential Unit Citation	7 Aug 1942 – 9 Dec 1942
YP-251 (HB *Foremost*)	Battle Star	9 Jul 1942
YP-284 (TC *Endeavor*)	Presidential Unit Citation	7 Aug 1942 – 9 Dec 1942
	Battle Star	25 Oct 1942
YP-346 (TC *Prospect*)	Presidential Unit Citation	7 Aug 1942 – 09 Dec 1942
YP-415 (BT *Swell*)	Battle Star	23 Nov 1943
YP-417 (FT *Calm*)	Battle Star	13 Apr 1943 – 20 Jun 1943
YP-421 (BT *Surf*)	Navy Unit Commendation	3 March – 10 June 1945
	Battle Star	15–29 Nov 1944
	Battle Star	26 Jun 1945 – 7 Jul 1945

YP-514 (TC *American Beauty*)	Battle Star	23 Nov 1943
YP-516 (TC *Queen Amelia*)	Battle Star	5 Apr 1943 – 16 Jun 1943
YP-517 (TC *St. Ann*)	Battle Star	5 Apr 1943 – 16 Jun 1943
	Battle Star	3–4 Dec 1943

The United States Marine Corps awarded the Presidential Unit Citation to the *YP-239*, *YP-284*, and *YP-346*.

Appendix H: Letter from the Secretary of the Navy to A. Donham Owen

Serial 77623

THE SECRETARY OF THE NAVY
WASHINGTON

Mr. A. Donham Owen
Russ Building
San Francisco, California

6 MAR 1945

Dear Mr. Owen:

    Soon after the outbreak of hostilities, and at a time when the menace to national defense and vital interests was most critical, your yacht PAT PENDING was made available to the Navy and became a contributing factor toward the furtherance of the war effort.

    The PAT PENDING has now been returned to you and it will no doubt be a matter of great pride and interest to you to know that the PAT PENDING gave valuable and excellent service in the important duties assigned to her.

    In recognition of the war service rendered by the PAT PENDING, you are authorized to place on the stack or in the vicinity of the bridge five chevrons, or one for each six months of service with the Navy.

    The Navy Department takes this opportunity to express its sincere appreciation and grateful thanks for your patriotic and generous contribution in the hour of the country's most urgent need.

Very sincerely yours,

James Forrestal

JAMES FORRESTAL

BIBLIOGRAPHY

Alexander, Joseph H. *Edson's Raiders: the 1st Marine Raider Battalion in World War II.* Annapolis, Md.: Naval Institute Press, 2001.

Bruhn, David D. *Wooden Ships and Iron Men: the U.S. Navy's Coastal and Inshore Minesweepers, and the Minecraft That Served in Vietnam, 1953-1976.* Westminster, Md.: Heritage Books, 2011.

——*Wooden Ships and Iron Men: the U.S. Navy's Coastal and Motor Minesweepers, 1941-1953.* Westminster, Md.: Heritage Books, 2009.

Bulkley, Robert J. *At Close Quarters PT Boats in the United States Navy.* Washington, D.C.: Naval History Division, 1962.

Building the Navy's Bases in World War II: History of the Bureau of Yards and Docks and the Civil Engineer Corps 1940-1946, Vol. 1 and 2. Washington, D.C.: Department of the Navy, Bureau of Yards and Docks, 1947.

Carter, Worrall Reed. *Beans, Bullets, and Black Oil: the Story of Fleet Logistics Afloat in the Pacific during World War II.* Washington, D.C.: Department of the Navy, 1953.

Christ, James F. *Battalion of the Damned: the 1st Marine Paratroopers at Gavutu and Bloody Ridge, 1942.* Annapolis, Md.: Naval Institute Press, 2007.

Cressman, Robert, J. *The Official Chronology of the U.S. Navy in World War II.* Annapolis, Md.: Naval Institute Press, 1999

Garfield, Brian. *The Thousand-Mile War: World War II in Alaska and the Aleutians.* Garden City, N.Y.: Doubleday, 1969.

Gilson, Ronald H. *An Island No More.* Gloucester, Mass: The author, 2006.

Hickman, Homer H. *Torpedo Junction: U-Boat War off America's East Coast, 1942.* Annapolis, Md.: Naval Institute Press, 1989.

Hoffman, Jon T., *From Makin to Bougainville: Marine Raiders in the Pacific War.* Washington, D.C.: History and Museums Division, Headquarters, U.S. Marine Corps, 1995.

Johnston, Richard. *Follow Me!: the Story of the Second Marine Division in World War II.* New York: Random House, 1948.

Kimura. *Issei: Japanese Immigrants in Hawaii.* Honolulu, University of Hawai'i Press, 1988.

Lee, Robert Edward. *Victory at Guadalcanal.* Novato, Calif: Presidio Press, 1981.

Lott, Arnold S. *Most Dangerous Sea*. Annapolis, Md.: Naval Institute Press, 1959.

MacArthur, Douglas. *Reports of General MacArthur, the Campaigns of MacArthur in the Pacific, Vol I*. Washington, D.C.: Center of Military History, U.S Army, 1994.

McClurg, Robert W. *On Boyington's Wing*. Bowie, Md.: Heritage Books, 2003.

Miller, John. *Guadalcanal: The First Offensive*. Washington, D.C.: Center of Military History, U.S. Army, 1995.

Millett, Allan R. and Maslowski, Peter, *For the Common Defense, a Military History of the United States of America*. New York: The Free Press, 1994.

Morison, Samuel Eliot. *History of United States Naval Operations in World War II, the Battle of the Atlantic, September 1939 - May 1943*. Boston, Mass.: Little, Brown, 1984.

——*History of United States Naval Operations in World War II, Breaking the Bismarcks Barrier, 22 July 1942-1 May 1944*. Boston, Mass.: Little, Brown, 1984.

——*History of United States Naval Operations in World War II, Coral Sea, Midway and Submarine Actions, May 1942-August 1942*. Boston, Mass.: Little, Brown, 1984.

——*History of United States Naval Operations in World War II, the Struggle for Guadalcanal, August 1942-February 1943*. Boston, Mass.: Little, Brown, 1984.

——*The Two-Ocean War*. Boston, Mass.: Little, Brown, 1963.

Moses, Sam. *At All Costs: How a Crippled Ship and Two American Merchant Mariners Turned the Tide of World War II*. New York: Random House, 2006.

Perkins, J. W. *Battle Stars and Naval Awards*. Seminole, Fla: The author, 2004.

Roscoe, Theodore. *United States Destroyer Operations in World War II*. Annapolis, Md: Naval Institute Press, 1953.

Rottman, Gordon L. *Guam 1941 & 1944: Loss and Reconquest*. Oxford: Osprey, 2004.

——*World War II Pacific Island Guide: a Geo-Military Study*. Westport, Conn.: Greenwood Press, 2002.

Tregaskis, Richard. *Guadalcanal Diary*. New York: Random House, 1943.

NOTES

GLOSSARY OF ACRONYMS USED IN CHAPTER NOTES:

CincPac	Commander-in-Chief, Pacific Fleet
COM 1	Commandant, First Naval District
Com7thFlt	Commander, Seventh Fleet
Com7thPhibFor	Commander, Seventh Amphibious Force
ComAirSoPacForce	Commander, Naval Air Force, South Pacific Force
ComAmpFor	Commander, Amphibious Force
ComCaribSeaFron	Commander, Caribbean Sea Frontier
ComCortDiv	Commander, Escort Division
ComEastSeaFron	Commander, Eastern Sea Frontier
ComGulfSeaFron	Commander, Gulf Sea Frontier
ComHawSeaFron	Commander, Hawaiian Sea Frontier
ComInShPat	Commander, Inshore Patrol
ComNorSeaFron	Commander, Northern Sea Frontier
ComNorWestSeaFron	Commander, Northwest Sea Frontier
ComPanSeaFron	Commander, Panama Sea Frontier
ComPatRon 42	Commander, Patrol Squadron Forty-two
ComPatWing 4	Commander, Patrol Wing Four
ComPhibForPac	Commander, Amphibious Force Pacific
ComServFor	Commander, Service Force
ComServRon	Commander, Service Squadron
ComSoWestPac	Commander, South West Pacific
ComSoPacFor	Commander, South Pacific Force
ComWestSeaFron	Commander, Western Sea Frontier
CTF	Commander, Task Force
CTG	Commander, Task Group
MTB Ron	Motor Torpedo Boat Squadron
NAS	Naval Air Station

PREFACE NOTES

1. George Johnson, BMCM, USN Retired, 8 June 2009 and 16 April 2011.
2. Thomas Kibble Hervey, *The Devil's Progress*: a poem (London: Lupton Relfe, 1830).

3. Ronald Gilson, 14 June 2009.
4. Ibid.
5. Millett and Maslowski, *For the Common Defense, a Military History of the United States of America*, p. 79-80.

CHAPTER 1 NOTES

1. Frank J. Guidone, "Tasimboko: Small Raid Changed Everything at Guadalcanal" in *Leatherneck Magazine* (August 2009).
2. Morison, *History of United States Naval Operations in World War II: the Struggle for Guadalcanal August 1942-February 1943*, p. 124; *Manley* and *Gregory, DANFS*; Hoffman, *From Makin to Bougainville: Marine Raiders in the Pacific War*, p. 13.
3. *Colhoun* and *Little, DANFS*.
4. Morison, *The Two-Ocean War*, p. 167-168; "Tokyo Express," *Wikipedia* (http://en.wikipedia.org/wiki/Tokyo_Express: accessed 20 June 2012).
5. *Manley, DANFS*.
6. Alexander, *Edson's Raiders: the 1st Marine Raider Battalion in World War II*, p. 120.
7. Morison, *The Two-Ocean War*, p. 164-165.
8. Morison, *The Struggle for Guadalcanal, August 1942-February 1943*, p. 15-16; *Guadalcanal: The U.S. Army Campaign of World War II* (http://www.history.army.mil/brochures/72-8/72-8.htm: accessed 19 February 2011).
9. Unified Port of San Diego sign honoring World War II Service of Tuna Fleet Update, 8 July 2008 (http://www.portofsandiego.org/recreation/939-sign-honors-world-war-ii-service-of-tuna-fleet.html: accessed 25 January 2011); August J. Felando, "The Errand Boys of the Pacific: Tuna Clippers & World War II," *Mains'l Haul, A Journal of Pacific Maritime History* (Winter/Spring 2008); August Felando, 29 November 2011; "'Yippie' Boats Defy Japanese 600 San Diego Fishermen See Battle Service," *San Diego Tribune* (23 July 1943).
10. Felando, "The Errand Boys of the Pacific: Tuna Clippers & World War II".
11. Vincent Battaglia interview, 3 March 1991, San Diego Historical Society Oral History Program (http://gondolin.ucsd.edu/sio/ceo-sdhsoh/OH_battaglia.html: accessed 24 January 2011); Richard Crawford, "S.D. fishermen became WWII's 'pork chop express,'" *San Diego Union-Tribune* (27 May 2010); Felando, "The Errand Boys of the Pacific: Tuna Clippers & World War II."
12. Kenneth G. Adams Diary.
13. COM 11 and Navy Yard Pearl Harbor War Diary, May 1942; *Almandite, DANFS*; Felando, "The Errand Boys of the Pacific: Tuna Clippers & World War II;" Kenneth G. Adams Diary; John Bunker, "Gasoline

Chapter 1 Notes {313}

Drums Fill Fish Holds," *San Diego Tribune* (27 February 1957); "Hulks of Tunaboats Lie at Guadalcanal," *San Diego Tribune* (28 February 1957); United States Pacific Fleet Organization 1 May 1945 (http://www.ibiblio.org/hyperwar/USN/OOB/PacFleet/Org-450501/index.html: accessed 12 January 2012).

14. COM 11 and Navy Yard Pearl Harbor War Diary, May 1942; Felando, "The Errand Boys of the Pacific: Tuna Clippers & World War II;" Kenneth G. Adams Diary.
15. ComSoPacFor War Diary, June 1942; "Life during Wartime: Vanuatu in World War II," (http://www.bigempire.com/sake/vanuatu_world_war.html: accessed 1 August 2012); Carter, *Beans, Bullets, and Black Oil: the Story of Fleet Logistics Afloat in the Pacific during World War II*, p. 7-9, 23; COM 14 memorandum to Vice Chief of Naval Operations, 28 June 1942.
16. ComSoPacFor War Diary, June 1942; COM 14 memorandum to Vice Chief of Naval Operations, 28 June 1942.
17. Battaglia interview; Felando, "The Errand Boys of the Pacific: Tuna Clippers & World War II;" CincPac and ComSoPacFor War Diary, June 1942.
18. Battaglia Interview; Joaquin (Jack) S. Theodore interview, 29 February 1992, San Diego Historical Society Oral History Program (http://gondolin.ucsd.edu/sio/ceo-sdhsoh/OH_theodore.html: accessed 21 January 2011); *Tucker*, NavSource (http://www.navsource.org/archives/05/374.htm: accessed 29 January 2011) and *DANFS*.
19. *Breese* War Diary, August 1942.
20. Theodore interview; *Manley, Helm*; Commander, Amphibious Force, South Pacific Force War Diary, August 1942; Navy Yard Pearl Harbor War Diary, June 1942; Commander, NAS Palmyra War Diary, July 1942.
21. Theodore interview; Morison, *The Struggle for Guadalcanal August 1942-February 1943*, p. 114; "Hulks of Tunaboats Lie at Guadalcanal," *San Diego Tribune* (28 February 1957).
22. Battaglia interview; Morison, *The Struggle for Guadalcanal August 1942-February 1943*, p. 114.
23. Guidone, "Tasimboko;" Morison, *The Struggle for Guadalcanal August 1942-February 1943*, p. 124.
24. Guidone, "Tasimboko;" *The Struggle for Guadalcanal August 1942-February 1943*, 124; *Manley, DANFS*; Hoffman, *From Makin to Bougainville*, p. 13; Tregaskis, *Guadalcanal Diary*, p. 206.
25. Guidone, "Tasimboko;" Morison, *The Struggle for Guadalcanal August 1942-February 1943*, p. 124; *Manley, DANFS*; Hoffman, *From Makin to Bougainville*, p. 13; Tregaskis, *Guadalcanal Diary*, p. 208-213.

26. *Manley, DANFS*; Theodore interview; Christ, *Battalion of the Damned: the 1st Marine Paratroopers at Gavutu and Bloody Ridge, 1942*, p. 191; Justice M. Chambers, *Edson's Raiders: The 1st Marine Raider Battalion in World War II* (Thesis), p. 131; "'Yippie' Boats Defy Japanese 600 San Diego Fishermen See Battle Service".
27. Battaglia interview; "'Yippie' Boats Defy Japanese 600 San Diego Fishermen See Battle Service".
28. Theodore interview; Felando, "The Errand Boys of the Pacific: Tuna Clippers & World War II;" "'Yippie' Boats Defy Japanese 600 San Diego Fishermen See Battle Service".
29. Christ, *Battalion of the Damned: The 1st Marine Paratroopers at Gavutu and Bloody Ridge, 1942*, p. 191.
30. Hall of Valor, *Military Times* (http://militarytimes.com/citations-medals-awards/recipient.php?recipientid=21168: accessed 29 January 2011); Felando, "The Errand Boys of the Pacific: Tuna Clippers & World War II."
31. Hall of Valor, *Military Times*; Felando, "The Errand Boys of the Pacific: Tuna Clippers & World War II."
32. Theodore interview.
33. Theodore interview; Alexander, *Edson's Raiders*, p. 131.
34. Battaglia interview.
35. Theodore interview.
36. Lee, *Victory at Guadalcanal*, p. 203-205; *Trevor, DANFS*.
37. *Office of Naval Intelligence, Navy Department, Combat Narratives, Miscellaneous Action in the Southern Pacific, 8/8/42-1/22/43*, p. 49-52; Cressman, *The Official Chronology of the U.S. Navy in World War II – 1942*; Lee, *Victory at Guadalcanal*, p. 203-205; David H. Lippman "World War II Plus 55" (http://usswashington.com/worldwar2plus55/dl25oc42.htm: accessed 7 February 2011).
38. *Combat Narratives, Miscellaneous Action in the Southern Pacific, 8/8/42-1/22/43*, p. 49-52.
39. *Combat Narratives*, p. 49-52; *Seminole, DANFS*; U.S. Department of State, *Background Note: Tonga*, 23 December 2010, (http://www.state.gov/r/pa/ei/bgn/16092.htm: accessed 22 February 2011); "Wreck of YP-284," *Wikipedia* (http://wikimapia.org/11291754/Wreck-of-YP-284: accessed 7 February 2011).
40. *Combat Narratives*, p. 49-52; *Seminole, DANFS*; U.S. Department of State, *Background Note: Tonga*, 23 December 2010; "Wreck of YP-284," *Wikipedia*.
41. *Seminole, DANFS*; Lee, *Victory at Guadalcanal*, p. 205; Felando, "The Errand Boys of the Pacific: Tuna Clippers & World War II;" "Wreck of YP-284," *Wikipedia*.

42. Cressman, *The Official Chronology of the U.S. Navy in World War II – 1942*; Amberjack, DANFS.
43. One Man's View by Leonard Skinner, 2001 (http://members.peak.org/~skinncr/oneman/onemansview.html: accessed 9 December 2011).
44. Battaglia interview; Morison, *The Two-Ocean War*, p. 164; "Guadalcanal Campaign," *Wikipedia* (http://en.wikipedia.org/wiki/Guadalcanal_Campaign: accessed 30 January 2011).
45. Bureau of Naval Personnel. Information Bulletin No. 317 (August 1943) & No. 326 (May 1944) (http://www.homeofheroes.com/members/02_NX/citations/03_wwii-nc/nc_06wwii_navyB.html: accessed 29 January 2011).
46. Unit Awards to the First Marine Division (http://www.ww2gyrene.org/spotlight_1stmardiv_awards.htm#DIVISION: accessed 6 February 2011); *United States Marine Corps Unit Awards Manual*, NAVMC 2922, MMMA, 21 April 2000.
47. Perkins, *Battle Stars and Naval Awards*, p. 4-88, 96.
48. *Isabel* (PY-10), *Siren* (PY-13), and *Southern Seas* (PY-32), "Patrol Yacht (PY) Index," NavSource (http://www.navsource.org/archives/12/13idx.htm: accessed 12 July 2012).
49. Ibid.
50. COMDT COGARD WASHINGTON message date-time-group 051852Z January 2001.

CHAPTER 2 NOTES

1. War Plan Rainbow (http://www.globalsecurity.org/military/ops/war-plan-rainbow.htm: accessed 21 July 2011).
2. Promulgation of Navy Basic War Plan-Rainbow No. 5 (WPL-46), Navy Department, Office of the Chief of Naval Operations, Op-12B-5-McC, (SC)A16(R-5), Serial 060512 of May 26, 1941.
3. Navy Basic War Plan-Rainbow No. 5; Amethyst, DANFS.
4. "Ernest Borgnine, Biographies in Naval History," Naval Historical Center (http://www.history.navy.mil/bios/borgnine_e.htm: accessed 17 February 2012).
5. "Privateers and Mariners in the Revolutionary War" (http://www.usmm.org/revolution.html: accessed 12 August 2012); Section Patrol Craft (SP) and Civilian Vessels (ID) Index (http://www.navsource.org/archives/12/17idx.htm: accessed 28 July 2011).
6. Navy Basic War Plan-Rainbow No. 5.
7. Ibid.
8. Navy Basic War Plan-Rainbow No. 5; "Casualties: U.S. Navy and Coast Guard Vessels, Sunk or Damaged Beyond Repair during World War II, 7 December 1941-1 October 1945," Naval History and Heritage

Command (http://www.history.navy.mil/faqs/faq82-1.htm: accessed 11 August 2012).
9. Navy Basic War Plan-Rainbow No. 5.
10. Ibid.
11. Ibid.
12. Ibid.
13. Bruhn, *Wooden Ships and Iron Men: The U.S. Navy's Coastal and Motor Minesweepers*, p. 27-30.

CHAPTER 3 NOTES

1. J. W. Wickham, "The Story of the Yippee Fleet" (http://www.wartimepress.com/archive-article.asp?TID=Task%20Force%204.0&MID=68&q=85&FID=742: accessed 28 June 2011).
2. Tim Colton, "Patrol Yachts (PY, PYc)" (http://shipbuildinghistory.com/history/smallships/py.htm: accessed 13 August 2012).
3. U.S. Coast Guard Headquarters (Public Information Division), *The Coast Guard at War: Transports & Escorts, Vol. I—Escorts* (http://www.ibiblio.org/hyperwar/USCG/V1-Escorts/index.html: accessed 5 August 2011).
4. Tim Colton, "Patrol and Training Craft (YP)" (http://shipbuildinghistory.com/history/smallships/yp.htm: accessed 14 August 2012).
5. Ibid.
6. NavSource, "Motor Torpedo Boat (PT) Index" (http://www.navsource.org/archives/12/05idx.htm: accessed 24 April 2011); NavSource, "Coastal Patrol Yacht (PYc)" (http://www.navsource.org/archives/12/14idx.htm: accessed 24 April 2011); NavSource, "Submarine Chaser (PC)" (http://www.navsource.org/archives/12/01idx.htm: accessed 25 April 2011).
7. Michael Shapiro, "Saving Kula Kai," *Hana Hou!* (October/November 2006); Kimura, *Issei: Japanese Immigrants in Hawaii*, p. 110-111; Donald M. Schug, "Hawai'i's Commercial Fishing Industry: 1820-1945" (http://evols.library.manoa.hawaii.edu/bitstream/handle/10524/637/JL35021.pdf?sequence=2: accessed 28 June 2011).
8. Shapiro, "Saving Kula Kai."
9. Schug, "Hawai'i's Commercial Fishing Industry."
10. "YP Vessels Yard Patrol Vessels Manned by Coast Guard crews, 1941-1946" (http://www.uscg.mil/history/webcutters/YP_Vessels.pdf: accessed 22 January 22, 2011); *The Coast Guard at War: Transports & Escorts, Vol. I—Escorts*.
11. J. W. Wickham, "The Story of the Yippee Fleet."
12. Ibid.
13. Ibid.
14. Ibid.

CHAPTER 4 NOTES

1. HIJMS Submarine *I-26*: Tabular Record of Movement by Bob Hackett and Sander Kingsepp (http://www.combinedfleet.com/I-26.htm: accessed 19 January 2012).
2. "Japanese submarine *I-26*," *Wikipedia* (http://en.wikipedia.org/wiki/Japanese_submarine_I-26#Patrols_on_the_US_and_Canadian_West_Coast: accessed 9 January 2012); The *Cynthia Olson* (http://www.artfiberglass.com/ship/co.html: accessed 19 January 2012).
3. "Type B1 submarine," *Wikipedia* (http://en.wikipedia.org/wiki/Type_B1_submarine: accessed 19 January 2012); "Japanese submarine *I-26*," *Wikipedia*; Hackett and Kingsepp, "HIJMS Submarine *I-26*."
4. Hackett and Kingsepp, "HIJMS Submarine *I-26*;" Donald J. Young, "Japanese Submarines Prowl the U.S. Pacific Coastline in 1941" (http://www.historynet.com/japanese-submarines-prowl-the-us-pacific-coastline-in-1941.htm: accessed 20 January 2012).
5. Young, "Japanese Submarines Prowl the U.S. Pacific Coastline in 1941."
6. California and the Second World War (http://www.militarymuseum.org/HistoryWWII.html: accessed 2 January 2012); Young, "Japanese Submarines Prowl the U.S. Pacific Coastline in 1941."
7. Young, "Japanese Submarines Prowl the U.S. Pacific Coastline in 1941."
8. Hackett and Kingsepp, "HIJMS Submarine *I-17*: Tabular Record of Movement" (http://www.combinedfleet.com/I-17.htm: accessed 21 January 2012); "Japanese Submarines Prowl the U.S. Pacific Coastline in 1941."
9. Hackett and Kingsepp, "HIJMS Submarine *I-17*;" Young, "Japanese Submarines Prowl the U.S. Pacific Coastline in 1941;" David Walkinshaw, "A Bit of History, U.S. Navy Patrol Squadrons" (http://www.vpnavy.com/vp44_history.html: accessed 22 January 2012).
10. Young, "Japanese Submarines Prowl the U.S. Pacific Coastline in 1941."
11. Bruhn, *Wooden Ships and Iron Men, The U.S. Navy's Coastal and Inshore Minesweepers, and the Minecraft That Served in Vietnam, 1953-1976*, p. 97; Cressman, *The Official Chronology of the U.S. Navy in World War II - 1941*.
12. Hackett and Kingsepp, "HIJMS Submarine *I-17*;" "Japanese Bombed Oregon, 27 September 2007" (http://www.homerleasite.com/Site/Blog/9E165B3C-6D80-11DC-81E9-003065F3F514.html: accessed 23 January 2012); Hackett and Kingsepp, "HIJMS Submarine *I-25*."
13. Hackett and Kingsepp, "HIJMS Submarine *I-23*: Tabular Record of Movement" (http://www.combinedfleet.com/I-23.htm: accessed 23 January 2012); Young, "Japanese Submarines Prowl the U.S. Pacific Coastline in 1941."

14. Hackett and Kingsepp, "HIJMS Submarine *I-19*" (http://www.combinedfleet.com/I-19.htm: accessed 23 January 2012); Young, "Japanese Submarines Prowl the U.S. Pacific Coastline in 1941;" "Planes Bomb Sub Raiders," *The Evening Tribune*, (Marysville, Ohio) 23 December 1941.
15. Hackett and Kingsepp, "HIJMS Submarine *I-25*."
16. Hackett and Kingsepp, "HIJMS Submarine *I-21*" (http://www.combinedfleet.com/I-21.htm: accessed 23 January 2012).
17. Ibid.
18. "SS *Montebello* Timeline," California Department of Fish and Game (http://www.dfg.ca.gov/ospr/Admin/Montebello/timeline-working.aspx: accessed 25 January 2012).
19. Donald J. Young, "West Coast War Zone," *World War II Magazine* (July 1998).
20. Young, "West Coast War Zone."
21. Ibid.
22. "The Discovery of *Montebello*, November 29, 1996" (http://www.militarymuseum.org/Montebello.html: accessed 24 January 2012).
23. "Scientists find no oil in sunken 1941 oil tanker off California coast," Newsnet 14 (http://www.newsnet14.com/?p=84542: accessed 9 February 2012).
24. Hackett and Kingsepp, "HIJMS Submarine *I-19*: Tabular Record of Movement;" Cressman, *The Official Chronology of the U.S. Navy in World War II - 1941*; Young, "Japanese Submarines Prowl the U.S. Pacific Coastline in 1941."
25. Ibid.
26. Ibid.
27. Ibid.
28. Ibid.
29. Cressman, *The Official Chronology of the U.S. Navy in World War II - 1941*.
30. Hackett and Kingsepp, "HIJMS Submarine *I-25*;" Hackett and Kingsepp, "HIJMS Submarine *I-19*."
31. Hackett and Kingsepp, "HIJMS Submarine *I-17*."
32. Hackett and Kingsepp, "HIJMS Submarine *I-25*;" Hackett and Kingsepp, "HIJMS Submarine *I-26*;" "U.S. Ships Sunk or Damaged in Pacific Area during World War II" (http://www.usmm.org/pacific.html); 2nd "American Merchant Ships Sunk in World War II" (http://www.armed-guard.com/sunk.html: both accessed 17 January 2012).

CHAPTER 5 NOTES

1. "Q-Ships (Anti-submarine vessels disguised as merchant vessels)," Naval Historical Center, Washington, D.C. (http://www.history.navy.mil/docs/wwii/q-ships.htm#anchor1557612: accessed 25 August 2012).
2. Section Base, San Pedro, Eleventh Naval District War Diary 3/1/42 to 9/30/42; "USS *YAG-6*" (http://www.navsource.org/archives/14/2006.htm: accessed 9 January 2012); *Vileehi, DANFS*; COM 11 War Diary, March 1942; Era, "Coast Guard Modeling, Database of Coast Guard Cutters" (http://www.coastguardmodeling.com/07A_Cutters-by-Era.html: accessed 9 January 2012).
3. COM 11 War Diary, March 1942; "Principal Civilian Officials and Naval Officers in Command 7 December 1941- 2 September 1945" (http://www.ibiblio.org/hyperwar/USN/USN-Chron/USN-Chron-I.html: accessed 19 August 2012).
4. Section Base, San Pedro War Diary, 3/1/42 to 9/30/42; COM 11 War Diary, March 1942.
5. "Her History *Norwester*" (http://norwestercharters.com/herhistory.html) and (http://reidboats.blogspot.com/2006_01_01_archive.html: accessed 31 December 2011).
6. "Her History *Norwester*."
7. August Felando, 20 August 2012.
8. Section Base, San Pedro War Diary, 3/1/42 to 9/30/42; "El Segundo, California," *Wikipedia* (http://en.wikipedia.org/wiki/El_Segundo,_California: accessed 9 January 2012).
9. Section Base, San Pedro War Diary, 3/1/42 to 9/30/42.
10. Ibid.
11. Naval Net Depot, Tiburon, "The California State Military Museum" (http://www.militarymuseum.org/Tiburon.html: accessed 12 January 2012); Naval History and Heritage Command, Naval History and Heritage Command, "The Great White Fleet" (http://www.history.navy.mil/faqs/faq42-1.htm: accessed 13 January 2012); Justin M. Ruhge, "Tiburon Naval Net Depot History" (Goleta Calif.: Goleta Valley Historical Society).
12. Naval Net Depot, Tiburon, "The California State Military Museum;" Naval History and Heritage Command, "The Great White Fleet."
13. Melville Owen, 19 November 2012.
14. COM 12 War Diary, March, May 1942.
15. Ibid., March and April 1942, April 1943.
16. Ibid., March, April, and May 1942.
17. Belvedere-Tiburon Landmarks Society Living History (http://www.landmarks-society.org/history/timelines.php: accessed 12 January 2012); Susan Smith, "NOAA's Fishery Research Laboratory at Tiburon: History

of the Site and Present Activities" (http://www.corpsfuds.com/reports/OTHER/J09CA1075historicDoc.pdf: accessed 12 January 2012); Naval Net Depot, Tiburon, "The California State Military Museum;" "The Great White Fleet;" Ruhge, "Tiburon Naval Net Depot History."
18. Melville Owen, 16 and 19 November 2012; NavSource, *Pat Pending*.
19. Melville Owen, 16 and 19 November 2012; Classic Yacht Association (http://classicyacht.org/fantails: accessed 31 October 2012).
20. ComWestSeaFron Operational Order No. 2-42, 1 April 1942.
21. Ibid; Morison, *The Two-Ocean* War, p. 132.
22. ComWestSeaFron War Diary, March 1942; Navy Yard Mare Island War Diary, March and April 1942; *Lapwing* (AVP-1) Class: Photographs (http://www.shipscribe.com/usnaux/AVP/AVP01-p.html: accessed 2 July 2012).
23. Commanding Officer, U.S. Fleet Training Base, San Clemente War Diary, June 1942; COM 11 War Diary, July 2012; ComWestSeaFron War Diary, March 1943.
24. Terry O. Roen, "Rear Adm. Curtis Hutchings, 93, Had Sharp Mind, Stellar Navy Career, Obituary," *Orlando Sentinel* (4 March 2005); "Vice Adm. Curtis Hutchings" (http://groups.yahoo.com/group/PBY/message/3435?var=1: accessed 2 July 2012); U.S. Pacific Fleet Service Force Utility Squadron Two Detachment War Diary, September 1942.
25. ComWestSeaFron War Diary, March 1943; Com 11 War Diary, April 1943; U.S. Naval & Drydock Repair Facility, San Juan War Diary May 1943; *Pelican, DANFS*.
26. "Q-Ships."
27. "U.S. Coast Guard Lightships & Those of the U.S. Lighthouse Service" (http://www.uscg.mil/history/WEBLIGHTSHIPS/LV88.asp: accessed 22 August 2012); "Lightship *SWIFTSURE* (LV-83, then WAL-508)," Historical Naval Ships Association (http://www.hnsa.org/ships/swiftsure.htm: accessed 22 August 2012); Tim Colton, comp., "Coastal Minesweepers (AMc) Built in WWII" (http://shipbuildinghistory.com/history/smallships/minesweepers2.htm: accessed 22 August 2012); Colton, "Patrol and Training Craft (YP)."
28. Jim Gill, "The Warship *Swiftsure*" (http://www.jacksjoint.com/swiftsure.htm: accessed 24 August 2012); Tim Colton, "U.S. Coast Guard Light Vessels (LV, WAL)" (http://shipbuildinghistory.com/history/smallships/wal.htm: accessed 24 August 2012); "Umatilla Reef Lightship Station History" (http://www.uscglightshipsailors.org/umatilla_reef_lv_88.htm: accessed 24 August 2012).
29. "Umatilla Reef Lightship Station History."
30. Ibid.
31. Ibid.

CHAPTER 6 NOTES

1. Garfield, *The Thousand-Mile War: World War II in Alaska and the Aleutians*, p. 12.
2. Ibid, p. 5.
3. Garfield, *The Thousand-Mile War*, p. 6-7; Cressman, *The Official Chronology of the U.S. Navy in World War II - 1942*; "The Doolittle Tokyo Raiders" (http://www.doolittleraider.com: accessed 14 October 2011).
4. Garfield, *The Thousand-Mile War*, p. 6-7; Cressman, *The Official Chronology of the U.S. Navy in World War II - 1942*.
5. Hackett and Kinsepp, "HIJMS Submarine *I-25*;" Hackett and Kinsepp, "HIJMS Submarine *I-26*."
6. Hackett and Kinsepp, "HIJMS Submarine *I-25*;" Hackett and Kinsepp, "HIJMS Submarine *I-26*."
7. CTF 8 War Diary, May 22, 1942 to May 31, 1942; Garfield, *The Thousand-Mile War*, p. 11-14; U.S. Navy Joint Intelligence Center, *The Aleutians Campaign, June 1942-August 1943* (Washington, D.C.: Naval Historical Center, Department of the Navy, 1993) (http://www.ibiblio.org/hyperwar/USN/USN-CN-Aleutians.html: accessed 18 July 2011); "U.S. Pacific Fleet and Pacific Ocean Areas Order of Battle" (http://www.zipcon.com/~kestral/usn.html: accessed 15 July 2011); "Task Force 8" (http://pacific.valka.cz/forces/tf8.htm#midway: accessed 15 July 2011).
8. Morison, *History of United States Naval Operations in World War II, Coral Sea, Midway and Submarine Actions, May 1942-August 1942*, p. 163-165; Garfield, *The Thousand-Mile War*, p. 45; USS *Charleston*, 1941 Cruise, diary entries, from the collection of N. G. Wade, CTC, USN (Ret.), crewmember November 1940-April 1941 (http://www.navsource.org/archives/12/120905118.pdf: accessed 2 August 2011).
9. Morison, *Coral Sea, Midway and Submarine Actions*, p. 163-165; Garfield, *The Thousand-Mile War*, p. 45; USS *Charleston*, 1941 Cruise, diary entries.
10. Morison, *Coral Sea, Midway and Submarine Actions*, p. 165; Garfield, *The Thousand-Mile War*, p. 56, 73; "Guide to the Olson & Wingc Marine Works Photographs and Scrapbook 1914-1970" (http://nwda-db.orbiscascade.org/findaid/ark:/80444/xv50635: accessed 17 July 2011).
11. ComNorWestSeaFron War Diary, May 1942.
12. Ibid.
13. CTF 8 War Diary, May 22 to May 31, 1942; ComPatWing 4 War Diary, 27 May to 30 June, 1942.
14. ComPatWing 4 War Diary, 27 May to 30 June, 1942.
15. CTF 8 War Diary, May 22, 1942 to May 31, 1942; ComNorWestSeaFron War Diary, May 1942; *Oriole, DANFS*.

16. CTF 8 Operational Plan 1-42 of 27 May 1942; *Onondaga, DANFS*; ComPatWing 4 War Diary, 27 May, 1942 to 30 June, 1942; Bulkley, *At Close Quarters: PT Boats in the United States Navy*, p. 261.
17. *Charleston* War Diary, May 1, 1942 to May 31, 1942.
18. CTF 8 War Diary, June 1942; CTF 8 Letter of Instruction to Commander Destroyer Striking Force, A16-1/TF8 Serial T06 of May 31, 1942.
19. Commander Task Group Eight and *Louisville* War Diary, June 1942; Morison, *Coral Sea, Midway and Submarine Actions*, p. 166-170.
20. Commander Task Group Eight and *Louisville* War Diary, June 1942; Morison, *Coral Sea, Midway and Submarine Actions*, p. 169, 175-176.
21. CTF 8 and ComNorWestSeaFron War Diary, June 1942; Morison, *Coral Sea, Midway and Submarine Actions*, p. 176.
22. ComPatWing 4 War Diary, 27 May, 1942 to 30 June, 1942.
23. Commander Task Group Eight and *Louisville* War Diary, June 1942; Bulkley, *At Close Quarters*, p. 261-262.
24. CTF 8 and ComNorWestSeaFron War Diary, June 1942; *Gillis* War Diary, 23 May, 1942 to 30 June 1942.
25. *Gillis* War Diary, 23 May, 1942 to 30 June 1942; ComNorWestSeaFron War Diary, June 1942.
26. *Gillis* War Diary, 23 May, 1942 to 30 June 1942; U.S. Navy Joint Intelligence Center, *The Aleutians Campaign*, p. 7.
27. ComNorWestSeaFron War Diary, June 1942; U.S. Navy Joint Intelligence Center, *The Aleutians Campaign*, p. 9; Morison, *Coral Sea, Midway and Submarine Actions*, p. 176-178; "Marine Exchange of Alaska" (http://www.mxak.org/community/northwestern/northwestern.html: accessed 2 September 2012); ComPatWing 4 War Diary, 27 May, 1942 to 30 June, 1942.
28. Ibid.
29. CTF 8 War Diary, June 1942.
30. Ibid.
31. Ibid.
32. Ibid.
33. Ibid.
34. ComPatWing 4 War Diary, 27 May, 1942 to 30 June, 1942; CTF 8 War Diary, June 1942; Bulkley, *At Close Quarters: PT Boats in the United States Navy* p. 261-262.
35. ComPatWing 4 War Diary, 27 May, 1942 to 30 June, 1942; CTF 8 War Diary, June 1942.
36. ComPatWing 4 War Diary, 27 May, 1942 to 30 June, 1942; *Gillis* War Diary, 23 May, 1942 to 30 June 1942.
37. Ibid.

38. ComNorWestSeaFron War Diary, May 1942; *Charleston* War Diary, June 1942; CTF 8 Operational Plan No. 4-42 dated 10 June 1942.
39. ComPatWing 4 War Diary, 27 May to 30 June, 1942; *Gillis* War Diary, 23 May to 30 June, 1942.
40. ComPatWing 4 War Diary, 27 May to 30 June, 1942; ComNorWestSeaFron War Diary, June 1942.
41. ComNorWestSeaFron War Diary and CTF 8 War Diary, June 1942.
42. Morison, *Coral Sea, Midway and Submarine Actions*, p. 162-163; Garfield, *The Thousand-Mile War*, p. 157.
43. Morison, *Coral Sea, Midway and Submarine Actions*, p. 162-163; Garfield, *The Thousand-Mile War*, p. 157.
44. ComNorWestSeaFron War Diary, June 1942; Magellan Ship Biographies (http://www.cimorelli.com/cgi-bin/magellanscripts/ship_bio1.asp?ShipName=Seine: accessed 17 July 2011).

CHAPTER 7 NOTES

1. Morison, *Coral Sea, Midway and Submarine Actions*, p. 70-72; "Hawaii's Comprehensive Wildlife Conservation Strategy, Northwestern Hawaiian Islands" (http://www.state.hi.us/dlnr/dofaw/cwcs/files/second%20revised%20draft/CHAPTER%206%20nwhi.pdf: accessed 9 February 2011).
2. "The Battle of Midway June 3 - 6, 1942, Preparations at Midway, Hyperwar Foundation (http://www.ibiblio.org/hyperwar/USN/USN-CN-Midway/USN-CN-Midway-2.html: accessed 17 January 2011); Morison, *Coral Sea, Midway and Submarine Actions*, p. 70-74.
3. "The Battle of Midway June 3 - 6, 1942;" "Battle of Midway: 4-7 June 1942 Composition of U. S. Forces" (http://www.ibiblio.org/hyperwar/PTO/TideTurns/Midway/Midway-OOB.html: accessed 17 January 2011); Cressman, *The Official Chronology of the U.S. Navy in World War II*, p. 99; ComPatWing 2 War Diary, June 1942.
4. Cressman, *The Official Chronology of the U.S. Navy in World War II - 1942*; Morison, *Coral Sea, Midway and Submarine Actions*, p. 70; Felando, "The Errand Boys of the Pacific: Tuna Clippers & World War II;" Lott, *Most Dangerous Sea*, p. 40.
5. Hall of Valor, *Military Times*.
6. Burl Burlingame, "The Midway diary of a naval aviator six minutes off Midway" (http://www.oocities.org/jvtvj/midway.html: accessed 5 November 2011).
7. Ibid.
8. Ibid.
9. Ibid.

10. "The Battle of Midway June 3 - 6, 1942;" *Hammann*, NavSource (http://www.navsource.org/archives/05/412.htm: accessed 11 February 2011); Morison, *Coral Sea, Midway and Submarine Actions*, p. 159; "Japanese submarine *I-168*," Wikipedia (http://en.wikipedia.org/wiki/Japanese_submarine_I-168: accessed 26 February 2011).
11. "Midway" (http://www.bartcop.com/midway.htm: accessed 6 November 2011).
12. CincPac War Diary, 6/1-30/42 and 10/1-31/42; *Allen* War Diary, December 1942.

CHAPTER 8 NOTES

1. U.S. National Parks Service, *War in the Pacific: Outbreak of the War* (http://www.nps.gov/history/history/online_books/npswapa/extContent/wapa/guides/outbreak/sec4.htm: accessed 28 July 2011).
2. Bruhn, *Wooden Ships and Iron Men: The U.S. Navy's Coastal and Motor Minesweepers, 1941-1953*, p. 17.
3. Ibid, p. 18; *Isabel*, *DANFS*; Lynna Kay Shuffield, "Thomas Charles Hart biographical sketch" (www.arlingtoncemetary.net: accessed 5 September 2012).
4. "USS *Isabel* (SP-521, later PY-10), 1917-1946," Naval Historical Center (http://www.history.navy.mil/photos/sh-usn/usnsh-i/py10.htm: accessed 5 September 2012); Kemp Tolley, "The Strange Mission of the *Lanikai*," NavSource (http://www.navsource.org/archives/12/130096.htm: accessed 5 September 2012).
5. *Isabel*, *DANFS*; Cressman, *The Official Chronology of the U.S. Navy in World War II - 1941*; "USS *Isabel* (PY-10)," Wikipedia (http://en.wikipedia.org/wiki/USS_Isabel_%28PY-10%29: accessed 6 September 2012).
6. Tolley, "The Strange Mission of the *Lanikai*."
7. Ibid.
8. Bruhn, *Wooden Ships and Iron Men: The U.S. Navy's Coastal and Motor Minesweepers, 1941-1953*, p. 18-19; *Isabel*, *DANFS*.
9. *Isabel* (SP-521, later PY-10), 1917-1946; Bob Hackett and Sander Kingsepp, "HIJMS Submarine *I-155*: Tabular Record of Movement" (http://www.combinedfleet.com/I-155.htm: accessed 5 September 2012); *Isabel*, *DANFS*.
10. "USS *Isabel* (SP-521, later PY-10), 1917-1946."
11. Bruhn, *Wooden Ships and Iron Men, Volume: The U.S. Navy's Coastal and Motor Minesweepers, 1941-1953*, p. 20.
12. Ibid, p. 21; Cressman, *The Official Chronology of the U.S. Navy in World War II - 1942*; Casualties: U.S. Navy and Coast Guard Vessels, Sunk or

Damaged Beyond Repair during World War II, 7 December 1941-1 October 1945.
13. Hall of Valor, *Military Times*.
14. Edward C. Whitman, "Submarines to Corregidor" (http://www.navy.mil/navydata/cno/n87/usw/issue_15/subs_corregidor.html: accessed 9 September 2012).
15. George K. Petritz Obituary, *Traverse City Record-Eagle* (24 December 2010); David X. Wright, "United States Asiatic Fleet Order of Battle, December 1941" (http://www.asiaticfleet.com/orbat.htm: accessed 9 August 2012); "State Summary of War Casualties from World War II for Navy, Marine Corps, and Coast Guard Personnel: Maine, U.S." (Washington, D.C.: Government Printing Office, 1946); Anne Stanton, "Escape from a Floating Hell," *Northern Express* (5 February 2004) (http://www.northernexpress.com/michigan/article-129-escape-from-a-floating-hell.html: accessed 6 September 2012); "*Oraku Maru* sank in Olongapo, WWII in Zambales" (http://www.angelfire.com/on4/zambalesforum/leyte_landing.htm: accessed 6 September 2012); Mark A. Kelso, *Oryoku Maru* (http://www.oryokumaru.net/oryokumaru.htm:accessed 8 September 2012).
16. Stanton, "Escape from a Floating Hell;" "*Oraku Maru* sank in Olongapo, WWII in Zambales."
17. Stanton, "Escape from a Floating Hell;" "*Oraku Maru* sank in Olongapo, WWII in Zambales."
18. *Oryoku Maru*, Wikipedia (http://en.wikipedia.org/wiki/Oryoku_Maru: accessed 8 September 2012).
19. Hall of Valor, *Military Times*.
20. Bruhn, *Wooden Ships and Iron Men: The U.S. Navy's Coastal and Motor Minesweepers, 1941-1953*, p. 22-23; Cressman, *The Official Chronology of the U.S. Navy in World War II - 1941*.
21. "A Guide to the War in the Pacific" (http://www.nps.gov/history/history/online_books/npswapa/extContent/wapa/guides/outbreak/sec7.htm: accessed 18 February 2012).
22. Department of the Navy, Central Division (Op13), Office of Government Islands (Washington, DC), Guam Island Command 8 December 1941.
23. "District Patrol Vessel / Craft (YP) Index," NavSource (http://www.navsource.org/archives/14/31idx.htm: accessed 18 February 2012); Rottman, *Guam 1941 & 1944: Loss and Reconquest*, p. 21.
24. "Roster of Guam Personnel, Center For Research Allied POWS Under The Japanese" (http://www.mansell.com/pow_resources/guam/guamroster.html: accessed 18 February 2012).

CHAPTER 9 NOTES

1. Brendan Coyle, "Of ghosts and submarines," *The Vancouver Sun* (18 August 2008).
2. U.S. Coast Guard, *The Coast Guard At War*, CGC *McLane* (WSC-146) (http://www.ibiblio.org/hyperwar/USN/ships/tande/WSC/wsc146.html: accessed 22 January 2011); COMDT COGARD WASHINGTON DC message date-time-group 051852Z JAN 07; Morison, *The Two-Ocean War*, p. 147-148; "New Life for Oldest Surviving Seattle-Built Halibut Schooner," *PugetSoundMagazine.com* (http://www.pugetsoundmagazine.com/articles/a001/10024.php: accessed 9 November 2012); Hal Bernton, "For tradition-rich halibut fisherman, the future looks prosperous," *The Seattle Times* (http://seattletimes.com/html/localnews/2011494392_halibut1m.html: accessed 9 November 9, 2012).
3. *The Coast Guard At War*, CGC *McLane*; Coyle, "Of ghosts and submarines."
4. Cressman, *The Official Chronology of the U.S. Navy in World War II - 1942*; Coyle, "Of ghosts and submarines."
5. *The Coast Guard At War Transports and Escorts*, CGC *McLane*; Coyle, "Of ghosts and submarines."
6. *The Coast Guard At War Transports and Escorts*, CGC *McLane*.
7. *The Coast Guard At War Transports and Escorts*, CGC *McLane*; Coyle, "Of ghosts and submarines."
8. *The Coast Guard At War*, CGC *McLane*; Perkins, *Battle Stars and Naval Awards*, p. 4-198.
9. U.S. Coast Guard Public Relations Division, "United States Coast Guard Book of Valor, A Fact Book on Medals and Decorations awarded to Coast Guardsmen for valor during World War II." (http://www.uscg.mil/history/awards/Book_of_Valor_WWII.asp: accessed 22 January 22, 2011).
10. USCG *McLane* (WSC-146) history (http://www.uscg.mil/history/webcutters/McLane1927.asp: accessed 22 January 2011); *The Coast Guard At War*, CGC *McLane*.
11. "The Death of Chief Photographer Sergei Mihailoff, USNR and the Soviet submarine L16" (http://www.researcheratlarge.com/Pacific/L16/: accessed 23 January 2011); ComNorSeaFron Secret Memorandum titled: Russian Submarine L16; Loss of, serial F-103023 of 23 October 1942; Victories and losses of Soviet submarines during World War II, Axis History Forum (http://forum.axishistory.com/viewtopic.php?highlight=&p=1034785: accessed 23 January 2011).
12. Coyle, "Of ghosts and submarines."
13. COMDT COGARD WASHINGTON message date-time-group 051852Z January 2001.

CHAPTER 10 NOTES

1. "*YP-389* and the Battle of the Atlantic," in *Archaeology* 64. No. 3 (May/June 2011) (http://www.archaeology.org/1105/features/world_war_II_YP389.html: accessed 8 July 2011); Joe Hoyt, "History and Disposition of the *U-701*" (http://sanctuaries.noaa.gov/missions/battleoftheatlantic/pdfs/u701_history.pdf: accessed 8 July 2011).
2. "All U-boats of WWII," U-boat.net (http://www.uboat.net/boats/listing.html) and Guðmundur Helgason, "Operation Drumbeat," U-boat.net (http://www.uboat.net/ops/drumbeat.htm: both accessed 20 September 2012); Morison, *History of United States Naval Operations in World War II, The Battle of the Atlantic*, p. 126-131.
3. Helgason, "Operation Drumbeat;" Morison, *The Battle of the Atlantic*, p. 126-131.
4. Morison, *The Battle of the Atlantic*, p. 126-131.
5. North Atlantic Naval Coastal Frontier War Diary, January 1942.
6. Augustus P. Johnston, oral history interview, 29 November 2002, Monmouth University DESA Oral History Project (http://library.monmouth.edu/spcol/DESA/Interviews/johnston.htm: accessed 8 July 2011).
7. COM1 Inshore Patrol War Diary, March 1942; COM 1 War Diary, May 1942; Commander, Section Base, Woods Hole War Diary, 9 May to 14 June 1942.
8. Ibid.
9. Ibid.
10. Ibid.
11. Ibid.
12. Ron Gilson, 14 June 2009; "*Aeolus* American Motor fishing vessel" (http://www.uboat.net/allies/merchants/ships/1736.html: accessed 27 August 2011).
13. "Top U-boat Aces, Heinz-Otto Schultze," U-boat.net (http://www.uboat.net/men/schultze_heinz-otto.htm: accessed 24 September 2012); Charles Dana Gibson, "Victim or Participant? Allied Fishing Fleets and U-boat Attacks in World Wars I and II" (http://www.cnrs-scrn.org/northern_mariner/vol01/tnm_1_4_1-18.pdf: accessed 27 August 2011); "FV *Aeolus* (+1942)" (http://www.wrecksite.eu/wreck.aspx?18037: accessed 27 August 2011); "*Foam* American Steam Trawler" (http://www.uboat.net/allies/merchants/ships/1661.html: accessed 27 August 2011); "*Aeolus* American Motor fishing vessel;" "*Ben and Josephine* American Motor fishing vessel" (http://www.uboat.net/allies/merchants/ships/1738.html: accessed 27 August 2011).

14. Hickman, *Torpedo Junction: U-Boat War off America's East Coast, 1942*, p. 8-10, 296; Moses, *At All Costs: How a Crippled Ship and Two American Merchant Mariners Turned the Tide of World War II*, 18-21.
15. North Atlantic Naval Coastal Frontier War Diary, January 1942; Hickman, *Torpedo Junction: U-Boat War off America's East Coast, 1942*, p. 296.
16. ComEastSeaFron War Diary, February 1942; Hickman, *Torpedo Junction: U-Boat War off America's East Coast, 1942*, p. 296.
17. John R. Lewis interview, Rutgers Oral History Archives of World War II (http://oralhistory.rutgers.edu/Interviews/lewis_john.html: accessed 8 July 2011).
18. Cressman, *The Official Chronology of the U.S. Navy in World War II - 1942*; "Fort Miles" (http://www.fortmiles.org/navy/hecp/#submarine: accessed 20 August 2011); COM 5 War Diary, April 1942.
19. "West Imboden," U-boat.net (http://uboat.net/allies/merchants/ships/1559.html: accessed 20 August 2011).
20. ComEastSeaFron War Diary, March through June 1942; North Atlantic Naval Coastal Frontier War Diary, January 1942.
21. ComEastSeaFron War Diary, March 1942.
22. ComEastSeaFron War Diary, February through April 1942.
23. ComEastSeaFron War Diary, April 1942.
24. ComEastSeaFron War Diary, March 1942; Gilson, *An Island No More*, p. 25.
25. Gilson, *An Island No More*, p. 61-62.
26. "District Patrol Vessel / Craft (YP) Index."
27. COM 3 ComInShPat War Diary, April 1942; Commander, Montauk Section War Diary, 3/8-31/1942 and May 1942; Commander, Ambrose Section War Diary, 3/25-31/1942 and May 1942.
28. Cressman, *The Official Chronology of the U.S. Navy in World War II - 1942*.
29. COM 3 ComInShPat War Diary, April 1942; Commander, Montauk Section War Diary, 3/8-31/1942 and May 1942; Commander, Ambrose Section War Diary, 3/25-31/1942 and May 1942.
30. Commander, Ambrose Section War Diary, May 1942.
31. "Douglas Elton Fairbanks, Jr.," Naval History and Heritage Command (http://www.history.navy.mil/bios/fairbanks_douge.htm: accessed 24 September 2012).
32. Commander Montauk Section and Commander Ambrose Section War Diary, May 1942.
33. Ibid.
34. ComEastSeaFron War Diary, June 1942.

35. Ibid; "Battle of the Atlantic Vessels of Interest, National Marine Sanctuaries" (http://sanctuaries.noaa.gov/missions/2011battleoftheatlantic/vessels.html: accessed 8 July 2011), "*YP-389*," NavSource (http://www.navsource.org/archives/11/03202.htm: accessed 10 August 2011); Eric Mills, "Another Piece of the Torpedo Junction Puzzle," *Naval History*, February 2010, p. 65.
36. COM 4 ComInShPat War Diary, May 1942; "USS *Jason*," Naval Historical Center (http://www.history.navy.mil/photos/sh-usn/usnsh-j/ac12.htm: accessed 26 September 2012).
37. ComEastSeaFron War Diary, June 1942; Hickman, *Torpedo Junction: U-Boat War off America's East Coast, 1942*, p. 261; "Fore River Shipyard Production Record" (http://www.hazegray.org/shipbuilding/quincy/fore2.htm: accessed 9 August 2011); "U.S. Naval Activities World War II By State" (http://www.ibiblio.org/hyperwar/USN/ref/USN-Act/NY.html: accessed 9 August 2011); "Ships Hit by U-boats in WWII," U-boat.net (http://www.uboat.net/allies/merchants/listing.php: accessed 25 September 2012); *The Niagara Falls Gazette* (26 June 1942).
38. ComEastSeaFron War Diary, June 1942.
39. Ibid; "SS *West Lashaway*," *Wikipedia* (http://en.wikipedia.org/wiki/SS_West_Lashaway: accessed 9 August 2011).
40. ComEastSeaFron War Diary, June 1942; "SS *F. W. Abrams*," Dive Hatteras (http://www.divehatteras.com/fwabrams.html: accessed 23 August 2011).
41. ComEastSeaFron War Diary, June 1942; Hickman, *Torpedo Junction: U-Boat War off America's East Coast, 1942*, p. 263-264; "German U-Boat Deck Guns" (http://www.uboataces.com/weapon-deck-gun.shtml: accessed 14 August 2011).
42. "Report of Interrogation of Survivors of *U-701*, Sunk by U.S. Army Attack Bomber on July 7, 1942" (http://www.uboatarchive.net/U-701INT.htm: accessed 8 July 2011); *U-701* - 3rd War Patrol Diary, translated by Capt. Jerry Mason, USN (Ret.) with the help of Ken Dunn and Rainer Kolbicz; History and Disposition of the *U-701*.
43. Report of Interrogation of Survivors of *U-701*; *U-701* - 3rd War Patrol Diary.
44. ComEastSeaFron War Diary, June 1942; Hickman, *Torpedo Junction: U-Boat War off America's East Coast, 1942*, p. 263-264; *YP-389* and the Battle of the Atlantic.
45. ComEastSeaFron War Diary, June 1942; Hickman, *Torpedo Junction: U-Boat War off America's East Coast, 1942*, p. 263-264.
46. ComEastSeaFron War Diary, June 1942.
47. Ibid; Enemy Action and Distress Diary for 18 June 1942; Report of Interrogation of Survivors of *U-701*.

48. History and Disposition of the *U-701*; "The Men - The Commander listing, Horst Degen" (http://www.uboat.net/men/commanders/197.html: accessed 11 August 2011); O.N.I. Interrogations Section memorandum Op-16-F-9 A16-2(4) of July 31, 1942, Subject: Prisoners of War; Request for Transfer of (http://www.uboatarchive.net/U-701NavyInterrogations.htm: accessed 11 August 2011); Mills, "Another Piece of the Torpedo Junction Puzzle," p. 66; "Fort Hunt," *Wikipedia* (http://fortwiki.com/Fort_Hunt: accessed 15 August 2011).
49. ComEastSeaFron War Diary, June 1942.
50. Catherine Kozak, "Footage taken of WWII Navy vessel sunk by U-boat," *The Virginian-Pilot* (10 September 2009) (http://hamptonroads.com/2009/09/footage-taken-wwii-navy-vessel-sunk-uboat: accessed 15 August 2011).
51. COM 4 ComInShPat War Diary, April and May 1942; Tim Colton, "Coastal Minesweepers (AMc) Built in WWII" (http://shipbuildinghistory.com/history/smallships/minesweepers2.htm: accessed 21 September 2012).
52. COM 4 ComInShPat War Diary, April and May 1942.
53. COM 4 ComInShPat War Diary, May 1942; "Ships Hit by U-boats in WWII."
54. COM 5 ComInShPat War Diary, March and April 1942; Commander Section Base, Morehead, South Carolina War Diary, March-June 1942.
55. COM 5 ComInShPat War Diary, April 1942; "Ships Hit by U-boats in WWII."
56. COM 15 War Diary, December 7, 1941 to June 1, 1942; Robert P. Sables, "Overdue Atlantic USS *Cythera* (PY 26)," NavSource (http://www.navsource.org/archives/12/170575s.htm: accessed 13 April 2012); ComEastSeaFron War Diary, May 1942.
57. COM 15 War Diary, December 7, 1941 to June 1, 1942; "Overdue Atlantic USS *Cythera* (PY 26);" ComEastSeaFron War Diary, May 1942.
58. COM 15 War Diary, December 7, 1941 to June 1, 1942; "Overdue Atlantic USS *Cythera* (PY 26)."
59. "Overdue Atlantic USS *Cythera* (PY 26);" *Rudderow, DANFS*.
60. "Overdue Atlantic USS *Cythera* (PY 26);" Mike McCarthy, "USS *Cythera* (PY-26), account of loss of the patrol yacht," Uboat.net (http://uboat.net/allies/merchants/1586.html: accessed 19 February 2012).
61. "Overdue Atlantic USS *Cythera* (PY 26);" "Top U-Boat Aces, Freiherr Siegfried von Forstner," U-boat.net (http://www.uboat.net/men/forstner.htm: accessed 29 May 2012).
62. COM 6 War Diary, March 1942; Commander, Section Base, Savannah, Georgia War Diary, May 1942; COM 6 ComInShPat War Diary, April 1942; "St. Johns River Lightship Station History, Lightship Sailors

Association" (http://www.uscglightshipsailors.org/st_johns_river_lightship_station_history.htm: accessed 28 September 2012).
63. COM 6 War Diary, March 1942; Commander, Section Base, Savannah, Georgia War Diary, May 1942; COM 6 ComInShPat War Diary, April 1942; "St. Johns River Lightship Station History, Lightship Sailors Association".
64. COM 6 ComInShPat War Diary, April 1942.
65. Ibid.
66. COM 6 ComInShPat War Diary, April 1942; Bruhn, *Wooden Ships and Iron Men: The U.S. Navy's Coastal and Motor Minesweepers, 1941-1953*, p. 31.

CHAPTER 11 NOTES

1. ComGulfSeaFron War Diary, April 1942.
2. Morison, *The Battle of the Atlantic*, p. 135; *Carnelian, DANFS*; "Nike, 1934, WPC-112" (http://www.uscg.mil/history/webcutters/Nike_1934.pdf: accessed 23 February 2012), ComGulfSeaFron and COM 7 War Diary, April 1942.
3. COM 7 War Diary, April 1942; Cressman, *The Official Chronology of the U.S. Navy in World War II - 1942*.
4. COM 7 War Diary, April 1942; COM 7 ComInShPat War Diary, July 1942.
5. COM 7 ComInShPat War Diary, July 1942.
6. Ibid.
7. COM 7 War Diary, April 1942; COM 7 ComInShPat War Diary, July 1942.
8. Ibid.
9. Ibid.
10. COM 8 ComInShPat War Diary, 7 December 1941 to 28 February 1942.
11. Ibid.
12. Ibid.
13. COM 8 ComInShPat War Diary, 7 December 1941 to 28 February 1942; "*Woodbury*, 1927 WSC-155" (http://www.uscg.mil/history/webcutters/Woodbury1927.pdf: accessed 23 February 2012); *Onyx, DANFS*.
14. COM 8 ComInShPat War Diary, 7 December 1941 to 28 February 1942.
15. Ibid.
16. COM 8 ComInShPat War Diary, May 1942.
17. Ibid.
18. Ibid.

19. COM 8 ComInShPat War Diary, May 1942; "Ships Hit by U-boats in WWII."
20. COM 8 ComInShPat War Diary, May 1942.
21. "Ships Hit by U-Boats in WWII;" Cressman, *The Official Chronology of the U.S. Navy in World War II - 1942*.
22. ComGulfSeaFron War Diary, July 1942; "*U-166*" (http://www.uscg.mil/history/uscghist/u166.asp: accessed 14 March 2012).
23. Commanding Officer, USS *PC-566* letter, Action with enemy submarine which torpedoed SS *Robert E. Lee* and rescue of survivors, Report of, dated August 5, 1942.
24. "USS *PC-566*," NavSource (http://www.navsource.org/archives/12/010566.htm: accessed 14 March 2012).
25. Ibid.
26. Ibid.
27. Commanding Officer, USS *PC-566* letter; ComGulfSeaFron War Diary, July 1942.
28. Commanding Officer, USS *PC-566* letter.
29. Ibid.
30. Ibid.
31. "Grumman G-44 Widgeon," *Wikipedia* (http://en.wikipedia.org/wiki/Grumman_G-44_Widgeon); "*U-171*" (U-boat.net, http://www.uboat.net/boats/u171.htm: both accessed 14 March 2012); COM 15 War Diary, December 7, 1941 to June 1, 1942.
32. Inshore Patrol – Pacific, Section Base, Balboa, Canal Zone War Diary, April 1942; COM 15 War Diary, December 7, 1941 to June 1, 1942.
33. Section Base, Cristobal, Canal Zone War Diary, April 1942.
34. COM 15 War Diary, December 7, 1941 to June 1, 1942; Felando, "The Errand Boys of the Pacific: Tuna Clippers & World War II."
35. COM 15 War Diary, December 7, 1941 to June 1, 1942.
36. COM 15 War Diary, December 7, 1941 to June 1, 1942; Felando, "The Errand Boys of the Pacific: Tuna Clippers & World War II."
37. COM 15 War Diary, December 7, 1941 to June 1, 1942.
38. Ibid.
39. Ibid.
40. Ibid.
41. Ibid.
42. Ibid.
43. Ibid.
44. Ibid.
45. Ibid.

46. "Mystery Of Sub Lost After Leaving Bermuda," *Bernews* (31 October 2011) (http://bernews.com/2011/10/mystery-of-sub-lost-after-leaving-bermuda: accessed 18 March 2012).
47. Ibid.
48. Ibid.
49. Ibid.
50. COM 15 War Diary, December 7, 1941 to June 1, 1942.
51. "History of Martinique," *Wikipedia* (http://en.wikipedia.org/wiki/History_of_Martinique: accessed 1 April 2012).
52. COM 15 War Diary, December 7, 1941 to June 1, 1942.
53. Ibid.
54. Ibid.
55. COM 15 War Diary, December 7, 1941 to June 1, 1942; COM 15 ComInShPat War Diary, April 1942; Section Base, Cristobal War Diary, March 1942; "District Patrol Vessel / Craft (YP) Index."
56. COM 15 War Diary, December 7, 1941 to June 1, 1942; COM 15 ComInShPat War Diary, April 1942; Inshore Patrol Pacific, Fifteenth Naval District War Diary, 4/1/41 to 6/30/42; COM 12 War Diary, May-June 1942.
57. COM 15 War Diary, December 7, 1941 to June 1, 1942; COM 15 ComInShPat War Diary, April 1942; Inshore Patrol Pacific, Fifteenth Naval District War Diary, 4/1/41 to 6/30/42; COM 12 War Diary, May-June 1942; United States Pacific Fleet Organization 1 May 1945.
58. COM 15 War Diary, December 7, 1941 to June 1, 1942; ComPanSeaFron War Diary, July 1942.
59. COM 15 War Diary, 12/7/1941 to 6/1/1942; Morison, *The Two-Ocean War*, p. 102.
60. "U.S. Ships Sunk or Damaged in Gulf of Mexico during World War II" (http://www.usmm.org/pacific.html: accessed 29 February 2012).
61. Section Base, Cristobal, Canal Zone War Diary, June 1942; Cressman, *The Official Chronology of the U.S. Navy in World War II - 1942*; "Ships Hit by Uboats in WWII."
62. Ibid.
63. Ibid.
64. Section Base, Cristobal, Canal Zone War Diary, June 1942.
65. Ibid.
66. Morison, *The Battle of the Atlantic*, p. 127.
67. Ibid, p. 144, 346-347.
68. COM 10 ComInShPat War Diary, 12/7/41 to 3/31/42.
69. Ibid; ComCaribSeaFron War Diary, 4/1/42 to 6/30/42.
70. COM 10 ComInShPat War Diary, 12/7/41 to 3/31/42, April-July 1942, and September 1942; Commanding Officer, Naval Operating Base,

Trinidad War Diary, July 1943; *Building the Navy's Bases in World War II,* p. 8-9, 14.
71. *Building the Navy's Bases in World War II,* p. 144-145, 147.
72. Ibid, p. 2:23, 25, 36.
73. Ibid.
74. Morison, *The Battle of the Atlantic,* p. 148.
75. "Most successful Convoy Attacks by a U-boat," Uboat.net (http://uboat.net/ops/convoys/most_successful.html: accessed 20 February 2012); Roscoe, *United States Destroyer Operations in World War II,* p. 134-135.
76. ComCaribSeaFron and ComGulfSeaFron War Diary, November 1942; Roscoe, *United States Destroyer Operations in World War II,* p. 134-135.
77. "Ships hit from convoy TAG-18," Uboat.net (http://uboat.net/ops/convoys/convoys.php?convoy=TAG-18: accessed 22 February 2012); "Ship's Master Lost, *Leda* - (1935-1942)," Auke Visser's International Esso Tankers site (http://www.aukevisser.nl/inter/id1053.htm: accessed 13 June 2012).
78. "Top U-boat Aces," Uboat.net (http://uboat.net/men/lassen.htm) and "Ships hit from convoy TAG-18" (both accessed 22 February 2012); "Ship's Master Lost, *Leda* - (1935-1942)."
79. *Lea* War Diary, November 1942; "Ships hit from convoy TAG-18;" "Ship's Master Lost, *Leda* - (1935-1942)."
80. *Lea* War Diary, November 1942.
81. *Lea* War Diary, November 1942; "Ships hit by U-boats in WWII."
82. *Lea* War Diary, November 1942.
83. *Navy and Marine Corps Awards Manual,* NAVPERS 15,790 (Rev. 1953).

CHAPTER 12 NOTES

1. Kenneth G. Adams Diary.
2. Kenneth G. Adams Diary; CincPac War Diary, August 1942.
3. Kenneth G. Adams Diary.
4. Ibid.
5. Kenneth G. Adams Diary; CincPac War Diary, November 1942.
6. Kenneth G. Adams Diary.
7. Kenneth G. Adams Diary; Miller, *Guadalcanal: The First Offensive,* p. 174-175; CincPac War Diary, November 1942.
8. Kenneth G. Adams Diary.
9. Felando, "The Errand Boys of the Pacific: Tuna Clippers & World War II;" *Building the Navy's Bases in World War II,* p. 192-195; *Pacific Fisherman* (December 1942), p. 53.
10. Carter, *Beans, Bullets, and Black Oil: the Story of Fleet Logistics Afloat in the Pacific during World War II,* p. 7-9, 23, 46.

11. Ibid, p. 9-10.
12. CincPac War Diary, November 1942.

CHAPTER 13 NOTES
1. "Kill or be Killed" (http://veteransbreakfastclub.com/?p=307: accessed 7 November 2011).
2. Bulkley, *At Close Quarters: PT Boats in the United States Navy*, p. 105.
3. "AmShip Lorain, Lorain OH" (http://shipbuildinghistory.com/history/shipyards/2large/inactive/amshiplorain.htm: accessed 5 November 2011).
4. *YP-417* War Diary, 12/15/42 to 2/28/43.
5. Ibid.
6. Ibid.
7. Ibid.
8. Ibid.
9. Ibid.
10. Nicholas John Lavnikevich interview by Eileen M. Hurst on 30 January 2004 (http://lcweb2.loc.gov/diglib/vhp/story/loc.natlib.afc2001001.31036/transcript?ID=sr0001: accessed 4 November 2011); Nicholas John Lavnikevich; John Clifford "Jack" Fitzgerald obituary, 18 April 2000 (http://articles.courant.com/2000-04-18/news/0004180411_1_virginia-m-fitzgerald-john-herbert-charlotte: accessed 4 November 2011).
11. Lavnikevich interview; Bulkley, *At Close Quarters*, p. 83, 95, 108-109; Morison, *History of United States Naval Operations in World War II, Breaking the Bismarcks Barrier 22 July 1942-1 May 1944*, p. 121.
12. Lavnikevich interview.
13. Lavnikevich interview; CincPac and ComAmpFor SoPacFor War Diary, April 1943; "WWII PT Boats, Bases, Tenders" (http://www.ptboats.org/20-04-05-squadrons-003.html: accessed 5 November 2011); "Lt. John F. Kennedy, USN," Naval Historical Center (http://www.history.navy.mil/faqs/faq60-2.htm: accessed 5 November 2011).
14. Lavnikevich interview.
15. ComSoPacFor and *Sonoma* War Diary, June 1943; *YP-417* War Diary 12/15/42 to 2/28/43; *Dixie* War Diary, 1/1/43 to 6/30/43, and December 1943; CincPac War Diary, January, February, March, and May 1943; U.S. Naval Forces Fiji Islands War Diary, December 1943; ComSoWestPac War Diary, February 1943; Commander Naval Bases Solomon Islands, Communication Order No. 9-43 dated 25 August 1943.
16. Miller, *Guadalcanal: The First Offensive*, p. 210, 215-216.
17. ComAirSoPacFor War Diary, 3/1/43 to 4/30/43; *Locust, DANFS*; "USS Taupata," NavSource (http://www.navsource.org/archives/14/2026.

htm: accessed 7 December 2011); *YP-518* Operations Log for April-June 1943; CincPac and ComAmpFor SoPacFor War Diary, April 1943; *Locust* and *Taupata, DANFS*.
18. ComAmpFor SoPacFor War Diary, April 1943.
19. *YP-518* Operations Log for April-June 1943.
20. Ibid.
21. Ibid.
22. USS *O'Bannon* Action Report – Air Attack on Blue Shipping, Guadalcanal area by Japanese, 16 June 1943.
23. Ibid; USS *LST-340* Action Report, 16 June 1943.
24. *Skylark, DANFS; YP-518* War Diary, 4/1/43 to 9/1/43; Commander Task Unit 32.4.4 Report; USS *O'Bannon* Report of Sinking of USS *Aludra* and USS *Deimos*.
25. Ibid.

CHAPTER 14 NOTES

1. Morison, *Breaking the Bismarcks Barrier*, p. 6, 8, 92; "Campaign Chronologies of the United States Marine Corps, Selected World War II Marine Corps Chronology 1941-1946" (http://www.tecom.usmc.mil/HD/Chronologies/Campaign/WWII_1941-1946.htm: accessed 12 November 2011).
2. Ibid, p. 6, 8, 92; "Campaign Chronologies of the United States Marine Corps, Selected World War II Marine Corps Chronology 1941-1946."
3. "Last Battles, In the Shadows, Australia's War 1939-1945;" Kent G. Budge, "Bougainville," *The Pacific War Online Encyclopedia* (http://pwencycl.kgbudge.com/B/o/Bougainville.htm: accessed 12 November 2011).
4. 3rd Marine Division Combat Report of Operations in the Bougainville Campaign, 1 November-28 December 1943.
5. Morison, *The Two-Ocean War*, p. 285-291; McClurg, *On Boyington's Wing*, p. 112, 121; "Admiral Arleigh A. Burke, USN" (http://navysite.de/people/aaburke.htm#top: accessed 13 November 2011).
6. "Battle of Bougainville: 37th Infantry Division's Battle for Hill 700" (http://www.historynet.com/battle-of-bougainville-37th-infantry-divisions-battle-for-hill-700.htm: accessed 12 November 2011).
7. Morison, *Breaking the Bismarcks Barrier*, p. 348.
8. 3rd Marine Division Combat Report on Operations in the Bougainville Campaign.
9. *YP-514* Deck Log, November 1943.
10. *YP-514* War Diary, January 1944.
11. *YP-514* War Diary, January 1944; Casualties: U.S. Navy and Coast Guard Vessels Sunk or Damaged Beyond Repair during World War II

7 December 1941-1 October 1945; *Building the Navy's Bases in World War II,* p. 194.
12. CTF 31, LST Flotilla Five, Amphibious Force South Pacific, and Advanced Naval Base, Torokina War Diary, November 1943; *YP-514* War Diary, January 1944.
13. LST Flotilla Five and Amphibious Force South Pacific War Diary, November 1943; Rottman, *World War 2 Pacific Island Guide: A Geo-Military Study,* p. 130-132.
14. CTF 31, *LST-449, YP-514,* LST Flotilla Five, Amphibious Force South Pacific, and *LST-472* War Diary, November 1943; USS *Renshaw* Report of Action, 21-25 November, dated 25 November 1943.
15. CTF 31, *Bennett, Sigourney, LST-449, LST-472,* and *YP-514* War Diary, November 1943.
16. USS *Renshaw* Report of Action; *YP-514* War Diary, January 1944.
17. Morison, *Breaking the Bismarcks Barrier,* p. 358.
18. Budge, "Bougainville."
19. Morison, *Breaking the Bismarcks Barrier,* p. 360-361.
20. ComDesRon 45, LCI(L) Group Fourteen, Flotilla Five, *LST-446,* and *LST-447* War Diary, December 1943; USS *Guest* Action Report dated 6 December, 1943.
21. ComDesRon 45 Action Report dated 14 December 1943.
22. ComDesRon 45 Action Report; *LST-446* War Diary, 1 December 1943 to 29 February 1944; USS *Guest* Action Report; USS *Renshaw* Action Report dated 4 December 1943; ComDesDiv 46 Report of action against enemy aircraft off Empress Augusta Bay on December 3, 1943.
23. J.W. Fryer, Jr., Executive Officer's Report included as Attachment B to Commanding Officer, USS *Guest* Action Report.
24. ComDesRon 45 Action Report.
25. USS *Guest* Action Report; USS *Fullam* Report of Anti-Aircraft Action of 11 December 1943; ComDesRon 45 Action Report; ComDesDiv 46 Action Report of 4 December 1943.
26. USS *Fullam* Report of Anti-Aircraft Action; Advanced Naval Base, Torokina, and LCI(L) Group Fourteen, Flotilla Five War Diary, December 1943; Morison, *Breaking the Bismarcks Barrier,* p. 341.
27. ComDesRon 45 and LCI(L) Group Fourteen, Flotilla Five War Diary, December 1943.
28. Morison, *Breaking the Bismarcks Barrier,* p. 364-365; CTF 31 War Diary, December 1943.

CHAPTER 15 NOTES

1. Morison, *Breaking the Bismarcks Barrier,* p. 369-370.
2. Ibid.

3. CTF 76 Operation Plans No. 3A-43 and No. 3B-43; *Rigel* War Diary, November 1943; "Battle of Milne Bay," *Wikipedia* (http://en.wikipedia.org/wiki/Battle_of_Milne_Bay: accessed 26 November 2011); "Battle of Buna, Australian War Memorial," (http://www.awm.gov.au/units/event_340.asp: accessed 26 November 2011); *Building the Navy's Bases in World War II*, p. 279; Peter Tare, "Along With Cousin Sam" (www.petertare.org/sam/body11.htm: accessed 28 November 2011); *Pacific Islands, Sailing Directions 1, Issue 1*, Great Britain Hydrographic Department.
4. Commander Southwest Pacific Force War Diary, March 1943; CTF 76 Operation Plans No. 3A-43 and No. 3B-43; Com7thFlt War Diary, June 1943.
5. Com7thPhipFor (CTF 76) Arawe Operation - report of, FE25/A16-3 Serial No. 0025.
6. Com7thAmpFor (CTF 76) Arawe Operation - report of; "Battle of Arawe," *Wikipedia* (http://en.wikipedia.org/wiki/Battle_of_Arawe: accessed 13 October 2012).
7. Com7thAmpFor (CTF 76) Arawe Operation - report of; "Battle of Arawe".
8. CTF-76 Operation Plan 3A-43; Commanding Officer, *LST-453*, Enemy Action, report of, FE25-LST 453/A16-3 Serial 03-43 of 15 December 1943.
9. CTF 76 and CTG 70.1 War Diary, December 1943; CTF 76 Movement Order No. NG 147-43; "*ML 817*'s New Guinea Operations," Naval Historical Society of Australia (http://www.navyhistory.org.au/ml-817s-new-guinea-operations: accessed 13 October 2012).
10. Frank O. Hough and John A. Crown, "The Campaign on New Britain" (http://www.ibiblio.org/hyperwar/USMC/USMC-M-NBrit/USMC-M-NBrit-5.html: accessed 27 November 2011).
11. Ibid.
12. Com7thPhibFor Cape Gloucester Operation – Report on; MacArthur, *Reports of General MacArthur, The Campaigns of MacArthur in the Pacific*, Vol I; CTF 76 War Diary, December 1943.
13. CTF 76 War Diary, December 1943; CTF OpPlan No. 3B-43; *SC-743* War Diary, December 1943 and January 1944; U.S. Naval Base, Gown War Diary, February 1943 and January 1944.

CHAPTER 16 NOTES

1. Morison, *Two-Ocean War*, p. 296; "Battle of Tarawa," *Wikipedia* (http://en.wikipedia.org/wiki/Battle_of_Tarawa: accessed 15 October 2012).
2. Carter, *Beans, Bullets, and Black Oil: the Story of Fleet Logistics Afloat in the Pacific during World War II*, p. 90-93.

3. CTF 16 and *Southern Seas* War Diary, November 1943.
4. Headquarters Fifth Defense Battalion, Reinforced, in the Field, Special Action Report S-3116 RET/hlm of 18 November 1943; *Southern Seas* and *Patapsco* War Diary, November 1943.
5. *The Capture of Makin* (Washington, D.C.: Center of Military History, U.S. Army, 1990), p. 132; James R. Stockman, *The Battle for Tarawa*, Appendix B: "Marine Casualties" (http://www.ibiblio.org/hyperwar/USMC/USMC-M-Tarawa/USMC-M-Tarawa-B.html: accessed 15 October 2012); Richard Johnston, *Follow Me!: The Story of The Second Marine Division in World War II*, p. 111.
6. CincPac and *LST-240* War Diary, December 1943.

CHAPTER 17 NOTES

1. O. R. Lodge, "The Recapture of Guam" (http://www.ibiblio.org/hyperwar/USMC/USMC-M-Guam/index.html: accessed 18 December 2011).
2. *William W. Burrows, DANFS*.
3. "Defoe Shipbuilding" (http://shipbuildinghistory.com/history/shipyards/2large/inactive/defoe.htm: accessed 12 September 2011); "*YP-42*," NavSource (http://www.navsource.org/archives/14/31042.htm: accessed 12 September 2011).
4. "USS *Hannibal*," NavSource (http://www.navsource.org/archives/09/49/49001.htm: accessed 15 December 2011); "Barrett Family Memoir" (http://barrettfamilymemoir.blogspot.com/2011/01/crew-of-survey-ship-hannibal-may-31.html: accessed 12 September 2011).
5. "Barrett Family Memoir."
6. Ibid.
7. Ibid.
8. Ibid.
9. "USS *Hannibal*," NavSource; *Bowditch*, *DANFS*; *Bowditch* War Diary, December 1943.
10. COM 11 and *Bowditch* War Diary, January 1944; CincPac and CTF 16 War Diary, February 1944.
11. *Bowditch* War Diary, February 1944; Morison, *The Two-Ocean War*, p. 296, 307; "USS *Liscome Bay*," NavSource (http://www.navsource.org/archives/03/056.htm: assessed 23 December 2011).
12. Commander Joint Expeditionary Force FLINTLOCK, 05A/A-16-3(3) serial 00180, Report of Amphibious Operations for the Capture of the Marshall Islands (Flintlock and Catchpole Operations); Morison, *The Two-Ocean War*, p. 307-312.
13. Commander Joint Expeditionary Force FLINTLOCK, 05A/A-16-3(3) serial 00180, Report of Amphibious Operations for the Capture of the

Marshall Islands (Flintlock and Catchpole Operations); Morison, *The Two-Ocean War*, p. 307-312.
14. *Bowditch* and *Gear* War Diary, July 1944; "USS *Oregon*," NavSource (http://www.navsource.org/archives/01/03a.htm: accessed 23 December 2011); United States Pacific Fleet Organization 1 May 1945.
15. Ibid.
16. Morison, *The Two-Ocean War*, p. 322; "The Battle of Saipan," The Stamford Historical Society (http://www.stamfordhistory.org/ww2_saipan.htm: accessed 16 October 2012).
17. CTF 52 Capture of Tinian – Report of, A16-3(3) Serial 0232 of 24 August 1944.
18. CTF 52 Capture of Tinian – Report of; *Bowditch* War Diary, July 1944; William W. Burrows, *DANFS*.
19. *Bryant* War Diary, August 1944.
20. ComServRon 12 War Diary, August 1944.
21. Morison, *The Two-Ocean War*, p. 421.

CHAPTER 18 NOTES

1. United States Strategic Bombing Survey, Interrogation of Japanese Officials, OpNav P-03-100, Naval Analysis Division, 13-14 November 1945 (http://www.ibiblio.org/hyperwar/AAF/USSBS/IJO/IJO-75.html: accessed 9 November 2011).
2. Morison, *The Two-Ocean War*, p. 30-345.
3. Morison, *The Two-Ocean War*, p. 432-435; "Battle of Leyte Gulf," *Wikipedia* (http://en.wikipedia.org/wiki/Battle_of_Leyte_Gulf: accessed 9 November 2011).
4. "Battle of Leyte Gulf," *Wikipedia*.
5. Cressman, *The Official Chronology of the U.S. Navy in World War II*; Building the Navy's Bases in World War II, p. 381-382.
6. Cressman, *The Official Chronology of the U.S. Navy in World War II - 1944*.
7. U.S. Pacific Fleet South Pacific Fleet Service Squadron War Diary, July 1944; ComServFor 7th Fleet War Diary, 10/1/44 to 11/30/44; Carter, *Beans, Bullets, and Black Oil: the Story of Fleet Logistics Afloat in the Pacific during World War II*, p. 237; ComCortDiv 16 War Diary, November 1944.
8. ComCortDiv 16 War Diary, November 1944.
9. *YP-421* Report of AA Action in Tacloban Harbor, Leyte Island, Philippines, on 23 November 1944.
10. *YP-421* Report of AA Action in Tacloban Harbor, Leyte Island, Philippines, on 24 November 1944.
11. "Battle of Leyte Gulf," *Wikipedia*.

CHAPTER 19 NOTES
1. Morison, *The Two-Ocean War*, p. 513-514.
2. "Battle for Iwo Jima, 1945," Naval History and Heritage Command (http://www.history.navy.mil/library/online/battleiwojima.htm: accessed 22 October 2012).
3. ComServRon 12 Operation Plan No. 1-45; *Sumner* War Diary, March 1945.
4. ComPhibForPac War Diary, March 1945; *Sumner* War Diary, March-May 1945.
5. *Valve* War Diary, May 1945.
6. ComServRon 12 and *LST-847* War Diary, May 1945.
7. "Battle for Iwo Jima, 1945."
8. Morison, *The Two-Ocean War*, p. 528; "Battle of Okinawa," *Wikipedia* (http://en.wikipedia.org/wiki/Battle_of_Okinawa: accessed 24 October 2012).
9. "Battle of Okinawa," *Wikipedia*.
10. "Defoe Shipbuilding;" Morison, *The Two-Ocean War*, p. 542, 544.
11. *Bowditch* War Diary, May 1945.
12. USS *PC-1603* Anti-Aircraft Action of 26 May 1945 – Report of; *Bowditch* War Diary, May 1945; "*PC-1603*," NavSource (http://www.navsource.org/archives/12/011603.htm: accessed 24 October 2012).
13. *Bowditch* War Diary, May 1945.
14. Ibid.
15. Perkins, *Battle Stars and Naval Awards*, p. 4-198.

CHAPTER 20 NOTES
1. CTG 78.2 Action Report-Balikpapan-Manggar-Borneo June 15-July 6, 1945.
2. Commanding Officer, Navy 1905 MEIU One War Diary, April 1943; "Mobile Explosives Investigation Unit No. 1, U.S. Navy, in Australia during WW2" (http://home.st.net.au/~dunn/usnavy/meiunitno1.htm: accessed 20 October 2012); "Philippines Work Earns Unit Honor for Salvage Group," *All Hands Naval Bulletin*, December 1945; Perkins, *Battle Stars and Naval Awards*, p. 6-32.
3. MTB Ron 33 War Diary, May 1945; "Leon Goldsworthy," *Wikipedia* (http://en.wikipedia.org/wiki/Leon_Goldsworthy: accessed 18 October 2012).
4. Bruhn, *Wooden Ships and Iron Men: The U.S. Navy's Coastal and Motor Minesweepers, 1941-1953*, p. 103-104.
5. Bruhn, *Wooden Ships and Iron Men: The U.S. Navy's Coastal and Motor Minesweepers, 1941-1953*, p. 114-115; "Leon Goldsworthy."

POSTSCRIPT NOTES

1. August Felando, 22 October 2012; *Pacific Fisherman* (March 1944), p. 72.
2. Melville Owen, 19 November 2012.
3. Ibid.
4. "NAVSHIPS 250-012 – Ship's Data U.S. Naval Vessels, Volume III – Auxiliary, District Craft and Unclassified Vessels (15 April 1945)" (http://www.alternatewars.com/Archives/Ships_Data_USN/Ships_Data.htm: accessed 19 October 2012).

Index

Abbott, Gordon, 135
Adams, Edward E., 296
Adams, Kenneth G., xix, 6, 8, 197-201
Agnew, Dwight A., 19
Alberg, David W., 131
Allen, William H., 158, 164
Altman, Frederick, 291
Anderson, Charles E., 79, 83
Anderson, Clifton R., 296
Andrews, Adolphus, 132, 138, 140-142, 153
Anotil, D. L., 303
Ascuito, Mike, 5
Aritomo, Goto, 120
Armstrong, Clarence W., 290
Arnett, Lowren Augustus, 121
Ashley, J. M., 190
Ashley, W. J., 168
Ashton, Henry Jay, 121
Austin, B. L., 226-227, 230
Australia, xv, 4, 9, 79, 115-116, 202, 211, 213, 219, 222, 239
Australian bases/forces/troops/Rendering Safe Mines Officers, xxv, 115, 220, 233, 256, 258, 270-271
Bacon, Lloyd, xx, 65
Baker, H., 212
Baker, Jr., Ray P., 149, 303
Baker, Walter E., 270
Barbey, Daniel E., 235
Barlage, Benjamin J., 291
Barnett, J. A., 190
Barr, Robert R., 291
Barrymore, John, 73
Barston, Jr., Burrows, 291
Battaglia, Vincent, xx, 6, 13, 15, 18
Battisti, A. T., 303

Battle of
　the Atlantic, 131
　(Sixth air battle of) Bougainville, 217, 227
　Cape St. George, 3, 226-227
　the Coral Sea, 80
　Iwo Jima, 261-264
　Java Sea, 115
　Kwajalein, 251
　Leyte Gulf, xxv, 256-258
　Manila Bay, 246
　Midway, xxiv, 83, 87, 96, 99-106, 123
　(naval battle of) Guadalcanal, 21-23
　Okinawa, xxv, 261, 264-267
　Philippine Sea, 255
　Pivot Forks, 222-223
　Savo Island, 1-3
　Second Battle for Henderson Field, 19
　Tarawa, 250
Beatie, W. C., 190
Beckerleg (Ensign), 190-191
Behrman, G., 303
Benton, Jr., H. P., 168
Bergen, Theodore L., 61
Binns, Donald Adair, 121
Blancq, M. J., 168
Bluma, Lawrence Edward, 121
Bohn, Donald F., 291
Bonsall, E. C., 303
Borgnine, Ernest, 40
Boyington, Gregory, 222
Branson, G., 238
Branyon, Howard H., 8, 10, 23
Brink, C. R., 74
Brister, Robert Earl, 157
Broadfoot, H. B., 168
Brocato, G. J., 8, 25
Broller, E., 179
Brown, James Monroe, 158
Bruce, John R., 8, 102
Bryon, Albert R., 295
Buckner, Jr., Simon B., 82, 85, 97
Bunker, Jr., William Logan, 157

Bunn, J. C., 252
Burke, Arleigh A., 3, 222, 226-227
Burns, Ralph, 127
Butler, William O., 85
Cahoon, Roger C., 291
Calhoun, William L., 202
California Maritime Academy, 65
Callin, John Elijah, 102
Canadian Airforce (RCAF), 123-127
Canepa, Larry, 19
Caroline Islands, Truk Atoll, 2, 109, 245, 250
Carpenter, J. K., 74
Carr, S. W., 135
Carroll, M. S., 8
Carter, Charles Harold, 158
Carter, Worrall R., 250
Cary, George A., 291
Chandler, Josiah B., 291
China, 111-112, 116, 128
Cho, Isamu, 267
Christensen, Stratton, 157
Churchill, Winston, 29, 268
Claudius, H. G., 173-175
Clusman (Lieutenant), 190
Coe, Herbert H., 291
Cogger, K. I., 264
Cole, Samuel O., 51
Cole, W. B., 151, 303
Collins (Ensign), 191
Combs, William B., 75
Corwin, A. A., 143
Crabb, Anderson J., 295
Crabb, V. W., 151, 303
Craig, C., 60
Crane, Francis G., 296
Creighton Robert D., 290
Crenshaw, Russell S., 163-164
Crosby, Bing, 65
Curtis, Allan Dwight, 74
Curtiss, Cyrus, 26
Dahlsted, Arthur Benedict, 121
Dana, Lawrence, 135

Daniels, A. N., 143
Dawnes, James W., 74
De Gaulle, Charles, 182
Dege, C. F., 166
Degen, Horst, 149-152
Deits, Donald W., 74
Dias, Pete, 8
Dieht, F. W., 166
DiPaixio, V., 8
Donitz, Karl, xxv, 131-132, 149-150, 160
Doolittle, James H., 79-80
Doucette, J. C., 303
Dutch East Indies, Java, 79, 114-115
Dutro, Harold William, 121
Eckert, Floyd E., 291
Edel, Adolph F., 154
Edson, Merritt A., 3, 13
Ekstrom, Olof, 53-55
Ellice Islands, Funafuti, 204, 224, 241-244
Elliman, George T., 295
Erickson (Lieutenant Junior Grade), 190
Estess, E. J., 155
Everson, J. H., 61
Fabian, Jr., Henry, 121
Fairbanks, Jr., Douglas Elton, 145
Farrow, Clark A., 50
Felando, August, xvii, xix, 63
Ferguson, Homer, 113
Ferrill, H. E., 154
Fijian Islands, 9-10, 202, 209
Fitzpatrick, Russell E., 165
Fitzsimmons, Jr., Lawrence G., 143
Foote, Arthur Earnest, 121
Foote (radioman), 50-51
Formosa (now Taiwan), 32, 113, 118-119
France/French
    Brest, 149, 181
    Brittany, 131
    Guiana, 33, 38, 183, 188
    Indochina, 111-112
    Lorient, 131, 149
    Morocco, 37

Polynesia, Bora Bora, 9, 199-202, 209
"Vichy," xxv, 181-183, 191-192, 200
West Indies/Antilles, 183
Freeman, Charles S., 73-74, 84
Freitas, Manuel, 5, 8
Frey, Charles W., 194
Gehres, Leslie E., 85, 93-95
German
    Group Hecht/Abwehr (intelligence) agents, 149-150
    Prisoner of War Camp Marlag und Milag Nord, 158
Ghormley, Robert L., 9, 10
Gilbert, Charles, 61
Gilbert Islands (Tarawa, Makin), xxv, 241-244, 250, 252
Goldman, A. B., 8
Goldsworthy, Leonard, xxv, 258, 270, 272
Goncalves, Fredrick, 47, 52
Gonsalves, Frank, 5, 7
Goodheart, W. J., 252
Gorham, John A., 295
Graham, Robert W., 159, 165
Greenslade, John W., 60, 66, 69
Greenwald, Harry, 56
Griswold, Oscar W., 231
Guidone, Frank J., xx, 1
Gwinn, Louis H., 60
Hall, James Joseph, 74
Hall, Jr., John L., 37
Halsey, Jr., William F. "Bull," 23, 48, 207, 212, 231
Halstead, Richard, 247-248
Hardegan, Reinhard, 160
Harkness, William L., 156-157
Harris, C. P., 303
Harris (Lieutenant Commander), 176
Harrison, W. H., 168
Hart, Thomas C., 32, 111-114
Haskell, S. B., 158
Haviland, J. W., 120
Hawaii/Hawaiian Islands
    French Frigate Shoals, 9-10, 25, 101, 106
    Gardner Pinnacles, Kure Island, Laysan, Necker, Pearl and Hermes
        Reef, 101-106
    Kewalo Basin, 42-43

Lisianski, 9, 101, 104, 106
Midway, xx, xvii, xxiv, 9, 25, 38, 79-81, 89, 96, 99-106
Hayes, William C., 296
Hayward, Jr., Griswold S., 296
Hazzard, George Alonzo, 102
Hendley, T. B., 168
Hensley, C. F., 303
Hero, Alvin, 165
Herrick, W. R., 143
Hessberg, A., 190
Heyward, Allard B., 159, 165
Hia, M., 303
Hicks, Jr., E. F., 74
Hill, Harry W., 250
Hoffman, George L., 165
Holmes, Ralston S., 60, 70
Holt, N. H., 303
Holtz, Edward L., 66
Hong Kong, 79, 110, 112
Hoover, John H., 190-191
Hotchkiss, Stuart T., 177, 185
Hudson, Richard L., 168
Huelsenbeck, Paul C., 212
Hull, Jack L., 84
Hull, Raymond M., 295
Impett, Jr., Vernon Grant, 75
Ingersoll, Royal E., 113
Ives, Warren C., 165
Jack, Raymond L., 157
Japanese
    Aircraft
        Betty (Mitsubishi G4M3) bomber, 230, 236
        Kamikaze, xxv, 257-258, 265-266
        Oscar (Nakajima Ki-43) fighter, 236
        Sally (Mitsubishi Ki-21-II) bomber, 236, 243, 259
        Val (Aichi D3A) dive bomber, 230, 236, 259-260, 267
        Zero (A6M5) fighter plane, 106, 215, 236
    Army
        32nd Army, 267
        43rd Division, 252
    Imperial General Headquarters, 49
    Imperial Japanese Navy (IJN)

1st Assault Unit, 20
B1 submarines, 48
Combined Fleet, 2, 80, 105, 245
Eighth Fleet, 2
First Mobile Fleet, 255
Prisoner of War Camps, 117, 221
Second Mobile Force, 89
Sixth Fleet, 48-49
South Seas Detachment/Fifth Defense Force, 120
Tokyo Express, 2-3, 14
Yokosuka E14Y seaplane, 48
Johansen, John E., 177, 185
Johnson, George, xix, xxi-xxiii
Johnson, John O., 137
Johnston Atoll, 8, 35
Jones, Arthur D., 291
Judson, Jr., Charles S., 61
Kadolph, Darnell, 118
Kakuta, Kakaji, 89
Kaufman, Charles E., 217
Kawaguchi, Kiyotake, 13
Keefe, Frank B., 113
Kerr, E. E., 168
Keller, R. K., 75
Kennedy, John F., 210
Killian, Frank, 143
Kimes, Kenneth, 51
King, Ernest J., 59, 70, 73, 138, 140-141, 180-181, 186
Kowski, J. P., 252
Kurita, Takeo, 255
Lampson, Everett W., 291
Lange, George A., 295
Lassen, Georg, 193-195
Lavnikevich, Nicholas J., xx, 209-211
LecLuyse, Charles L., 291
Lehman (Electrican's Mate First), 16
Linder, Robert L., 291
Lobred, Leonard K., 290
Logan, Charles W., 135
Long, A. W., 165
Long, R. J., 303
Lowry, William M., 74

Index

MacArthur, Douglas, 113, 116, 119, 233, 241, 254, 256
MacLean, C. F., 303
MacPherson, G. L., 303
Madruga, Edward X., xv, 5, 7-8, 202
Madruga, Joseph, xv, 202
Mansfield, Marshall, 56
Marden (Lieutenant), 238
Mariana Islands, 109-110, 219, 241, 245-256, 252-254, 264
    Guam, xv, xxiv, 26, 32, 79, 109-110, 119-121, 245, 252-254, 263, 265, 268
    Saipan, xv, xxv, 32, 109-110, 119-120, 245-246, 252-253
    Tinian, 109-110, 245, 252-253
Marshall Islands, 49, 100, 109, 204, 219, 241, 245, 250-252, 255
Martin, Thomas F., 66
Mascarenhas, Antonio/Anthony, 5, 7, 273
Massello, Edmond J., 134
Masselo, E. J., 212
Matsumura, Kanji, 53
McCain, John, S., 11, 70
McClean, Jr., Odber R., 135
McGillivray, Stuart, 50
McKee (Mr. & Mrs.), 95
McKellar, R. M., 149, 303
McMillin, George J., 120
Mecleary, H. B., 153
Merrill, Anson, 222
Michelsen, Jens P., 194
Mitchell, David A., 134
Moler, B. F., 51
Moore, E. B., 291
Moore, J. D., 168
Morcott, W. J., 5, 7
Morgan, M. S., 8
Munroe, Frank, 61
Murch, R. L., 303
Murphy, John, 17, 23, 297-298
Navy/Naval Commands
    Air Station
        Alameda, 50
        Clark Field, 111
        Corpus Christi, 167-168
        Dutch Harbor, 82, 89-91

Kodiak, 82, 93, 96
Midway, 99, 106
Palmyra, 10
Pensacola, 169, 171
Sitka, 82
Squantum, 136
Coastal/Sea Frontiers, 29-30, 32-37
Construction Battalion ("Seabees"), 225, 231, 263
Destroyer
    Division
        Eleven, 81
        Seventy, Eighty-three, 70
    Squadron
        Twenty-two, 224
        Twenty-three, 222, 226-230
        Thirty-three, 180
        Forty-five, 227
Fleet
    United States Fleet, 59, 111, 138, 186
        Asiatic Fleet, xxiv, 32, 111-112, 114, 116
        Atlantic Fleet (the former "Scouting Force"), 35, 72, 111, 175, 180-181
        "Great White," 65
        Pacific Fleet (the former "Battle Fleet"), xxvi, 9, 22, 36, 58, 65, 80-81, 97, 111, 157, 175, 261
            Service Force, 202-204, 241-246, 250, 252, 258, 269-270
            Transportation Division Twelve, 1, 3
            Fifth Fleet, 255
            Seventh Fleet, 258, 260-261
Motor Torpedo Boat Squadron, 9, 210
    One, 101
    Two, 180, 210
    Three, 19, 116
    Nine, 210
Naval Hydrographic Office, 248-250
Naval Operating Base
    Guadalcanal, 20
    Guantanamo, 33
    Leyte, 256
    Newfoundland, 32
    Newport, 138, 140, 148, 155
    Norfolk, 32, 38

Trinidad, 33, 191, 195
Patrol
    OS2U-3 Kingfisher aircraft, 136
    Squadrons (VP)
        bomber (VPB), 35
        Thirty-one, 191
        Forty-one, Forty-two, Forty-three, 94
        Forty-four, 50-51
    Wing Four, 82-96
Q-Ship Program, 59, 70-73
Section Base
    Astoria, Oregon; Coos Bay, Oregon; Neah Bay, Washington; Port Angeles, Washington; Port Townsend, Washington; Seattle, Washington, 74-75
    Balboa, Panama, 176
    Bar Harbor, Maine; Portland, Maine; Portsmouth, New Hampshire; Rockland, Maine; Woods Hole, Massachusetts, 134-135
    Boston, Massachusetts, xxi, 134
    Burrwood, Louisiana; Corpus Christi, Texas; Galveston, Texas; Mobile, Alabama; Sabine Pass, Texas, 168-170, 172
    Cape May, New Jersey, 153-154
    Charleston, South Carolina, 159
    Cordova, Dutch Harbor, Ketchikan, Kodiak, Sitka, Alaska, 84
    Cristobal, Panama, 176-177, 184, 188, 208
    Eureka, California, 67
    Key West, Mayport, St. Petersburg, Florida, 159-160, 164-166
    Little Creek, Virginia, 139
    New London, Connecticut; Tompkinsville, New York, 143-144, 147
    Morehead City, North Carolina, 148, 155
    Port Everglades, Florida, 165, 208
    San Diego, San Pedro, California, 61, 63-64
    San Juan, Puerto; St. Thomas, Virgin Islands; Teteron Bay, Trinidad, 190-191
    Savannah, Georgia; Southport, North Carolina, 158
Submarine Division Forty-one, 86
Tiburon Net Depot, xiv, 65, 67-69
Training
    U.S. Fleet Training Base, San Clemente Island, 71
    Great Lakes Naval Training Station, 137
Underwater Demolition Team 11/Mobile Explosives Investigation Unit, 269-272
War Plan-Rainbow No. 5, xxlv, 29-38

Nazarsky, W. W., 303
Neely, H. W., 190-191
Nestor, J. L., 120
Nevle, Gerard, 17, 23, 297-299
New Britain, 2-3, 233-239
New Caledonia, Noumea, xv, 9, 53, 199-200, 202, 204, 209-210, 212
New Hebrides
    Efate, 9-10, 200-202, 204, 224
    Espiritu Santo, 4, 10-12, 200-201, 210, 213-214, 216, 224, 242
Newell, Jr., Fred Rising, 116-117
New Zealand, Auckland, 10, 198-199
    8th Brigade Group of the 3rd Division, 224
    251st Coastal Artillery, 62nd Radar Squadron, 227
Nichols, J. T. G., 135
Nicola, Raphael M., 291
Nienau, Albert H., 286
Nimitz, Chester, xxiv, 2, 9, 81, 85, 89, 94, 96, 99, 101, 241, 245, 250
Nishino, Kozo, 49-52, 57
Nolan, James Clair, xx, 103-105
O'Donnell, James B., 207, 212
Okinawa, xv, xxv, 25, 219, 246, 261-262, 264-268, 274-275
Olds, John R., 291
Operation
    CHERRY BLOSSOM (Cape Torokina, Bougainville Assault), 220
    DEXTERITY (Arawe and Cape Gloucester, New Britain Assault), 233, 236-239
    FLINTLOCK (Kwajalein, Marshall Islands Assault), 251
    FORAGER (Saipan, Guam and Tinian, Mariana Islands Assault), 245
    GALVANIC (Tarawa and Makin, Gilbert Islands Assault), 241
    NEULAND ("New Territory;" German operation), 189
    PAUKENSCHLAG ("Drumbeat;" German operation), 131
    TEN-GO (Japanese kamikaze attacks at Okinawa), 265
Osterhaus, Hugo W., 70
Owen, Don, 65, 69, 273-274, 307
Owen, Melville, xiv, xix-xx, 66, 69
Page, Jr., Alfred, F., 134, 165
Paine, George P., 217
Palmyra Atoll, 8, 10, 35, 197
Papua/New Guinea, xv, 2-4, 79, 219, 233-238, 241, 245, 254-255, 258
Paris, W. E., 143
Parker, Ralph C., 81-85, 96
Parnell, Roy C., 16-17

Parris, (Ensign), 168
Pash, Virgil, 8, 198-199
Payne, Jr., John Walker, 112-113
Pennington, R. W., 50
Perdue (Lieutenant Commander), 176
Petritz, George K., xx, 117-119, 301
Philip, Robert L., 291
Philippine Islands
    Cavite, 38, 114-115
    Corregidor, 26, 79, 115-117, 301
    Far Eastern Air Force, 114
    Filipino guerrilla Camp D, 118
    Lingayen, 272
    Luzon, 26, 35, 113, 118, 219, 261
    Manila/Manila Bay, 79, 111, 113-117, 119, 246, 270, 301
    Tacloban Harbor, 256-259
Philips, Roderick Johnstone, 147-153, 303
Pierce, M. R., 60
Podries, Anthony Joseph, 121
Potts, Fred, 50
Prickett, Hiram Jefferson, 121
Pringle, Louie, 56
Pye, William S., 226
Quincy, Richard, 53
Rasch, Philip J., 295
Rasmussen, Christian, 5, 8, 20, 197
Rasmussen, John F., 74
Raymond, Fred L., 116-117, 301
Reeves, George, 8
Reeves, Jr., John W., 96
Reich, Herman, 61
Reynolds, William, 99
Rhea, J. W., 185
Robert, Georges A. M. J., 183
Rockwell, Francis W., 114, 116
Roos, Bo, 62
Roosevelt, Franklin D., xxiv, 70, 111-113, 115, 256
Roosevelt, Theodore, 65
Roper, Walter Gordon, 157
Rosa, Victor, 5, 7-8, 202
Roth, Eli B., 168
Rudderow, Thomas W., 157

Rupertus, William H., 239
Russell, Allen, 135
Russell, Jane, 56
Ryan, Joseph, 56
Sadler, Frank H., 176, 178-180
Saltmarsh, Ernest O., 168
Samoan Islands,
    Feta Feta (a branch of the Marine Corps) Guard, 198
    Tutuila Island/Pago Pago Harbor, 10, 197-198, 205, 209, 212, 224
Sanders, M. R., 159
Saunders, Philip Earl, 120-121
Sauvain, Edward B., 290
Savidge, Richard G., 215, 217
Schmidt, Harry, 262-263
Schumann (Lieutenant), 190
Schultze, Heinz-Otto, 137
Scull, H. M., 241
Scott, Joseph, 55
Sesselman, W. J., 303
Shannon, G. E., 8
Sharp, Alexander, 264
Shibata, Genichi, 52, 56
Shigemitsu, Mamoru, 245
Shimizu, Mitsumi, 48-49, 57
Ships and Craft
    Allied or Foreign
        Australian
            Merkur, 237
        British
            anti-submarine trawlers, 141
            British Freedom, 152
            Cyclops, 132, 138
            Gypsum Express, 194, 196
            HMS *Aurania*, 160
            HMS *Duhamel*, HMS *Hertfordshire*, HMS *Norwich City*, HMS *St. Zero, San Demetrio, Splendour*, 155
            HMS *Kingston Ceylonite*, 152
            Kent, 187
            Yochow, 259
        Canadian
            Christian J. Kampmann, 193, 196
            HMCS *Edmunston*, 81

HMCS *Quatsino*, 125
Columbian, *Envoy* and *Zaroma*, 187
Dutch
- HNMS *TM-23*, 196
- *Van Cloon*, 115

French
- *Barfluer* and *Jeanne d'Arc*, 183
- *Surcouf*, xxv, 181-183

German
- *U-66, U-109, U-125, U-128*, 131
- *U-123*, 73, 131-132, 138, 159-160
- *U-129*, 195-196
- *U-130*, 131-132
- *U-159, U-504*, 187
- *U-160*, 193-194
- *U-166*, 163, 172-175
- *U-171*, 175
- *U-402*, xxv, 158
- *U-404, U-552, U-576*, 155
- *U-432*, 137
- *U-506*, 172
- *U-507*, 171
- *U-588*, 144, 147
- *U-701*, xxv, 149-152
- *U-752*, 154
- *U-754*, 139, 144

Honduran, *Ontario*, 171

Japanese
- *aku* boats ("Hawaiian sampans"), 42-43
- Imperial Navy (IJN)
    - *Akagi, Hiryu, Kaga, Soryu*, 105
    - *Akatsuki, Ikazuchi, Shiratsuyo*, 19, 21
    - *Hatsuyuki, Murakumo, Yudachi*, 1
    - *Hijo, Shokaku, Taiho*, 255
    - *I-6*, 48
    - *I-9, I-15*, 49
    - *I-10*, 48-49
    - *I-17*, 49-51, 55, 57
    - *I-19*, 49, 52-53, 55
    - *I-21*, 49, 52-54
    - *I-23*, 47, 49, 52, 55-56
    - *I-25*, 49, 52-53, 55, 57-58, 80-81, 128

Index {357}

       I-26, 47-49, 55, 57, 80-81
       I-55, 115
       Junyo, Ryujo, 89
       Kamikawa Maru, 113
       Katori, 49
       Makinami and *Onami*, 226-227
       RO-32, xxiv, 27, 123, 127-128
       RO-103, 216
       Sendai, xxvi, 14-15, 18
    "Hell Ships" *Brazil Maru, Enoura Maru, Oryoku Maru*, 117-119
Norwegian
    Astrell, 196
    Bidevind, Lancing, Tamesis, 152-155
    Frisco, 132
    Thorshavet, 194
Panamanian
    Friar Rock, 132
    Leda, 194
Soviet, submarines *L-16* and *Shch-138*, 128
Spanish, *Zorossai*, 181
U.S. Coast Guard
    Alert, Ariadne, Daphne, Perseus, Pulaski, 70
    Aurora, Bonham, Cyane, Haida, 86
    Boutwell, 169-172
    Cahoone, 64, 70
    Calypso, Cuyahoga, Dione, Legare, 155
    CG-6, CG-475, 196
    CG-123, CG-194, 184
    CG-135, 145
    CG-462, CG-481, 152
    CG-466, 170
    CG-471, 155
    CG-477, 147, 155
    Colfax, 195-196
    Diligence, 64
    Dorothy, 170
    Hermes, 63, 70
    McLane, xxiv, 27, 123-128
    Nemaha, 90
    Onondaga, 86, 90
    Rush, 155, 196
    Shawnee, 51, 70

    St. Johns Lightship, 159-160
    Tuckahoe, 170-172
    Woodbine, 252
U.S. Merchant Marine/Civilian Craft
    Absaroka, 55-56
    Aeolus (fishing vessel), 137
    Agwiworld, 47, 52
    Alcoa Puritan, 171
    American, 187
    Andrew Jackson, 179
    Ardmore, F. H. Bedford, Jr., Benjamin Bourn, City Service Kansas, Edward L. Doheny, Domino, Gulfpride, Peter Hurll, Meton, Moldova, Nishmaha, Pan Gulf, Paulsboro, Felix Taussig, 196
    Aurora, 172
    Barbara Olson, 55
    Ben and Josephine (fishing vessel), 137
    Coast Trader, 81
    Connecticut, 57
    Copiapo, 179
    Cynthia Olson, 47-48
    Dartmouth, Ida & Joseph, Natalie III (fishing vessels), 142
    Dorothy Philips, 56
    Eagle (Q-Ship), 70, 196
    Ed Moran and *Theo Moran*, 208
    Emidio, 50-52
    Esparta, 160
    Esso Baton Rouge, Oklahoma, 159
    Esso Augusta, 152
    F. W. Abrams, 148
    Foam (fishing vessel), 137
    Forest Dream, 128
    Frank S. Grinnell, Gertrude L. Thebaud, Mary W., Serafina N., Three Sisters (fishing vessels), 142
    Gulfamerica, 160
    Gulf King, 172
    H. M. Storey, 52
    Idaho, 53
    Larry Doheny, 51, 53
    Irene and May (fishing vessel), 155
    J. C. Donnell, K. R. Kingsbury, 63
    Jason, 147
    L. P. St. Clair, Lurline, 48

Matthew P. Deady, 258
Mindi, 208
Montebello, 53-54
Morlen, 90-91
Nathaniel Currier, 215
Nira Luckenbach, 11
Northwestern, 91-92
Otho, 144
Peter Sylvester, 214
Pipestone County, 155
Plow City, 144, 147
President Coolidge, 201
President Fillmore, 90
Robert C. Tuttle, 152
Robert E. Lee, 163, 173-175
Samoa, 49-50
Santore, 152
Seneca (Pennsylvania Nautical School Ship), 157
Sixaola, Solon Turman, 187
Standard Service, 63
Thompson Lykes, 181-182
Tiger, 139
Underwriter (pilot boat), 163, 174
Virginia I (fishing vessel), 81
West Lashaway, 148
William H. Berg, 57
William Rockefeller, 152

U.S. C&GS/National Oceanic and Atmospheric Administration (NOAA)
   Nancy Foster, 131
   Oceanographer, 155

U.S. Navy
   amphibious
      Higgins boats, 2, 14, 187-188, 202
      Hunter Liggett, 129
      LCI-61, LCI-63, LCI-328, LCI-332, 224
      LCI-62, LCI-64, LCI-222, 227
      LCI-335, LCI-336, 224, 227
      LCI-1078, 267
      LCT-1061, 261, 263
      LST-240, LST-268, 244
      LST-334, 224, 227, 230
      LST-390, LST-397, LST-446, LST-472, 224, 227

LST-398, LST-449, 224, 226-227
LST-447, 224-227
LST-453, 237, 239
LST-847, 264
auxiliary/service/support/miscellaneous
Aludra, 215-217
Amycus, 237
APc-2, APc-15, 239
Asterion (Q-Ship), 70
Atik (Q-Ship), 70, 72
Bellatrix, Fuller, 13
Big Horn, Irene Forsyte (Q-Ships), 70, 73
Bowditch, 249-253, 265, 267
Cascade, Patapsco, Phaon, Vestal, 242-243
Celeno, Deimus, Schley, 215
De Kalb, 157
Gear, 252
Hannibal, 246-250
Hydrographer, 254, 293
Kaloli, 101, 197
Keokuk, 250
Locust, Taupata, 214
Menkar, 129
Normandie II (Q-Ship), 71-72
Ramapo, 121
Rigel, 235
Robert L. Barnes, 120-121
Sabine, 88
Seminole, 19-21
Sepulga, 208-209
Sioux, 224, 227-228
Sumner, 261, 263-264
Valve, 263
Woodcock, 186
Zuni, 252
combatant
aircraft carrier
Enterprise, 48-49, 81, 105-106, 251
Essex, Saratoga, 251
Hornet, 79, 81, 105, 118
Lexington, 80
Yorktown, 80-81, 105-106

Index {361}

battleship
    Arizona, 8
    Oregon, 252
cruiser
    Honolulu, St. Louis, 81, 88
    Indianapolis, 81, 88, 92, 96
    Louisville, 81
    Nashville, 81, 88, 92-93
destroyer
    Allen, 106, 157
    Bainbridge, 152
    Barry, Tattnall, 181
    Bennett, 224, 226-227, 229-230
    Braine, Terry, 227, 229
    Brooks, Case, Dent, Gilmer, Kane, Sands, 88
    Bryant, 253
    Clark, 101
    Cole, Dallas, Dickerson, Dupont, Hamilton (later DMS-18), *Herbert, Roper, Upshur*, 155
    Converse, 230
    Conway, Saufley, Waller, 224
    Conyngham, Shaw, 236
    Edwards, 252
    Fullam, 227, 229-230
    Goff, 183
    Gridley, 81, 88, 92-93
    Guest, 227-228
    Hammann, 105
    Helm, 12
    Humphreys, 81, 88
    McCall, 81, 88, 157
    O'Bannon, 216
    Peary, Pillsbury, 114
    Reid, 81-82, 236
    Renshaw, 224, 227
    Sigourney, 224, 226
    Talbot, 70, 90
    Tucker, 10-12
destroyer-transport
    Colhoun, Gregory, Little, 1-2
    Manley, McKean, 1, 13-14
gunboat

Index

  Charleston, 82-83, 85-87, 95
  Erie, 177-178, 180
  Luzon and *Oahu*, 116
  Niagara, 187
 motor torpedo (PT) boat,
  PT-8, 142, 154, 279
  PT-20, PT-21, PT-22, PT-24, PT-25, PT-26, PT-27, PT-28, PT-29, PT-30, 101
  PT-37, PT-39, PT-45, PT-61, 19
  PT-56, PT-157, PT-159, PT-160, PT-162, 210
  PT-69, 143, 279
  PT-70, 279
  PT-109, 210
 patrol craft, *Eagle*-class *PE-48*, 145
 seaplane, Catalina PBY, 50, 82-95, 99, 102-103, 106, 112, 174
 seaplane tender
  Ballard, Thornton, 101
  Casco, Williamson, 86
  Curtiss SOC Seagull floatplane, 71
  Gillis, 86, 90-91, 93-96
  Hulbert, 94-95
  Pelican, 70-72
 Sloop-of-war *Lackawanna*, 99
 submarine chaser (PC/SC),
  PC-64, PC-507, PC-826, 145
  PC-454, PC-456, PC-509, 180
  PC-458, 180, 188
  PC-460, 180, 187
  PC-469, PC-559, PC-561, 193, 196
  PC-495, 193-194, 196
  PC-519, 163, 174
  PC-566, 163, 172-175
  PC-627, PC-1119, PC-1121, SC-521, SC-700, SC-738, SC-740, SC-749, SC-750, 208
  PC-1127, 250
  PC-1396, 267
  PC-1603, 266-267
  SC-640, 214
  SC-743, 239
  SC-1317, 244
mine warfare
 minelayer (DM)

Index {363}

Breese, Gamble, 11
Preble, Pruitt, Sicard, 102
Tracy, 11, 102
minesweeper (AM),
   Bittern, 114
   Oriole, 85-86
   Penguin, 119-120
   Quail, Tanager, 116
   Salute, 272
   Sheldrake, 242
   Skylark, 216
   Vireo, 101
   base (AMb), 31, 35, 60, 68
      AMb-1, 135
      AMb-2, AMb-5, AMb-8, 66
      AMb-3, AMb-7, AMb-9, AMb-11, AMb-12, AMb-13, AMb-14, 67
      AMb-4, 67, 285
      AMb-6, 67, 176, 185, 285
      AMb-10, 185
      AMb-16, 67, 185
      AMb-17, 134, 285
      AMb-18, 285
      AMb-19, AMb-20, AMb-21, 134-135, 285
      AMb-22, 134-135
      AMb-27, 134
   coastal (AMc),
      Accentor, Bulwark, Chimango, Cotinga, Fulmar, Puffin (ex-dragger *Mary Jane*), *Valor,* 135
      Acme, Assertive, Demand, Dominant, Limpkin, Lorikeet, Victor, 143
      Affray, Agile, Frigate Bird (ex-*Star of San Pedro*), *Goshawk* (ex-trawler *Penobscot*), *Liberator, Nightingale* (ex-purse seiner *St. Francis*), *Phoebe* (ex-*Western Robin*), *Pintail* (ex-fishing vessel *Three Star*), 74
      Barbet, Brambling, 177, 185
      Blue Jay (ex-dragger *Charles J. Ashley*), *Canary* (ex-fishing vessel *John G. Murley*), *Egret* (ex-fishing vessel *Julia Eleanor*), *Flamingo* (ex-dragger *Harriet N. Eldridge*), *Roller, Skimmer,* 154
      Bold, Combat, Detector, Kingbird (ex-*Governor*

        Saltonstall), Skipper, Trident, Vigor, 134
        Bunting (ex-*Vagabond*), *Chatterer* (ex-*Sea Breeze*), *Grosbeak* (ex-fishing vessel *Del Rio*), *Hornbill* (ex-fishing vessel *J. A. Martinolich*), *Killdeer* (ex-purse seiner *Vindicator*), *Waxbill* (ex-purse seiner *Leslie J. Fulton*), 66
        Courlan, 167-168, 171
        Courser (ex-*Nancy Rose*), *Firecrest* (ex-purse seiner *S. G. Giuseppe*), *Grouse* (ex-*New Bol*), *Plover* (ex-trawler *Sea Rover*), 61
        Crow (ex-purse seiner *Jadran*), *Radiant*, 75
        Develin, 167-168, 172
        Exultant, Fearless, 159
        Governor, 134, 165
        Guide, Summit, Tapacola, 165
        Ideal, 143, 165
        Kestrel (ex-fishing vessel *Chanco*), 155
        Longspur (ex-fishing vessel *New Ambassador*), 176
        Pipit (ex-fishing vessel *Spartan*), 176
        Ostrich, 167-168, 170
        Roadrunner (ex-seiner *Treasure Island*), 61, 63
        Sanderling (ex-purse seiner *Conti di Savoia*), 60
        Stalwart, 166
        Turaco, 159-160, 165
    destroyer-minesweeper (DMS)
        Forrest, 267
        Hamilton, 196
        Hopkins, 201
        Trever, Zane, 19-20
    yard (motor) minesweeper
        YMS-10, 208, 272
        YMS-39, YMS-47, YMS-49, YMS-50, YMS-51, YMS-84, YMS-314, YMS-329, YMS-334, YMS-335, YMS-339, YMS-363, YMS-364, YMS-365, YMS-368, YMS-481, 272
        YMS-70, 208
        YMS-290, 244
        YMS-328 (later John Wayne's *Wild Goose*), 62
        YMS-357, 261
submarine
    Drum, 184
    "S-boat," 35, 86, 125

S-21, 183
S-27, 88
S-34, S-35, 85
Sealion, 114
Shark, 115
yacht
    coastal patrol (PYc),
        Agate, 176, 180, 276, 295
        Alabaster, 154, 295
        Amber, 75, 276, 295
        Amethyst, 55-56, 61, 70, 295
        Brave, 286, 296
        Captor, 70, 276, 296
        Chalcedony, 39, 295
        Emerald, 159, 165-167, 276, 295
        Gallant, 134, 143, 276, 295
        Iolite, 143, 190, 287, 295-296
        Jasper, 60, 295
        Moonstone, 26, 177, 180, 295
        Onyx, 167-168, 171-172, 276, 295
        Opal, 190-191, 295
        Patriot, 39, 276, 296
        Sapphire, 143-145, 147, 295
        Topaz, 176, 180, 276, 295
        Truant, 40, 295
        Vagrant, 283, 295
        PYcs mentioned in Appendix C: *Andradite, Aquamarine, Ability, Colleen, Cymophane, Felicia, Garnet, Lash, Leader, Marnell, Mentor, Palace, Peridot, Perseverance, Phenakite, Pyrope, Rhodolite, Sard, Sardonyx, Sturdy, Tourist, Valiant, Venture*, 295-296
        PYcs mentioned in Postscript and Appendix C: *Black Douglas, Carolita, Impetuous, Olivin, Paragon, Persistent, Retort, Sea Scout*, 275-276, 295-296
    converted
        Fisheries II, Maryanne, 26, 31, 109, 116-119, 301-302
    patrol (PY),
        Almandite, 6, 293
        Argus, Azurlite, Beryl, Coral, Girasol, Mizpah, Wenonah, 293
        Carnelian, 165, 167, 293
        Crystal, 101, 106, 293
        Cythera, xxv, 26, 156-158, 293

{366} Index

  Hydrographer, 254, 293
  Isabel, 26, 111-113, 114-116, 293, 305
  Jade, 177, 180, 183, 276, 293
  Marcasite, 276, 293
  Ruby, 158, 293
  Siren, 26, 134, 136, 193-196, 293, 305,
  Southern Seas, 26, 242, 244, 293, 305
  Sylph, 40, 143, 293
  Tourmaline, 155, 293
  Turquoise, 190-191, 293
  Zircon, 143-144, 293
yard patrol craft (YP), 30-31, 35, 39, 41-45
 YP Squadron One and YP Squadron Two, 184
 YP (ex-*Bendora*), YP (ex-*Northern Light*), YP (ex-F/V *Hiram*), YP (ex-M.V. *Point Reyes*), YP (ex-*Washington*), 84
 YP-3, *YP-10*, 184-185, 277
 YP-7, 74, 277
 YP-8, 139, 144, 184-185, 277
 YP-9, 143, 145, 277
 YP-11, 139, 154, 275, 277
 YP-12, 143, 277
 YP-13, 184-185, 277
 YP-14, 167-168, 277
 YP-15, 139-140, 278
 YP-16, *YP-17*, 26, 109, 120-121, 278
 YP-18, 184-185, 278
 YP-19, 139-140, 167-168, 278
 YP-24, 159, 278
 YP-26, 26, 176-177, 184, 188, 278
 YP-27, 139-140, 276, 278
 YP-28, 190-191, 278
 YP-31, 159-160, 278
 YP-32, 159, 278
 YP-33, 61, 64, 276, 278
 YP-34, 61, 63, 278
 YP-37, *YP-39*, 60, 276, 278
 YP-38, 60, 278
 YP-41, xxv, 26-27, 246-249, 252-253, 265-268, 278, 305
 YP-42, xxv, 26-27, 246-247, 249, 252-253, 261, 263-264, 266, 268, 278, 305
 YP-45, 167-169, 276, 278
 YP-46, *YP-48*, 176-177, 184, 278

Index {367}

YP-47, 26, 143, 278
YP-49, 138-139, 154, 278
YP-52, 139, 278
YP-56, xxv, 26-27, 169, 246-247, 249, 252-254, 265-266, 268, 278, 305
YP-59, 140, 278
YP-63, 191, 278
YP-64, 190-191, 278
YP-72, 26, 82-85, 90, 279
YP-73, 26, 82, 84, 276, 279
YP-74, 26, 82, 84, 90, 279
YP-77, 26, 279
YP-83, YP-84, 75, 85, 275-276, 279
YP-85, YP-93, 84, 279
YP-86, 84-85, 275, 279
YP-87, 75, 279
YP-88, 26, 84-85, 279
YP-89, YP-90, 75, 279
YP-92, 84, 97, 279
YP-94, YP-95, 26, 84-85, 275-276, 279
YP-96, 74, 85, 276, 279
YP-97, 26, 109, 116-117, 279
YP-98, 167-168, 279
YP-104, YP-106, 143, 279
YP-110, 154, 279
YP-111, 61, 275, 279
YP-112, YP-113, 67, 279
YP-114, 67, 276, 280
YP-115, YP-116, YP-117, YP-118, YP-120, YP-121, YP-124, YP-125, YP-126, YP-129, YP-137, YP-138, YP-139, YP-141, YP-145, 67, 280
YP-119, xix, 65-69, 273-274, 280
YP-122, YP-127, YP-130, YP-134, YP-135, YP-140, YP-142, YP-143, 68, 280
YP-123, 8, 67, 280
YP-128, 26-27, 280
YP-131, YP-132, 67, 69, 276, 280
YP-136, 67, 275, 280
YP-147, 61, 67, 280
YP-148, 84-85, 280
YP-149, 75, 85, 280
YP-150, 74, 280

Index

YP-151, YP-155, 84-85, 90, 281
YP-152, 84-85, 281
YP-153, 75, 85, 281
YP-154, 74, 85, 276, 281
YP-156, YP-159, YP-160, YP-161, 168-169, 275-276, 281
YP-157, 168-169, 171-172, 276, 281
YP-158, 168-169, 281
YP-162, 168-169, 172, 281
YP-164, 61, 63, 276, 281
YP-165, xix, 61-62, 276, 281
YP-166, 74, 276, 281
YP-173, YP-174, 8, 281
YP-175, 142, 144-145, 276, 281
YP-178, 142, 144, 281
YP-180, 142, 276, 281
YP-183, 26, 281
YP-186, 8, 281
YP-188, 168-170, 276, 281
YP-189, 143, 145, 275, 281
YP-196, 168, 275, 281
YP-197, 84-85, 281
YP-198, 74, 281
YP-199, YP-200, 75, 275, 282
YP-202, 190, 275, 282
YP-203, 190, 282
YP-204, 142, 275, 282
YP-205, 26, 190, 282
YP-206, 142, 275, 282
YP-208, 142, 190, 282
YP-209, 176, 184-185, 282
YP-210, YP-211, YP-212, YP-213, YP-215, 134-135, 275-276, 282
YP-216, 135, 159, 276, 282
YP-217, 159, 276, 282
YP-218, 159, 165, 275, 282
YP-219, 159, 191, 193, 282
YP-221, 154, 275, 282
YP-222, 134, 282
YP-224, 190, 282
YP-225, YP-226, 8, 282
YP-228, 135, 275, 282
YP-230, 144-145, 276, 282

Index {369}

YP-231, *YP-232*, 165-166, 275, 282
YP-233, 238, 282
YP-235, 25-26, 274, 282
YP-236, xvii, 26-27, 237-239, 282, 305
YP-237, 8-9, 102, 186, 197, 282
YP-238, 186, 282
YP-239, xvii, 1, 3, 8-15, 21-25, 102, 186, 204, 274, 282, 305-306
YP-240, 8-10, 186, 282
YP-241, 159, 176, 184-185, 282
YP-248, 165-166, 275, 283
YP-249, 142-143, 275, 283
YP-250, 84, 275, 283
YP-251, xxiv, 26-27, 84, 123-129, 283, 305
YP-252, *YP-253*, *YP-256*, 143, 283
YP-254, 143, 145, 275, 283
YP-257, 143, 276, 283
YP-259, 154-155, 276, 283
YP-262, *YP-263*, 274-276, 283
YP-265, 144, 276, 283
YP-269, 274, 283
YP-270, 26, 283
YP-271, *YP-272*, 165-166, 275, 283
YP-274, 134, 276, 283
YP-275, 61, 275, 283
YP-277, 8-9, 25-26, 101-102, 186, 274, 283
YP-278, *YP-283*, 238, 283
YP-279, 25-26, 274, 283
YP-280, 188, 274, 283
YP-281, 25-26, 188, 274, 283
YP-284, xvii, 8-11, 19-27, 101-106, 186, 197, 204, 274, 283, 305-306
YP-287, 184-185, 283
YP-288, *YP-291*, 188, 283
YP-289, xv, 8-10, 25, 186, 202, 274, 283
YP-290, 8-10, 101-102, 105, 186, 202, 204, 283
YP-292, 8-10, 186, 283
YP-294, *YP-299*, 184-185, 284
YP-295, *YP-301*, *YP-302*, *YP-305*, *YP-310*, *YP-311*, *YP-312*, *YP-313*, *YP-314*, *YP-315*, *YP-317*, *YP-321*, *YP-322*, *YP-326*, 184-186, 275-276, 284
YP-327, 8, 284

Index

YP-331, 26, 165-166, 275, 284
YP-332, *YP-340*, 165-166, 275-276, 284-285
YP-333, *YP-338*, 74, 85, 275-276, 284
YP-334, 142, 147, 154, 275, 284
YP-335, 142, 275, 284
YP-336, 26, 284
YP-337, 74, 284
YP-345, xvii, 8-9, 25-26, 101-102, 106-107, 274, 285
YP-346, xvii, xxvi, 1, 3-25, 204, 274, 285, 297-299, 305-306
YP-347, 6, 8, 197-202, 285
YP-348, 8-9, 102, 197, 199, 285
YP-349, 8, 285
YP-350, 8-9, 101-102, 285
YP-352, 165, 275, 285
YP-354, 142, 285
YP-356, *YP-358*, *YP-359*, 165, 275, 285
YP-357, 165, 276, 285
YP-360, 66, 68, 285
YP-361, *YP-365*, *YP-367*, *YP-369*, *YP-371*, 67, 285
YP-362, *YP-370*, 67, 276, 285
YP-363, *YP-366*, 66, 285
YP-364, 67, 176, 185, 276, 285
YP-368, 185, 285
YP-372, 67-68, 285
YP-374, 67, 185, 285
YP-375, 133-134, 142, 285
YP-377, *YP-378*, *YP-379*, 134-135, 275-276, 285
YP-380, 134-135, 285
YP-381, 67, 285
YP-382, 67-68, 276, 285
YP-383, 26, 185, 276, 285
YP-384, *YP-385*, 66, 68, 276, 285
YP-386, 66, 68, 276, 285
YP-387, 26, 143, 145, 147, 285
YP-388, 144, 147, 149, 285, 303
YP-389, xxv, 26, 131, 144-153, 286, 303
YP-392, *YP-393*, *YP-394*, 165, 275, 286
YP-395, 166, 286
YP-396, 74, 85, 275, 286
YP-397, 74, 76-77, 85, 286
YP-398, 165, 275, 286
YP-401, 84-85, 286

YP-403, 165, 286
YP-405, 26, 165, 286
YP-408, 165, 275, 286
YP-414, 208, 212, 286
YP-415, 26-27, 212, 223-226, 231, 286, 305
YP-416, 212, 276, 286
YP-417, 26-27, 207-211, 276, 286, 305
YP-418, 208, 212, 276, 286
YP-419, 212, 286
YP-420, 212, 276, 286
YP-421, xxv, 26-27, 208-209, 212, 258-260, 269-270, 274, 286, 305
YP-422, 26, 212, 275, 286
YP-423, 212, 276, 286
YP-426, 26, 286
YP-430, 142, 275, 286
YP-436, *YP-442*, 191, 275, 287
YP-437, 142, 275, 287
YP-438, xxi-xxiii, 26, 142, 287
YP-445, 142, 191, 275, 287
YP-451, 165, 287
YP-452, 165, 275, 287
YP-453, 26, 166, 287
YP-454, 143, 190, 275, 287
YP-456, 26, 275, 287
YP-481, *YP-492*, 26, 288
YP-503, 274, 276, 288
YP-514, xvii, 26-27, 204-205, 216-217, 223-226, 231, 288, 305
YP-515, 214, 217, 288
YP-516, xvii, 26-27, 205, 207, 214-215, 217, 288, 305
YP-517, xvii, 26-27, 205, 207, 214-215, 217, 227-231, 288, 305
YP-518, 205, 214-217, 288
YP-519, 205, 288
YP-520, 25, 274-275, 288
YP-577, 26, 289
YP-610, 191, 290
YP-617, 290
YP-625, 44, 291
YPs mentioned in Appendix A: *YP-2, 6, 20, 21, 22, 23, 25, 29, 30, 36, 40, 43, 44, 50, 51, 53, 54, 57, 60, 61, 62, 65, 66, 67, 68, 69, 71, 76, 78, 79, 80, 81, 82, 91, 99, 100, 101, 102, 103, 105, 107, 109, 144, 146, 167, 169, 170, 171, 172, 179, 181,*

Index

182, 185, 192, 193, 195, 201, 214, 223, 227, 234, 242, 243, 244, 245, 246, 255, 258, 264, 266, 267, 268, 276, 282, 285, 286, 296, 303, 306, 307, 308, 309, 316, 319, 320, 323, 324, 325, 328, 330, 341, 342, 343, 344, 351, 355, 399, 400, 404, 407, 411, 424, 425, 427, 429, 439, 440, 444, 446, 448, 449, 450, 455, 459, 465, 472, 485, 504, 512, 513, 522, 523, 525, 528, 532, 533, 539, 545, 550, 551, 552, 553, 554, 555, 556, 557, 559, 560, 561, 562, 564, 565, 567, 569, 571, 575, 576, 578, 580, 581, 583, 584, 585, 586, 587, 588, 589, 590, 591, 592, 595, 596, 597, 598, 599, 604, 605, 607, 611, 614, 615, 616, 617, 618, 619, 620, 621, 622, 623, 624, 626, 627, 628, 629, 630, 631, 632, 633, 634, 635, 636, 637, 638, 639, 640, 641, 642, 643, 644, 645, 646, 277-291

YPs mentioned in Postscript and Appendix A: *YP-4, 5, 35, 55, 58, 70, 75, 108, 133, 163, 168, 176, 177, 184, 187, 190, 191, 194, 207, 220, 229, 247, 260, 261, 273, 293, 297, 298, 300, 304, 318, 329, 339, 353, 373, 376, 390, 391, 402, 406, 409, 410, 412, 413, 428, 431, 432, 433, 434, 435, 441, 443, 447, 457, 458, 460, 461, 462, 463, 464, 466, 467, 468, 469, 470, 471, 473, 474, 475, 476, 477, 478, 479, 480, 482, 483, 484, 486, 487, 488, 489, 490, 491, 493, 494, 495, 496, 497, 498, 499, 500, 501, 502, 505, 506, 507, 508, 509, 510, 511, 521, 524, 526, 527, 529, 530, 531, 534, 535, 536, 537, 538, 540, 542, 543, 544, 546, 547, 548, 549, 558, 563, 566, 568, 570, 572, 573, 574, 579, 582, 593, 594, 600, 601, 602, 603, 606, 608, 609 612, 613, 275-276, 277-291*

Simons, Manley H., 155
Smith, Erwin E., 295
Smith, W. A., 303
Smith, W. W., 96
Soares, Eddie, 5
Solomon Islands
    Bougainville Island, xv, 2-3, 12, 129, 212, 217, 219-231, 233-234
    Guadalcanal Island Area,
        Aola Bay, 201, 212
        Florida Island, 4, 19, 21, 25, 201, 211
        Gavutu and Tanambogo Islands, 4, 25
        Henderson Field, 2, 4-5, 13, 19, 21-23, 201, 209, 212-213, 215
        "Ironbottom Sound," 19
        Kukum, 1, 3-4, 13-14, 201, 214, 227
        Lunga Point/Airfield, 4, 9, 13-15, 18, 20-21, 201-202, 214-216
        Savo Island, 1-2, 19, 216

Tasimboko Village, 1, 3-4, 13-14, 23
Tulagi Island, xv, xxvi, 1-4, 12-25, 201, 207, 209-216, 297-298
New Georgia Island (Munda, Rabaul, and Cape Torokina), 4, 210, 212, 219-231, 234
San Cristobal Island, 12, 210, 214
Ulawa Island, 214, 217
Vella Lavella Island, 221, 223, 226-227

Srez, William, 53-54
Stark, Harold R., 113
Steckel, A. M., 165
Stevens, Herbert, 56
Stevenson, W. E., 74
Stiles, Jr., W. H., 158
Stoneleigh, D. R., 134, 143
Strand, Lowell Hall, 117, 301-302
Sullivan, Cornelius M, 143, 293
Swartz (Lieutenant), 238
Swayze, H. P., 168
Symington (Ensign), 190
Tagami, Meiji, 57
Tarleton, W. W., 168
Tarrant, William T., 134
Theobald, Robert A., 81-82, 85-86, 88-94, 96
Theodore, Joaquin S., xx, 5-6, 8, 10-11, 15-18
Thieme, Robert I., 74
Thomsen, Neils P., 124-129
Tidman, W. H., 8
Tonga Islands, 9-10, 204
Townsend, Homer Lamar, 120-121
Toyoda, Soemu, 245, 255
Treasury Islands, 223-228
Truman, Harry S., 268
Tunmer, G., 303
Turbitt, John G., 74
Turner, Richmond K., 11, 216
United States
  Army
    3rd Army, 158
    6th Army, 256
    7th Infantry Division, 251-252, 264
    10th Army, 264
    14th Army Corps, 213, 231

14th Infantry Regiment, 188
27th Infantry Division, 243, 252, 264
37th Infantry Division, 220, 222
77th Infantry Division, 253, 264
96th Division, 264
American Division, 213, 219, 231
Fort
    Davis, 188
    Drum, Frank, Hughes, Mills, 115
    Glenn, 91
    Hunt, 152
    Jackson, 171
    MacArthur, 56
    Mears, 89-91
    Morgan, 168-169
    Pierce, 166-167
Tugs *Cape Horn*, *Invader*, *Shasta* (ex-tuna clippers), 177-187
Army Air Force (USAAF), 10, 37, 132, 236
    A29, 152, 174
    B17, 93, 103, 116
    B24, 96, 243
    B25, 79
    B26, 93
    B29, 245
    Bombardment Squadron 36, 86
    Eleventh, 85
    P38, 236
Coast Guard
    J4F amphibious aircraft, 175
    station
        Ocracoke Island, 148, 151
        Port Townsend and Swiftsure Banks, 76
        Toms River, 154
        Trumbell, 145
Coast and Geodetic Survey (USC&GS), 74, 155, 254
Fish and Wildlife Service (FWS), 41, 73-75, 84, 168, 277, 281-282
Lighthouse Service, 76-77
Marine(s)
    Marine Division
        1st Marines, 4, 12, 24, 213, 219, 239, 264
        2nd Marines, 243, 250, 252-253
        3rd Marines, 220, 222-223, 231, 253, 262-263

4th Marines, 251-253, 261, 263
5th Marines, 261-263
6th Marines, 264
9th and 21st Marines, 223
10th Marines, 20
1st Raider Battalion, 1, 13-14
I Amphibious Corps, 228
2nd Raider Regiment, 223
4th Raider Battalion, 219
19th Regiment, 231
Aircraft Group 23, 14
Fighter Squadron
  121, 21
  214, 221
Ushijima, Mitsuru, 267
Vandegrift, Alexander, 12
Varley, Ed, 7-8
Vaughn, Charles, 17, 23, 297-298
Visser, Richard G., 246-249
von Forstner, Siegfried, 158
Wainwright, Jonathon M., 115-117
Wake Island, 79, 100-101, 255
Walker, Jr., Hiram S., 154
Walker, Richard E., 74, 76, 286
Warmington, Harry C., 159
Warms, William F., 168
Watson, Adolphus E., 153
Wash, Jack Lawrence, 121
Wayne, John, xix, 61-62
Welker, Arnold W., 291
White, H. G., 193
White, L. A., 303
Whitford, Marcus L., 143
Whitney (Lieutenant Junior Grade), 190
Wickham, J. W., xx, 39
Williams, William W., 291
Wilson, Charles Fredrick, 74
Wilson, R., 151, 303
Witte, Helmut, 187
Winters, R. A., 51
Wood, Malcolm L., 296
Woods Hole Oceanographic Institution, 134-135, 248

Wright (Ensign), 168
Wright, Harold, 84
Würdemann, Erich, 172
Yamada, Yusuke, 20
Yamamoto, Isoroku, 9, 80-81, 96, 103, 105-106
Yokota, Minoru, 47-48
Zacharias, Casper L., 157

About the Author

Commander David D. Bruhn, U.S. Navy (Retired) served twenty-two years on active duty and two in the Naval Reserve, as both an enlisted man and as an officer, between 1977 and 2001.

Following completion of basic training, he served as a sonar technician aboard USS *Miller* (FF 1091) and USS *Leftwich* (DD 984). He was commissioned in 1983 following graduation from California State University at Chico. His initial assignment was to USS *Excel* (MSO 439), serving as supply officer, damage control assistant, and chief engineer. He then served in USS *Thach* (FFG 43) as chief engineer and Destroyer Squadron Thirteen as material officer.

After graduation from the Naval Postgraduate School, Commander Bruhn was assigned to Secretary of the Navy and Chief of Naval Operation staffs as a budget analyst and resources planner before attending the Naval War College in 1996, following which he commanded the mine countermeasures ships USS *Gladiator* (MCM 11) and USS *Dextrous* (MCM 13) in the Persian Gulf.

Commander Bruhn's final assignment was executive assistant to a senior (SES 4) government service executive at the Ballistic Missile Defense Organization in Washington, D.C.

Following military service, he was a high school teacher and track coach for ten years, and is now a USA Track & Field official. He lives in northern California with his wife Nancy and has two sons, David and Michael.

www.ingramcontent.com/pod-product-compliance
Lightning Source LLC
Chambersburg PA
CBHW071948220426
43662CB00009B/1039